Adobe® Dreamweaver® CS6

# CLASSROOM IN A BOOK®

The official training workbook from Adobe Systems

Adobe Press books are published by Peachpit, a division of Pearson Education located in Berkeley, California. For the latest on Adobe Press books, go to www.adobepress.com. To report errors, please send a note to errata@peachpit.com. For information on getting permission for reprints and excerpts, contact permissions@peachpit.com.

Writer: James J. Maivald
Project Editor: Nancy Peterson
Production Editor: Cory Borman
Development Editor: Robyn G. Thomas
Technical Editors: Clint Funk, Catherine Palmer
Copyeditor: Scout Festa
Compositor: Kim Scott, Bumpy Design
Indexer: Joy Dean Lee
Media Producer: Eric Geoffroy
Cover Design: Eddie Yuen
Interior Design: Mimi Heft

Printed and bound in the United States of America

ISBN-13:      978-0-321-82245-1
ISBN-10:          0-321-82245-5

9 8 7 6 5 4 3 2 1

# WHAT'S ON THE DISC

**Here is an overview of the contents of the Classroom in a Book disc**

The *Adobe Dreamweaver CS6 Classroom in a Book* disc includes the lesson files that you'll need to complete the exercises in this book, as well as other content to help you learn more about Adobe Dreamweaver CS6 and use it with greater efficiency and ease. The diagram below represents the contents of the disc, which should help you locate the files you need.

## Lesson files

Each lesson has its own folder inside the Lessons folder. You will need to copy these lesson folders to your hard drive before you can begin each lesson.

## Learn by Video bonus tutorials

A bonus 2-hour set of *Adobe Dreamweaver CS6: Learn by Video* tutorials are included on this disc, from video2brain and Adobe Press. Learn by Video is one of the most critically acclaimed training products on Adobe software and is the only Adobe-approved video courseware for the Adobe Certified Associate Level certification.

## Online resources

Links to Adobe Community Help, product Help and Support pages, Adobe certification programs, Adobe TV, and other useful online resources can be found inside a handy HTML file. Just open it in your web browser and click the links, including a special link to this book's product page where you can access updates and bonus material.

# CONTENTS

# GETTING STARTED

Adobe® Dreamweaver® CS6 is the industry-leading web authoring program. Whether you create websites for a living or plan to create one for your own business, Dreamweaver offers all the tools you need to get professional-quality results.

## About *Classroom in a Book*

*Adobe Dreamweaver CS6 Classroom in a Book®* is part of the official training series for graphics and publishing software developed with the support of Adobe product experts.

The lessons are designed so that you can learn at your own pace. If you're new to Dreamweaver, you'll learn the fundamentals of putting the program to work. If you are an experienced user, you'll find that *Classroom in a Book* teaches many advanced features, including tips and techniques for using the latest version of Dreamweaver.

Although each lesson includes step-by-step instructions for creating a specific project, you'll have room for exploration and experimentation. You can follow the book from start to finish, or complete only those lessons that correspond to your interests and needs. Each lesson concludes with a Review section containing questions and answers on the subjects you've covered.

## TinyURLs

In several points in the book, we reference external information available on the Internet. The uniform resource locators (URLs) for this information are often long and unwieldy, so we have provided custom TinyURLs in their place for your convenience. Unfortunately, the TinyURLs sometimes expire over time and no longer function. If you find that a TinyURL doesn't work, look up the actual URL provided in the Appendix.

# Prerequisites

Before using *Adobe Dreamweaver CS6 Classroom in a Book*, you should have a working knowledge of your computer and its operating system. Be sure you know how to use the mouse, standard menus and commands, and also how to open, save, and close files. If you need to review these techniques, see the printed or online documentation that was included with your Microsoft Windows or Apple Macintosh operating system.

# Installing the program

Before you perform any exercises in this book, verify that your computer system meets the hardware requirements for Dreamweaver CS6, that it's correctly configured, and that all required software is installed.

Adobe Dreamweaver CS6 software must be purchased separately; it is not included with the lesson files that accompany this book. For system requirements, go to www.adobe.com/products/dreamweaver/tech-specs.html.

Install Dreamweaver CS6 onto your hard drive from the Adobe Dreamweaver CS6 application DVD (you cannot run the program from the disc) or from the installation files you downloaded from Adobe. For complete instructions on installing the software, see the Adobe Dreamweaver CS6 Read Me file on the application DVD or on the web at www.adobe.com/support.

Make sure your serial number is accessible before installing the application.

# Copying the *Classroom in a Book* files

The *Adobe Dreamweaver CS6 Classroom in a Book* DVD includes folders containing all the electronic files for the lessons in the book. Each lesson has its own folder; you must copy the folders to your hard drive to complete the lessons. It is recommended that you copy all lesson folders to your hard drive at once, but to conserve space on your hard disk, you can install individual folders for each lesson as you need them. It is vitally important that you store all lesson folders within a single folder on your hard drive. If you follow the recommended lesson order, this master folder will serve as the local site root folder, as described more fully in Lesson 4, "Creating a Page Layout."

To install the *Classroom in a Book* files:

1   Insert the *Adobe Dreamweaver CS6 Classroom in a Book* DVD into your computer's optical disc drive.

**2** Navigate to the CD/DVD drive on your computer.

**3** If you intend to complete all lessons in the book in order, drag the Lessons folder to your computer hard drive. Otherwise, skip to step 5.

The Lessons folder contains all the individual lesson folders and other assets needed for the training.

**4** Rename the Lessons folder **DW-CS6**.

This folder will be used as the local site root folder.

**5** If you desire to perform one or more lessons individually, copy each lesson folder to your hard drive separately, as needed. Then, proceed to the "Jumpstart" section for more instructions. Do not copy one lesson folder into any other lesson folder.

*The files and folders for each lesson cannot be used interchangeably.* For specific instructions, see the following section.

## Recommended lesson order

The training herein is designed to take you from A to Z in basic to intermediate website design, development, and production. Each new lesson builds on previous exercises, using the files and assets you create to develop an entire website. It is recommended that you perform each lesson in sequential order to achieve a successful result and the most complete understanding of all aspects of web design.

The ideal training scenario will start in Lesson 1 and proceed through the entire book to Lesson 15. Since each lesson builds essential files and content for the next, once you start this scenario you shouldn't skip any lessons, or even individual exercises. While ideal, this method may not be a practicable scenario for every user. So, if desired, individual lessons can be accomplished using the jumpstart method described in the next section.

## Jumpstart

For users who don't have the time or inclination to perform each lesson in the book in sequence, or who are having difficulty with a particular lesson, a jumpstart method is included to facilitate the performance of individual lessons in or out of sequence. Once you start using the jumpstart method, you will have to use this method for all subsequent lessons. For example, if you want to jumpstart Lesson 6, you will have to jumpstart Lesson 7, too. In many instances, essential files needed for subsequent exercises were built in earlier lessons and exercises and may not be present in a jumpstart environment.

Each lesson folder includes all the files and assets needed to complete the exercises contained within that lesson. Each folder contains finished files, staged files, and customized Template and Library files, but not always a complete set of files that may have been used or completed in other lessons. You may think these folders contain seemingly duplicative materials. But these duplicate files and assets, in most cases, cannot be used interchangeably in other lessons and exercises. Doing so will probably cause you to fail to achieve the goal of the exercise.

The jumpstart method for completing individual lessons treats each folder as a stand-alone website. To jumpstart a lesson, copy the lesson folder to your hard drive and create a new site for that lesson using the Site Setup dialog box. Do not define sites using subfolders of existing sites. Keep your jumpstart sites and assets in their original folders to avoid conflicts. One suggestion is to organize the lesson folders, as well as your own site folders, in a single *web* or *sites* master folder near the root of your hard drive. But avoid using the Dreamweaver application folder or any folders that contain a web server, like Apache, ColdFusion, or Internet Information Services (IIS) (which are described more fully in Lessons 13 and 14).

Feel free to use the jumpstart method for all lessons, if you prefer.

To set up a jumpstart site, do the following:

1   Choose Site > New Site.

    The Site Setup dialog box appears.

2   In the Site Name field, enter the name of the lesson, such as **lesson06**.

3   Click the Browse ( 🗀 ) icon next to the Local Site Folder field. Navigate to the desired lesson folder you copied from the *Adobe Dreamweaver CS6 Classroom in a Book* DVD and click Select/Choose.

4   Click the arrow (▶) next to the Advanced Settings category to reveal the tabs listed there. Select the Local Info category.

5   Click the Browse icon next to the Default Images Folder field. When the dialog box opens, navigate to the Images folder contained within the lesson folder and click Select/Choose.

6   In the Site Setup dialog box, click Save.

7   The name of the currently active website will appear in the Files panel's site pop-up menu. If necessary, press F8/Cmd-Shift-F to display the Files panel, and select the desired website you wish to work on from the Show menu.

These steps will have to be repeated for each lesson you wish to jumpstart. For a more complete description of how to set up a site in Dreamweaver, see Lesson 4. Remember, if you use the jumpstart method for all lessons, you may not end up with a complete set of site files in any individual folder when you are finished.

# Setting up the workspace

Dreamweaver includes a number of workspaces to accommodate various computer configurations and individual workflows. For this book the Designer workspace is recommended.

1 In Dreamweaver CS6, locate the Application bar. If necessary, choose Window > Application Bar to display it.

2 The default workspace is called Designer. If it is not displayed, use the pop-up menu in the Application bar to choose it.

3 If the default workspace has been modified and certain toolbars and panels are not visible (as they appear in the figures in the book), you can select Window > Workspace > Reset Designer to restore the default configuration.

Most of the figures in this book show the Designer workspace. When you finish the lessons in this book, experiment with various workspaces to find the one that you prefer.

For a more complete description of the Dreamweaver workspaces, see Lesson 1, "Customizing Your Workspace."

# Windows vs. Macintosh instructions

In most cases, Dreamweaver performs identically in both Windows and Mac OS X. Minor differences exist between the two versions, mostly due to platform-specific issues out of the control of the program. Most of these are simply differences in keyboard shortcuts, how dialog boxes are displayed, and how buttons are named. Screen shots may alternate between platforms throughout the book. Where specific commands differ, they are noted within the text. Windows commands are listed first, followed by the Macintosh equivalent, such as Ctrl-C/Cmd-C. Common abbreviations are used for all commands whenever possible, as follows:

| WINDOWS | MACINTOSH |
|---|---|
| Control = Ctrl | Command = Cmd |
| Alternate = Alt | Option = Opt |

# Finding Dreamweaver information

For complete, up-to-date information about Dreamweaver panels, tools, and other application features, visit the Adobe website. Choose Help > Dreamweaver Help. The Adobe Help application opens and downloads the latest Help files from the

Adobe Community Help website. These files are cached locally so you can access them even when you are not connected to the Internet. You can also download a PDF version of the Dreamweaver Help files from the Adobe Help application.

For additional information resources, such as tips, techniques, and the latest product information, visit www.adobe.com/support/dreamweaver to access the Adobe Community Help page.

## Checking for updates

Adobe periodically provides software updates. You can obtain these updates using Adobe Updater if you have an active Internet connection.

1  In Dreamweaver, choose Help > Updates. The Adobe Updater automatically checks for updates for your Adobe software.

2  In the Adobe Updater dialog box, select the updates you want to install, and then click Download And Install Updates to install them.

For book updates and bonus material, visit the book's page on the web at www.peachpit.com/dwcs6cib.

## Additional resources

*Adobe Dreamweaver CS6 Classroom in a Book* is not meant to replace documentation that comes with the program or to be a comprehensive reference for every feature. Only the commands and options used in the lessons are explained in this book. For comprehensive information about program features and tutorials, please refer to these resources:

**Adobe Community Help:** Community Help brings together active Adobe product users, Adobe product team members, authors, and experts to give you the most useful, relevant, and up-to-date information about Adobe products.

**To Access Community Help**: To invoke Help, press F1 or choose Help > Dreamweaver Help.

Adobe content is updated based on community feedback and contributions. You can add comments to content and forums (including links to web content), publish your own content using Community Publishing, or contribute Cookbook recipes. Find out how to contribute at www.adobe.com/community/publishing/download.html.

See community.adobe.com/help/profile/faq.html for answers to frequently asked questions about Community Help.

**Adobe Dreamweaver CS6 Help and Support:** www.adobe.com/support/dreamweaver is where you can find and browse Help and Support content on adobe.com.

**Adobe Forums:** forums.adobe.com lets you tap into peer-to-peer discussions, questions, and answers on Adobe products.

**Adobe TV:** tv.adobe.com is an online video resource for expert instruction and inspiration about Adobe products, including a How To channel to get you started with your product.

**Adobe Design Center:** www.adobe.com/designcenter offers thoughtful articles on design and design issues, a gallery showcasing the work of top-notch designers, tutorials, and more.

**Adobe Developer Connection:** www.adobe.com/devnet is your source for technical articles, code samples, and how-to videos that cover Adobe developer products and technologies.

**Resources for educators:** www.adobe.com/education offers a treasure trove of information for instructors who teach classes on Adobe software. Find solutions for education at all levels, including free curricula that use an integrated approach to teaching Adobe software and can be used to prepare for the Adobe Certified Associate exams.

Also check out these useful links:

**Adobe Marketplace & Exchange:** www.adobe.com/cfusion/exchange is a central resource for finding tools, services, extensions, code samples, and more to supplement and extend your Adobe products.

**Adobe Dreamweaver CS6 product home page:** www.adobe.com/products/dreamweaver

**Adobe Labs:** labs.adobe.com gives you access to early builds of cutting-edge technology, as well as forums where you can interact both with the Adobe development teams building that technology and with other like-minded members of the community.

# Adobe certification

The Adobe training and certification programs are designed to help Adobe customers improve and promote their product-proficiency skills. There are four levels of certification:

- Adobe Certified Associate (ACA)
- Adobe Certified Expert (ACE)

- Adobe Certified Instructor (ACI)

- Adobe Authorized Training Center (AATC)

The Adobe Certified Associate (ACA) credential certifies that individuals have the entry-level skills to plan, design, build, and maintain effective communications using different forms of digital media.

The Adobe Certified Expert program is a way for expert users to upgrade their credentials. You can use Adobe certification as a catalyst for getting a raise, finding a job, or promoting your expertise.

If you are an ACE-level instructor, the Adobe Certified Instructor program takes your skills to the next level and gives you access to a wide range of Adobe resources.

Adobe Authorized Training Centers offer instructor-led courses and training on Adobe products, employing only Adobe Certified Instructors. A directory of AATCs is available at partners.adobe.com.

For information on the Adobe Certified programs, visit www.adobe.com/support/certification/index.html.

# 1 CUSTOMIZING YOUR WORKSPACE

## Lesson Overview

In this lesson, you'll familiarize yourself with the Dreamweaver CS6 (Creative Suite 6) program interface and learn how to do the following:

- Switch document views
- Work with panels
- Select a workspace layout
- Adjust toolbars
- Personalize preferences
- Create custom keyboard shortcuts
- Use the Property inspector

 This lesson will take about 20 minutes to complete. Before beginning, make sure you have copied the files for Lesson 1 to your hard drive as described in the "Getting Started" section at the beginning of the book.

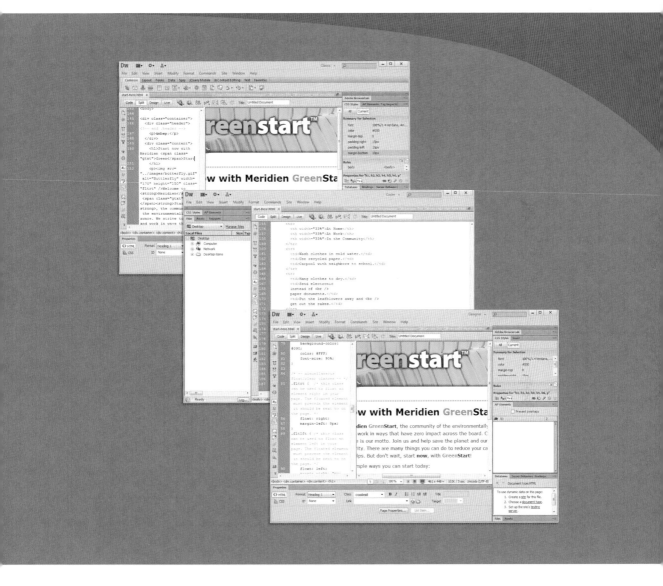

Dreamweaver offers a customizable and easy-to-use
WYSIWYG HTML editor that doesn't compromise
when it comes to power and flexibility. You'd probably
need a dozen programs to perform all the tasks that
Dreamweaver can do—and none of them would be
as fun to use.

# Touring the workspace

Dreamweaver is the industry-leading Hypertext Markup Language (HTML) editor, with good reasons for its popularity. The program offers an incredible array of design and code-editing tools. Dreamweaver offers something for everyone.

Coders love the variety of enhancements built into the Code view environment, and developers enjoy the program's support for ASP, PHP, ColdFusion, and JavaScript, among other programming languages. Designers marvel at seeing their text and graphics appear in an accurate What You See Is What You Get (WYSIWYG) depiction as they work, saving hours of time previewing pages in browsers. Novices certainly appreciate the program's simple-to-use and power-packed interface. No matter what type of user you are, if you use Dreamweaver you don't have to compromise.

The Dreamweaver interface features a vast array of user-configurable panels and toolbars. Take a moment to familiarize yourself with the names of these components.

**A** Menu bar
**B** Application bar
**C** Workspace menu
**D** Document tab
**E** Document toolbar
**F** Coding toolbar
**G** Code view
**H** Design view
**I** Insert panel
**J** CSS Styles panel
**K** Tag selectors
**L** Property inspector
**M** Files panel

You'd think a program with this much to offer would be dense, slow, and unwieldy, but you'd be wrong. Dreamweaver provides much of its power via dockable panels and toolbars you can display or hide and arrange in innumerable combinations to create your ideal workspace.

This lesson introduces you to the Dreamweaver interface and gets you in touch with some of the power hiding under the hood. If you want to follow along on the tour, choose File > Open. In the lesson01 folder, choose **start-here.html**. Click Open.

# Switching and splitting views

Dreamweaver offers dedicated environments for coders and designers as well as a composite option that blends both together.

## Design view

Design view focuses the Dreamweaver workspace on its WYSIWYG editor, which provides a close, but not perfect, depiction of the webpage as it would appear in a browser. To activate Design view, click the Design view button in the Document toolbar.

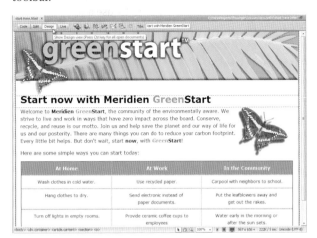

Design view

## Code view

Code view focuses the Dreamweaver workspace exclusively on the HTML code and a variety of code-editing productivity tools. To access Code view, click the Code view button in the Document toolbar.

Code view

## Split view

Split view provides a composite workspace that gives you access to both the design and the code simultaneously. Changes made in either window update in the other instantly. To access Split view, click the Split view button in the Document toolbar. To take advantage of the expanded width of the new flat-panel displays, Dreamweaver splits the workspace vertically, by default.

Split view

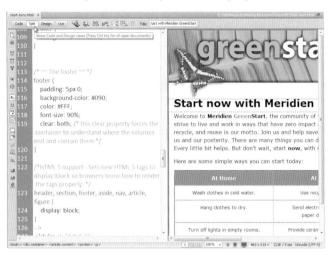

You can also split the screen horizontally by disabling the vertical split in the view menu. To disable this feature, choose View > Split Vertically.

Split view horizontally

# Working with panels

Although you can access most commands from the menus, Dreamweaver scatters much of its power in user-selectable panels and toolbars. You can display, hide, arrange, and dock panels at will around the screen. You can even move them to a second or third video display if you desire.

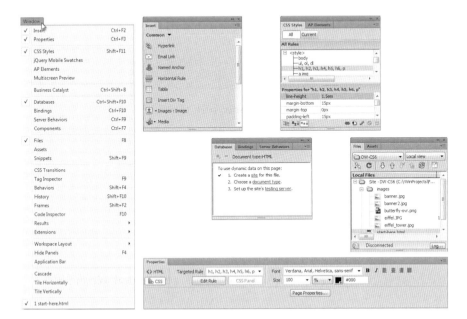

Standard panel grouping

The Window menu lists all the available panels. If you do not see a specific panel on the screen, choose it from the Window menu. A check mark appears in the menu to indicate that the panel is open. Occasionally, one panel may lie behind another on the screen and be difficult to locate. In such situations, simply choose the desired panel in the Window menu and it will rise to the top of the stack.

## Minimizing

To create room for other panels or to access obscured areas of the workspace, you can minimize or expand individual panels in place. To minimize a panel, double-click the tab containing the panel name. To expand the panel, double-click the tab again.

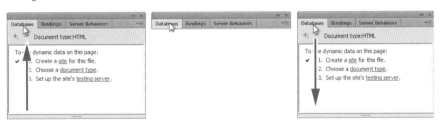

Minimizing floating panel by double-clicking the tab

You can also minimize or expand one panel within a stack of panels individually by double-clicking its tab.

Minimizing one panel in
a stack using its tab

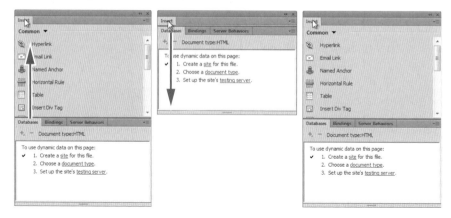

To recover more screen real estate, you can minimize panel groups or stacks down to icons by double-clicking the title bar. You can also minimize the panels to icons by clicking the double arrow (▶▶) icon in the panel title bar. When panels are minimized to icons, you access any of the individual panels by clicking its icon or button. The selected panel will appear on the left or right of your layout wherever room permits.

Minimizing sequence
to icons

## Floating

A panel grouped with other panels can be floated separately. To float a panel, drag it from the group by its tab.

Pulling a panel out by
its tab

## Dragging

You can reorder a panel tab by dragging it to the desired position within the group.

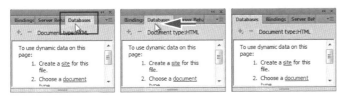

Dragging a tab to change its position

To reposition panels, groups, and stacks in the workspace, simply drag them by the title bar.

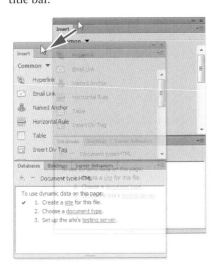

Dragging a whole panel group or stack to a new position

## Grouping, stacking, and docking

You can create custom groups by dragging one panel into another. When you've moved the panel to the correct position, Dreamweaver highlights the area, called the drop zone, in blue (as shown in the following figure). Release the mouse button to create the new group.

Creating new groups

In some cases, you may want to keep both panels visible simultaneously. To stack panels, drag the desired tab to the top or bottom of another panel. When you see the blue drop zone appear, release the mouse button.

Creating panel stacks

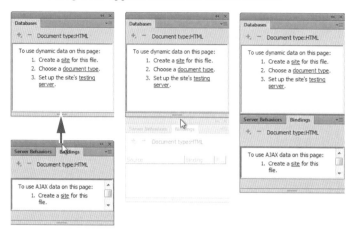

Floating panels can be docked to the right, left, or bottom of the Dreamweaver workspace. To dock a panel, group, or stack, drag its title bar to the edge on which you wish to dock. When you see the blue drop zone appear, release the mouse button.

Docking panels

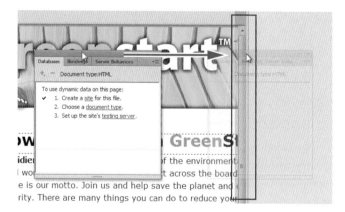

# Selecting a workspace layout

A quick way to customize the program environment is to use one of the prebuilt workspaces in Dreamweaver. These workspaces have been optimized by experts to put the tools you need at your fingertips.

Dreamweaver CS6 includes 11 prebuilt workspaces. To access these workspaces, choose them from the Workspace menu located in the Application bar.

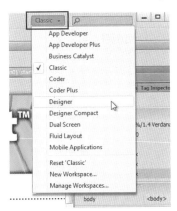

Workspace menu

Longtime users of Dreamweaver may choose the Classic workspace, which displays the panels and toolbars they're accustomed to seeing and using in previous Dreamweaver versions.

Classic workspace

The Coder workspace produces a workspace that focuses Dreamweaver on the HTML code and its code-editing tools.

Coder workspace

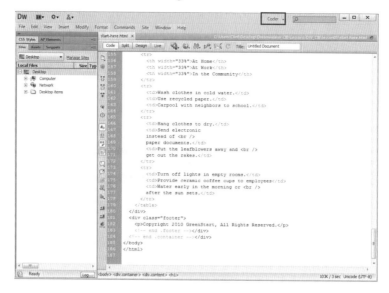

The Designer workspace provides the optimum environment for visual designers.

Designer workspace

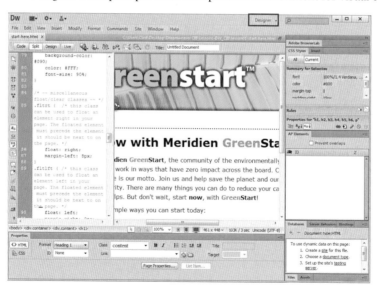

# Adjusting toolbars

Some program features are so handy you may want them available all the time in the form of a toolbar. Three of the toolbars—Style Rendering, Document, and Standard—appear horizontally at the top of the document window. The Coding toolbar, however, appears vertically, but only in the Code view window. You will explore the capabilities of these toolbars in later exercises.

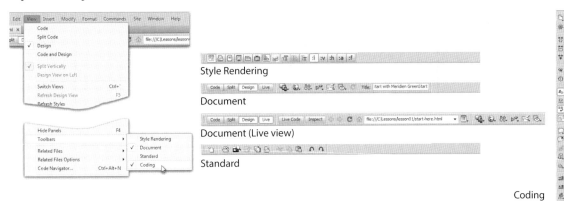

Style Rendering

Document

Document (Live view)

Standard

Coding

Display the desired toolbar by selecting it from the View menu.

# Personalizing preferences

As you continue to work with Dreamweaver, you will devise your own optimal workspace of panels and toolbars for each activity. You can store these configurations in a custom workspace of your own naming.

To save a custom workspace, create your desired configuration, choose New Workspace from the Workspace menu in the Application bar, and then give it a custom name.

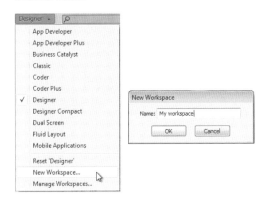

Saving a custom workspace

# Creating custom keyboard shortcuts

Another power feature of Dreamweaver is the capability of creating your own keyboard shortcuts as well as editing existing ones. Keyboard shortcuts are loaded and preserved independent of custom workspaces.

Is there a command you can't live without that doesn't have a keyboard shortcut? Create it yourself. Try this:

1 Choose Edit > Keyboard Shortcuts/Dreamweaver > Keyboard Shortcuts.

2 Click the Duplicate Set button to create a new set of shortcuts.

3 Enter a name in the Name Of Duplicate Set field. Click OK.

4 Choose Menu commands from the Commands menu.

5 Select Save All from the File command list.

Note that the Save All command does not have an existing shortcut, although you will use this command frequently in Dreamweaver.

6 Insert the cursor in the Press Key field. Press Ctrl-Alt-S/Cmd-Opt-S.

Note the error message indicating that the keyboard combination you chose is already assigned to a command. Although we could reassign the combination, let's choose a different one.

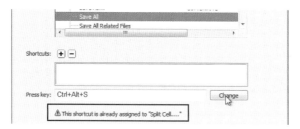

**7** Press Ctrl-Alt-Shift-S/Cmd-Ctrl-S.

This combination is not currently being used, so let's assign it to the Save All command.

**8** Click the Change button.

The new shortcut is now assigned to the Save All command.

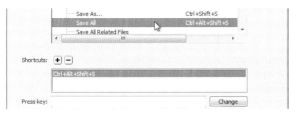

**9** Click OK to save the change.

You have created your own keyboard shortcut—one you will use in upcoming lessons.

# Using the Property inspector

One tool that is vital to your workflow is the Property inspector. This panel typically appears at the bottom of the workspace. The Property inspector is context driven and adapts to the type of element you select.

## Using the HTML tab

Insert the cursor into any text content on your page, and the Property inspector provides a means to quickly assign some basic HTML codes and formatting. When the HTML button is selected, you can apply heading or paragraph tags, as well as bold, italics, bullets, numbers, and indenting, among other formatting and attributes.

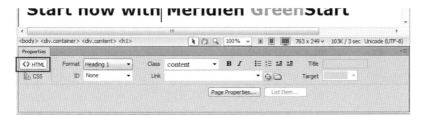

HTML Property inspector

## Using the CSS tab

Click the CSS (cascading style sheet) button to quickly access commands to assign or edit CSS formatting.

CSS Property inspector

## Image properties

Select an image in a webpage to access the image-based attributes and formatting control of the Property inspector.

Image Property inspector

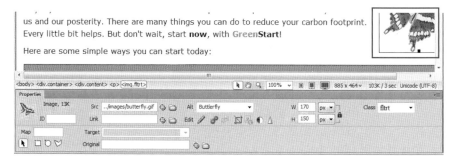

## Table properties

To access table properties, insert your cursor in a table and then click the table tag selector at the bottom of the document window.

Table Property inspector

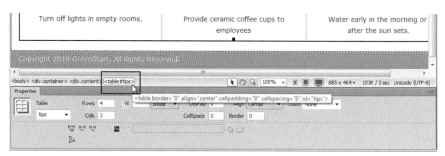

## Review questions

1  Where can you access the command to display or hide any panel?

2  Where can you find the Code, Design, and Split view buttons?

3  What can be saved in a workspace?

4  Do workspaces also load keyboard shortcuts?

5  What happens in the Property inspector when you insert the cursor into various elements on the webpage?

## Review answers

1  All panels are listed in the Window menu.

2  These buttons are components of the Document toolbar.

3  Workspaces can save the configuration of the document window, the open panels, and the panels' size and position on the screen.

4  No, keyboard shortcuts are loaded and preserved independently of a workspace.

5  The Property inspector adapts to the selected element, displaying pertinent information and formatting commands.

# 2 HTML BASICS

## Lesson Overview

In this lesson, you'll familiarize yourself with HTML and learn how to do the following:

- Write HTML code by hand
- Understand HTML syntax
- Insert code elements
- Format text
- Add HTML structure
- Create HTML with Dreamweaver

 This lesson will take about 45 minutes to complete. There are no support files for this lesson.

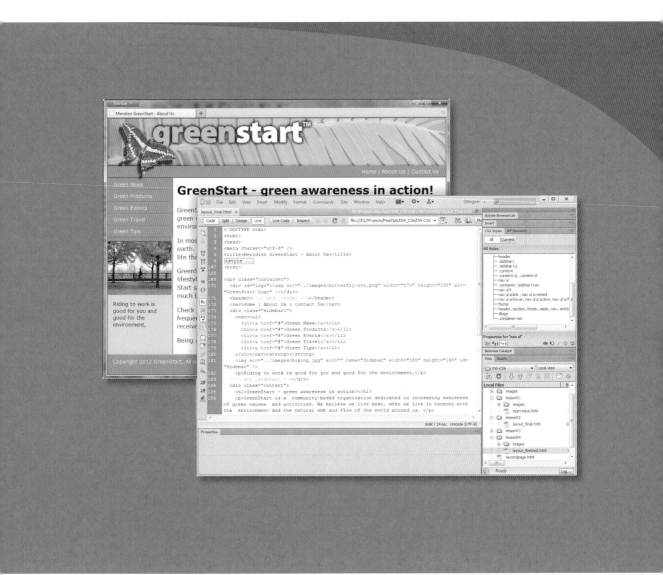

HTML is the backbone of the web, the skeleton of your webpage. It is the structure and substance of the Internet, although it is usually unseen except by the web designer. Without it, the web would not exist. Dreamweaver has many features that help you access, create, and edit HTML code quickly and effectively.

# What is HTML?

"What other programs can open a Dreamweaver file?"

This question was asked by a student in a Dreamweaver class; although it might seem obvious to an experienced developer, it illustrates a basic problem in teaching and learning web design. Most people confuse the program with the technology. They assume that the extension .htm or .html belongs to Dreamweaver or Adobe. Print designers are used to working with files ending with .ai, .psd, .indd, and so on. These are proprietary file formats created by programs that have specific capabilities and limitations. The goal in most of these cases is to create a final printed piece. The program in which the file was created provides the power to interpret the code that produces the printed page. Designers have learned over time that opening these file formats in a different program may produce unacceptable results or even damage the file.

On the other hand, the goal of the web designer is to create a webpage for display in a browser. The power and functionality of the originating program have little bearing on the resulting browser display, because the display is contingent on the HTML code and how the browser interprets it. Although a program may write good or bad code, it's the browser that does all the hard work.

The web is based on the HyperText Markup Language (HTML). The language and the file format don't belong to any individual program or company. In fact, it is a nonproprietary, plain-text language that can be edited in any text editor, in any operating system, and on any computer. Dreamweaver is an HTML editor at its core, although it is much more than this. But to maximize the potential of Dreamweaver, you first need to have a good understanding of what HTML is and what it can and can't do. This chapter is intended as a concise primer for HTML and its capabilities and as a foundation for understanding Dreamweaver.

# Where did HTML begin?

HTML and the first browser were invented in the early 1990s by Tim Berners-Lee, a scientist working at the CERN (Conseil Européen pour la Recherche Nucléaire, which is French for European Council for Nuclear Research) particle physics laboratory in Geneva, Switzerland. He intended the technology as a means for sharing technical papers and information via the fledgling Internet that existed at the time. He shared his HTML and browser inventions openly as an attempt to get the scientific community and others to adopt it and engage in the development themselves. The fact that he did not copyright or try to sell his work started a trend for openness and camaraderie on the web that continues to this day.

The language that Berners-Lee created over 20 years ago was a much simpler construct of what we use now, but HTML is still surprisingly easy to learn and master. At the time of this writing, HTML is at version 4.01, which was officially adopted in 1999. It consists of around 90 *tags*, such as `html`, `head`, `body`, `h1`, `p`, and so on. The tag is written between angle brackets, as in `<p>`, `<h1>`, and `<table>`. These tags are used to enclose, or *mark up*, text and graphics to enable a browser to display them in a particular way. HTML code is considered properly *balanced* when the markup contains both an opening tag (`<...>`) and a closing tag (`</...>`). When two matching tags appear this way, they are referred to as an *element*.

Some elements are used to create page structures, others to format text, and yet others to enable interactivity and programmability. Even though Dreamweaver obviates the need for writing most of the code manually, the ability to read and interpret HTML code is still a recommended skill for any burgeoning web designer. And sometimes, writing the code by hand is the only way to find an error in your webpage.

Here you see the basic structure of a webpage:

# Basic HTML Code Structure

Properly structured, or balanced, HTML markup consists of an opening tag and a closing tag. Tags are enclosed within angle brackets. You create a closing tag by typing a forward slash (/) after the opening bracket and then repeating the original tag. Empty tags, like the horizontal rule, can be written in an abbreviated fashion, as shown above.

You may be surprised to learn that the only words from this code that display in the web browser are "Welcome to my first webpage." The rest of the code creates the page structure and text formatting. Like an iceberg, most of the content of the actual webpage remains out of sight.

# Writing your own HTML code

The idea of writing code may sound difficult or at least tedious, but creating a web-page is actually much easier than you think. In the next few exercises, you will learn how HTML works by creating a basic webpage and adding and formatting some simple text content:

1 Launch Notepad (Windows) or TextEdit (Mac).

2 Enter the following code in the empty document window:

```
<html>
<body>
Welcome to my first webpage
</body>
</html>
```

3 Save the file to the desktop as **firstpage.html**.

4 Launch Chrome, Firefox, Internet Explorer, Safari, or another installed web browser.

5 Choose File > Open. Navigate to the desktop, select **firstpage.html**, and then click OK/Open.

Congratulations, you just created your first webpage. As you can see, it doesn't take much code to create a serviceable webpage.

Text editor                                              Browser

## Understanding HTML syntax

Next you'll add content to your new webpage to learn some important aspects of HTML code syntax.

1 Switch back to the text editor, but don't close the browser.

2 Insert your cursor at the end of the text "Welcome to my first webpage," and press Enter/Return to insert a paragraph return.

3 Type **Making webpages is fun**, then press the spacebar five times to insert five spaces. Finish by typing **and easy!** on the same line.

**Note:** Feel free to use any text editor for these exercises, but be sure to save your files as plain text.

▶ **Tip:** In TextEdit, you may need to choose Format > Format As Plain Text before you can save the file as .html.

**Note:** Some text editors may try to change the .html extension or prompt you to confirm the choice.

**4** Save the file.

**5** Switch to the browser, and refresh the window to load the updated page.

As you can see, the browser is displaying the new text, but it's ignoring the paragraph return between the two lines as well as the extra spaces. In fact, you could add hundreds of paragraph returns between the lines and dozens of spaces between each word, and the browser display would be no different. That's because the browser is programmed to ignore extra white space and honor only HTML code elements. By inserting a tag here and there, you can easily create the desired text display.

## Inserting HTML code

In this exercise, you will insert HTML tags to produce the correct text display:

**1** Switch back to the text editor.

**2** Add the tags to the text as follows:

`<p>`Making webpages is fun      and easy!`</p>`

To add extra spacing or other special characters within a line of text, HTML provides code elements called *entities*. Entities are entered into the code differently than tags. For example, the method for inserting a nonbreaking space is to type the ` ` entity.

**3** Replace the five spaces in the text with nonbreaking spaces, so that the code looks like the following sample:

`<p>`Making webpages is fun**     **and easy!`</p>`

**4** Save the file. Switch to the browser and reload or refresh the page display.

The browser is now showing the paragraph return and desired spacing.

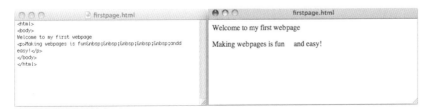

**Note:** A good rule of thumb regarding the use of entities is whether you can enter a character using the standard 101-key keyboard. If the character doesn't appear, you'll probably have to use an entity.

Because the tags and entities were added, the browser can display the desired paragraph structure and spacing.

## Formatting text with HTML

Tags often serve multiple purposes. Besides creating paragraph structures and creating white space as demonstrated earlier, they can impart basic text formatting, as well as identify the relative importance of the page content. For example, HTML provides six heading tags (<h1> to <h6>) you can use to set headings off from normal paragraphs. The tags not only format the text differently than paragraph text, they also impart additional meaning. Heading tags are automatically formatted in bold and often at a larger relative size. The number of the heading also plays a role: Using the <h1> tag identifies the heading as being the largest and highest in importance by default. In this exercise, you will add a heading tag to the first line:

1   Switch back to the text editor.

2   Add the tags to the text as follows:

    **<h1>**Welcome to my first webpage**</h1>**

3   Save the file. Switch to the browser and reload or refresh the page display.

    Note how the text changed. It is now larger and formatted in boldface.

Web designers use heading tags to identify the importance of specific content and to help improve their site rankings on Google, Yahoo, and other search engines.

## Applying inline formatting

So far, all the tags you have used work as paragraph or stand alone elements. These are referred to as *block* elements. HTML also provides the ability to apply formatting and structure to content that's contained within the flow of another tag, or *inline*. A typical use of inline code would be to apply bold or italic styling to a word or to a portion of a paragraph. In this exercise, you will apply inline formatting:

1   Switch back to the text editor.

2   Add the tags to the text as follows:

    <p>Making webpages is fun     
    **<strong><em>**and easy!**</em></strong>**</p>

3   Save the file. Switch to the browser and reload or refresh the page display.

Most formatting, both inline and otherwise, is properly applied using cascading style sheets (CSS). The <strong> and <em> tags are among the few still acceptable ways to apply inline formatting using strictly HTML code elements. Technically, these elements are more intended to add semantic meaning to text content, but

**Note:** Pay special attention to how the tags are nested so that you close them properly. Notice how the <em> tag is closed before the <strong> tag is closed.

the effect is the same: The text still appears by default as bold or italic. There is an industry-supported move to separate the content from its presentation, or formatting. See Chapter 3, "CSS Basics," for a full explanation of the strategy and application of CSS in standards-based web design.

The tags <strong> and <em> are used in place of the tags <b> (bold) and <i> (italic) because they provide enhanced semantic meaning for visitors with disabilities or visual impairment, but the result to the average user is identical.

## Adding structure

Most webpages feature at least three fundamental elements: a root (typically <html>), <head>, and <body>. These elements create the essential underlying structure of the webpage. The root element contains all the code and content and is used to declare to the browser, and any browser applications, what types of code elements to expect within the page. The <body> element holds all the visible content, such as text, tables, images, movies, and so on. The <head> element holds code that performs vital background tasks, including styling, external links, and other information.

The sample page you created doesn't have a <head> element. A webpage can exist without this section, but adding any advanced functionality to this page without one would be difficult. In this exercise, you will add <head> and <title> elements to your webpage:

1  Switch back to the text editor.

2  Add the tags and content to the text as follows:

    <html>

    <head>

    <title>HTML Basics for Fun and Profit</title>

    </head>

    <body>

3  Save the file. Switch to the browser and reload or refresh the page display.

Did you notice what changed? It may not be obvious at first. Look at the title bar of the browser window. The words "HTML Basics for Fun and Profit" now magically appear above your webpage. By adding the <title> element, you have created this display. But it's not just a cool trick; it's good for your business, too.

Google, Yahoo, and the other search engines catalog the `<title>` element of each page and use it, among other criteria, to rank webpages. The content of the title is one of the items typically displayed within the results of a search. A well-titled page could be ranked higher than one with a bad title or one with none at all. Keep your titles short but meaningful. For example, the title "ABC Home Page" doesn't really convey any useful information. A better title might be "Welcome to the Home Page of ABC Corporation." Check out other websites (especially peers or competitors) to see how they title their own pages.

The content of the `<title>` tag will appear in the browser title bar when the page is refreshed.

## Writing HTML in Dreamweaver

So the inevitable question is, "If I can write HTML in any text editor, why do I need to use Dreamweaver?" Although a complete answer awaits you in the following 13 chapters, the question begs for a quick demonstration. In this exercise, you will re-create the same webpage using Dreamweaver:

1 Launch Dreamweaver CS6.

2 Choose File > New.

3 In the New Document window, select Blank Page from the first column.

4 Select HTML from the Page Type column and <none> from the Layout column. Click Create.

   A new document window opens in Dreamweaver. The window may default to one of three displays: Code view, Design view, or Split view.

5 If it's not already selected, click the Code view button in the upper-left corner of the document window.

   The first thing you should notice in the Code view window is that Dreamweaver has provided a huge head start over using the text editor. The basic structure of the page is already in place, including the root, head, body, and title tags, among others. The only thing Dreamweaver makes you do is add the content itself.

Code view
Split view
Design view

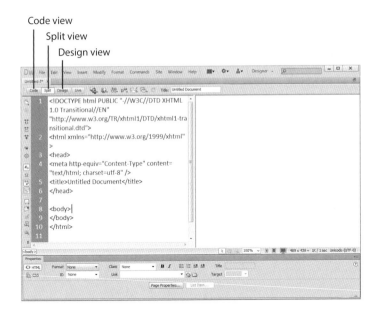

The advantages of using Dreamweaver to create HTML are evident from the very beginning: Much of the page structure is already created.

**6** Insert the cursor after the opening <body> tag, and type **Welcome to my second page** following the tag.

Dreamweaver makes it a simple matter to format the first line as a heading 1.

**7** Move the cursor to the beginning of the text "Welcome to my second page," and type **<** to start the <h1> code element.

Note how Dreamweaver automatically opens a drop-down list of compatible code elements. This is Dreamweaver's code hinting feature. When activated, code hinting provides a drop-down list of applicable HTML, CSS, JavaScript, and other supported coding elements.

**8** Type **h** and observe the Code hint window.

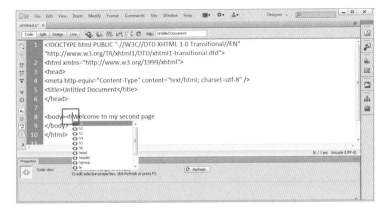

Dreamweaver filters the code hint list to elements that start with "h".

9   In the code hint list, double-click **h1** to insert it in the code. Type **>** to close the element.

10  Move the cursor to the end of the text. Type **</** at the end of the sentence.

Note how Dreamweaver closes the <h1> element automatically. But most coders add the tags as they write, in the following way:

11  Press Enter/Return to insert a line break. Type **<.**

12  Type **p** and press Enter/Return to insert the paragraph element. Type **>** to close the tag.

13  Type **Making webpages in Dreamweaver is even more fun!** Then type **</** to close the <p> element.

Tired of hand-coding yet? Dreamweaver offers multiple ways to format your content.

14  Select the word "more." In the Property inspector, click the B button, and then the I button to apply the <strong> and <em> tags to the text.

These tags produce the appearance of bold and italic formatting on the selected text.

## Something missing?

When you reached for the B and I buttons in step 14, were they missing? When you make changes in Code view, the Property inspector occasionally needs to be refreshed before you can access the formatting commands featured there. Simply click the Refresh button, and the formatting commands will reappear.

Only two more tasks remain before your new page is complete. Note that Dreamweaver created the <title> element and inserted the text "Untitled Document" within it. You could select the text within the code window and enter a new title, or you could change it using another built-in feature.

15  Locate the Title field at the top of the document window, and select the "Untitled Document" text.

16  Type **HTML Basics, Page 2** in the Title field.

**17** Press Enter/Return to complete the title.

Note that the new title text appears in the code, replacing the original content. It's time to save the file and preview it in the browser.

**18** Choose File > Save. Navigate to the desktop. Name the file **secondpage**, and click Save.

Dreamweaver adds the proper extension (.html) automatically.

**19** Choose File > Preview in Browser.

The completed page appears in the browser window.

You have just completed two webpages—one by hand and the other using Dreamweaver. In both cases, you can see how HTML played a central role in the whole process. To learn more about this technology, go to www.w3schools.com or check out any of the books listed in the following sidebar.

## Recommended books on HTML

*HTML, XHTML, and CSS3: Visual QuickStart Guide, Seventh Edition*, Elizabeth Castro and Bruce Hyslop (Peachpit Press, 2012) ISBN: 0-321-71961-1

*HTML and XHTML Pocket Reference*, Jennifer Niederst Robbins (O'Reilly, 2009) ISBN: 978-0-596-80586-9

*Head First HTML with CSS & XHTML*, Elisabeth and Eric Freeman (O'Reilly, 2005) ISBN: 978-0-596-10197-8

# Frequently used HTML 4 codes

HTML code elements serve specific purposes. Tags can create structures, apply formatting, identify logical content, or generate interactivity. Tags that create stand-alone structures are called block elements; the ones that perform their work within the body of another tag are called inline elements.

## HTML tags

The following table shows some of the most frequently used HTML tags. To get the most out of Dreamweaver and your webpages, it helps to understand the nature of these elements and how they are used. Remember, some tags can serve multiple purposes.

**Table 2.1** Frequently used HTML tags

| TAG | DESCRIPTION | STRUCTURAL | BLOCK | INLINE |
|---|---|:---:|:---:|:---:|
| `<!--...-->` | HTML comment. Allows you to add notes within the HTML code that are not displayed within the browser. | • | | |
| `<a>` | Anchor. Creates a hyperlink. | | | • |
| `<blockquote>` | Quotation. Creates a stand-alone, indented paragraph. | | • | |
| `<body>` | Designates the document body. Contains the visible portions of the webpage content. | • | | |
| `<br />` | Break. Inserts a line break without creating a new paragraph. | • | | |
| `<div>` | Division. Used to divide page content into discernible groupings. Used extensively to simulate columnar layouts. | • | • | |
| `<em>` | Emphasis. Adds semantic emphasis. Displays as italics by default. | | | • |
| `<form>` | Designates an HTML form. | • | • | |
| `<h1>` to `<h6>` | Headings. Creates bold headings. Implies hierarchical semantic value. | | • | |
| `<head>` | Designates the document head. Contains code that performs background functions, such as meta tags, scripts, styling, links, and other information not displayed on the page. | • | | |

| TAG | DESCRIPTION | STRUCTURAL | BLOCK | INLINE |
|---|---|:---:|:---:|:---:|
| <hr /> | Horizontal rule. Empty element that generates a horizontal line. | • | • | |
| <html> | Root element of most webpages. Contains an entire webpage, except in certain cases where server-based code must load before the opening <html> tag. | • | | |
| <iframe> | Inline frame. A structural element that can contain another document. | • | | • |
| <img /> | Image. | • | | • |
| <input /> | Input element for a form such as a text field. | • | | • |
| <li> | List item. | | • | |
| <link /> | Designates the relationship between a document and an external resource. | • | | |
| <meta /> | Metadata. | • | | |
| <ol> | Ordered list. Defines a numbered list. | • | • | |
| <p> | Paragraph. Creates a stand-alone paragraph. | | • | |
| <script> | Script. Contains scripting elements or points to an external script. | • | | |
| <span> | Designates a section of an element. Provides a means of applying special formatting or emphasis to a portion of an element. | | | • |
| <strong> | Adds semantic emphasis. Displays as bold by default. | | | • |
| <style> | Calls CSS style rules. | • | | |
| <table> | Designates an HTML table. | • | • | |
| <td> | Table data. Designates a table cell. | • | | |
| <textarea> | Multi-line text input element for a form. | • | • | |
| <th> | Table header. | • | | |
| <title> | Title. | • | | |
| <tr> | Table row. | • | | |
| <ul> | Unordered list. Defines a bulleted list. | • | • | |

## HTML character entities

Entities exist for every letter and character. If a symbol can't be entered directly from the keyboard, it can be inserted by typing the name or numeric value listed in the following table:

**Table 2.2** HTML character entities

| CHARACTER | DESCRIPTION | NAME | NUMBER |
|---|---|---|---|
| © | Copyright | &copy; | &#169; |
| ® | Registered trademark | &reg; | &#174; |
| ™ | Trademark | | &#153; |
| • | Bullet | | &#149; |
| – | En dash | | &#150; |
| — | Em dash | | &#151; |
| | Nonbreaking space |   |   |

# Introducing HTML5

The current version of HTML has been around for over 10 years and has not kept pace with many of the advances in technology, such as cell phones and other mobile devices. The World Wide Web Consortium (W3C), the standards organization responsible for maintaining and updating HTML and other web standards, has been working diligently on updating the language and released the first working draft of HTML5 in January 2008. The latest update was published in March 2012, but a final version may not be ready for several more years. So, what does that mean for current or up-and-coming web designers? Not much—yet.

Websites and their developers change and adapt to current technologies and market realities quickly, but the underlying technologies progress at a more glacial pace. Browser manufacturers are already supporting many of the new features of HTML5 today. Early adopters will attract developers and users who are interested in the latest and greatest, which means that older, non-HTML5-compliant browsers will be abandoned as these new features are implemented in the majority of popular websites. Some say the full transition won't happen until 2020 or later; others think it will happen more quickly. In any case, backward-compatibility to HTML 4.01 will be certain well into the future, so your older pages and sites won't suddenly explode or disappear.

## What's new in HTML5

Every new version of HTML has made changes to both the number and the purpose of the elements that make up the language. HTML 4.01 consists of approximately 90 elements. Some of these elements have been deprecated or removed altogether, and new ones have been adopted or proposed.

Many of the changes to the list revolve around supporting new technologies or different types of content models. Some changes simply reflect customs or techniques that have been popularized within the developer community since the previous version of HTML was adopted. Other changes simplify the way code is created and make it easier to write and faster to disseminate.

## HTML5 tags

The following table shows some of the important new tags in HTML5, which, at the moment, consists of over 100 tags. Almost 30 old tags have been deprecated, which means HTML5 features nearly 50 new elements in total. The exercises in this book use many of these new HTML5 elements as appropriate and will explain the elements' intended role on the web. Take a few moments to familiarize yourself with these tags and their descriptions.

**Table 2.3** Important new HTML5 tags

| TAG | DESCRIPTION | STRUCTURAL | BLOCK | INLINE |
|-----|-------------|:----------:|:-----:|:------:|
| `<article>` | Designates independent, self-contained content, which can be distributed independently from the rest of the site. | • | • | |
| `<aside>` | Designates sidebar content that is related to the surrounding content. | • | • | |
| `<audio>` | Designates multimedia content, sounds, music, or other audio streams. | • | | • |
| `<canvas>` | Designates graphics content created using a script. | • | | |
| `<figure>` | Designates a section of stand-alone content containing an image or video. | • | • | |
| `<figcaption>` | Designates a caption for a `<figure>` element. | • | | • |
| `<footer>` | Designates a footer of a document or section. | • | • | |

*continued on next page*

*continued from previous page*

| TAG | DESCRIPTION | STRUCTURAL | BLOCK | INLINE |
|---|---|:---:|:---:|:---:|
| <header> | Designates the introduction of a document or section. | • | • | |
| <hgroup> | Designates a set of <h1> to <h6> elements when a heading has multiple levels. | • | | |
| <nav> | Designates a section of navigation. | • | • | |
| <section> | Designates a section in a document, such as a chapter, a header, a footer, or any other section of the document. | • | • | |
| <source> | Designates media resources for media elements. A child element of <video> or <audio> elements. Multiple sources can be defined for browsers that do not support the default resource. | • | | • |
| <track> | Designates text tracks used in media players. | • | | |
| <video> | Designates video content, such as a movie clip or other video stream. | • | | |

## Semantic web design

Many of the changes to HTML have been done to support the concept of *semantic web design*, or designing webpages using elements and structures that provide or possess intrinsic meaning. For example, it has led to the introduction of many new elements, such as <article>, <section>, <header>, and <footer>. It is a movement that has important ramifications for the future and usability of HTML and for the interoperability of websites on the Internet. At the moment, each webpage stands alone on the web. The content may link to other pages and sites, but there's really no way to combine or collect the information available on multiple pages or multiple sites in a coherent manner. Search engines do their best to index the content that appears on every site, but much of it is lost because of the nature and structure of old HTML code.

HTML was initially designed as a presentation language. In other words, it was intended to display technical documents in a browser in a readable and predict-able manner. If you look carefully at the original specifications of HTML, it looks like a list of items you would put in a college research paper: headings, paragraphs, quoted material, tables, numbered and bulleted lists, and so on.

The Internet before HTML looked more like MS DOS or the OS X Terminal applications. There was no formatting, no graphics, and no color. The element list in the first version of HTML basically identified how the content would be displayed. The tags did not convey any intrinsic meaning or significance. For example, using a heading tag displayed a particular line of text in bold, but it didn't tell you what relationship the heading had to the following text or to the story as a whole. Was it a title or merely a subheading?

HTML5 has added a significant number of new tags to help us add meaning to our markup. Tags like `<header>`, `<footer>`, `<article>`, and `<section>` allow you for the first time to identify specific content without having to resort to additional attributes, such as `<div class="header">...</div>`. The end result is simpler code and less of it. But most of all, the addition of semantic meaning to your code will allow you and other developers to connect the content from one page to another in new and exciting ways—many of which haven't even been invented yet.

## New techniques and technologies

HTML5 has also revisited the basic nature of the language to take back some of the functions that over the years have been increasingly done with third-party plug-ins and external programming. If you are new to web design, this transition will be painless, because you have nothing to relearn and no bad habits to break. If you already have experience building webpages and applications, this book will guide you safely through some of these waters and introduce the new technologies and techniques in a logical and straightforward way. But best of all, semantic web design doesn't mean you have to trash all of your old sites and rebuild everything from scratch. Valid HTML 4 code will remain valid for the foreseeable future. HTML5 was intended to make your task easier by allowing you to do more, with less work. So let's get started!

## HTML5 references

To learn more about HTML5, check out www.w3.org/TR/2011/WD-html5-20110525/.

To see the complete list of HTML5 elements, check out www.w3schools.com/html5/html5_reference.asp.

To learn more about W3C, check out www.w3.org.

## Review questions

**1**  What programs can open HTML files?

**2**  What does a markup language do?

**3**  True or false? HTML5 is not very different from HTML 4.

**4**  What are the three main parts of most webpages?

**5**  What's the difference between a block element and an inline element?

# Review answers

**1** HTML is a plain-text language that can be opened and edited in any text editor and viewed in any web browser.

**2** A markup language places tags contained within brackets < > around plain-text content to pass information concerning structure and formatting from one application to another.

**3** False. Over 30 tags have been deprecated from HTML 4, and almost 50 new tags have been added to HTML5. That means almost half of the entire language has changed since it was released in 1998.

**4** Most webpages are composed of three sections: a root, head, and body.

**5** A block element creates a stand-alone element. An inline element can exist within another element.

# 3 CSS BASICS

## Lesson Overview

In this lesson, you'll familiarize yourself with CSS and learn how to do the following:

- CSS (cascading style sheets) terms and terminology
- The difference between HTML and CSS formatting
- How the cascade, inheritance, descendant, and specificity theories affect how browsers apply CSS formatting
- How CSS can format objects
- New features and capabilities of CSS3

 This lesson should take 1 hour and 15 minutes to complete. Before beginning, make sure you have copied the files for Lesson 3 to your hard drive as described in the "Getting Started" section at the beginning of the book. If you are starting from scratch in this lesson, use the method described in the "Jumpstart" section of "Getting Started."

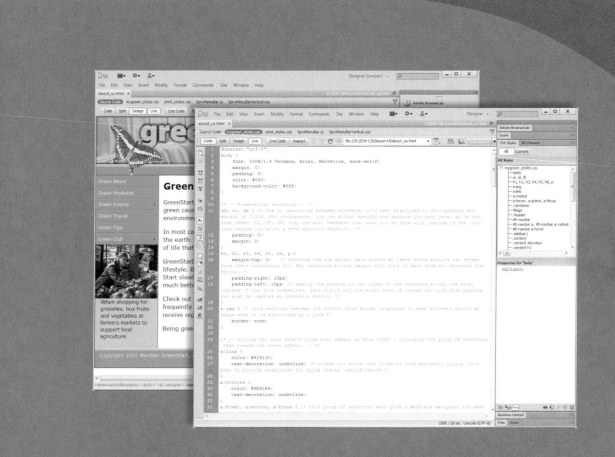

CSS controls the look and feel of a webpage. The language and syntax is complex, powerful, and endlessly adaptable; it takes time and dedication to learn and years to master. A modern web designer can't live without it.

# What is CSS?

HTML was never intended to be a design medium. Other than bold and italic, version 1.0 lacked a standardized way to load fonts or format text. Formatting commands were added along the way up to version 3 of HTML to address these limitations, but these changes still weren't enough. Designers resorted to various tricks to produce the desired results. For example, they used HTML tables to simulate multicolumn and complex layouts for text and graphics, and they used images when they wanted to display typefaces other than Times or Helvetica.

Using the expanded table mode in Dreamweaver (top), you can see how this webpage relies on tables and images to produce the final design (bottom).

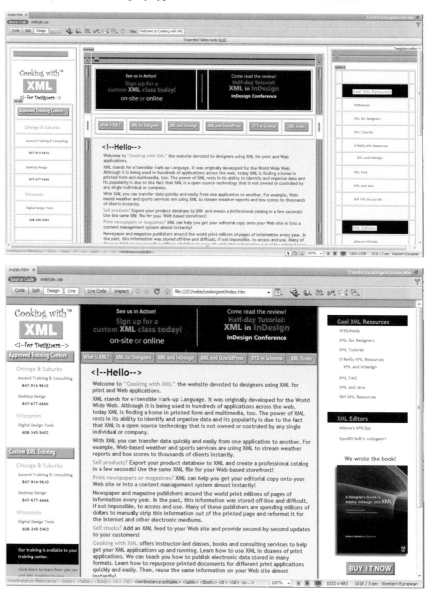

HTML-based formatting was so misguided a concept that it was deprecated from the language entirely in favor of cascading style sheets (CSS). CSS avoids all the problems of HTML formatting, while saving time and money, too. Using CSS lets you strip the HTML code down to its essential content and structure and then apply the formatting separately, so you can more easily tailor the webpage to specific applications.

# HTML vs. CSS formatting

When comparing HTML-based formatting to CSS-based formatting, it's easy to see how CSS produces vast efficiencies in time and effort. In the following exercise, you'll explore the power and efficacy of CSS by editing two webpages: one formatted by HTML, the other by CSS:

1  Launch Dreamweaver CS6, if it is not currently running.

2  Choose File > Open.

3  Navigate to the lesson03 folder and open **html_formatting.html**.

4  Click the Split view button. If necessary, select View > Split Vertically to split the Code view and Design view windows vertically, side by side.

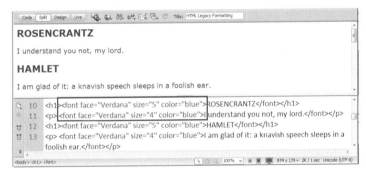

Each element of the content is formatted individually using the deprecated <font> tag. Note the attribute color="blue" in each <h1> and <p> element.

5  Replace the word blue with **green** in each line in which it appears. Click in the Design view window to update the display.

The text displays in green now. As you can see, formatting using the obsolete <font> tag is not only slow, but prone to error, too. Make a mistake, like typing **greeen** or **geen**, and the browser will ignore the color formatting altogether.

6  Open **CSS_formatting.html** from the lesson03 folder.

**7** If it's not currently selected, click the Split view button.

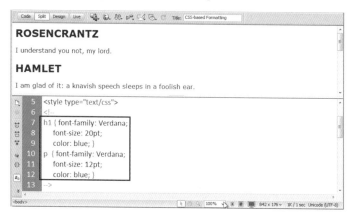

The content of the file is identical to the previous document, except that it's formatted by CSS. The code that formats the HTML elements appears in the `<head>` section of this file. Note that the code contains two `color: blue;` attributes.

**8** Select the word `blue` in the code `h1 { color: blue; }` and type **green** to replace it. Click in the Design view window to update the display.

In Design view, all the heading elements display in green. The paragraph elements remain blue.

**9** Select the word `blue` in the code `p { color: blue; }` and type **green** to replace it. Click in the Design view window to update the display.

In Design view, the paragraph elements have changed to green.

In this exercise, CSS accomplished the color change with two simple edits, whereas the HTML `<font>` tag required you to edit *every* line. Are you beginning to understand why the W3C deprecated the `<font>` tag in favor of cascading style sheets? This exercise highlights just a small sampling of the formatting power and productivity enhancements offered by CSS that can't be matched by HTML alone.

# HTML defaults

Each of the nearly 100 HTML tags comes right out of the box with one or more default formats, characteristics, or behaviors. So even if you do nothing, the text will already be formatted in a certain way. One of the essential tasks in mastering CSS is learning and understanding these defaults. Let's take a look.

1   Open **HTML_defaults.html** from the lesson03 folder. If necessary, select
    Design view to preview the contents of the file.

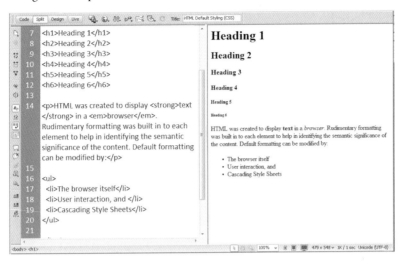

The file contains the full range of HTML headings and text elements. Each
element exhibits basic styling for traits such as size, font, and spacing, among
others.

2   If necessary, click the Split view button. In the Code view window, locate the
    <head> section and try to identify any code that may be formatting the HTML
    elements.

A quick look will tell you that there is no obvious styling information in the file, but
the text still displays different kinds of formatting. So where does it come from?
And what are the settings?

The answer is: it depends. HTML elements draw characteristics from multiple
sources. The first place to look is the W3C, the web standards organization that
establishes Internet specifications and protocols. You can find a default style sheet
at www.w3.org/TR/CSS21/sample.html that defines the standard formatting and
behaviors of all HTML 4 elements. This is the style sheet on which all browser vendors base their default rendering of HTML elements.

To save time and give you a bit of a head start, the following table pulls together
some of the most common defaults.

**Table 3.1** Common HTML defaults

| ITEM | DESCRIPTION |
|------|-------------|
| Background | In most browsers, the page background color is white. The background of <div>, <table>, <td>, <th>, and most other tags is transparent. |
| Headings | Headings <h1> through <h6> are bolded and aligned to the left. The six heading tags apply differing font size attributes, with <h1> the largest and <h6> the smallest. |
| Body text | Outside of a table cell, text aligns to the left and starts at the top of the page. |
| Table cell text | Text within table cells <td> aligns horizontally to the left and vertically to the center. |
| Table header | Text within header cells <th> is bolded and aligned horizontally and vertically to the center. This default is not honored by all browsers. |
| Fonts | Text color is black. Default typeface and font is specified and supplied by the browser (or by browser preferences specified by the manufacturer and then by the user). |
| Margins | Spacing external to the element box. Many HTML elements feature some form of margin spacing. |
| Padding | Spacing between the box border and the content. According to the default style sheet, no element features default padding. |

Although it's nice to know which browsers are the most popular among the general public, it's crucial that before you build and test your pages, you identify the browsers that visitors in your target audience use.

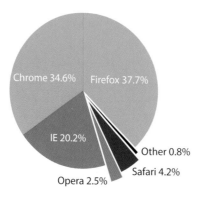

The next task is to identify the browser (and its version) that is displaying the HTML. That's because browsers frequently differ in the way they interpret, or render, HTML elements and CSS formatting. Unfortunately, even different versions of the same browser can produce wide variations from identical code.

The best practice is to build and test your webpages to make sure that they work properly in the browsers employed by the majority of web users—especially the browsers preferred by your own visitors. In January 2012, the W3C published statistics, shown in the image above, identifying the most popular browsers.

Although this chart shows the basic breakdown in the browser world, it obscures the fact that multiple versions of each browser are still being used. This is important to know, because older browser versions are less likely to support the latest

HTML and CSS features and effects. To make matters more complicated, although these statistics are valid for the Internet overall, the statistics for your own site may vary wildly.

# CSS box model

The browser normally reads the HTML code, interprets its structure and formatting, and then displays the webpage. CSS does its work by stepping between HTML and the browser, redefining how each element should be rendered. It imposes an imaginary box around each element and then enables you to format almost every aspect of how that box and its contents are displayed.

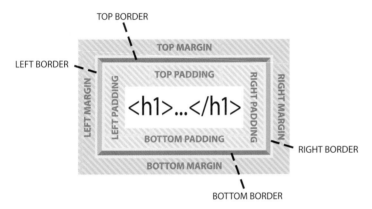

The box model is a programmatic construct imposed by CSS that enables you to format, or redefine, the default settings of any HTML element.

CSS permits you to specify fonts, line spacing, colors, borders, background shading and graphics, margins, and padding, among other things. In most instances these boxes are invisible, and although CSS gives you the ability to format them, it does not require you to do so.

1  Launch Dreamweaver, if necessary. Open **boxmodel.html** from the lesson03 folder.

2  Click the Split view button to divide the workspace between the Code view and Design view windows.

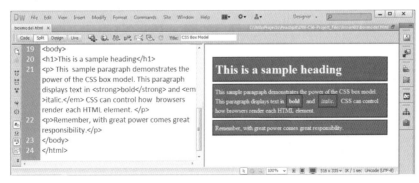

The file's sample HTML code contains a heading and two paragraphs with sample text that is formatted to illustrate some of the properties of the CSS box model. The text displays visible borders, background colors, margins, and padding.

## Content vs. presentation

A basic tenet in web standards today is the separation of the *content* (text, images, lists, and so on) from its *presentation* (formatting). Here is identical HTML content, side by side. We've removed the CSS formatting entirely from the file on the left. Although the text on the left is not wholly unformatted, it's easy to see the power of CSS to transform HTML code.

The working specifications found at www.w3.org/TR/css3-box describe how the box model is supposed to render documents in various media.

# Formatting text

You can apply CSS formatting in three ways: *inline*, *embedded* (in an internal style sheet), or *linked* (via an external style sheet). A CSS formatting instruction is called a *rule*. A rule consists of two parts—a *selector* and one or more *declarations*. The selector identifies what element, or combination of elements, is to be formatted; the declaration, or declarations, contains the formatting specifications. CSS rules can redefine any existing HTML element, as well as define two custom selector modifiers called "class" and "ID."

A rule can also combine selectors to target multiple elements at once or to target specific instances within a page where elements appear in unique ways, such as when one element is nested within another.

Applying a CSS rule is not a simple matter of selecting some text and applying a paragraph or character style, as in Adobe InDesign or Adobe Illustrator. CSS rules can affect single words, paragraphs of text, or combinations of text and objects. A single rule can affect an entire page. A rule can be specified to begin and end abruptly, or to format content continuously until changed by a subsequent rule.

**Sample CSS Rule Construction**

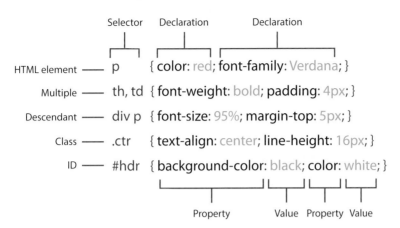

These sample rules demonstrate some typical constructions used in selectors and declarations. The way the selector is written determines how the styling is applied and how the rules interact with one another.

There are many factors that come into play in how a CSS rule performs its job. To help you better understand how it all works, the exercises in the following sections illustrate four main CSS concepts, which we'll refer to as theories: cascade, inheritance, descendant, and specificity.

## Cascade theory

The cascade theory describes how the order and placement of rules in the style sheet or on the page affects the application of styling. In other words, if two rules conflict, which one wins out? Let's take a look at how cascade influences CSS formatting.

1 Open **cascade.html** from the lesson03 folder.

   The file contains HTML headings formatted in red.

2 Click the Split view button, if necessary, and observe the CSS rules in the `<head>` section of the code.

Note that the code contains two CSS rules that are identical except that they apply different colors: red or blue. Both rules want to format the same elements, but only one will be honored.

Obviously, the second rule won. Why? Because the second rule is the last one declared, which makes it the closest one to the actual content.

**3** Select the rule h1 { color: blue; }.

**4** Select Edit > Cut.

**5** Insert the cursor at the end of the h1 { color: red; } rule.

**6** Select Edit > Paste.

You have switched the order of the rules.

**7** Click in the Design view window to refresh the preview display.

The headings now display in blue.

Both *proximity* and the *order* in which rules appear within the markup are powerful factors in how CSS is applied. When you try to determine which CSS rule will be honored and which formatting will be applied, browsers typically use the following order of hierarchy, with #3 being the most powerful.

1. Browser defaults.

2. External or embedded (in the <head> section) style sheets. If both are present, the one declared last supersedes the earlier entry in conflicts.

3. Inline styles (within the HTML element itself).

## Inheritance theory

The inheritance theory describes how one rule can be affected by one or more previously declared rules. Inheritance can affect rules of the same name as well as rules that format parent elements or elements that nest one inside another. Let's take a look at how inheritance influences CSS formatting.

**1** Open **inheritance.html** from the lesson03 folder. In Split view, observe the CSS code.

First, notice that there are two CSS rules that format <h1> elements. Can you tell, by looking at the Design view window, which of the rules is formatting the <h1> text? If you said both of them, you're the winner.

At first glance, you may think that there are two separate rules for <h1> and, technically, that's true. But if you look closer, you'll see that the second rule doesn't contradict the first. It's not resetting the color attribute; it's declaring a new one. In other words, since both rules do something different, both will be honored. All <h1> elements will be formatted as blue and Verdana.

Far from being a mistake or an unintended consequence, the ability to build rich and elaborate formatting using multiple rules is one of the most powerful and complex aspects of cascading style sheets.

2 Observe the rules formatting the h2, h3, and p elements.

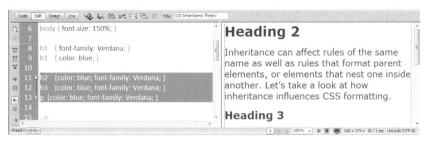

All the rules include the statement {color: blue; font-family: Verdana; }. Redundant code should be avoided whenever possible. It adds to the size of the code as well as to the time it takes to download and process it. By using inheritance, you can create the same effect with a single rule. Instead of applying the styling to each element individually, you simply apply it to the parent element that contains them—in this case, <div>.

3 Select the h2 selector, and type **div** to replace it.

This change applies the style to the parent and, therefore, to all of its contents, too.

4 Delete the rules formatting the elements h3 and p.

5 Click in the Design view window to refresh the display.

All the elements remain formatted as blue Verdana. One rule is now formatting three different elements. Let's take it one step further. You may have also noticed that the two h1 rules combined create the same styling applied by the new div rule.

**6**  Select and delete both h1 rules. Click in the Design view window to refresh the display; it should look exactly the same.

All the text is now formatted by the single CSS rule
`div { color: blue; font-family: Verdana; }`.

## Descendant theory

The descendant theory describes how formatting can target a particular element based on its position relative to other elements. By constructing a selector using multiple elements, in addition to ID and class attributes, you can target the formatting to specific instances of text as it appears within your webpage. Let's take a look at how descendant selectors influence CSS formatting.

**1**  Open **descendant.html** from the lesson03 folder. In Split view, observe the CSS code and the structure of the HTML content.

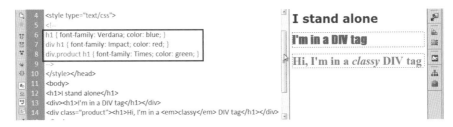

The page contains three h1 elements. The elements appear in three different ways: alone, within a div, and within a div that features an applied class attribute. In addition to the HTML markup, there are also three CSS rules that apply various types of styling to these elements.

What is interesting about these rules is that they don't always apply styling directly to the h1 elements, but to h1 elements as they appear within the HTML structure. Note how the first <h1> element is formatted as blue Verdana.

**2**  In the Code view window, select the entire first <h1> element.

**3**  Select Edit > Copy.

**4**  Insert the cursor after the closing tag of the code `<h1>I'm in a DIV tag</h1>`.

**5**  Select Edit > Paste. Click in the Design view window to refresh the display.

The new `<h1>` element appears, formatted as red Impact, exactly like the other `<h1>` element within the same `<div>`. What happened to blue Verdana? The CSS automatically differentiates stand-alone h1 elements from those that appear within a `<div>`. In other words, you don't have to apply a special format or change an existing one. Just move the element into the proper structure or location within the code, and it formats itself. Cool. Let's try it again.

6   In the Code view window, insert the cursor after the closing tag of `<h1>Hi, I'm in a <em>classy</em> DIV tag</h1>`.

7   Select Edit > Paste. Click in the Design view window to refresh the display.

The `<h1>` element appears, formatted as green Times. Once again the pasted text matches the formatting applied to the other h1 element within the `<div>`, its original styling ignored altogether.

## Specificity theory

Specificity describes how browsers determine what formatting to apply when two or more rules conflict. Some refer to this as *weight*—giving certain rules more priority based on order, proximity, inheritance, and descendant relationships. Such conflicts are the bane of most web designers' existence and can waste hours of time in troubleshooting errors in CSS formatting. Let's take a look at how specificity affects the weight of some sample rules.

1   Open **specificity.html** from the lesson03 folder. In Split view, observe the CSS code and the structure of the HTML content. Then, note the appearance of the text in the Design view window.

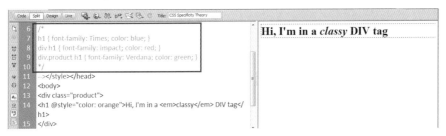

There are three CSS rules in the <head> section of the file. All of them potentially could format the <h1> element on the page. But, at the moment, none of the rules is actually formatting the text.

Do you see the slash and asterisk (/*) at the beginning of the CSS markup? This notation is used to create a comment within CSS code and effectively disables the rules that follow. The commented code ends with a similar notation reversing the order of the slash and the asterisk (*/). In Dreamweaver, commented code usually appears grayed out.

Also, note that the opening tag of the <h1> element features an attribute: @style. This inline CSS style markup has been disabled by appending the @ symbol to the beginning of the word. You can re-enable all the CSS styling by merely deleting the /* and */ notations, along with the @ symbol within the attribute.

But before you do this, can you determine—based on the syntax and order of the rules—what formatting will apply to the sample text? For example, will the text appear in Times, Impact, or Verdana? Will it be blue, red, green, or orange? Let's see.

2   Select the notation /* at the beginning of the CSS code and delete it.

3   Select the notation */ at the end of the CSS code and delete it.

4   Select the @ symbol in the <h1> attribute and delete it.

5   Click in the Design view window to refresh the display.

If you picked the inline style markup inserted within the <h1> tag itself as the winner, you are at the head of the class. The text displays in orange as specified. But did you notice that the inline style doesn't specify a typeface? So, then why does the text display in the typeface Verdana?

Although inline styles trump any other formatting, CSS rules don't always work alone. As mentioned earlier, CSS rules may style more than one HTML element at a time, and some rules may overlap or inherit styling from one another. In this case, the <h1> element is picking up the font family from one of the other rules. Can you determine which one?

6   Select and delete the entire inline style markup within the `<h1>` tag: `style="color: orange"`.

7   Click in the Design view window to refresh the display.

The last line of text is now wholly formatted by the `div.product h1` rule. Can you explain why? The notation `.product` within the selector refers to the `class="product"` attribute, which is assigned to the `<h1>` element. Classes are used to apply CSS styling to text when other methods can't produce the desired effect or when you need to override specific defaults. You'll explore classes more fully later in this lesson.

Each of the theories described here has a role to play in how CSS styling is applied through your webpage and across your site. When the style sheet is loaded, the browser will use the following hierarchy—with number 4 being the most powerful—to determine how the styles are applied, especially when rules conflict:

1.  Cascade

2.  Inheritance

3.  Descendant structure

4.  Specificity

Of course, knowing this hierarchy doesn't help much when you are faced with a CSS conflict on a page with dozens or perhaps hundreds of rules. In such cases, Dreamweaver comes to the rescue with a fantastic feature named Code Navigator.

## Code Navigator

The Code Navigator is an editing tool within Dreamweaver that allows you to instantly inspect an HTML element and assess its CSS-based formatting. When activated, it will display all the CSS rules that have some role in formatting an element, and it will list the order of their cascade application and specificity. The Code Navigator works in both Code view and Design view.

1   If necessary, open **specificity.html** as modified in the previous exercise. In Split view, observe the CSS code and the structure of the HTML content.

```
1  <!DOCTYPE HTML>
2  <head>
3  <title>CSS Specificity Theory</title>
4  <style type="text/css">
5  <!--
6
7  h1 { font-family: Times; color: blue; }
8  div h1 { font-family: Impact; color: red; }
9  div.product h1 { font-family: Verdana; color: green; }
```

Hi, I'm a *classy* DIV tag

Although this file is simple in nature, it features three CSS rules that may format the `<h1>` element. In an actual webpage, the possibility of styling conflicts grows with each new rule added. But with the Code Navigator, sussing out such problems becomes child's play.

**2** In Design view, insert the cursor in the heading text.

```
2  <head>
3  <title>CSS Specificity Theory</title>
4  <style type="text/css">
5  <!--
6
7  h1 { font-family: Times; color: blue; }
8  div h1 { font-family: Impact; color: red; }
9  div.product h1 { font-family: Verdana; color: green; }
```

Hi, I'm a *classy* DIV tag

Click indicator to bring up the Code Navigator.

After a moment, an icon that looks like a ship's wheel appears. This icon provides instant access to the Code Navigator.

**Note:** You can also access the Code Navigator by right-clicking the element and selecting View > Code Navigator from the context menu, or by pressing Alt-Ctrl-N/ Opt-Cmd-N.

**3** Click the Code Navigator icon.

```
2  <head>
3  <title>CSS Specificity Theory</title>
4  <style type="text/css">
5  <!--
6
7  h1 { font-family: Times; color: blue; }
8  div h1 { font-family: Impact; color: red; }
9  div.product h1 { font-family: Verdana; color: green; }
10
```

Hi, I'm a *classy* DIV tag

specificity.html
  h1
  div h1
  div.product h1

Alt+click to show    Disable indicator

A small window appears, displaying a list of three CSS rules that apply to this heading. The sequence of rules in the list indicates both their cascade order and their specificity. When rules conflict, rules farther down in the list override rules that are higher up. Remember, elements may inherit styling from one or more rules, and default styling may be overridden by more-specific settings.

The `div.product h1` rule appears at the bottom of the Code Navigator display, indicating that its specifications are probably styling this element. But many factors can influence which of the rules may win. Sometimes it's simply the order in which rules are declared in the style sheet that determines which one is actually applied. As you saw earlier, changing the order of rules can often affect how the rules work.

**4** In the Code view window, select the entire
`div.product h1 { font-family: Verdana; color: green; }` rule.

**5** Select Edit > Cut.

**6** Insert the cursor in front of the `h1 { font-family: Times; color: blue; }` rule.

**7** Select Edit > Paste. Press Enter/Return, if necessary, to insert a line break.

**8** Click in the Design view window to refresh the display.

The styling did not change.

**9** In Code view, insert the cursor into the text of the <h1> element. Activate the Code Navigator.

Although the rule was moved to the top of the style sheet, the display of rules did not change, because the div.product h1 rule has a higher specificity than the other two rules. In this instance, it would win no matter where it was placed in the code, but its specificity can easily be changed by modifying the selector.

**10** Select and delete the class notation .product in the selector.

**11** Click in the Design view window to refresh the display.

```
7  div h1 { font-family: Verdana; color: green; }
8  h1 { font-family: Times; color: blue; }
9  div h1 { font-family: Impact; color: red; }
```

Hi, I'm a *classy* DIV tag

Did you notice how the styling changed?

**12** Insert the cursor in the heading and activate the Code Navigator.

By removing the class notation from its selector, the rule now has equal value to the div h1 { font-family: Impact; color: red; } rule. But, since this rule is the last one declared in the code, it now takes precedence in the cascade. Is it starting to make more sense? Don't worry—it will over time. Until that time, just remember that the rule that appears last in the Code Navigator has the most influence on any particular element.

# Formatting objects

The last concept you'll explore in this lesson is also the most complex and prone to error: object formatting. Consider object formatting as specifications directed at modifying an element's size, background, borders, margins, padding, and positioning. Since CSS can redefine any HTML element, object formatting basically can be applied to any tag, although it's most commonly directed at the <div> element.

By default, all elements start at the top of the browser screen and appear consecutively one after the other from left to right, top to bottom. *Block* elements generate their own line or paragraph breaks; *inline* elements appear at the point of insertion.

CSS can break all of these default constraints and let you size, format, and position elements almost any way you want them.

Size is one of the most basic specifications for an HTML element. CSS can control both the width and the height of an element, with varying degrees of success. All specifications can be expressed in *relative* terms (percentages, ems, or exs) or in *absolute* terms (pixels, inches, points, centimeters, and so on).

## Width

Setting the width of an HTML element is simple. Let's take a look at an example.

1 Open **width.html** from the lesson03 folder.

2 View the page in Split view, and observe the CSS code and HTML structure.

By default, block elements occupy 100 percent of the width of the browser window. Otherwise, CSS can define element measurements in absolute or relative terms.

The file contains four `<div>` elements, formatted with a mixture of relative and absolute width settings.

Box 1 is unformatted to demonstrate how block elements display by default. It will occupy 100% of the width of the browser window. By contrast, the CSS specifications for Box 2 set the width to 50%. The percentage specifies what portion of the screen the element will fill. Relative measurements allow the elements to automatically adapt to changes to the width of the browser. For example, if you were to drag the divider between the Code view and Design view windows left or right, Box 2 would always display at half the width of the Design view window.

Element widths set to percentages will adapt automatically to changes in the browser window, maintaining their relative dimension within the space. Absolute measurements don't react to changes in the browser window.

Box 3 is formatted to a fixed measurement of 200 pixels. It will maintain this width no matter what happens to the size of the browser screen. This is a popular method with many designers because it allows them to tightly control the size and shape of page components. But it doesn't easily account for users' interaction with your page. For example, a fixed-width layout can't adapt to user requests for increases or decreases in font size. Such requests can often break page layouts when they're based in pixels or other absolute measurements.

The last `<div>` demonstrates a system that is kind of an amalgam of both relative and absolute measurements. It is formatted to a width of 10 ems. The em is a measurement that is more familiar to print designers. It's based on the size of the typeface and font being used. In other words, use a large font and the em gets bigger; use a small font and the em gets smaller. It even changes based on whether the font is a condensed or expanded face. In web design, the em (and ex) takes its cue from the base font defined in the `<body>` tag, the default font of the webpage itself.

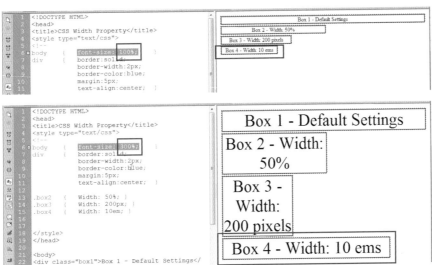

Widths specified in ems allow your page elements to adapt to user requests for increases or decreases in font size.

If you were to change the `font-size` property in the `body` rule from 100% to 300%, the fourth `<div>` would automatically scale up three times larger, preserving the relationship of the container's size relative to the text. The elements formatted in pixels or percentages would not change at all.

## Height

Ideally, you should be able to specify the height of all elements the same way you do the width. Unfortunately, the reality is not so simple. Past browser support for the `height` property was not consistent or reliable. Today, modern browsers shouldn't present many surprises if you're working in absolute measurements, like pixels, points, inches, and so on. Relative measurements in ems or exs probably won't disappoint either. But measurements in percentages require a small workaround, or hack, to make most browsers honor them.

1　Open **height.html** from the lesson03 folder. Display the file in Split view, and observe the CSS and HTML code.

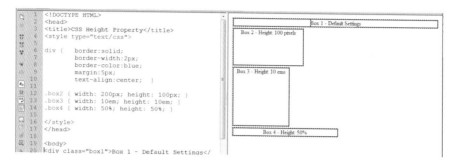

The file contains four `<div>` elements employing examples of both relative and absolute height settings. Box 1 demonstrates the default behavior of block elements; it takes up only as much height as the content contained within it requires. Box 2 is set to a height of 100 pixels; it will remain at this fixed height regardless of changes to the screen size or orientation. Box 3 is set to a height of 10 ems. Although the em is a relative measurement, the height doesn't take its cue from the screen size; instead it's dependent on the size of the base font, as described earlier. Change the default font size and the `<div>` reacts accordingly.

So far, so good. The `height` property seems to be pretty straightforward and works as expected in the first three elements. But Box 4 is the one that's going to cause all the trouble. It's set to a height of 50%, and you'd expect it to be taking up half the height of the screen. But, as you can see in the Design view window, it's no taller than Box 1. What's the problem?

Most browsers, and even Dreamweaver's Design view window, ignore heights set in percentages. The reasons for this have to do with how browsers calculate the size of the page window. Basically, it boils down to the fact that browsers calculate width but don't calculate height. This behavior doesn't affect fixed measurements or measurements set in ems or exs, but it does mess up percentages. This is where the aforementioned HTML hack comes in.

2　Insert the cursor at the beginning of the CSS markup.

3　Type **html, body { height: 100% }**.

Adding the `height` property to the root elements of your webpage gives the browser the information it needs to calculate any element heights set in percentages. But to see the results, you'll have to use Live view or preview the page in an actual browser.

**4** Click the Live view button to enable Live view.

**Note:** In most applications, height won't be strictly observed by any element. By default, it is intended to be a fluid specification that allows an element to automatically adapt to the space requirements of its content.

Box 4 now occupies 50% of the height of the Design view window.

Although browser support is much better today, it's vital to test all your design settings in all the popular browsers to ensure that the pages display properly.

## Borders and backgrounds

Each element can feature four individually formatted borders (top, bottom, left, and right). These are handy for creating boxed elements, but you can also place them at the top or bottom (or both) of paragraphs in place of <hr/> (horizontal rule) elements to separate text areas.

**1** Open **borders.html** from the lesson03 folder. Display the file in Split view, and observe the CSS and HTML code.

```
1  <!DOCTYPE HTML>
2  <head>
3  <title>CSS Border Effects</title>
4  <style type="text/css">
5  <!--
6  body {
7      margin-left: 50px;
8      font-family: "Trebuchet MS", Verdana,
   Tahoma, Arial, Helvetica, sans-serif;
9      margin-right: 100px;
10     margin-top: 50px;
11 }
12 h1 {
13     border-left-width: 35px;
14     border-left-style: solid;
15     border-left-color: #000;
16     padding-left: 10px;
```

**Borders Create Great Effects**

Use borders for more than boxes. Add them to the top
and bottom of paragraphs to replace horizontal rules,
or...

To create 3D buttons!

The file contains three examples of text elements formatted with border effects. As you can see, borders can be used for more than just creating boxes. Here you see them used as graphical accents to paragraphs and even to simulate a three-dimensional button effect.

It's also important to point out that there is no extraneous markup within the actual content; all the effects are generated by CSS code alone. That means you can quickly adjust, turn on, and turn off effects, and you can move the content easily without having to worry about graphical elements cluttering up the code.

By default, all element backgrounds are transparent, but CSS enables you to format them with colors, images, or both. If both are used, the image will appear above, or in front of, the color. This behavior allows you to use an image with a transparent background to create layered graphical effects. If the image fills the visible space or is set to repeat, it may obscure the color entirely.

2   Open **backgrounds.html** from the lesson03 folder. Display the file in Split view, and observe the CSS and HTML code.

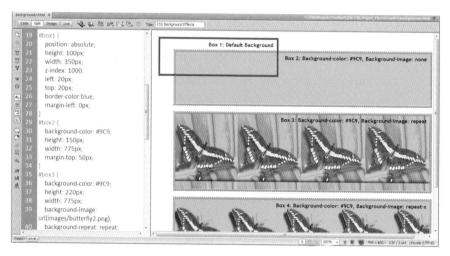

The file contains several examples of CSS background effects. Borders have been added to the <div> elements to make the effects easier to see.

Box 1 displays the default HTML transparent background. Box 2 depicts a background with a solid color. Box 3 shows a background image that repeats in both directions along the x-axis and y-axis. It also features a background color, but it's completely obscured by the repeating image. Box 4 also shows a background image, but its transparency and drop-shadow effect allow you to see the background color around the edges of the image.

Be sure to fully test any background treatments. In some applications, CSS background specifications are not fully supported or are supported inconsistently.

## Margins and padding

Margins create space outside an element—between one element and another; padding adds spacing between the content of an element and its border, whether or not it's visible. The effective use of such spacing is vital in the overall design of your webpage.

1   Open **margins_padding.html** from the lesson03 folder. Display the file in Split view, and observe the CSS and HTML code.

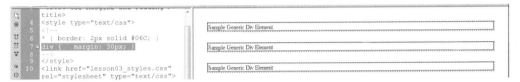

The file contains several `<div>` elements stacked one on top of the other, sample text headings, and paragraph elements. All the elements display the default HTML formatting for margins and padding. Borders have been applied to all the elements to make the spacing effects easier to see.

To add spacing between `<div>` elements, you'll now add a margin specification.

2   Insert the cursor in the CSS section of the code. Type **div { margin: 30px; }**.

3   Click to refresh the Design view window.

The `<div>` elements are now spaced 30 pixels apart. By using the notation `margin: 30px`, you added 30 pixels to all four sides, but that doesn't mean you'll see 60 pixels between the elements. When two adjacent elements both have margins, the settings don't combine; instead, browsers use only the larger of any two settings.

Padding is used to put spacing between an element's content and its border.

4   In the `div` rule, insert the cursor after the `margin: 30px;` notation.

5   Press Enter/Return to insert a new line. Type **padding: 30px;**.

6   Click to refresh the Design view window.

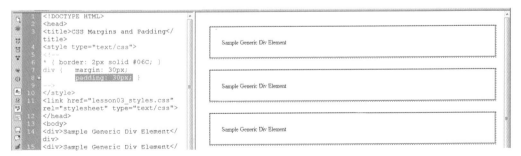

You can see 30 pixels of padding appear within each `<div>` element. Since padding is applied within the element boundaries, it will combine with margin settings to affect the overall spacing that appears between elements. Padding can also affect the specified width of an element and must be factored into the design of your page components.

Unlike the <div> element, text elements, such as <p>, <h1> through <h6>, <ol>, and <ul>, already have margin settings applied to them, as you can see from the sample text within the page. Many designers abhor these default specifications, especially because they may vary among browsers. Instead, they start off most projects by purposely removing these settings in a technique that's called *normalization*. In other words, they declare a list of common elements and reset their default specifications to more desirable, consistent settings, as you'll do now.

7   In the CSS section, create a new line after the div rule.

8   Type **p, h1, h2, h3, h4, h5, h6, li { margin: 0px }**.

9   Click to refresh the Design view window.

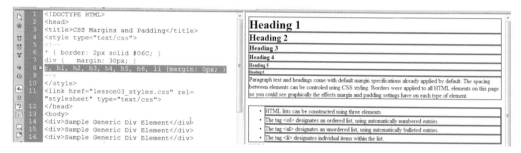

The text elements now display without the default spacing. Using zero margins may be a bit extreme for your own tastes, but you get the picture. As you become more comfortable with CSS and webpage design, you can develop your own default specifications and implement them in this way.

## Positioning

By default, all elements start at the top of the browser screen and appear consecutively one after the other from left to right, top to bottom. Block elements generate their own line or paragraph breaks; inline elements appear at the point of insertion.

CSS can break all these default constraints and let you place elements almost anywhere you want them to be. As with other object formatting, positioning can be specified in *relative* terms (such as left, right, center, and so on) or by *absolute* coordinates measured in pixels, inches, centimeters, or other standard measurement systems. Using CSS, you can even layer one element above or below another to create amazing graphical effects. By using positioning commands carefully, you can create a variety of page layouts, including popular multicolumn designs.

1. Open **positioning.html** from the lesson03 folder. Display the file in Split view, and observe the CSS and HTML code.

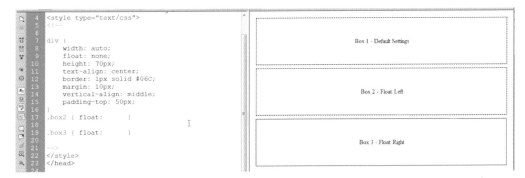

The file contains three `<div>` elements; they are stacked one on top of the other and occupy the full width of the Design view window, in the default manner of all block elements. Using CSS, you can control the placement of these elements. But first, you'll have to reduce the width so that more than one item can fit side by side.

2. In the `div` rule, change the `width` property from `auto` to **30%**.

3. Click to refresh the Design view window.

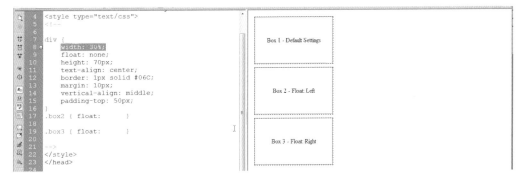

The `<div>` elements resize but remain stacked. There are several methods that can be used to position elements on the screen, but the *float* method is by far the most popular.

4. In the `div` rule, change the `float` property from `none` to **left**.

5. Click to refresh the Design view window.

All three `<div>` elements now display in a single row, side by side. Using class attributes, you can control each `<div>` individually.

6  In the `div` rule, change the `float` property from `left` to **none**.

7  In the `.box2` rule, change the `float` property from `none` to **left**.

8  In the `.box3` rule, change the `float` property from `none` to **right**.

9  Click to refresh the Design view window.

The page now contains a mix of default and float specifications. Box 1 displays on a line of its own, in the default manner. Box 2 appears on the next line, aligned to the left side of the screen as specified. Box 3 appears on the right side of the screen, but on the same line as Box 2. In subsequent lessons, you will learn how to combine different float attributes with various width, height, margin, and padding settings to create sophisticated layouts for your website designs.

Unfortunately, as powerful as CSS positioning seems to be, it is the one aspect of CSS that is most prone to misinterpretation by the various browsers in use today. Commands and formatting that work fine in one browser can be translated differently or totally ignored—with tragic results—in another. In fact, formatting that works fine on one page of your website can fail on another page containing a different mix of code elements.

# Multiples, classes, and IDs, oh my!

By taking advantage of the cascade, inheritance, descendant, and specificity theories, you can target formatting to almost any element anywhere on a webpage. But CSS offers a few more ways to optimize and customize the formatting even further.

## Applying formatting to multiple elements

To speed things up, CSS allows you to apply formatting to multiple elements at once by listing each in the selector, separated by commas. For example, the formatting in these rules:

```
h1 { font-family: Verdana; color: blue; }
h2 { font-family: Verdana; color: blue; }
h3 { font-family: Verdana; color: blue; }
```

can also be expressed like this:

```
h1, h2, h3 { font-family: Verdana; color: blue; }
```

## Creating class attributes

Frequently, you will want to create unique formatting to apply to objects, paragraphs, phrases, words, or even individual characters appearing within a webpage. To accomplish this, CSS allows you make your own custom attributes, called *class* and *ID*.

Class attributes may be applied to any number of elements on a page, whereas ID attributes may appear only once. If you are a print designer, think of classes as similar to a combination of Adobe InDesign's paragraph, character, and object styles. Class and ID names can be a single word, an abbreviation, any combination of letters and numbers, or almost anything, but they may not start with a number or contain spaces. While it's not strictly prohibited, you should avoid using HTML attribute names.

● **Note:** Dreamweaver will warn you when you enter a name that's inappropriate.

To declare a CSS class selector, insert a period before the name within the style sheet, like this:

```
.intro
.copyright
```

Then, you apply the CSS class to an entire HTML element as an attribute, like this:

```
<p class="intro">Type intro text here.</p>
```

or to individual characters or words inline, like this:

```
Here is <span class="copyright">some text</span> formatted
differently.
```

## Creating ID attributes

HTML designates ID as a unique attribute. Therefore, a specific ID should not be assigned to more than one element per page. In the past, many web designers used ID attributes to point at specific components within the page, such as the header, the footer, or articles. With the advent of HTML5 elements—header, footer, aside, article, and so on—the use of ID and class attributes for this purpose is less necessary than it was. But IDs can still be used to identify specific text elements, images, and tables to assist you in building powerful hypertext navigation within your page and site. You will learn more about using IDs this way in Lesson 9, "Working with Navigation."

To declare an ID attribute in a CSS style sheet, insert a number sign, or hash mark, before the name, like this:

```
#contact_info
#disclaimer
```

You apply the CSS ID to an entire HTML element as an attribute, like this:

```
<div id="contact_info"></div>
<div id="disclaimer"></div>
```

# CSS3 overview and support

The Internet doesn't stand still for long. Technologies and standards are evolving and changing constantly. The members of the W3C have been working diligently to adapt the web to the latest realities, which include powerful mobile devices, large flat-panel displays, and HD video—all of which seem to get better and cheaper every day. This is the urgency currently driving the development of HTML5 and CSS3.

Although these standards have not been officially adopted, browser vendors are already implementing many of their features and techniques. If you feel adventuresome and would like to live on the edge, Dreamweaver won't leave you in the lurch. The program already provides ample support for the current mix of HTML5 elements and CSS3 formatting, and as new features and capabilities are developed, you can count on Adobe to add them to the program as quickly as possible.

As you work through the upcoming lessons, you will be introduced to many of these new and exciting techniques and actually implement many of the more stable HTML5 and CSS3 features within your own sample pages.

## CSS3 features and effects

There are over two dozen new features in CSS3. Many are ready now and have been implemented in all the modern browsers; others are still experimental and are supported less fully. Among the new features, you will find

- Rounded corners and border effects

- Box and text shadows

- Transparency and translucency

- Gradient fills

- Multicolumn text elements

All these features and more can be implemented via Dreamweaver today. The program will even assist you in building vendor-specific markup when necessary. To give you a quick tour of some of the coolest features and effects brewing in CSS3, we'll take a look at a sample file.

1   Open **css3_demo.html** from the lesson03 folder. Display the file in Split view, and observe the CSS and HTML code.

Many of the new effects can't be previewed directly in Design view, so you'll need to use Live view or preview the page in an actual browser.

**2** Click the Live view button to preview all the CSS3 effects.

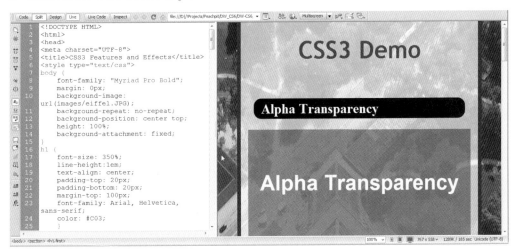

The file contains a hodgepodge of features and effects that may surprise and even delight you—but don't get too excited. Although many of these features are already supported in Dreamweaver and will work fine in modern browsers, there's still a lot of older hardware and software out there that can turn your dream site into a nightmare. And, there's at least one additional twist.

Some of the new CSS3 features have not been standardized, and certain browsers may not recognize the default markup generated by Dreamweaver. In these instances, you may have to include specific vendor commands to make them work properly. These commands are preceded by a vendor prefix, such as −ie, −moz, and −webkit. If you look carefully in the code of the demo file, you'll be able to find examples of these within the CSS markup.

## Additional CSS support

CSS formatting and application is so complex and powerful that this short lesson can't cover all aspects of the subject. For a full examination of CSS, check out the following books:

- *Bulletproof Web Design: Improving Flexibility and Protecting Against Worst-Case Scenarios with HTML5 and CSS3 (3rd edition)*, Dan Cederholm (New Riders Press, 2012) ISBN: 978-0-321-80835-6

- *CSS: The Missing Manual*, David Sawyer McFarland (O'Reilly Media, 2009) ISBN: 978-0-596-80244-8

- *Stylin' with CSS: A Designer's Guide (2nd edition)*, Charles Wyke-Smith (New Riders Press, 2007) ISBN: 978-0-321-52556-7

- *The Art & Science of CSS*, Jonathan Snook, Steve Smith, Jina Bolton, Cameron Adams, and David Johnson (SitePoint, 2007) ISBN: 978-0-975-84197-6

# Review questions

1  Should you still use HTML-based formatting?

2  What does CSS impose on each HTML element?

3  True or false? If you do nothing, HTML elements will feature no formatting or structure.

4  What four "theories" affect the application of CSS formatting?

5  What is the difference between block and inline elements?

6  True or false? CSS3 features are all experimental, and you should not use them at all.

# Review answers

1  No. HTML-based formatting was deprecated in 1997 when HTML 4 was adopted. Industry best practices recommend using CSS-based formatting instead.

2  CSS imposes an imaginary box on each element and can then apply borders, background colors and images, margins, padding, and other types of formatting.

3  False. Even if you do nothing, many HTML elements feature built-in formatting.

4  The four theories that affect CSS formatting are cascade, inheritance, descendant, and specificity.

5  Block elements create stand-alone structures; inline elements appear at the insertion point.

6  False. Many CSS3 features are already supported by modern browsers and can be used today.

# 4

# CREATING A PAGE LAYOUT

## Lesson Overview

In this lesson, you'll learn the following:

- The basics of webpage design

- How to create design thumbnails and wireframes

- How to insert and format new components into a predefined CSS layout

- How to use the Code Navigator to identify CSS formatting

- How to check for browser compatibility

 This lesson should take 1 hour to complete. Before beginning, make sure you have copied the files for Lesson 4 to your hard drive as described in the "Getting Started" section at the beginning of the book. If you are starting from scratch in this lesson, use the method described in the "Jumpstart" section of "Getting Started."

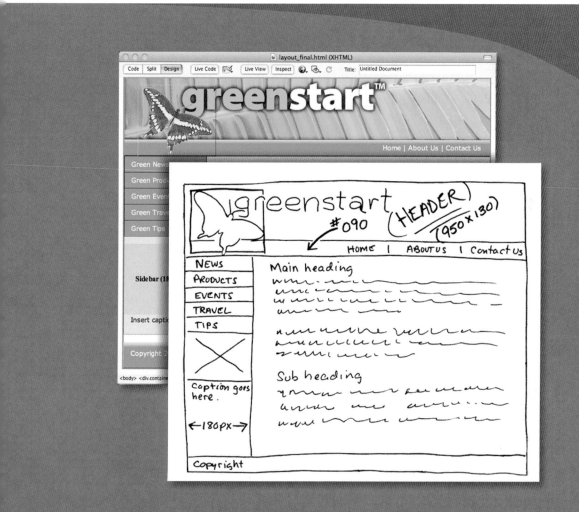

Whether you use thumbnails and wireframes or just a vivid imagination, Dreamweaver can quickly turn design concepts into complete, standards-based CSS layouts.

# Web design basics

Before you begin any web design project for yourself or for a client, there are three important questions you need to answer:

- What is the purpose of the website?
- Who is the customer?
- How do they get here?

## What is the purpose of the website?

Will the website sell or support a product or service? Is your site for entertainment or games? Will you provide information or news? Will you need a shopping cart or database? Do you need to accept credit card payments or electronic transfers? Knowing the purpose of the website tells you what type of content you'll be developing and working with and what types of technologies you'll need to incorporate.

## Who is the customer?

Are the customers adults, children, seniors, professionals, hobbyists, men, women, everyone? Knowing *who* your market will be is vital to the overall design and functionality of your site. A site intended for children probably needs more animation, interactivity, and bright engaging colors. Adults will want serious content and in-depth analysis. Seniors may need larger type and other accessibility enhancements.

Could two sites be more different than Google and Yahoo? Yet they both perform the same service.

A good first step is to check out the competition. Is there an existing website performing the same service or selling the same product? Are they successful? You don't have to mimic others just because they're doing the same thing. Look at Google and Yahoo. They perform the same basic service, but their site designs couldn't be more different from one another.

## How do they get here?

This sounds like an odd question when speaking of the Internet. But, just as with a brick-and-mortar business, your online customers can come to you in a variety of ways. For example, are they accessing your site on a desktop computer, laptop, tablet, or cell phone? Are they using high-speed Internet, wireless, or dial-up service? What browser do they most like to use, and what is the size and resolution of the display? These answers will tell you a lot about what kind of experience your customers will expect. Dial-up and cell phone users may not want to see a lot of graphics or video, while users with large flat-panel displays and high-speed connections may demand as much bang and sizzle as you can send at them.

So, where do you get this information? Some you'll have to get through painstaking research and demographic analysis. Some you'll get from educated guesses based on your own tastes and understanding of your market. But a lot of it is actually available on the Internet itself. W3Schools, for one, keeps track of tons of statistics regarding access and usage, all updated regularly:

- **w3schools.com/browsers/browsers_stats.asp**: Provides more information about browser statistics.

- **w3schools.com/browsers/browsers_os.asp**: Gives the breakdown on operating systems. In 2011, they started to track the usage of mobile devices on the Internet.

- **w3schools.com/browsers/browsers_display.asp**: Lets you find out the latest information on the resolutions, or size, of screens using the Internet.

If you are redesigning an existing site, your web hosting service itself may provide valuable statistics on historical traffic patterns and even the visitors themselves. If you host your own site, third-party tools are available, like Google Analytics and Adobe Omniture, which you can incorporate into your code to do the tracking for you for free or for a small fee.

When you boil down all the statistics, this is what you will find as of the beginning of 2012. Windows (80 to 90 percent) dominates the Internet, with most users divided almost equally between Firefox (37 percent) and Google Chrome (33 percent), with various versions of Internet Explorer (22 percent) taking third position. The vast majority of browsers are set to a resolution *higher* than 1024 pixels by 768 pixels. If it weren't for the growth in usage of cell phones and smartphones for accessing the Internet, these statistics would be great news for most web designers and developers. Designing a website that can look good and work effectively for both flat-panel displays and cell phones is a tall order.

Each day, more people are using cell phones and other mobile devices to access the Internet. Some users may use them now to access the Internet more frequently than they use desktop computers. This presents a nagging problem to web designers. For one thing, cell phone screens are a fraction of the size of even the smallest flat-panel display. How do you cram a two- or three-column page design into a meager 200 to 300 pixels? Another problem is that many device manufacturers have decided to follow Apple's decision to drop support for Flash-based content on their mobile devices. Keep all these statistics in mind as you go through the process of designing your site.

Many of the concepts of print design are not applicable to the web, because you are not in control of the user's experience. A page carefully designed for a typical flat panel is basically useless on a cell phone.

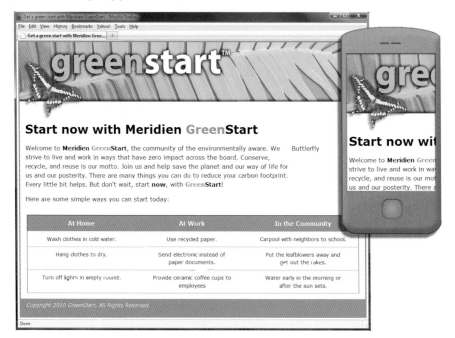

## Scenario

For the purposes of this book you will be working to develop a website for Meridien GreenStart, a fictitious community-based organization dedicated to green investment and action. This website will offer a variety of products and services and require a broad range of webpage types, including dynamic pages using server-based technologies like PHP.

Your customers come from a broad demographic including all ages and education levels. They are people who are concerned about environmental conditions and who are dedicated to conservation, recycling, and the reuse of natural and human resources.

Your marketing research indicates that most of your customers use desktop computers or laptops, connecting via high-speed Internet services, but that you can expect 10 to 20 percent of your visitors via cell phone and other mobile devices.

# Working with thumbnails and wireframes

The next step, after you have nailed down the answers to the three questions about your website purpose, customer demographic, and access model, is to determine how many pages you'll need, what those pages will do, and finally, what they will look like.

## Creating thumbnails

Many web designers start by drawing thumbnails with pencil and paper. Think of thumbnails as a graphical shopping list of the pages you'll need to create for the website. Thumbnails can also help you work out the basic website navigation structure. Draw lines between the thumbnails showing how your navigation will connect them.

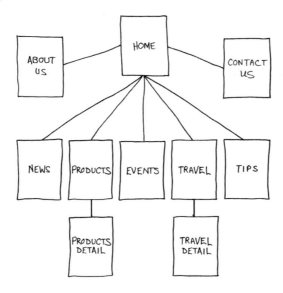

Thumbnails list the pages that need to be built and how they are connected to each other.

Most sites are divided into levels. Typically, the first level includes all the pages in your main navigation menu, the ones a visitor can reach directly from the home page. The second level includes pages you can reach only through specific actions or from specific locations, say from a shopping cart or product detail page.

## Creating a page design

Once you've figured out what your site needs in terms of pages, products, and services, you can then turn to what those pages will look like. Make a list of components you want on each page, such as headers and footers, navigation, and areas for the main content and the sidebars (if any). Put aside any items that won't be needed on every page. What other factors do you need to consider?

1. Header (includes banner and logo)
2. Footer (copyright info)
3. Horizontal navigation (for internal reference, i.e., Home, About Us, Contact Us)
4. Vertical navigation (links to products and services)
5. Main content (one-column with chance of two or more)

Do you have a company logo, business identity, graphic imagery, or color scheme you want to accent? Do you have publications, brochures, or current advertising campaigns you want to emulate? It helps to gather them all in one place so you can see everything all at once on a desk or conference table. If you're lucky, a theme will rise organically from this collage.

Once you've created your checklist of the components that you'll need on each page, sketch out several rough layouts that work for these components. Most designers settle on one basic page design that is a compromise between flexibility and sizzle. Some site designs may naturally lean toward using more than one basic layout. But resist the urge to design each page separately. Minimizing the number of page designs may sound like a major limitation, but it's key to producing a professional-looking site. It's the reason why some professionals, like doctors and airline pilots, wear uniforms. Using a consistent page design, or template, lends a sense of professionalism and gives confidence to your visitor.

Wireframes allow you to experiment with page designs quickly and easily without wasting time with code.

While you figure out what your pages will look like, you'll have to address the size and placement of the basic components. Where you put a component can drastically affect its impact and usefulness. In print, designers know that the upper-left corner of a layout is considered one of the "power positions," a place where you want to locate important aspects of a design, such as a logo or title. This is because in western culture we read from left to right, top to bottom. The second power position is the lower-right corner because this is the last thing your eyes will see when you're finished reading.

Unfortunately, in web design this theory doesn't work so well because of one simple reason: You can never be certain how the user is seeing your design. Are they on a 20-inch flat panel or a 2-inch cell phone?

In most instances, the only thing you can be certain of is that the user can see the upper-left corner of any page. Do you want to waste this position by slapping the company logo here? Or, make the site more useful by slipping in a navigation menu? This is one of the key predicaments of the web designer. Do you go for design sizzle, workable utility, or something in between?

## Creating wireframes

After you pick the winning design, wireframing is a fast way to work out the structure of each page in the site. A wireframe is like a thumbnail, but bigger, that sketches out each page and fills in more details about the components, such as actual link names and main headings. This step helps to catch or anticipate problems before you smack into them when working in the code.

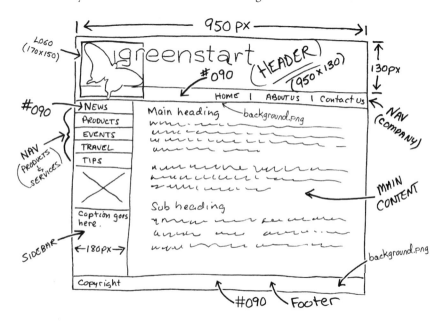

The wireframe for the final design should identify the components and feature markup for content, color, and dimensions.

Once the basic concepts are worked out, many designers take an extra step and create a full-size mockup or "proof of concept" using a program like Adobe Fireworks, Photoshop, or even Illustrator. It's a handy thing to do because you'll find that some clients just aren't comfortable giving an approval based only on pencil sketches. The advantage here is that all these programs allow you to export the results to full-size images (JPEG, GIF, or PNG) that can be viewed in a browser. Such mockups are as good as seeing the real thing but may take only a fraction of the time to produce.

In some cases, creating a mockup in Photoshop, Fireworks, or Illustrator can save hours of tedious coding to receive a needed approval.

▶ **Tip:** For years, designers have started the design process in Fireworks, where they can create a fully functional mockup (with menus, links, and hotspots) that can then be exported to a CSS-based HTML layout and then edited in Dreamweaver.

# Defining a Dreamweaver site

From this point forward, the lessons in this book function within a Dreamweaver site. You will create webpages from scratch and use existing files and resources that are stored on your hard drive, which combined make up what's called your *local* site. When you are ready to upload your site to the Internet (see Lesson 16, "Publishing to the Web"), you publish your completed files to a web host server, which then becomes your *remote* site. The folder structures and files of the local and remote sites are usually mirrors of each other.

First, let's set up your local site:

1 Launch Adobe Dreamweaver CS6, if necessary.

2 Choose Site > New Site. The Site Setup dialog box appears.

   If you've used any previous version of Dreamweaver, you will notice that the Site Setup dialog box has been slightly redesigned. Along with the options for creating a standard Dreamweaver site, the dialog offers the ability to create a site based on the services offered by Adobe Business Catalyst. Business Catalyst is an online, hosted application that allows you to build and manage rich, dynamic web-based businesses. To learn more about the capabilities of Business Catalyst, check out www.BusinessCatalyst.com.

   To create a standard website in Dreamweaver CS6, you need only name it and select the local site folder. Site names typically relate to a specific project or client and will appear in the Files panel. This name is intended for your own purposes, so there are no limitations to the name you can choose. It's a good idea to use a name that clearly describes the purpose of the website.

**3** In the Site Name field, type **DW-CS6**.

**4** Next to the Local Site Folder field, click the folder ( 📁 ) icon. When the Choose Root Folder dialog box opens, navigate to the DW-CS6 folder containing the lesson files you copied from the *Adobe Dreamweaver CS6 Classroom in a Book* CD and click Select/Choose.

You could click Save at this time and begin working on your new website, but we'll add one more piece of handy information.

**5** Click the arrow (▶) next to the Advanced Settings category to reveal the tabs listed there. Select the Local Info category.

Although it's not required, a good policy for site management is to store different file types in separate folders. For example, many websites provide individual folders for images, PDFs, video, and so on. Dreamweaver assists in this endeavor by including an option for a Default Images folder. Later, as you insert images from other places on your computer, Dreamweaver will use this setting to automatically move the images into the site structure.

**6** Next to the Default Images Folder field, click the folder ( 📁 ) icon. When the dialog box opens, navigate to the DW-CS6/images folder containing the files you copied from the *Adobe Dreamweaver CS6 Classroom in a Book* CD and click Select/Choose.

You've entered all the information required to begin your new site. In subsequent lessons, you'll add more information to enable you to upload files to your remote site and test dynamic webpages.

**7** In the Site Setup dialog box, click Save.

The site name DW-CS6 now appears in the site list pop-up menu in the Files panel.

Setting up a site is a crucial first step in beginning any project in Dreamweaver. Knowing where the site root folder is located helps Dreamweaver determine link pathways and enables many site-wide options, such as Find and Replace.

## Using the Welcome screen

The Dreamweaver Welcome screen provides quick access to recent pages, easy creation of a range of page types, and a direct connection to several key Help topics. The Welcome screen appears when you first start the program or when no other documents are open. Let's use the Welcome screen to explore ways to create and open documents.

**1** In the Create New column of the Welcome screen, click HTML to create a new, blank HTML page instantly.

**2** Choose File > Close.

The Welcome screen reappears.

**3** In the Open A Recent Item section of the Welcome screen, click the Open button. This allows you to browse for files to open in Dreamweaver. Click Cancel.

The Welcome screen shows you a list of up to nine of your recently opened files; however, your installation may not display any used files at this point. Choosing a file from this list is a quick alternative to choosing File > Open when you want to edit an existing page you have recently opened or created.

You will use the Welcome screen several times in this book. When you've completed the lessons in this book, you may prefer not to use the Welcome screen or even see it. If so, you can disable it by selecting the Don't Show Again option in the lower left of the window. You can re-enable the Welcome screen in the General category of the Dreamweaver Preferences panel.

## Previewing your completed file

To understand the layout you will work on in this lesson, preview the completed page in Dreamweaver.

**1** In Dreamweaver CS6, press F8/Shift-Cmd-F to open the Files panel, and select DW-CS6 from the site list.

**2** In the Files panel, expand the Lesson04 folder.

**3** Double-click **layout_finished.html** to open it.

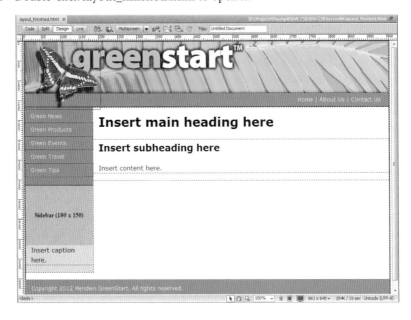

This page represents the completed layout you will create in this lesson. It is based on the wireframe drawings made earlier in this lesson and uses one of the new HTML5 CSS layouts available in Dreamweaver. Take a few moments to familiarize yourself with the design and components on the page. Can you determine what makes this layout different from existing HTML 4-based designs? You will learn the differences as you work through this lesson.

4  Choose File > Close.

## Modifying an existing CSS layout

The predefined CSS layouts provided by Dreamweaver are always a good start-ing point. They are easy to modify and adaptable to most projects. Using a Dreamweaver CSS layout, you will create a proof-of-concept page to match the final wireframe design. This page will then be used to create the main project tem-plate in subsequent lessons. Let's find the layout that best matches the wireframe.

**Note:** If for some reason you can't or don't want to use an HTML5-based layout, see the sidebar "Alternate HTML 4 workflow" later in this lesson.

1  Choose File > New.

2  Choose Blank Page > HTML in the New Page dialog box.

Dreamweaver CS6 offers 16 standard HTML 4 layouts and two HTML5 CSS layouts. Although the HTML5 layouts use some of the new semantic content elements, they are nearly identical to the HTML 4 designs. Unless you need to support an installed base of older browsers (like IE5 & 6), there's little to worry about using the newer layouts. Let's choose one of the HTML5 layouts that best fits the needs of the new site.

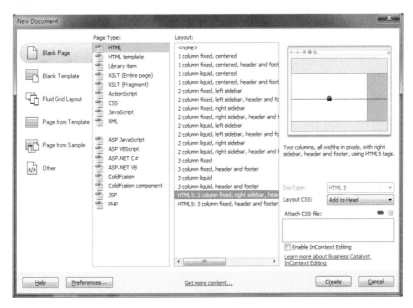

The layout "HTML5: 2 column fixed, right sidebar, header and footer" has the most in common with the target design. The only difference is that the sidebar element is aligned to the right of the layout instead of to the left. You will align this element to the left later in this lesson.

3  Select **HTML5: 2 column fixed, right sidebar, header and footer** from the layout list. Click Open/Create.

4  Switch to Design view, if necessary.

5  Insert the cursor anywhere in the page content. Observe the names and order of the tag selectors at the bottom of the document window.

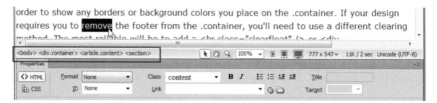

The display order of elements in the tag selector directly correlates to the page's code structure. Elements appearing to the left are parents, or containers, of all elements to the right. The element farthest to the left is the highest in the page structure. As you can see, the <body> element is highest and <div.container> is second.

As you click around the page sections, you will be able to determine the HTML structure without having to delve into the Code view window at all. In many ways, the tag selector interface makes the job of identifying the HTML skeleton much easier, especially in complex page designs.

## Semantics is all in the name

You will see several elements that you may not be familiar with yet, such as <section>, <article>, <aside>, and <nav>. These are some of the new *semantic* elements being introduced in HTML5. In the past, you would have seen <div> elements identified and differentiated with class or id attributes, such as <div class="header"> or <div id="nav">, to make it possible to apply CSS styling. HTML5 has simplified this construction down to <header> and <nav>. By using elements that are named for specific tasks or types of content, you can streamline code construction while achieving other benefits as well. For example, as search engines, such as Google and Yahoo, are optimized for HTML5, they will be able to locate and identify specific types of content on each page more quickly, making your site more useful and easier to browse.

The page consists of four main content elements, three subsections, and a single element that wraps around all the others. All but one of these are new HTML5 elements, including `<header>`, `<footer>`, `<nav>`, `<aside>`, `<article>`, and `<section>`. The only `<div>` elements in this layout are being used to hold the sidebar content and to hold everything together. Using these new elements means that you can apply complex CSS styling while reducing the complexity of the code overall. You can still use `class` and `id` attributes, but the new semantic elements reduce the need for this technique.

To understand exactly how much this design depends on CSS, it's sometimes a good idea to shut off CSS styling.

**6**  Choose View > Style Rendering > Display Styles to disable CSS styling in Design view.

Style display is typically on by default (showing a check mark in the menu). By clicking this option in the menu, you'll toggle CSS styling off temporarily.

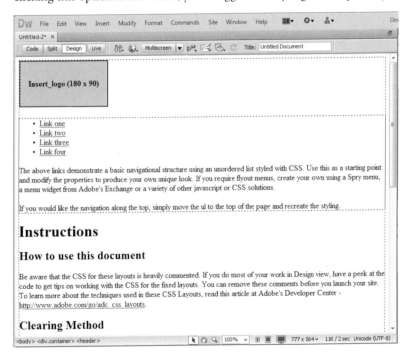

**7**  Note the identity and order of each page component.

Without CSS, the HTML skeleton is exposed for all to see. It's instructive to know what the page will look like if somehow the cascading style sheet is disabled or not supported by a particular browser. Now it's easier to identify the page components and their structure. Although it is not strictly required, items that display higher on the page, like `<header>`, usually are inserted before other elements that appear lower, like `<footer>`.

Another important aspect you should notice is the navigation menu. Without the CSS styling, the navigation menu reverted back to a simple bulleted, or unordered, list with hyperlinks. Not too long ago this menu would have been built with images and complex rollover animation. If the images failed to load, the menu usually became a jumbled, unusable mess. The hyperlinks continued to work, but without the images there were no words to tell the user what they were clicking. But navigation built on text-based lists, on the other hand, will always be usable, even without styling.

**8**  Choose View > Style Rendering > Display Styles to turn on CSS styling again.

It's a good idea to get into the habit of saving files before you modify any settings or add content. Dreamweaver doesn't offer a backup or recovered-file feature; if it crashes before you save, all your work in any open, unsaved file will be lost. Get into the habit of saving your files on a regular basis. It will prevent the loss of data and important changes to your files.

**9**  Choose File > Save. In the Save As dialog box, navigate to the site root folder, if necessary. Name the file **mylayout.html** and click Save.

Dreamweaver normally saves HTML files to the default folder specified in the site definition, but it's a good idea to double-check the destination to make sure your files end up in the right place. All HTML pages created for the final site will be saved in the site root folder.

## Adding a background image to the header

CSS styles are the current standard for all web styling and layout. In the following exercises, you'll apply background colors and a background image to a page section, adjust element alignment and the page width, and modify several text properties. All these changes are accomplished using Dreamweaver's CSS Styles panel.

If you start at the top of the page and work down, the first step would be to insert the graphical banner that appears in the final design. You could insert the banner directly into the header, but adding it as a background image has the advantage of leaving that element open for other content. It will also allow the design to be more adaptable to other applications, like cell phones and mobile devices.

**1**  Select the image placeholder *Insert_logo (180x90)* in the header. Press Delete.

When you delete the image placeholder, the empty header will collapse to a fraction of its former size because it has no CSS height specification.

**2**  Choose Window > CSS Styles to display the CSS Styles panel, if necessary.

**3**  In the CSS Styles panel, double-click the `header` rule to edit it.

The "CSS Rule Definition for header" dialog box appears.

# Alternate HTML 4 workflow

HTML5 is coming on strong all over the Internet and for most applications the suggested workflow will work perfectly well. But HTML5 is not the current web standard and some pages or components may not display properly on certain older browsers and devices. If you'd rather work with code and structures that are more tried and true, feel free to substitute one of the HTML 4-based layouts still offered by Dreamweaver. We suggest the layout "2-Column fixed, left sidebar, header and footer."

However, if you use this layout you'll have to adapt the steps within all the following lessons and exercises to this layout. For example, HTML 4 doesn't use the new semantic elements, such as the following:

```
<header>...</header>
<footer>...</footer>
<section>...</section>
<article>...<article>
<nav>...</nav>
```

Instead, substitute a generic `<div>` element and use a `class` attribute that identifies the component:

```
<div class="header">...</div>
<div class="footer">...</div>
<div class="section">...</div>
<div class="article">...</div>
<div class="nav">...</div>
```

You'll also have to adapt the CSS styling for the HTML 4 elements. In most cases, Dreamweaver will supply many of the rules you'll need with the layout or will build the appropriate selector name for you automatically by using the class name in place of the HTML5 component (`header`, `footer`, `nav`, and so on).

That way, the CSS rule **header {color:#090}** becomes instead **.header { color: #090 }**.

With all the caveats out of the way, the ugly truth is that even when you use standard HTML 4 code and components, older browsers and certain devices will still fail to render them properly. Some web designers believe that the longer we persist in using the older code, the longer the older software and devices will hang around making our lives difficult and delaying the inevitable adoption of HTML5. These designers say we should abandon the older standards and force users to upgrade as soon as possible.

The final decision is yours or your company's to make. In most cases, the problems you experience with HTML5 will be minor flaws—a font that's too big or too small—not a complete meltdown.

For more information about the differences between HTML 4 and HTML5, check out the following links:

http://tinyurl.com/html-differences

http://tinyurl.com/html-differences-1

http://tinyurl.com/html-differences-2

**4** In the Background category of the *"CSS Rule Definition for header"* dialog box, click the Browse button next to the Background-image field.

**5** Select **banner.jpg** and note the dimensions of the image in the preview.

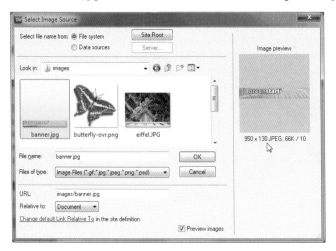

The image is 950 by 130 pixels.

**6** Click OK/Choose to select the background image.

Background images repeat both vertically and horizontally by default. This isn't a problem at the moment, but to ensure that this setting doesn't cause any undesirable effects in the future, you'll need to change the repeat behavior.

**7** Choose no-repeat from the Background-repeat menu.

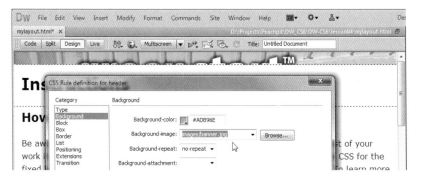

**8** Click Apply to view the results.

The header is wide enough but not tall enough to display the entire background image. Since background images aren't truly inserted into an element, they have no effect (positive or negative) on the size of a container. To ensure that the `<div>` is large enough to display the entire image, you need to add a height specification to the header rule.

**9** In the Box category, type **130** in the Height field and choose px from the pop-up menu to the right of the Height field. Click Apply.

The background appears fully in the `<header>` element. Note that the image is slightly narrower than the container. We'll adjust the width of the layout later. We don't want to set the width on the `<header>` element itself. You learned in Lesson 3 that the width of block elements, like `<header>`, defaults to the entire width of their parent element. Before clicking OK, we need to add some finishing touches to the element.

The `<header>` element contains a background color that doesn't match your site color scheme. Let's apply one that does.

**10** In the Background category, type **#090** in the Background-color field. Click OK.

You won't see the background color unless the background image fails to load.

**11** Choose File > Save.

## Inserting new components

The wireframe design shows two new elements that don't exist in the current layout. The first contains the butterfly image, the second the horizontal navigation bar. Did you notice that the butterfly actually overlaps both the header and the horizontal navigation bar? There are several ways to achieve this effect. In this case, an absolutely positioned (AP) `<div>` will work nicely.

**1** Insert the cursor into the header, if necessary. Select the `<header>` tag selector. Press the Left Arrow key.

This procedure should insert the cursor before the opening `<header>` tag. If you had pressed the Right Arrow key, the cursor would move outside the closing `</header>` tag instead. Remember this technique—you'll use it

**Note:** To better understand how this technique works, try this step in Split view.

frequently in Dreamweaver when you want to insert the cursor in a specific location before or after a code element without resorting to Code view.

● **Note:** AP divs were used extensively in the past to create highly structured, fixed-layout web designs. This technique has declined dramatically in recent years as the need to support cell phones and other mobile devices has increased. For certain applications, AP divs are still handy.

2   Choose Insert > Layout Objects > AP Div.

An AP div will appear at the top left of the header. Note the ID (#apDiv1) assigned to the new div in the tag selector. A corresponding rule has been added to the CSS Styles panel.

In previous versions of HTML, an AP div would have been assigned its size and position using inline HTML attributes. In a concession to new CSS-based web standards, these specifications are now applied by CSS via a unique ID created by Dreamweaver at the moment you insert the element.

3   Click the <div#apDiv1> tag selector.

The Property inspector displays the specifications for <div#apDiv1>. Note the element's width and height. Another property to be aware of is the z-index. This setting determines whether the element displays above or below another object. By default, all elements have a z-index of zero (0). On the other hand, the AP div has a z-index of 1, which means it will appear above all the other elements on the page. All the values displayed in the Property inspector are actually stored in the #apDiv1 rule that was generated automatically by Dreamweaver.

4   Insert the cursor into <div#apDiv1>.

5   Choose Insert > Image. Select **butterfly-ovr.png** from the images folder. Observe the dimensions of the image: 170 pixels by 158 pixels.

6  Click OK/Choose.

The Image Tag Accessibility Attributes dialog box appears.

7  Type **GreenStart Logo** in the Alternate text field in the Image Tag Accessibility Attributes dialog box. Click OK.

The butterfly appears in the AP div.

## Testing special image effects

You may have noticed that the butterfly displays a partially translucent drop shadow. The PNG file type supports *alpha* transparency, making this 3D effect possible. Unfortunately, older browsers may not support alpha transparency and other PNG features. If you use PNG files with such effects, always test them in your target browsers to make sure the desired effects are supported. If not, remove the effect or replace the file with a similar image saved as a different file type (GIF or JPEG).

You'll notice that the AP div is slightly wider than the butterfly image. Although the extra space shouldn't cause any trouble, it's a good idea to match the dimensions of the container to the image.

8  Double-click the #apDiv1 rule in the CSS Styles panel.

The "CSS Rule definition for *#apDiv1*" dialog box appears.

9  In the Box category, change the width to **170 px**. Change the height to **158 px**.

The <div> dimensions now match the height and width of the image.

10  Deselect the Same For All check boxes for Margins.

11  Type **10 px** in the Top margin field. Type **30 px** in the Left margin field. Click OK.

When the rule definition dialog box vanishes, <div#apDiv1> appears floating over the header, 10 pixels from the top and 30 pixels to the left of its original position.

An AP div acts like a free agent. It ignores the other page components and can even be positioned above or below other <div> elements and content.

The <div#apDiv1> is complete. Now, let's add another new component that will hold the horizontal navigation shown in the site design specs. The vertical navigation menu will hold links to the organization's products and services. The horizontal navigation will be used to link back to the organization's home page, mission statement, and contact information.

In HTML 4, you probably would have inserted the links into another `<div>` element and used a `class` or `id` attribute to differentiate it from the other `<div>` elements in the file. Instead, HTML5 provides a new element geared specifically toward such components: `<nav>`.

**12** Insert the cursor back into the header. Click the `<header>` tag selector. Press the Right Arrow key.

The cursor should now appear after the ending `</header>` tag.

**13** Press Ctrl-T/Cmd-T to activate the Tag Editor.

The Tag Editor appears, allowing you to add HTML components or edit existing tags without having to switch to Code view.

● **Note:** The `<nav>` element is new in HTML5. If you need to use HTML 4 code and structures, see the sidebar "Alternate HTML 4 workflow" earlier in this lesson.

**14** Type **nav**. Press Return/Enter as necessary to complete the tag.

An empty `<nav>` element has been inserted into the code, and the cursor has been inserted within this element—ready for you to enter any content.

**15** In the Property inspector, select Paragraph from the Format pop-up menu. Type **Home | About Us | Contact Us** in the new `<p>` element as placeholders for navigation links.

You will convert these to actual hyperlinks in Lesson 9, "Working with Navigation." For now, let's create a new CSS rule to format this element.

**16** Select the `<p>` tag selector at the bottom of the document window.

**17** In the CSS Styles panel, click the New CSS Rule button.

**18** If necessary, select Compound from the Selector Type menu.

The Selector Name window should display `.container nav p`.

**19** Click the Less Specific button to remove the notation `.container` from the selector name.

The Selector Name window should display `nav p`.

**20** Click OK to create the rule.

The "CSS Rule Definition for *nav p*" dialog box should appear.

**21** In the Type category, type **90** in the Font-size field and select the percentage sign (%) from the pop-up list. Type **#FFC** in the Color field. Select Bold from the Font-weight field.

**22** In the Background category, type **#090** in the Background-color field.

**23** In the Block category, select Right from the Text-align field.

**24** In the Box category, deselect the Same For All check box for Padding. Enter **5 px** in the Top padding field. Enter **20 px** in the Right padding field. Enter **5 px** in the Bottom padding field.

**25** In the Border category, deselect the Same For All check boxes for Style, Width, and Color. Enter the following values only in the corresponding Bottom border fields: **solid**, **2 px**, **#060**.

▶ **Tip:** To enter separate values in the Bottom field, remember to deselect the Same For All check boxes in each section first.

**26** Click OK in the CSS Rule Definition dialog box. Press Ctrl-S/Cmd-S to save the file.

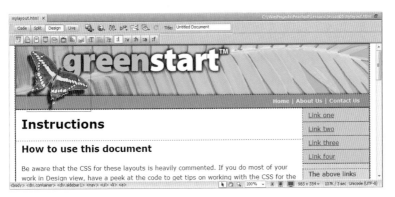

The new <nav> element appears below the header fully formatted and filled with your placeholder text aligned to the right.

# Changing element alignment

The proposed design calls for the sidebar to appear on the left side of the layout, but this layout puts it on the right. Dreamweaver does offer HTML 4 layouts that match the design criteria much more closely, but it was hard to resist working with an HTML5 layout and all the new semantic elements. Besides, adjusting the layout is a lot easier than you may think.

1   In Design view, insert the cursor anywhere in the right sidebar.

2   Click the Code Navigator ( ) icon, or right-click in the sidebar and select the Code Navigator option from the context menu.

The Code Navigator window opens, displaying all CSS rule names that may affect the selected element.

3   Identify the rule that aligns the sidebar to the right.

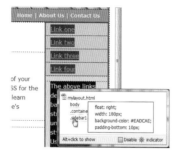

The obvious culprit is the `.sidebar1` rule, which contains the declaration `float: right`.

4   In the CSS Styles panel, double-click the `.sidebar1` rule to edit it.

5   In the Box category, change the `float` property from `right` to `left`.

6   Click Apply to preview the change.

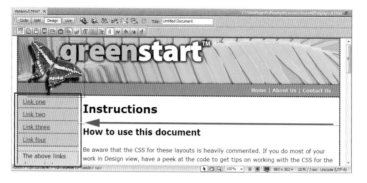

The sidebar moves to the left side of the layout.

7   Click OK and save the file.

# Modifying the page width and background color

Before you convert this file into the project template, let's tighten up the formatting and the placeholder content. For example, the overall width has to be modified to match the banner image. Before you can adjust the width, you'll first have to identify the CSS rule that controls the page width.

1  If necessary, select View > Rulers > Show or press Alt-Ctrl-R/Opt-Cmd-R to display the rulers in the Design window.

   You can use the rulers to measure the width and height of HTML elements or images. The orientation of the rulers defaults to the upper-left corner of the Design window. To give you more flexibility, you can set this zero point anywhere in the Design window.

2  Position the cursor over the axis point of the horizontal and vertical rulers. Drag the crosshairs to the upper-left corner of the header element in the current layout. Note the width of the layout.

   Using the ruler, you can see that the layout is between 960 and 970 pixels wide.

3  Insert the cursor into any content area of the layout.

   Observe the tag selector display to locate any elements that may control the width of the entire page; it would have to be an element that contains all the other elements. The only elements that fit this criterion are `<body>` and `<div.container>`.

4  Click the Code Navigator (⚙) icon, or right-click in the sidebar and select Code Navigator from the context menu.

   The Code Navigator window opens, displaying all CSS rule names that may affect the selected element.

5  Move the cursor over the `body` and `.container` rules to locate the specification that may control the page width.

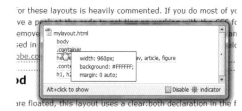

Can you identify the rule that controls the width of the entire page? The `.container` rule contains the declaration `width: 960px`. By now you should be getting good at CSS forensics using the tag selector interface and the Code Navigator.

**6** Double-click the `.container` rule in the CSS Styles panel.

**7** In the Box category, change the width to **950 px**. Click OK.

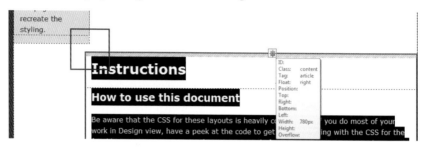

The `<div.container>` element now matches the width of the banner image, but you may have experienced an unintended consequence when you changed the overall width. In our example, the main content area shifted down below the sidebar. To understand what happened, you'll have to do a quick investigation.

**8** In the CSS Styles panel, click the `.content` rule and check its properties. Note its width: 780 pixels.

**9** Click the `.sidebar1` rule and check its width: 180 pixels.

Combined, the two `<div>` elements total 960 pixels, the same as the original layout width. The elements are too wide to sit side by side in the main container and thereby prompted the unexpected shift. This type of error is common in web design and is easily fixed by adjusting the width of either of the two child elements.

**10** Click the `.content` rule in the CSS Styles panel. In the Properties section of the panel, change the width to **770 px**.

The <div.content> element returns to its intended position. This was a good reminder that the size, placement, and specifications of page elements have important interactions that can affect the final design and display of your elements and of the entire page.

The current background color of the page detracts from the overall design. Let's remove it.

11 Double-click the body rule. In the Background category, change the Background-color to **#FFF**. Click OK.

Note that the absence of the background color gives the impression that the page's content area drifts off into the wide expanse. You could give <div.container> a different background color, or you could simply add a border to give the content elements a definitive edge. For this application, a thin border makes the most sense.

12 Double-click the .container rule. In the Border category, if necessary select the Same For All check boxes and enter the following values for all border fields: **solid**, **2px**, and **#060**. Click OK.

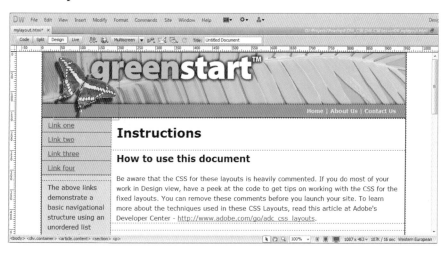

A dark green border appears around the page edge.

13 Save the file.

# Modifying existing content and formatting

As you can see, the CSS layout comes equipped with a vertical navigation menu. The generic hyperlinks are simply placeholders waiting for your final content. Let's change the placeholder text in the menu to match the pages outlined in the thumbnails created earlier, and modify the colors to match the site color scheme.

1 Select the placeholder text *Link one* in the first menu button. Type **Green News**. Change *Link two* to read **Green Products**. Change *Link three* to read **Green Events**. Change *Link four* to read **Green Travel**.

One of the advantages of using bulleted lists as navigational menus is that it's easy to insert new links.

2 With the cursor still at the end of the words *Green Travel*, press Enter/Return. Type **Green Tips**.

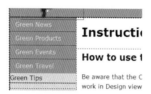

The new text appears in what looks like a button structure, but the background color doesn't match and the text doesn't align with other menu items. You could probably figure out what's wrong in Design view, but in this case, the problem may be identified faster in Code view.

3 Click the `<li>` tag selector for the new link item, select Code view. Observe the menu items and compare the first four with the last. Can you see the difference?

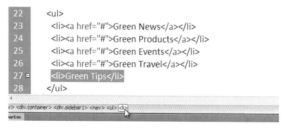

The difference is obvious in Code view. The last item is formatted with the `<li>` element like the others—as part of the bulleted list—but it doesn't feature the markup `<a href="#">` used in the other items to create the hyperlink placeholder. For *Green Tips* to look like the other menu items, you have to add a hyperlink, or at least a similar placeholder.

**4** Select the text *Green Tips.* In the Link field of the HTML Property inspector, type # and press Enter/Return.

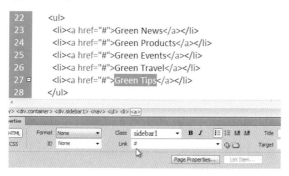

The code in all the items is identical now.

**5** Select Design view.

All the menu items are identically formatted now. You'll learn more about how to format text with CSS to create a dynamic HTML menu in Lesson 5, "Working with Cascading Style Sheets."

The current menu color doesn't match the site color scheme. To change the color, you'll have to use the Code Navigator to find which CSS rule controls this formatting.

**6** Insert the cursor into any of the menu items.

**7** Click the Code Navigator ( ) icon, or right-click in the menu and select Code Navigator from the context menu.

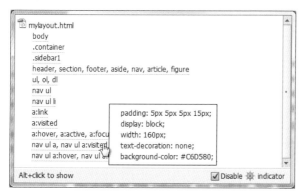

The Code Navigator window opens, displaying a list of 12 CSS rules that affect the targeted element. In some cases, the rules listed may only affect the element in a roundabout way, as in the body rule, which affects *all* HTML elements on the page.

**8** Check each of the rules and note which ones format aspects of the menu items.

Remember, more than one rule can, and probably will, format each page element. You're looking for a background color that's applied to the menu items themselves. Be careful. There's probably more than one background color in the listed rules, so if you find one, it's important to determine whether it actually affects the menu or something else.

**9** Examine each rule until you find the pertinent styling.

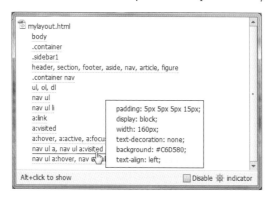

The .sidebar1 rule specifies a background color, but it affects the whole <div> element and not just the menu. The one you're actually looking for is applied by the rule nav ul a, nav ul a:visited. If you parsed the meaning of the rule selector, it tells you that it specifies the background color for an <a> (hyperlink) element that is contained in a <ul> (unordered list) element that is contained in a <nav> element. The second half of the selector then styles the *visited* state of the hyperlink, too. Sound right?

**10** Locate the rule nav ul a, nav ul a:visited in the CSS Styles panel and select it. In the Properties section of the panel, change the existing background color to **#090**.

The background color of the menu items now matches the horizontal <nav> element. But the black text is difficult to read against the green background color. As you see in the horizontal menu, a lighter color would be more appropriate. You can use the Properties section of the CSS Styles panel to add, as well as edit, element properties.

**11** Click the Add Property link in the Properties section of the CSS Styles panel.

**Note:** No matter how you create or modify the formatting, Dreamweaver updates the CSS markup wherever needed.

A new property field appears.

**12** Choose Color from the Property field menu. Type **#FFC** in the Value field.

The link text does not change color as expected. Unfortunately, Dreamweaver missed a problem in the style sheet. The text display in Design view is currently honoring the formatting in the a:link rule, which applies default formatting to hyperlinks on the page. According to the Code Navigator, the nav ul a, nav ul a:visited rule is more specific, and that's why it's listed lower in the Code Navigator display. The selectors a and a:link are supposed to be equivalent. They both format the default state of hyperlinks, but in the case of this display, a:link is being given precedence. Luckily, there's an easy fix.

**Note:** The CSS notation a:link is one of four pseudo-selectors that are used to format various default hyperlink behaviors. You will learn more about these pseudo-selectors in Lesson 9, "Working with Navigation."

**13** In the CSS Styles panel, right-click the nav ul a, nav ul a:visited rule and select Edit Selector from the context menu, or simply click the name and edit it in the panel list.

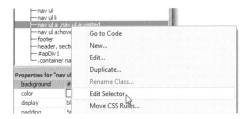

**14** Change the first half of the selector name to `nav ul a:link, nav ul a:visited`, and press Enter/Return to complete the selector.

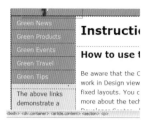

The link text in the vertical menu now displays in the desired color.

**15** Save the file.

# Inserting an image placeholder

The sidebar will feature photos, captions, and short blurbs on environmental topics. Let's insert a placeholder image and caption below the vertical menu.

**1** Insert the cursor into the text directly below the vertical menu. Click the <p> tag selector.

The placeholder image should not be inserted within the <p> element. If it were, it would inherit any margins, padding, and other formatting applied to the paragraph, which could cause it to disrupt the layout.

▶ **Tip:** Use Split view whenever you're unsure where the cursor is inserted.

**2** Press the Left Arrow key.

As you have seen in earlier exercises, the cursor moves to the left of the opening <p> tag in the code but stays within the <aside> element.

● **Note:** The alternate HTML 4 layout doesn't use the <aside> element. The <p> element is inserted directly following the vertical menu.

**3** Choose Insert > Image Objects > Image Placeholder.

The Image Placeholder dialog box appears.

**4** In the Image Placeholder dialog box, type **Sidebar** in the Name field.

Type **180** in the Width field.

Type **150** in the Height field.

Click OK.

An image placeholder appears in `<div.sidebar1>` below the vertical menu.

5  Select all the text below the image placeholder. Type **Insert caption here**.

The caption placeholder replaces the text.

6  Press Ctrl-S/Cmd-S to save.

## Inserting placeholder text

Let's simplify the layout by replacing the existing headings and text in the main content area.

1  Double-click to select the heading *Instructions*. Type **Insert main heading here** to replace the text.

2  Select the heading *How to use this document*. Type **Insert subheading here** to replace the text.

3  Select the placeholder text in that same `<section>` element. Type **Insert content here** to replace it.

4  Select and delete the remaining three `<section>` elements and all their content.

5  Press Ctrl-S/Cmd-S to save.

## Modifying the footer

Let's reformat the footer and insert the copyright information.

1  Double-click the `<footer>` rule in the CSS Styles panel.

2  In the Type category, enter **90%** in the Font-size field and **#FFC** in the Color field.

3  In the Background category, type **#090** into the Background-color field. Click OK.

4  Select the placeholder text in the footer. Type **Copyright 2012 Meridien GreenStart. All rights reserved**.

**5** Press Ctrl-S/Cmd-S to save.

The basic page layout is complete.

# Checking browser compatibility

The CSS layouts included with Dreamweaver have been thoroughly tested to work flawlessly in all modern browsers. However, during the lesson you made major modifications to the original layout. These changes could have ramifications in the compatibility of the code in certain browsers. Before you use this page as your project template, you should check its compatibility.

**1** If necessary, open **mylayout.html** in Dreamweaver.

**2** Choose File > Check Page > Browser Compatibility.

When the Report box opens, there should be no issues listed.

**3** To collapse the report, double-click the Browser Compatibility tab in the Report panel; or to close the entire tab group, right-click the tab and choose Close Tab Group from the context menu.

Congratulations. You created a workable basic page layout for your project template and learned how to insert additional components, image placeholders, text, and headings; adjust CSS formatting; and check for browser compatibility. In the upcoming lessons, you will work further on this file to complete the site template, tweak the CSS formatting and set up the template structure.

## Review questions

1  What three questions should you ask before starting any web design project?

2  What is the purpose of using thumbnails and wireframes?

3  What is the advantage of inserting the banner as a background image?

4  How can you insert the cursor before or after an element without using Code view?

5  How does the Code Navigator assist in designing your website layout?

6  What advantages can be had by using HTML5-based markup?

## Review answers

1  What is the purpose of the website? Who is the customer? How did they get here? These questions, and their answers, are essential in helping you develop the design, content, and strategy of your site.

2  Thumbnails and wireframes are quick techniques for roughing out the design and structure of your site without having to waste lots of time coding sample pages.

3  By inserting the banner or other large graphics as a background image, you leave the container free for other content.

4  Select an element using its tag selector, and press the Left Arrow or Right Arrow key to move the cursor before or after the selected element.

5  The Code Navigator serves the role of a CSS detective. It allows you to investigate what CSS rules are formatting a selected element and how they are applied.

6  HTML5 has introduced new semantic elements that help to streamline code creation and styling. These elements also allow search engines, like Google and Yahoo, to index your pages more quickly and effectively.

# 5 WORKING WITH CASCADING STYLE SHEETS

## Lesson Overview

In this lesson, you'll work with cascading style sheets (CSS) in Dreamweaver and do the following:

- Manage CSS rules using the CSS Styles panel
- Learn about the theory and strategy of CSS rule design
- Create new CSS rules
- Create and apply custom CSS classes
- Create descendant selectors
- Create styles for page layout elements
- Move CSS rules to an external style sheet
- Create style sheets for print applications

 This lesson will take about 2 hours to complete. Before beginning, make sure you have copied the files for Lesson 5 to your hard drive as described in the "Getting Started" section at the beginning of the book. If you are starting from scratch in this lesson, use the method described in the "Jumpstart" section of "Getting Started."

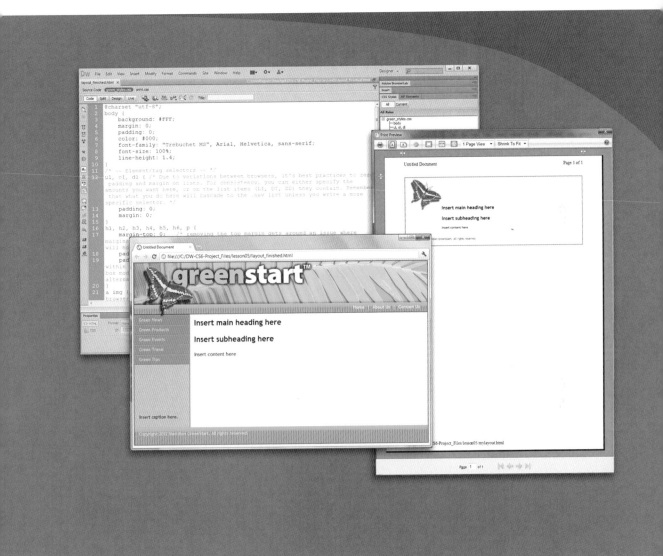

Today, pages designed in compliance with web standards separate the content from the formatting. Stored in a cascading style sheet (CSS), the formatting can be quickly changed and substituted for specific applications and devices.

# Previewing the completed file

**Note:** The process of opening a file on your local hard drive may differ depending on the browser you choose to use. If the suggested command does not work as described, consult the appropriate Help materials.

To see the finished page you'll create in this lesson, you can preview it in a browser.

1 Launch your favorite browser. Select File > Open or press Ctrl-O/Cmd-O.

2 Navigate to the lesson05 folder. Select **layout_finished.html** and click OK/Open.

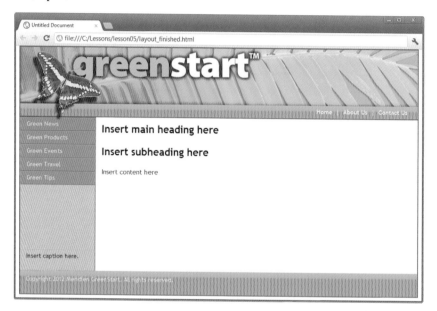

The page loads in the browser window. Note the layout, various colors, and other formats applied to the text and page elements—all created by cascading style sheets (CSS).

## Working with the CSS Styles panel

In Lesson 4, "Creating a Page Layout," you used one of the CSS layouts provided by Dreamweaver to start building your project site template page. These layouts come equipped with an underlying structure and a set of predefined CSS rules that establish the basic design and formatting of the page components and content. In the upcoming exercises in this lesson, you'll modify these rules and add new ones to complete the site design. But before you proceed, it's vital to your role as a designer to understand the existing structure and formatting before you can effectively complete your tasks. It's important to take a few minutes to examine the rules and understand what role they perform in the current document.

1  Open **mylayout.html** from the site root folder, if necessary. Or, if you are
   starting from scratch in this exercise, see the "Jumpstart" instructions in the
   "Getting Started" section at the beginning of the book.

2  If the CSS Styles panel isn't visible, select Window > CSS Styles to display it.

   The CSS Styles panel displays the `<style>` tag, indicating that the style sheet is
   embedded in the `<head>` section of the document.

3  Select Code view and locate the `<head>` section (starting at line 3). Locate the
   `<style type="text/css">` element (line 6) and examine the subsequent code
   entries.

► **Tip:** If you don't see
line numbers along the
side of your Code view
window, choose View >
Code View Options >
Line Numbers to turn
on this feature.

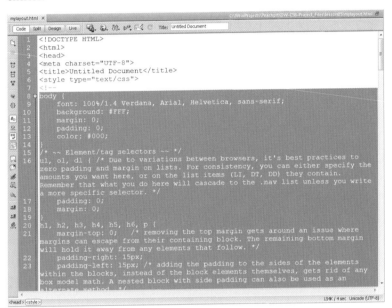

● **Note:** The CSS
markup is contained
within an HTML
`<!-- -->` comment
entry. That's because
CSS is not considered
valid HTML markup and
may not be supported
in some applications
or devices. Using the
comment structure
allows such applications
to ignore the CSS.

All the CSS rules displayed in the list are contained within the `<style>`
element.

4  Note the names and order of the selectors within the CSS code.

5  In the CSS Styles panel, expand and examine the list of rules.

   The list shows the same selector names in the same order you saw in Code view.
   There is a one-to-one relationship between the CSS code and the CSS Styles
   panel. When you create new rules or edit existing ones, Dreamweaver makes
   all the changes in the code for you, saving you time and reducing the possibility
   of code-entry errors. The CSS Styles panel is just one of the many productivity
   enhancements that you'll use and master in this book.

You should have 20 rules at this time—18 that came with the CSS layout, and 2 you made yourself in the previous lesson. The order of your rules may vary from that shown in the figure below. The CSS Styles panel makes it easy to reorder the list.

● **Note:** The names and order of styles in your panel may vary from those pictured.

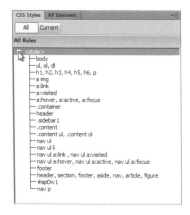

In the last lesson, you created `<div#apDiv1>` and inserted it into the layout. The `#apDiv1` rule applies to the `<div>` holding the butterfly logo and appears in the code between `<div.container>` and `<header>`. But as you can see in the CSS Styles panel above, the rule reference appears near the bottom of all the rules. In this instance, moving this rule within the style sheet will not affect how it formats the element but it will make it easier to find if you need to edit it later.

● **Note:** Before you move any other rules, you should first understand what function each one performs and how they relate to one another.

**6** Select the `#apDiv1` rule and drag it directly underneath the `.container` rule.

Dreamweaver has moved the rule within the list, but that's not all. It has also rewritten the code in the embedded style sheet, moving the rule to its new position. Arranging related rules together can save time later when you need to format specific elements or components. But be on the lookout for unintended consequences. Moving rules in the list can upset the established cascade or inheritance relationships you have already created. Review Lesson 3, "CSS Basics," if you need a refresher on these theories.

**7** Select the body rule in the CSS Styles panel. Observe the properties and values that appear in the Property section of the panel.

Most of these settings came with the layout, although you changed the background color in the last lesson. Note that the margins and padding are set to zero.

**8** Select the ul, ol, dl rule and observe the values that appear.

As in the body rule, this rule sets all margin and padding values to zero. Do you know why? An experienced web designer could select each rule in turn and probably figure out the reasons for each of the formats and settings. But you don't need to resort to hiring a consultant when Dreamweaver provides much of the information you need already.

**9** Right-click the ul, ol, dl rule and choose Go To Code from the context menu.

If you are in Design view, Dreamweaver will display the document in Split view and then focus on the section of code that contains the ul, ol, dl rule. In Code view, it will jump to the appropriate lines that contain the rule. Observe the text between the opening /* and closing */ notation. This is the way you add comments to cascading style sheets. Like HTML comments, this text usually provides behind-the-scenes information that will not be displayed within the browser or affect any elements. Comments are a good way to leave handy reminders within the body of the webpage or to leave notes to yourself or others explaining why you wrote the code in a particular fashion. You'll notice that some of the comments are used to introduce a set of rules, and others are embedded in the rules themselves.

**10** Scroll down through the style sheet and study the comments, paying close attention to the embedded ones.

The more you understand what these predefined rules are doing, the better results you can achieve for your final site. Here's what you'll find: the body, header, .container, .sidebar1, .content, and footer rules define the basic structural elements of the page. The rules a:img, a:link, a:visited, a:hover, a:active, and a:focus set up the appearance and performance of the default hyperlink behavior; nav ul, nav ul li, nav ul a:link, nav ul a:visited, nav ul a:hover, nav ul a:active, and nav ul a:focus define the look and behavior of the vertical menu. The remaining rules are intended to reset default formatting or add some desired styling as outlined in the embedded comments.

For the most part, there's nothing unacceptable or fatal in the current order of the rules, but keeping related rules together will pay productivity dividends later when the style sheet gets more complicated. It will help you find specific rules quickly and help remind you what you have already styled within your page.

● **Note:** When moving rules using the CSS Styles panel, the position of comments that are not embedded may not be preserved.

**11** Using the CSS Styles panel, reorder the rules in the list, as necessary, so they match the order shown in the figure below.

Now that you are more aware of the rules and rule order, remember that it's a good practice to take special care with rule order when you create new styles from this point forward.

**12** Save the file.

# Working with type

One of the first basic choices any designer must make for a website is selecting the default typeface or typefaces. The typeface can evoke all sorts of feelings in your visitors, ranging from security to elegance to sheer fun and humor. Some designers may use multiple typefaces for different purposes throughout the site. Others select a single base typeface that may match their normal corporate themes or culture. CSS gives you tremendous control over page appearance.

## Selecting a font group

● **Note:** You learned in Lesson 3 that the body rule is the parent of all the visible page elements. When you apply styles to body, all child elements will inherit these specifications by default.

In this exercise, you will learn how to apply a global site typeface by editing a single rule.

**1** If necessary, open **mylayout.html** and select Design view.

**2** In the CSS Styles panel, double-click the body rule.

**3** When the "CSS Rule Definition for *body*" dialog box opens, observe the entry displayed in the Font-family field: Verdana, Arial, Helvetica, sans-serif.

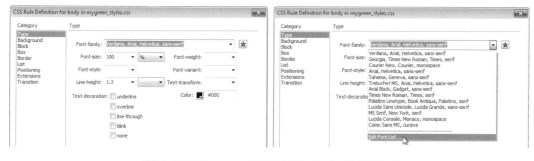

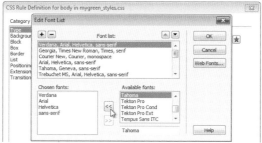

The field displays *three* typefaces and a design category. Why? Can't Dreamweaver make up its mind?

The answer is a simple but ingenious solution to a problem that has nagged the web from the very beginning: The fonts you see in your browser are not actually part of the webpage or the server; they are supplied by the computer that's *browsing* the site. Although most computers have many fonts in common, they don't all have the same fonts. What this means is that if you choose a specific font and it isn't installed on the visitor's computer, your carefully designed and formatted webpage could immediately and tragically appear in Courier or some other equally undesirable typeface.

Normal browser display                    Same page in Courier

The solution is to specify fonts in groups; the browser is given a second, third, and perhaps fourth (or more) choice to default to before it picks for itself (egads!). Some call this technique *degrading gracefully.*

Dreamweaver CS6 offers more than a dozen predefined font groups. If you don't see a combination you like, you can select the Edit Font List option at the bottom of the Font-family field menu and create your own.

But before you start building your own group, remember this: Once you pick *your* favorite font, try to figure out what fonts are installed on your *visitors'* computers and add them to the list. For example, you may prefer the font Hoefelter Allgemeine Bold Condensed, but it's unlikely that a majority of web users have it installed on their computers. By all means, select Hoefelter as your first choice, just don't forget to slip in some of the more tried-and-true fonts, such as Arial, Helvetica, Tahoma, Times New Roman, Trebuchet MS, Verdana, and finally, serif and sans serif.

4   From the Font-family menu, choose Trebuchet MS, Arial, Helvetica, sans-serif. Click OK.

You have successfully changed the basic font of the entire webpage by editing one rule. All the text on the page now displays in Trebuchet MS. If Trebuchet MS is *not* available on a visitor's computer, the page will default to Arial, then to Helvetica, and then to a sans serif font.

## Altering font size

In addition to changing the font, you can also alter text size with CSS. In the body rule, the font size is set to 100%. This sets the default size of all HTML elements on the page. Headings, paragraphs, and list elements are all sized relative to this setting. All elements on the page will inherit this setting unless it's overridden by a more specific rule.

Font size can convey the relative importance of the content on the page. Headings are typically larger than the text they introduce for that reason. This page is divided into two areas: the main content and the sidebar. To give the main content more emphasis, let's reduce the size of the text that appears under the vertical menu.

1   Insert the cursor in the caption under the vertical menu. Observe the tag selectors at the bottom of the document window. Identify the element that contains this caption.

The caption is a <p> element contained in the <aside> element, which is contained in the <div.sidebar1> element. To reduce the text size, you could create a new compound rule to format any of those elements. But before you choose which element you want to format, let's examine any potential conflicts that may arise from that decision.

Creating a rule for the `<p>` element would target paragraphs within the sidebar but ignore any other elements you wish to insert there. You could format `<div.sidebar1>` itself; the specifications would certainly affect both headings and paragraphs, but they also would apply to every element in the sidebar, including the vertical menu. In this instance, the best option would be to create a new rule that formats the `<aside>` element. Such a rule would narrowly target the styling to content contained therein and ignore the vertical menu altogether.

2   Select `<aside>` from the tag selector at the bottom of the document window, and click the New CSS Rule ( ⊕ ) icon.

3   In the New CSS Rule dialog box, select Compound from the Selector Type drop-down menu.

The Selector Name field displays `.container .sidebar1 aside`.

4   Click the Less Specific button once to remove the `.container` class. Click OK.

5   In the "CSS Rule Definition For *.sidebar1 aside*" dialog box, type **90** in the Font-size field and choose % from the unit of measurement menu. Click OK.

    The text in the `<aside>` element now displays at 90 percent of its original size.

6   Choose File > Save.

# Using images for graphical effects

Many designers resort to images to add graphical flair when code-based techniques can be problematic. But large images can consume too much Internet bandwidth and make pages slow to load and respond. In some cases, a strategically designed small image can be used to create interesting 3D shapes and effects. In this exercise, you will learn how to create a three-dimensional effect with the help of a tiny image graphic and the CSS `background` property.

1   Select Design view, if necessary.

2   In the CSS Styles panel, double-click the `nav p` rule.

3   Select the Background category. Click the Browse button next to the Background-image field.

    The Select Image Source dialog box appears.

▶ **Tip:** By using a compound selector, you are targeting only `<aside>` elements that appear in `<div.sidebar1>`, which will prevent any unwanted inheritance issue if an `<aside>` element exists elsewhere in the page.

**4** Navigate to DW-CS6 > images and select **background.png**. Observe the image dimensions and preview.

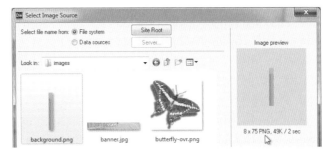

The image is 8 pixels by 75 pixels and 49 kilobytes in size. Notice the lighter shade of green at the top of the graphic. Since the page is 950 pixels wide, you know that this graphic could never fill the horizontal menu unless it were copied and pasted hundreds of times. But you don't need to resort to such antics if you simply use the `background-repeat` property.

**5** Click OK/Choose. Click Apply.

**Tip:** When a graphic provides a textural effect along with shading, like **background.png**, it's import that it is tall enough or wide enough to fill the entire element as necessary. Note that this graphic is much taller than the element it was inserted into.

The background image repeats automatically—both vertically and horizontally—to fill the entire horizontal menu seamlessly, giving the menu a three-dimensional appearance and an interesting textural effect. Some graphics, like this one, are not designed to repeat in both directions. This graphic was intended to create a rounded 3D effect for the top edge of a page element, so you shouldn't let it repeat vertically at all. CSS allows you to control the repeat function and limit it to either the vertical or horizontal axis.

**6** Choose repeat-x from the Background-repeat field menu. Click OK.

The graphic will repeat only horizontally now; it automatically aligns to the top of the <nav> element by default. Let's add the same background to the <footer> element too.

**7** Double-click the `footer` rule to edit it.

**8** In the Background-image field, browse and select **background.png**. Choose repeat-x from the Background-repeat field menu. Click OK.

The background image fills the <footer> element.

**9** Choose File > Save.

# Creating new CSS rules

In most of the previous exercises, you edited the rules that were predefined in the CSS layout. In the next exercise, you will learn how to create your own custom rules for HTML elements, classes, and IDs.

## Creating descendant selectors

The predefined style sheet declares a rule for multiple elements that will affect all h1, h2, h3, h4, h5, h6, and p tags no matter where they appear on the page. But if you want to target a style at a specific tag within a specific element, it requires a *descendant* selector. Dreamweaver makes it easy to create such rules. In this exercise, you will create a descendant selector that will target specific CSS styling to the <h1> element in the main content area.

1   Insert the cursor in the main heading in the main content area. Note the names and order of the tag selectors at the bottom of the document window.

The heading is an <h1> element sitting in <article.content> sitting in <div. container> sitting in the <body> element. As described earlier in this chapter, when creating new rules take care about where they appear in the style sheet. Rules at the top of the sheet can pass formatting to rules appearing later (using inheritance) or cancel settings because of higher specificity. Inserting a rule in the wrong place could cause the browsers to ignore it altogether.

2   Select the .content rule in the CSS Styles panel.

Because you selected the .content rule first, Dreamweaver will insert the new rule immediately following it in the style sheet.

3   In the CSS Styles panel, click the New CSS Rule (⊞) icon. If the Compound selector type is not displayed, choose it from the Selector Type menu.

The New CSS Rule dialog box opens. Typically, when the cursor is inserted into page content, the dialog box defaults to the Compound selector type and displays a descendant selector based on the location of the cursor—in this case, .container .content h1.

> **Note:** When the cursor is inserted into the page content, Dreamweaver will always create the compound selector for you, even if the Compound option is not displayed when the dialog box first appears.

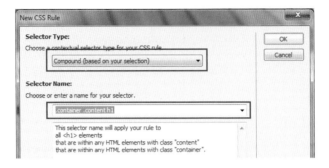

If you remember the CSS syntax you learned in Lesson 3, you know that this new rule will affect <h1> elements, but only when they appear within an element formatted with a class of .content and when both appear within an element formatted with a class of .container. The great thing about this rule is that it will leave all other <h1> elements unaffected.

Since there will only be one <article.content> element in this page design, there's no need for such specificity in the rule. Whenever possible, rules should be simplified to reduce the total amount of code that needs to be downloaded. In this case, it's only the notation .container that isn't needed, but unnecessary code adds up across the entire site (and Internet) overall.

4   In the New CSS Rule dialog box, click the Less Specific button. Click OK.

The word .container is removed from the Selector Name field.

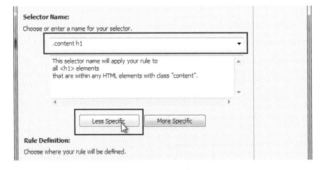

5   In the Type category of the "CSS Rule Definition For .content h1" dialog box, enter **200%** in the Font-size field.

6   In the Box category, deselect Same For All in the Margin section and enter **10px** in the Top margin field only. Enter **5px** in the Bottom margin field. Click OK.

The main heading doesn't change in size but appears 10 pixels lower on the page. Note that the new rule was inserted directly after the .content rule in the CSS Styles panel.

7   Save the file.

# Creating custom classes

CSS class attributes allow you to apply custom formatting to a specific element or to a portion of a specific element. Let's create a class that will allow you to apply the logo color to text in the file.

1   In the CSS Styles panel, click the New CSS Rule icon.

2   Choose Class from the Selector Type menu. Type **green** in the Selector Name field. Click OK.

**Tip:** When the desired styling doesn't appear as expected, use the Code Navigator to suss out the conflict.

3   In the "CSS Rule Definition For *.green*" dialog box, type **#090** in the Color field of the Type category. Click OK.

The `.green` rule is added to the style sheet. In most instances, a `class` attribute has a higher specificity than the default styling applied to any given element and will override it, so it shouldn't matter where in the style sheet it appears.

Dreamweaver makes it easy to apply classes. Let's apply the class to an entire element.

4   Insert the cursor anywhere in the `<h1>` element in `<article.content>`. Make sure the cursor is flashing in the element and that no text is selected.

5   In the Property inspector, choose `green` from the Class menu.

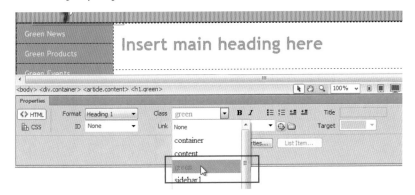

**Note:** You may need to refresh the page display to see the updated tag selector.

**Tip:** In some cases, you may have to click the appropriate tag selector before selecting the class from the Property inspector.

All the text in the `<h1>` element is now formatted in the color #090 (green). At the bottom of the document window, `<h1.green>` now displays in the tag selector.

6   Switch to Code view. Examine the opening tag of the `<h1>` element.

The rule is applied as an attribute to the tag as `<h1 class="green">`. When the cursor is inserted in an existing element, Dreamweaver assumes you want to apply the class to the entire element.

Now, let's remove the CSS class from the element.

**7** Insert the cursor anywhere in the formatted <h1> element in Code view.

Even while you are in Code view, the tag selector displays <h1.green> and green appears in the Class menu of the Property inspector.

**8** Choose None from the Class menu of the Property inspector.

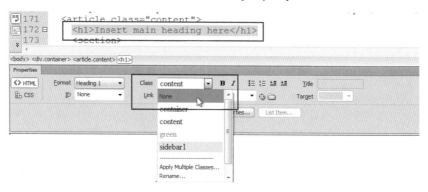

The class attribute is removed from the code. The tag selector now displays a plain <h1> tag. Although you applied None, the Class menu shows content instead of None, indicating the class attribute assigned to the parent element containing the <h1>.

Next let's apply a class to a range of text.

**9** Select the words *main heading* in the <h1> element. Choose green from the Class menu in the Property inspector.

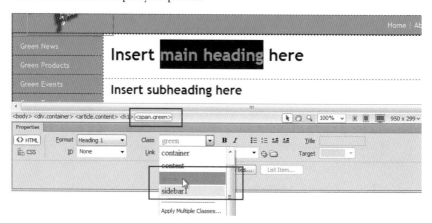

The class is applied to the selected text using the notation <span class= "green">. The span tag has no default formatting of its own and is intended to create custom inline styling like this.

Now remove the class.

**10** Switch to Design view. Insert the cursor anywhere in the formatted text. Choose None from the Class menu.

The text returns to the original formatting. When the cursor is inserted in a class-formatted element, Dreamweaver assumes you want to remove the formatting from the entire range of text.

**11** Save the file.

▶ **Tip:** Class attributes can be applied and removed in either Design or Code view.

## Creating custom IDs

The CSS id attribute is given the highest specific weight in CSS styling because it is used to identify *unique* content on a webpage and therefore should trump all other styling. The AP div containing the butterfly logo is a good example of a unique element. The <div#apDiv1> is positioned at a carefully specified location on the page, and you can be pretty certain you'll have only one such <div> on each page. Let's modify the existing rule for this element to reflect its use in the layout.

**1** Select the #apDiv1 rule in the CSS Styles panel. Right-click the selector name and choose Edit Selector from the context menu.

The selector name becomes editable in the panel list.

**2** Change the name to **#logo**. Press Enter/Return to complete the editing process.

The rule name changes, but it no longer formats <div#apDiv1>. The layout reflects the default behavior of an unformatted <div> element—without height and width and other key attributes applied—and it expands to the full width of <div.container> and pushes the <header> element down below the height of the butterfly image.

To restore the layout to its intended appearance, you have to assign the new #logo rule to <div#apDiv1>.

**3** Insert the cursor in <div#apDiv1> or click the butterfly to select it. Then, click the <div#apDiv1> tag selector at the bottom of the document window.

The Property inspector displays the properties of <div#apDiv1>. Note the ID displayed in the Property inspector.

**4** Open the ID pop-up menu.

Note that the menu has two apparent options: `apDiv1` and `logo`.

**Note:** On a Mac, you may not be able to access the ID pop-up menu at all if no unassigned IDs are available.

**5** Choose `logo` from the ID field pop-up menu.

Reformatted, `<div#logo>` resumes its former size and positioning.

Classes can be used as many times as you want, but an ID is supposed to be used only once per page. Although you could conceivably type the same ID multiple times manually yourself, Dreamweaver won't offer any help in your attempt at rule breaking. You can demonstrate this functionality with a simple test.

**6** Examine the CSS Styles panel and note the available class and ID selectors.

There are four classes and one ID selector defined in the panel.

**7** Insert the cursor in `<div#logo>`. Click the `<div#logo>` tag selector.

The Property inspector reflects the specifications applied to `<div#logo>`.

## A `<div>` apart

An AP `div` is treated differently from normal `<div>` elements. You see this difference as soon as you insert an AP `div` into a document: Dreamweaver creates a rule for it automatically and assigns it attributes for width, height, position, and z-index, and it then displays these specifications in the Property inspector. This doesn't happen with a normal `div`. In fact, the special treatment persists even after the rule is created. If you change the `id` attribute of the AP `div` in the Property inspector, Dreamweaver will update the name of the rule in the CSS Styles panel at the same time.

However, the reverse is not true. If you change the rule name using the style sheet (as you did in this lesson), Dreamweaver does not change the ID on the element itself. The program leaves this chore up to you.

**8** Open the ID field pop-up menu and examine the available IDs.

The only ID available is logo. What happened to apDiv1? The original name apDiv1 no longer appears in the style sheet and therefore won't appear in the pop-up menu. Additionally, as each ID stored in the style sheet is used in your layout, Dreamweaver interactively removes it from the menu to prevent you from accidentally using it a second time.

Don't take this behavior to mean that there's a law saying id and class attributes must appear in the style sheet before you can use them within a page. Many designers create these attributes first and then define them later, or use them to differentiate specific page structures, or to create hyperlink destinations. Some class and id attributes may never appear in the style sheets or pop-up menus. The Dreamweaver menus are intended to make it easier to assign classes and IDs that already exist, not to limit your creativity.

**9** In the Class field menu, choose green.

The tag selector displays <div#logo.green>. As you can see, it's possible to assign both an id and a class attribute to an element at the same time, which may come in handy in certain situations.

**10** Insert the cursor in the horizontal menu <nav>. Click the <nav> tag selector.

**11** In the Property inspector, open the ID menu and examine the available IDs.

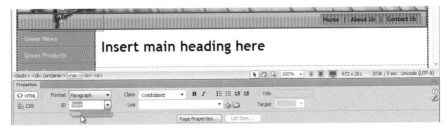

The only available ID option is None because logo is already assigned.

**12** Open the Class field menu. Examine the available class attributes.

Note that all class attributes are available. The Dreamweaver interface allows you to apply class attributes to multiple elements, but it prevents you from applying id attributes more than once.

**13** Close the Class menu without making a selection.

**14** Save the file.

You should now know some of the differences between classes and IDs, as well as how to create, edit, and assign them to elements on your page. Next, you'll learn how to combine these attributes using CSS to create interactive behaviors for hyperlinks.

## Creating an interactive menu

By combining descendant selectors, classes, and IDs, you can produce amazing behaviors from seemingly static elements.

**1** If necessary, switch to Design view and click the Live view button.

The document window will preview the layout as it would appear in a browser. Videos, Flash animation, and JavaScript behaviors will all perform as they would on the Internet.

**2** Position the cursor over the vertical navigation menu in the sidebar. Observe the behavior and appearance of the menu items.

● **Note:** *Rollover* refers back to the time when the computer mouse contained a ball that mechanically produced the cursor movement on your screen.

As the mouse moves over each button, the cursor icon changes to the hand pointer, indicating that the menu items are formatted as hyperlinks. The buttons also change color momentarily as the mouse passes, or rolls, over each, producing a dramatic graphical experience. These *rollover* effects are all enabled by HTML hyperlink behaviors and can be formatted by CSS.

**3** Position the mouse cursor over the items in the horizontal navigation menu in `<nav>`. Observe the behavior and appearance of the menu items, if any.

The pointer and background color do not change. The items are not formatted as hyperlinks.

**4** Click the Live view button to return to the normal document display.

**5** Select the word *Home* in the <nav> element. Do not select the spaces on either side of the word or the vertical bars, or pipes, that separate the words.

**6** Type **#** in the Link field of the Property inspector. Press Enter/Return.

Adding a hash mark (#) in the Link field creates a hyperlink placeholder and will allow you to create and test the necessary formatting for the horizontal navigation menu without having to create an actual link. Note that the text now displays the formatting of a typical text hyperlink.

**7** Add hyperlink placeholders to the items *About Us* and *Contact Us*.

Be sure to select both words in each item before applying the placeholder. If you don't, each word will be treated as separate links instead of as one.

Correct          Incorrect

To make the horizontal menu look more like the vertical one, you'll have to remove the underscore and change the text color. Let's start with the underscore.

**8** Insert the cursor in any of the hyperlinks in the horizontal <nav> element. Select the nav p rule in the CSS Styles panel. Click the New CSS Rule icon.

**9** Choose Compound from the Selector Type menu, if necessary.

The Selector Name field displays `.container nav p a`.

**Note:** Dreamweaver prevents you from making changes to your content in the Design view window while Live view is enabled, but you may edit the CSS. If desired, you can change both the content and styling using the Code view window at any time.

**Note:** Since the horizontal and vertical menus are based on the same HTML5 <nav> element, you should be aware that this rule applies styling that could be inherited by both. Watch for any undesirable side effects.

## Hyperlink pseudoclasses

In all, the <a> element makes available four *states,* or distinct behaviors, that can be modified by CSS using what are called *pseudoclasses*. A pseudoclass is a CSS feature that can add special effects or functionality to certain selectors, such as the <a> anchor tag:

- The a:link pseudoclass creates the default display and behavior of the hyperlink. The a:link pseudoclass in many cases is interchangeable with the a selector in CSS rules. However, as you already experienced earlier, a:link is *more* specific and may override specifications assigned to the less specific a selector if both are used in the style sheet.

- The a:visited pseudoclass applies formatting after the link has been visited by the browser. This specification is reset whenever the browser cache or history is deleted.

- The a:hover pseudoclass applies formatting when the cursor passes over the link.

- The a:active pseudoclass formats the link when the mouse clicks it.

When used, the pseudoclasses must be declared in the order as listed above to be effective. Remember, whether declared in the style sheet or not, each state has a set of default formats and behaviors.

**10** In the New CSS Rule dialog box, click the Less Specific button.

The `.container` class is removed from the Selector Name field. The class notation `.container` is not needed in this instance.

When a link has been used, it usually changes color, indicating that you visited that destination earlier. This is the normal, or default, behavior of hyperlinks. However, in the vertical and horizontal menus, we do not want the links to change their appearance after you click them. To prevent or reset this behavior, you can create a compound rule that will format both states of the link at once.

**11** If necessary, insert the cursor in the Selector Name field. Press Ctrl-A/Cmd-A to select the entire selector name. Press Ctrl-C/Cmd-C to copy the selector.

**12** Press the Right Arrow key to move the cursor to the end of the selector text. Type `:link` to add it at the end of the selector name.

The new selector `nav p a:link` is more specific and will preclude any potential inheritance from the default `a:link` rule appearing elsewhere in the style sheet, as happened with the vertical menu earlier.

**13** If necessary, move the cursor to the end of the selector text. Type a comma (,) and press the spacebar to insert a space. Press Ctrl-V/Cmd-V to paste the selector from the clipboard.

**14** Type `:visited` at the end of the pasted selector.

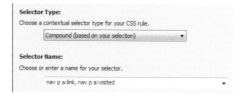

The selector should now appear as `nav p a:link, nav p a:visited` in the Selector Name field. The comma works like the word "and" allowing you to include two or more selectors in one name. By combining these two selectors into one rule, you are formatting the default properties of both hyperlink states at once.

**15** Click OK.

The new `nav p a:link, nav p a:visited` rule appears in the CSS Styles panel below the `nav p` rule.

**16** In the Type category's Text Decoration option, select **none**. Click Apply.

The underscore is removed from the hyperlinks. Now let's change the default hyperlink text color.

**17** Type **#FFC** in the Color field. Click OK.

The blue hyperlink text color is replaced by pale yellow (#FFC), which is easier to see on the green background. Let's test the hyperlink properties of the items in the horizontal menu.

18 Click the Live view button. Position the cursor over the hyperlink placeholders in the horizontal menu.

The mouse icon changes to the hand pointer, indicating that the text is formatted as a hyperlink. But these hyperlinks have none of the flair of the vertical menu, with its changing background color. As explained, that interactive behavior is controlled by the pseudoclass a:hover. Let's use this selector to create a similar behavior.

19 Click the Live view button to return to the normal document display. Save the file.

# Modifying hyperlink behavior

In this exercise, you will modify the default hyperlink behavior and add interactivity.

1 Insert the cursor in any one of the hyperlinks in the horizontal menu. You don't need to select any characters in the link. Select the nav p a:link, nav p a:visited rule in the CSS Styles panel. Click the New CSS Rule icon.

The New CSS Rule dialog box appears with the Compound selector type displayed and the text .container nav p a entered in the Selector Name field.

● **Note:** The a:hover state inherits much of its formatting from a or a:link. In most cases, you only need to declare values for formatting that will change when this state is activated.

2 Make sure the Compound selector type is selected in the New CSS Rule dialog box. Edit the Selector Name to say **nav p a:hover, nav p a:active**, and click OK.

The new nav p a:hover, nav p a:active rule appears in the CSS Styles panel. The "CSS Rule Definition for *nav p a:hover, nav p a:active*" dialog box appears.

3 In the Type category's Color field, type **#FFF**.

In the Background category's Background-color field, type **#060**. Click OK.

4 Activate Live view, and test the hyperlink behavior in the horizontal menu.

The background behind the hyperlink text changes to dark green as the mouse passes over it. This is a good start, but you may notice that the color change doesn't extend to the top or bottom edges of the <nav> or even to the pipes dividing one link from another. You can create a more interesting effect by adding a little padding to the element.

▷ **Tip:** Do you know why you added space to padding and not to margins? Adding space to the margins won't work because margins add space outside the background color.

**5** Deactivate Live view. Double-click the `nav p a:hover, nav p a:active` rule to edit it.

**6** In the Box category, enter **5px** in the Padding field and make sure that the Same For All check box is selected. Click OK.

**7** Activate Live view and test the hyperlink behavior in the horizontal menu.

The background color of each link now extends five pixels all around the hyperlink. Unfortunately, there's an unintended consequence: Not only does the padding cause the background to extend five pixels out from the text on either side of the link, but it also causes the other text to shift five pixels from its default position whenever the `a:hover` state is activated. Luckily, the solution to this problem is quite simple. Have you figured out what you need to do?

● **Note:** The Trash Can icon in the CSS Styles panel is context sensitive. It can be used to delete a rule property or the entire rule, depending on how it is invoked. Before using it, note the tooltip that appears when the cursor hovers over it.

**8** In the CSS Styles panel Properties section, select the `padding` property for the rule `nav p a:hover, nav p a:active`. Click the Delete CSS Property (🗑) icon at the bottom of the panel.

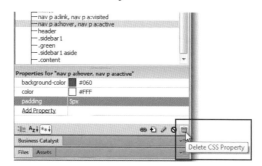

**9** Double-click the `nav p a:link, nav p a:visited` rule to edit it. In the Box category, enter **5px** in the Padding field, with the Same For All option selected. Click OK.

**10** Activate Live view and test the hyperlink behavior in the horizontal menu.

When the mouse moves over the links, the background color extends five pixels around the link without shifting. Do you understand why you added the padding to the default hyperlink? By adding padding to the default state, the hover state automatically inherits the extra padding and allows the background color to work as desired, without shifting the text.

**11** Save the file.

Congratulations. You've created your own version of the interactive navigation menu in the horizontal <nav> element. But you may have noticed that the pre-defined background color selection for the `a:hover` state in the vertical menu doesn't match the color of the horizontal menu. To be consistent, the colors used in the site should adhere to the overall site theme.

## Modifying existing hyperlink behavior

As you gain more experience in web design and working with CSS, identifying design inconsistencies and knowing how to correct them becomes easier. Since you know that the *hover* state is responsible for creating the interactive link behavior, it should be a simple matter to change the background color in the vertical menu. The first step is to assess what rules pertain specifically to the vertical menu itself.

**1**   Insert the cursor into one of the vertical menu items. Observe the names and the order of elements in the tag selector display.

The vertical menu is using a `<ul>` (unordered list) element inserted in an HTML5 `<nav>` element.

**2**   Locate any rules in the CSS Styles panel that format the `<nav>` element. Is there an `a:hover` pseudoclass associated with it?

The CSS Styles panel displays the `nav ul a:hover, nav ul a:active, nav ul a:focus` rule that formats the hyperlink behavior you're looking for.

**3**   Double-click the `nav ul a:hover, nav ul a:active, nav ul a:focus` rule to edit it. In the Background category, change the background color to **#060**. Click OK.

**4**   Using Live view, test the behavior of the vertical menu.

The background color of the vertical menu now matches the horizontal menu and the site color scheme.

**5**   Save the file.

## Adding visual appeal to menus

Another popular CSS trick that can give menus a bit more visual interest is to vary the border colors. By applying different colors to each border, you can give the buttons a 3D appearance. As in the previous exercise, you first need to locate the rules formatting the elements.

**1**   Insert the cursor in one of the menu items and examine the tag selector display.

The menu buttons are built using `<nav>`, `<ul>`, `<li>`, and `<a>` elements. By now, you should know that the `<ul>` element creates the entire list—not the individual items or buttons—and that you can eliminate it as a suspect. The `<li>` element creates list items.

**2**   Select the `nav ul li` rule in the CSS Styles panel. Observe the attributes displayed in the Properties section of the panel.

The `nav ul li` rule formats the basic structure of the menu button.

**3**   Double-click the `nav ul li` rule.

**4** Select the Border category in "CSS Rule Definition For *nav ul li*."
Enter **solid**, **1px**, **#0C0** in the Top border fields.
Enter **solid**, **1px**, **#060**  in the Right border fields.
Enter **solid**, **1px**, **#060** in the Bottom border fields.
Enter **solid**, **1px**, **#0C0** in the Left border fields. Click OK.

Before                              After

By adding lighter colors to the top and left and darker colors to the right and bottom, you have created a subtle but effective three-dimensional effect.

**5** Save the file.

## Creating faux columns

Although multicolumn designs are very popular on the web, HTML and CSS have no built-in commands to produce true column structures in a webpage. Instead, columnar designs—like the one used in the Dreamweaver CSS layouts—are simulated by using several types of HTML elements and various formatting techniques, usually combining margins and the float attribute. HTML5 and CSS3 can display text in multiple columns, but for the time being, the page layouts themselves will still depend on the older techniques.

Unfortunately, these methods have their limitations and downsides. For example, one of the problems with the layout used in this lesson is getting both columns to display at the same height. Either one column or the other will almost always be shorter. Since the sidebar has a background color, there will be a visible gap at the bottom as content is added to the main page.

There are methods, using JavaScript and other coding tricks, to force columns to display at equal height, but these are not fully supported by all browsers and could cause your page to break unexpectedly. Many designers sidestep the issue altogether simply by refusing to use background colors. Then no one will notice any discrepancy.

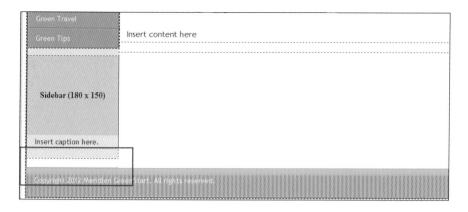

It's difficult, using only CSS formatting, to get all the columns to appear to be the same length in multicolumn designs.

Instead, you will create the effect of a full-height sidebar column by using a background graphic combined with the CSS `repeat` function. This technique works well with fixed-width website designs, like this one.

1  Insert the cursor in `<div.sidebar1>` below the vertical menu. Examine the tag selector display.

   The `<div.sidebar1>` element is within `<div.container>`, and both are contained in the body element.

2  Select the `.sidebar1` rule in the CSS Styles panel. Examine its properties.

   The `.sidebar1` rule applies a background color to the sidebar. Since the background color assigned to the `<div>` appears already to be failing to extend to the bottom of the document, the `.sidebar1` rule is not the solution to this problem. Since `<div.container>` holds the sidebar as well as the main content, it's an obvious candidate for the faux column. First, it's a good idea to remove the background color from the sidebar if it's not producing the desired results.

3  Select the background color reference in the Properties section of the CSS Styles panel. Click the Delete CSS Property (🗑) icon at the bottom of the panel.

   Now, you'll modify the `.container` rule to produce the desired background effect for the sidebar.

4  Double-click the `.container` rule. In the Background category, click the Browse button. Select **divider.png** from the default images folder. Click OK/Choose.

5  Choose repeat-y in the Background-repeat field menu. Click OK.

   A graphic 182 pixels wide appears at the left edge of `<div.container>` and extends from the top to the bottom. Since the other structural elements are contained entirely within `<div.container>`, the background appears behind them and is visible only where appropriate.

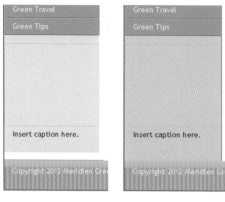

Before                  After

Let's make a couple of additional tweaks to the sidebar. First, let's remove the extra space that appears between the menu and the image placeholder. You'll need to identify the rule or rules that may be creating this styling.

6   Insert the cursor in the last button of the vertical menu. Right-click the button and choose Code Navigator from the context menu.

The Code Navigator appears, displaying a list of 12 CSS rules affecting this item. Chances are a margin setting is producing the spacing effect.

7   Scan the rules for a bottom-margin setting.

The nav ul rule features a bottom-margin of 15 pixels.

8   Select the nav ul rule in the CSS Styles panel. Select the bottom-margin setting in the Properties section. Click the Delete CSS Property (🗑) icon.

The gap between the menu and the image placeholder closes up. Finally, let's make the text in the vertical menu match that in the horizontal menu.

9   Double-click the rule nav ul.

10  In the Type category, enter **90%** in the Font-size field. Click OK.

11  Save the file.

## Moving rules to an external style sheet

When prototyping a webpage design, it's more practical to keep the CSS embedded. It makes the process of testing and uploading quick and simple. But an internal style sheet can style only one page. An external style sheet can be linked to any number of pages and, for most web applications, is the normal and preferred workflow. Before this page is put into production as a template, it's a good idea to move the CSS styles from the <head> section of the document to an external CSS style sheet. Dreamweaver provides the means to handle that task quickly and easily.

1   In the CSS Styles panel, select the first defined style: body. Hold the Shift key and select the last style.

● **Note:** The last style in your style sheet may differ from the figure. Remember to select the last one.

2   In the CSS Styles panel, choose Move CSS Rules from the Options menu in the upper-right corner of the panel.

You could also right-click the selected area to access the Move CSS Rules option from the context menu.

3   When the Move To External Style Sheet dialog box appears, choose A New Style Sheet in the Move Rules To options. Click OK.

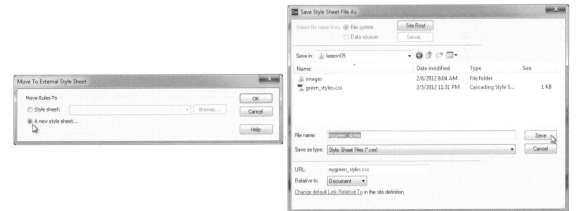

The Save Style Sheet File As dialog box appears.

4   Navigate to the site root folder, if necessary. Type **mygreen_styles** in the File Name field. Click Save.

Dreamweaver adds the .css extension to the filename, moves the selected styles from the `<head>` area to the newly defined style sheet, and simultaneously inserts a link to the style sheet. Note at the top of the document window that Dreamweaver now displays the name of the external style sheet in the Related Files interface.

The last chore is to remove the no-longer-needed `<style>` tag.

▶ **Tip:** If the reference does not disappear, you can right-click it and choose Delete from the context menu.

5   In the CSS Styles panel, click the `<style>` notation and then press Delete or click the Trash Can icon.

6   Choose File > Save All. Or, press Ctrl-Alt-Shift-S/Cmd-Ctrl-S to access the keyboard shortcut for the Save All command you created in Lesson 1, "Customizing Your Workspace."

▶ **Tip:** Once you move the CSS to an external file, remember to use the Save All command moving forward. Pressing Ctrl-S/ Cmd-S saves only the top document in the Dreamweaver interface. Other files that are open and referenced that have been changed are not automatically saved.

# Creating style sheets for other media

Current best practices call for the separation of presentation (CSS) from content (the HTML tags, text, and other page elements). The reason is simple: By separating the formatting, which may only be relevant for one type of medium, one HTML document can be formatted instantly for multiple purposes. More than one style sheet can be linked to a page. By creating and attaching style sheets optimized for other media, the specific browsing application can select the appropriate style sheet and formatting for its own needs. For example, the style sheet created and applied in the previous exercises was designed for a typical computer display. In this exercise, you'll convert a CSS screen-media file to one optimized for printing devices.

Today, designers frequently include a "Print" link on pages heavy with text or for sales receipts so that users can send the information to a printer more effectively. *Print* style sheets often adjust colors to work better for laser and inkjet printers, hide unneeded page elements, or adjust page sizes and layouts to be more suitable for printing.

When the print queue is activated, the printing application checks for a print-media style sheet. If one is present, the relevant CSS rules are taken into account. If not, the printer defers to the rules in the existing "screen" or "all-media" style sheets or to the CSS defaults for print output.

## Displaying the Style Rendering toolbar

If no media-type attribute appears in a style sheet, the browser or web application assumes that the CSS styles are intended for screen display. By default, Dreamweaver's Design view also defaults to screen styles and will ignore other media types. However, you have the ability to switch what media type is rendered in Design view by using the Style Rendering toolbar. That way, you can preview how different media types will render without having to access those applications or workflows.

1  If necessary, open the **mylayout.html** file by double-clicking its filename in the Files panel.

2  Choose View > Toolbars > Style Rendering.

The Style Rendering toolbar appears above the document window. Leave it visible for the next exercise.

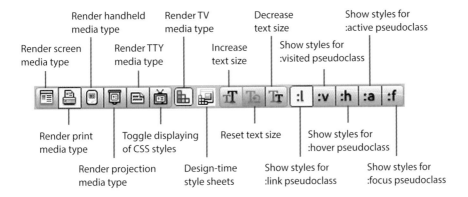

## Converting an existing style sheet for print

Although you can develop a print style sheet from scratch, it's usually much faster to convert an existing screen-media style sheet. The first step is to save the existing external style sheet under a new name.

1  In the Files panel, double-click **mygreen_styles.css** to open it.

2  Choose File > Save As.

3  When the Save As dialog box opens, type **print_styles.css** in the File Name/Save As field. Make sure the site root folder is targeted. Click Save.

4  If necessary, open **mylayout.html** from the site root folder. In the CSS Styles panel, click the Attach Style Sheet (⊕) icon.

The Attach External Style Sheet dialog box opens.

5  Click Browse.

The Select Style Sheet File dialog box appears.

6  Select **print_styles.css** from the site root folder. Click OK/Choose.

**7** In the Attach External Style Sheet dialog box, select the Link option for the Add As value. From the Media field menu, choose print. Click OK.

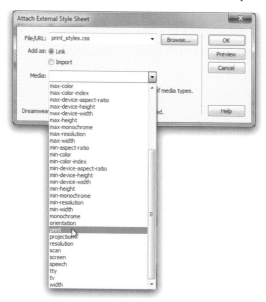

**8** In the CSS Styles panel, click the All button, if necessary.

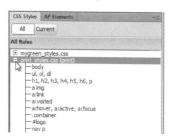

A new entry—**print_styles.css**—has been added. At the moment, both style sheets are identical. You will modify the print style sheet in the next exercise.

**9** Close **print_styles.css** and **mygreen_styles.css**.

**10** Save **mylayout.html**.

## Hiding unwanted page components

Using the Style Rendering toolbar, you can see your document rendered according to the print-media style rules.

**Note:** Remember to click the Render Screen Media Type icon when you're ready to work on screen-media formatting again.

**1** In the Style Rendering toolbar, click the Render Print Media Type (🖶) icon.

One of the main differences between screen and print media is that interactive items on a webpage are often meaningless in print. This would include all navigation elements in the horizontal and vertical menus. Using the print-media style sheet, you can hide unwanted portions of a page. Let's start with the horizontal and vertical menus. Before you can hide these menus, we need to create a new rule.

2   Insert the cursor in one of the links in the horizontal menu.

3   Click the `<nav>` tag selector at the bottom of the document window.

4   In the CSS Styles panel, click the New CSS Rule icon.

The New CSS Rule dialog box appears.

5   If necessary, select the Compound selector type.

The Selector name `.container nav` appears in the field.

6   Click OK.

This rule will apply to both the horizontal and the vertical menus.

7   In the Block category, select None from the Display menu. Click OK.

Both `<nav>` elements disappear from the document window. No, they haven't been deleted; Dreamweaver has simply stopped rendering them temporarily as long as the Render Print Media Type icon is selected.

The content in the rest of the `<div.sidebar1>` is also not needed for printing. Let's turn it off, too.

8   In the **print_styles.css** rule list, double-click the `.sidebar1` rule.

9   In the Block category, choose None from the Display field menu. Click OK.

The sidebar vanishes, and the main content expands to the full width of the `<div.container>`. The background image is visible under the content and may make it harder to read the text.

10  In the **print_styles.css** rule list, double-click `.container`.

11  In the Background category, delete the `divider.png` image reference in the Background-image field. Delete `repeat-y` from the Background-repeat field. Click Apply.

Note that the background image continues to display in `<div.container>`. Deleting the image reference is not enough. Although the print application defers to the print-media style sheet, formatting is still inherited from all referenced CSS style sheets. Even though you deleted the background image reference in the print style sheet, it's still applied in the screen styles. It won't disappear until you reset the rule by choosing none. This goes for other such rules, too.

**12** Choose none from the Background-image field menu. Click Apply.

The background image vanishes. Let's check the page in Live view.

**13** Click OK to complete the change. Click the Live view button.

Although the Style Rendering toolbar is set to Print, Dreamweaver ignores the print-media styles and renders the page for the screen. That's because Live view is intended for browser preview only and can't render print-based styling. To properly test the page, you have to use the print preview function in an actual browser.

**14** Save all files. Choose File > Preview in Browser and select your preferred browser.

**15** Once the page has loaded in the browser, activate print preview.

As you can see, the print application converted the text to black and automatically dropped all the background images and colors, but it is still printing the butterfly logo and the page borders. Let's eliminate the border.

**16** In the **print_styles.css** rules, double-click .container. In the Border category, if necessary, select the Same For All option in the Style section. Choose none from the Top Style field. Click OK.

**17** Save all files.

**18** Choose File > Preview in Browser and select your preferred browser.

**19** Once the page has loaded in the browser, activate print preview.

The border has been removed successfully.

**20** Save All files.

**Note:** Some browsers have a different technique to access the print preview mode. You may need to choose File > Print first and access the preview function from within the Print dialog box.

**Note:** From the preview, you may assume that all print applications will convert text to black and drop background colors and images, but don't be fooled. Always test this functionality in all browsers first to see what other styles you need to modify for printing.

As you can see, it's easy to adapt a screen style sheet for print. You should know enough now to keep the butterfly logo from printing, too. Take a few minutes here and see if you can do it.

## Removing unneeded styles

Even with the changes you made in the previous exercises, many rules in the two style sheets are identical. It doesn't make sense to keep two sets of styles that do the same job. Whenever you can remove unneeded code from your pages, you should do so. It reduces file size and allows the pages to download and respond more quickly. Let's remove from the print-media sheet any rules that haven't changed or that don't pertain anymore. You can delete unneeded styles using the CSS Styles panel. But be careful—even though a rule hasn't changed doesn't mean it's not needed for print rendering.

1   In Dreamweaver, select all rules that format the nav ul menu in **print_styles.css**. Click the Delete CSS Rule icon, or right-click the selected rules and choose Delete from the context menu. Click Yes to delete multiple rules.

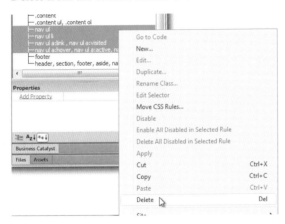

Since the vertical menu isn't displayed, there's no need for those rules. In fact, you can remove all the rules that format hyperlink behavior.

2   Select all hyperlink rules in **print_styles.css** and delete them, this includes rules that style a, a:link, a:visited, a:hover, and a:active properties.

Don't worry. You don't need these styles, because the hyperlinks in the horizontal and vertical menus are not printing, and the other rules are still identical to the ones in the screen styles and will be inherited, if supported by the print application. After deleting any rules, make sure you test the page in the browser and in the print application.

3   Save all files.

**4** Click the Render Screen Media Type (⊞) icon. Observe the screen display in Design view.

Dreamweaver renders the document for the web.

**5** Click the Render For Print Media Type (🖶) icon.

Dreamweaver renders the screen using the print style sheet. You have adapted a screen-media style sheet to render a webpage more appropriately in print.

You have completed the basic design of the page that will be used as the project template, and you have adapted it to print media. In the next lesson, you will learn how to convert this layout into a dynamic web template.

# Review questions

1 How do you attach an existing external style sheet to a webpage?

2 How can you target a specific type of formatting to content in a webpage?

3 What method can you use to hide specific content on a webpage?

4 How do you apply an existing CSS class to a page element?

5 What is the purpose of creating style sheets for different media?

# Review answers

1 In the CSS Styles panel, choose Attach Style Sheet. In the Attach External Style Sheet dialog box, choose the desired CSS file and select the media type.

2 You can create a custom class or ID using descendant selectors to target formatting to specific elements or element configurations on a page.

3 In the style sheet, set the Block `display` property of the element, class, or ID to `none` to hide any content you don't want to display.

4 One method is to select the element and then choose the desired style from the Class menu in the Property inspector.

5 Creating and attaching style sheets for different types of media enables the page to adapt to applications other than web browsers, such as print applications.

# 6 WORKING WITH TEMPLATES

## Lesson Overview

In this lesson, you'll learn how to work faster, make updating easier, and be more productive. You'll use Dreamweaver templates, library items, and server-side includes to do the following:

- Create a Dreamweaver template
- Insert editable regions
- Produce child pages
- Update templates and child pages
- Create, insert, and update library items
- Create, insert, and update server-side includes

 This lesson will take about 1 hour and 15 minutes to complete. Before beginning, make sure you have copied the files for Lesson 6 to your hard drive as described in the "Getting Started" section at the beginning of the book. If you are starting from scratch in this lesson, use the method described in the "Jumpstart" section of "Getting Started."

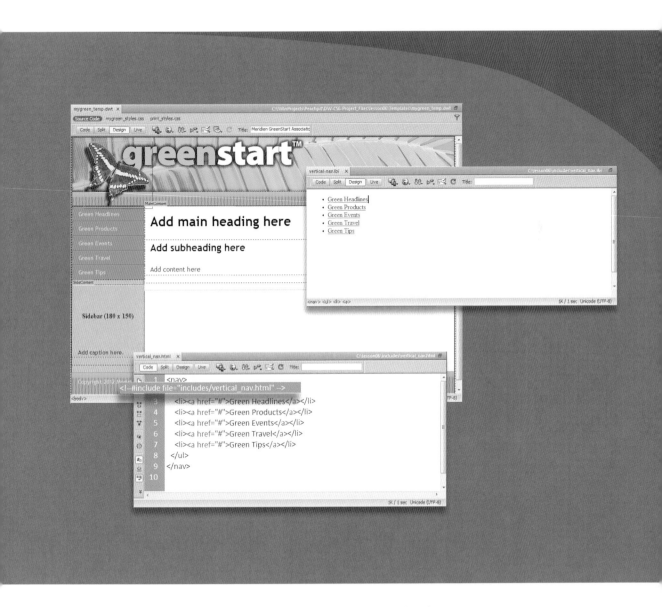

Dreamweaver's productivity tools and site management capabilities are among its most useful features
for a busy designer.

# Previewing completed files

To better understand the topics in this lesson, let's preview in a browser the page you will complete.

**1** Launch Adobe Dreamweaver CS6.

**2** If necessary, press Ctrl-Shift-F/Cmd-Shift-F to open the Files panel, and select DW-CS6 from the site list.

**3** In the Files panel, expand the lesson06 folder. Double-click **template_finished.html** to open it. Observe the design and structure of this page.

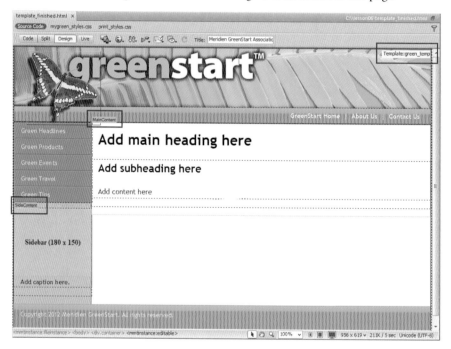

This page was created from a template; Dreamweaver displays the name of the parent file in the upper-right corner of the document window. The layout is identical to the page completed in Lesson 5, "Working with Cascading Style Sheets," with some notable exceptions. There are two areas on the page that display blue tabs and borders. These areas, or *editable regions*, represent the most significant differences between your own layout and the finished template-based one.

**4** Move the cursor over <header>. Note the mouse icon Dreamweaver displays.

The (⊘) icon signifies that the area is locked and uneditable.

5   Select the placeholder *Add main heading here* in `<article.content>`. Type **Get a fresh start with GreenStart** to replace the text. Save the file.

The `<article.content>` element is contained in one of the blue editable areas labeled *MainContent*, which allows you to select and change content within it.

6   Select File > Preview in a Browser. Select your default browser.

The browser display won't give you any clues as to how this page differs from the one you created earlier—that's the beauty of a template-based page. For all intents and purposes, a template-based page is just a normal HTML file. The extra code elements that enable its special features are basically comments added and read only by Dreamweaver and other web-aware applications and should never affect the performance or display in a browser.

7   Close your browser and return to Dreamweaver. Close **template_finished.html**.

# Creating a template from an existing layout

A template is a type of master page from which related child pages are produced. Templates are useful for setting up and maintaining the overall look and feel of a website, while providing a means for quickly and easily producing site content. A template is different from the pages you have already completed; it contains areas that are editable and other areas that are not. Templates enable a workgroup environment where page content can be created and edited by several people on the team, while the web designer is able to control the page design and specific elements that must remain unchanged.

Although you can create a template from a blank page, it is far more practical, and common, to convert an existing page into a template. In this exercise, you'll create a template from your existing layout.

1   Launch Dreamweaver CS6.

2   If necessary, open the **mylayout.html** file (which was complete at the end of Lesson 5) by double-clicking its filename in the root folder of the DW-CS6 website in the Files panel. Or, if you are starting from scratch in this exercise, see the "Jumpstart" instructions in the "Getting Started" section at the beginning of the book.

The first step for converting an existing page to a template is to save the page as a template.

3   Choose File > Save as Template.

Because of their special nature, templates are stored in their own folder, **Templates**, which Dreamweaver automatically creates at the site root level.

**Note:** If you don't feel confident working with your own layout, use the method described in the "Jumpstart" section of "Getting Started" at the beginning of the book and open **mylayout.html**, provided in the lesson06 folder.

4  When the Save As Template dialog box appears, choose DW-CS6 in the Site pop-up menu. Leave the Description field empty. (If you have more than one template in a site, a description may be useful.) Type **mygreen_temp** in the Save As field. Click Save.

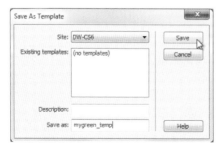

An untitled dialog box appears asking whether you want to update links.

5  Click Yes to update the links.

Since the template is saved in a subfolder, updating the links in the code is necessary so that they will continue to work properly when you create child pages later.

Although the page still looks exactly the same, you can identify a template in two ways. First, the title bar displays <<*Template*>>. Second, the file extension is .dwt, which stands for *Dreamweaver template*.

A template is *dynamic,* meaning that Dreamweaver maintains a connection to all pages within the site that are derived from it. Whenever you add or change content within the dynamic regions of the page and save it, Dreamweaver passes those changes to all the child pages automatically, keeping them up to date. But a template shouldn't be completely dynamic. Some sections of the page should contain areas where you can insert unique content. Dreamweaver allows you to designate these areas of the page as *editable.*

## Inserting editable regions

When you first create a template, Dreamweaver treats all the existing content as part of the master design. Child pages created from the template would be exact duplicates, except that the content would be locked and uneditable. This is great for repetitive features of a page, such as the navigation components, logos, copyright and contact information, and so on, but it's also bad because it stops you from adding unique content to each child page. You get around this barrier by defining editable regions in the template. Dreamweaver creates one editable region automatically for the `<title>` element in the `<head>` section of the page; you have to create the rest.

First, give some thought to which areas of the page should be part of the template and which should be open for editing. At the moment, two sections of your current layout need to be editable: `<article.content>` and a part of `<div.sidebar1>`. Although editable regions don't have to be limited to such elements, they are easier to manage.

1  Insert the cursor in `<article.content>`. Click the `<article.content>` tag selector.

2  Choose Insert > Template Objects > Editable Region.

3  In the New Editable Region dialog box, type **MainContent** in the Name field. Click OK.

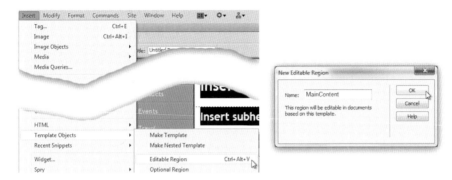

Each editable region must have a unique name, but there are no other special conventions. However, keeping them short and descriptive is a good practice. The name is used solely within Dreamweaver and has no other bearing on the HTML code. In Design view, you will see the name in a blue tab above the designated area, identifying it as an editable region.

You also need to add an editable region to `<div.sidebar1>`. It contains an image placeholder and caption that you can customize on each page. But it also includes the vertical menu, which will hold the main navigation links for the site. In most cases, you'll want to leave such components in the locked regions of the page, where the template can update them as needed. Luckily, the sidebar is divided between two distinct elements: `<nav>` and `<aside>`. In this case, you'll add the editable region to the `<aside>` element.

> **Note:** If you are building this template using an alternative HTML 4 layout suggested in Lesson 4, "Creating a Page Layout," it is suggested that you apply these steps to `<div.aside>` instead.

4  Insert the cursor in `<aside>`. Click the `<aside>` tag selector.

5  Choose Insert > Template Objects > Editable Region.

6  In the New Editable Region dialog box, type **SideContent** in the Name field. Click OK.

Adding a title to each page is a good practice. Each title should reflect the specific content or purpose of the page. But many designers also append the name of the company or organization to help build more corporate or organizational awareness. Adding the name in the template will save time typing it in each child page later.

**7** In the Title field of the document toolbar, select the placeholder text *Untitled Document.* Type **Meridien GreenStart Association – Add Title Here** to replace the text.

**8** Press Enter/Return to complete the title. Choose File > Save.

**9** Choose File > Close.

**Note:** The Update Template Pages dialog box may appear when you save the file. Since there are no template pages yet, click Don't Update.

You now have two editable regions, plus an editable title that can be changed as needed when you create new child pages using this template. The template is linked to your style sheet files, so any changes in those files will also be reflected in all child pages made from this template.

# Producing child pages

**Warning:** If you open a template in a text editor, all the code is editable, including the code for the non-editable regions of the page.

Child pages are the *raison d'être* for Dreamweaver templates. Once a child page has been created from a template, only the content within the editable regions can be modified in the child page. The rest of the page remains locked. This behavior is supported only within Dreamweaver and other web-aware HTML editors. If you open the page in a text editor, like Notepad or TextEdit, the code is fully editable.

The decision to use Dreamweaver templates for a site should be made at the beginning of the design process so that all the pages in the site can be made as child pages of the template. That's the purpose of the layout you've built up to this point: to create the basic structure of your site template.

**1** Choose File > New, or press Ctrl-N/Cmd-N.

The New Document dialog box appears.

**2** In the New Document dialog box, select the Page From Template option. Select DW-CS6 in the Site list, if necessary. Select **mygreen_temp** in the Template For Site *"DW-CS6"* list.

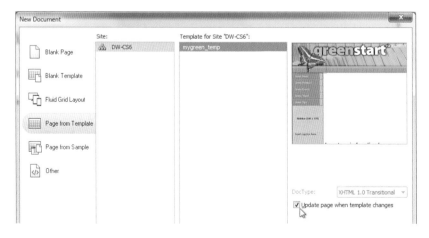

**3** Select the Update Page When Template Changes option, if necessary. Click Create.

Dreamweaver creates a new page based on the template. Note the name of the template file displayed in the upper-right corner of the document window. Before modifying the page, you should save it.

**4** Choose File > Save. In the Save As dialog box, navigate to the root folder for your project site. Type **about_us.html** in the File Name field. Click Save.

**5** Move the cursor over the different page areas.

Certain areas, such as the header, menu bar, and footer, are locked and cannot be modified. The content in the editable regions can be changed.

**6** In the Title field, select the placeholder text *Add Title Here*. Type **About Us** and press Enter/Return.

**7** Select the placeholder text *Insert main heading here* in the MainContent editable region. Type **About Meridien GreenStart** to replace the text.

**8** Select the placeholder text *Insert subheading here* in the MainContent editable region. Type **GreenStart – green awareness in action!** to replace the text.

**9** In the Files panel, double-click **content-aboutus.rtf** in the lesson06 folder to open the file.

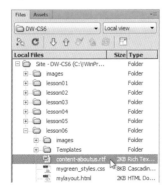

The file will open in a compatible program, such as WordPad or TextEdit.

**10** Press Ctrl-A/Cmd-A to select all the text. Press Ctrl-C/Cmd-C to copy the text.

**11** Switch back to Dreamweaver. Select the placeholder text *Insert content here* in the MainContent region. Press Ctrl-V/Cmd-V to paste the text.

The pasted text will replace the placeholder copy.

**12** In the SideContent region, double-click the image placeholder. In the Select Image Source dialog box, select **shopping.jpg** from the default images folder. Click OK.

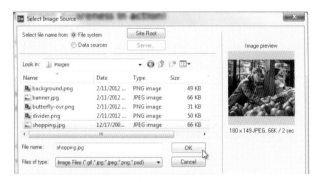

**13** Select the placeholder text *Insert caption here* and replace the text with **When shopping for groceries, buy fruits and vegetables at farmers markets to support local agriculture.**

**14** Save the file.

**15** Click the Live view button to preview the page.

As you can see, there is no indication that this template child page is any different from any other standard webpage. Editable regions don't limit the content you can insert into them; it can include text, images, tables, video, and so on.

16 Click the Live view button to return to standard document display. Choose File > Close.

## Updating a template

Templates can automatically update any child pages made from that template. But only areas outside the editable regions will be updated. Let's make some changes in the template to learn how a template is updated.

1 Choose Window > Assets.

The Assets panel appears. Typically, it is grouped with the Files panel. The Assets panel gives you immediate access to a variety of components and content available to your website.

2 In the Assets panel, click the Template category ( ) icon. Click the refresh ( ) icon if no templates appear in the list.

The panel changes to display list and preview windows for site templates. The name of your template appears in the list.

3 Right-click **mygreen_temp** and choose Edit from the context menu.

The template opens.

4 Select the text *Home* in the horizontal menu. Type **GreenStart Home** to replace the text.

5 Select the text *News* in the vertical menu. Type **Headlines** to replace the text.

**6** Select and replace the text *Insert* with the word **Add** wherever it appears in the MainContent or SideContent editable regions.

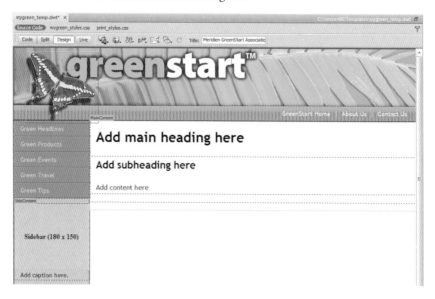

**7** Save the file.

The Update Template Files dialog box appears. The filename **about_us.html** appears in the update list.

**8** Click the Update button.

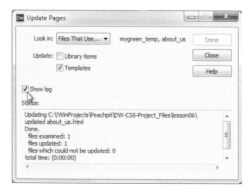

The Update Pages dialog box appears. Select the Show Log option at the bottom of the dialog box to display a report detailing which pages were successfully updated and which ones were not.

**9** Close the Update Pages dialog box.

**10** Choose File > Open Recent > **about_us.html**. Observe the page and note any changes.

The changes made to the horizontal and vertical menus are reflected in this file, but the changes to the sidebar and main content areas were ignored, and the content you added to both areas remain unaltered. That way, you can safely make changes and add content to the editable regions without worrying that the template will delete all your hard work. At the same time, the boilerplate elements of the header, footer, and horizontal menu all remain consistently formatted and up to date based on the status of the template.

**11** Click the document tab for **mygreen_temp.dwt** at the top of the document window to switch to the template file.

**12** Delete the word *GreenStart* from the Home link in the horizontal menu.

**13** Save the template and update related files.

**14** Click the tab for **about_us.html** to switch back. Observe the page and note any changes.

The horizontal menu has been updated. Dreamweaver even updates linked documents that are open at the time. The only concern is that the changes have not been saved; the document tab shows an asterisk, which means the file has been changed and is unsaved. If Dreamweaver or your computer were to crash at this moment, the changes would be lost and you would have to update the page manually or wait until the next time you make changes to the template to take advantage of the automatic update feature.

▶ **Tip:** Always use the Save All command whenever you have multiple files open that have been updated by a template.

**15** Select File > Save All.

# Using library items

Library items are reusable bits of HTML—paragraphs, links, copyright notices, tables, images, navigation bars, and so on—that you use frequently but not on every page within a website and therefore would not necessarily include in the site template. You can use existing page elements or create original library items from scratch and add copies of them where needed. A library item is a like a template, only on a small scale. As with templates, when you make and save changes to a library item, Dreamweaver automatically updates every page that uses that item. In fact, they are so similar in behavior that some workflows may favor library items over templates altogether.

## Creating a library item

In this exercise, you'll experiment by creating an alternative workflow model using library items in place of a site template.

**1** Open **about_us.html**, if necessary. Select File > Save As.

**2** Save the file as **library_test.html**.

A new tab appears at the top of the document window for the new file. It's an exact copy of the existing About Us page, down to its link to the site template. To implement the new workflow properly, you'll need to detach it from the template first.

3   Select Modify > Templates > Detach from Template.

The new file is no longer connected to the template. The editable regions have been removed, and you can modify them freely. Without a link to a site template, you won't be able to update changes to the common features of the page quickly and easily. Instead, they'll have to be made page by page, manually. Or, you could implement common page elements using library items.

4   Insert the cursor in the vertical menu. Click the <nav> tag selector.

5   Choose Window > Assets to display the Assets panel, if necessary.

6   Click the Library category (📖) icon.

No items appear in the library for this lesson.

7   Click the New Library Item (🗗) icon at the bottom of the panel.

A dialog box appears explaining that the library item may not look the same when placed in other documents because style sheet information is not included.

8   Click OK. Type **vertical-nav** in the Library Item Name field.

When you click OK, Dreamweaver does three things simultaneously. First, it creates a library item from the selected menu code and inserts an *Untitled* reference to it in the Library list, allowing you to name it. Second, it replaces the existing menu with the library item code. And third, it creates a folder called Library at the site root level to store this and other items. In Lesson 16, "Publishing to the Web," you will learn more about what files need to be uploaded, or published, to the Internet.

● **Note:** The Library folder doesn't need to be uploaded to the server.

9   Save the file.

Working with library items is similar to using a template. You insert the library item on each page as desired and then update the items as needed. To test this functionality, you'll make a copy of the current page.

10  Select File > Save As. Name the file **library_copy.html**.

**11** Close **library_copy.html**.

The original file, **library_test.html**, is still open.

**12** Click on the vertical menu. Position the cursor over the vertical menu. Observe the menu display.

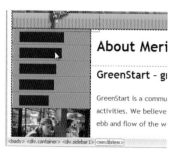

The link text is obscured, indicating that the menu is basically uneditable. The `<nav>` element has been replaced by `<mm.libitem>`. This is how Dreamweaver displays a library item.

**13** Click the `<mm.libitem>` tag selector. Switch to Code view. Insert your cursor in the selected code.

```
20    </nav>
21    <div class="sidebar1"><!-- #BeginLibraryItem "/Library/vertical-nav.lbi" --><nav>
22       <ul>
23          <li><a href="#">Green News</a></li>
24          <li><a href="#">Green Products</a></li>
25          <li><a href="#">Green Events</a></li>
26          <li><a href="#">Green Travel</a></li>
27          <li><a href="#">Green Tips</a></li>
28       </ul>
29    </nav><!-- #EndLibraryItem --><aside> <img name="Sidebar" src="images/shopping.jpg
      height="149" alt="">
30       <p> When shopping for groceries, buy fruits and vegetables at farmers markets to su
```

Note that the library item still contains the same code for the menu, although it's highlighted in a different color and enclosed in some special markup. The opening tag is

```
<!-- #BeginLibraryItem "/Library/vertical-nav.lbi" -->
```

The closing tag is

```
<!-- #EndLibraryItem -->
```

But be careful. Although the library item is locked in Design view, Dreamweaver doesn't prevent you from editing the code in Code view.

● **Note:** A dialog box may appear at any time in this or the next two steps warning you that the changes you made will be discarded the next time you update the page from the template. For the purpose of this exercise, click OK/Yes to preserve the manual changes.

**14** Select the text *News* in the code. Type **Headlines** to replace the text.

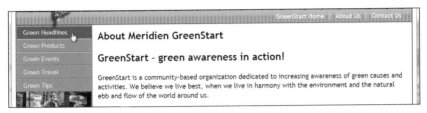

**15** Save the file and select File > Preview in Browser. Select a browser from the list.

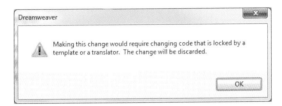

The browser displays the page with the edited menu. You may be wondering why no warning dialogs appeared and why you weren't prevented from making the change in the first place. But the news isn't entirely bad. Dreamweaver is keeping track of the library item and your edits, intentional or otherwise. As you will see shortly, the change you made will be short-lived.

**16** Choose File > Close All.

Finally, a dialog appears warning you that you have made changes to code that was locked. It further explains that the original code will be restored the next time you update the template or library item.

● **Note:** The manual change to the library item will remain in the menu for the time being.

**17** Click OK to preserve your manual edits. Save all changes.

**18** Right-click `vertical-nav` in the Library list and choose Update Site from the context menu.

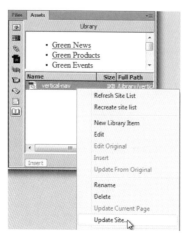

The Update Pages dialog box appears.

**19** Click Start.

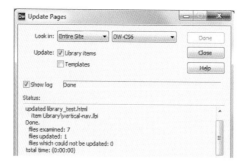

Dreamweaver updates any pages in the site that use the library item and reports the results of the process. At least one page should be updated. The **library_ copy.html** file contains the unedited menu, so it should not have to be updated.

**20** Click Close to exit the dialog box.

**21** Click **library_test.html** in the Welcome Screen to reopen the file.

**22** Click the Live view button to preview the page.

The menu has been restored to the original code. Library items allow you to insert repeatable content throughout the site and update it without having to open the files individually.

## Updating library items

Templates, library items, and server-side includes exist for one reason: to make it easy to update webpage content. Let's update the menu library item.

1   In the Library category list in the Assets panel, double-click to open the `vertical-nav` item, or right-click the item in the list and select Edit in the context menu.

    The vertical menu opens without formatting as a bulleted list. Formatting is applied via CSS in the actual page layout. The library item is not a stand-alone webpage; it merely contains the `<nav>` element itself and no other code.

2   Switch to Code view. Select the text *News* and type **Headlines** to replace it.

3   Choose File > Save.

    The Update Library Items dialog box appears.

4   Click Update.

    The Update Pages dialog box appears and reports which pages were successfully updated and which ones were not.

5   Click to close the Update Pages dialog box.

6   Click the Live view button. Observe the vertical menu.

    The vertical menu has been updated successfully. Let's check **library_copy.html**.

7   Select the Files panel, and double-click **library_copy.html** to open that file. Observe the vertical menu in Live view.

    The menu in the template was updated too.

8   Save all files.

You've successfully used library items to add repetitive content to your webpages. As you can see, using library items and templates can save you a lot of time when you want to change and update more than one page. But Dreamweaver still has one more trick up its productivity sleeve: server-side includes.

## Using server-side includes

Server-side includes (SSIs) are like library items in some ways. They are reusable bits of HTML—paragraphs, links, copyright notices, navigation bars, tables, images, and so on—that you use frequently. The main differences between library items and SSIs are in the way they are handled in the page code and then managed within the site.

For example, a complete copy of the library item must be inserted in the page's code *before* it's uploaded to the web. (That's why the library items themselves don't have to be stored on the server.) Then, each affected page must be updated and then uploaded before the change takes effect on the Internet.

Unlike library items, SSIs must be stored on the web, preferably in your site folder. In fact, the code the SSI contains doesn't appear anywhere in the page itself, only a reference to its filename and path location. The SSI appears only when the page is accessed by a visitor and rendered by the browser. This function has advantages and disadvantages.

On the upside, server-side includes are the most efficient and timesaving way to add reusable HTML code elements to a large number of pages. They are faster and easier to work with than either templates or library items. The reason is simple: It only takes a single file containing a menu or piece of important content—once edited and uploaded—to update the entire site.

On the downside, dozens or even hundreds of pages on your site could depend on one file to operate correctly. Any error in the code or path name, even a minor one, could cause your entire site to fail. For small sites, library items can be a perfectly workable solution. For large sites, it would be hard to live without SSIs.

In this exercise, you will create an SSI and add it to a page in your site.

## Creating server-side includes

An SSI is almost identical to a library item—it's an HTML file stripped clean of any superfluous code. In this exercise, you will create an SSI from the code creating the vertical menu. First, you'll have to make the menu editable again.

1   Open the file **library_test.html**, if necessary. In Design view, right-click the vertical menu. Select Detach From Original in the context menu.

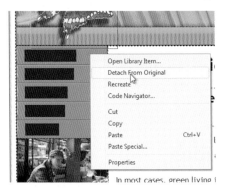

A dialog box appears explaining that if you make this item editable, it will no longer be possible to automatically update it when the original changes.

**2**  Click OK.

The markup for the library item is removed, making the menu editable.

**3**  Select the <nav> tag selector. Switch to Code view. Select Edit > Copy or press Ctrl-C/Cmd-C to copy the code for the vertical menu.

**4**  Choose File > New. Select Blank Page from the Category section. In the Page Type list, choose HTML. In the Layout list, select <none>. Click Create.

**5**  Switch to Code view, if necessary.

Note that the Untitled document is a completely formed webpage. However, none of the existing HTML code is needed for the SSI and could actually cause trouble if inserted into another page.

**6**  Press Ctrl-A/Cmd-A to select all the code in the new file. Press Delete.

The code is deleted, leaving an empty window. The menu code is still in memory.

**7**  Select Edit > Paste.

> ● **Note:** If you copy elements in Code view, you must be in Code view to paste them.

**8**  Choose File > Save. Navigate to the site root folder. In the Save As dialog box, click the Create New Folder button. Name the folder **includes**. Select the newly created **includes** folder, if necessary. Name the file **vertical-nav.html**. Click Save.

**9**  Close **vertical-nav.html**.

You have completed the SSI for the vertical menu. In the next exercise, you will learn how to insert it into a webpage.

## Inserting server-side includes

On a live website, you must upload the "includes" files or folder to the server along with the normal pages of your site. A command inserted in the code of any page on your site would make a *call* to the server to add the HTML include in the indicated location. The include command will look something like this:

```
<!--#include file="includes/vertical-nav.html" -->
```

You can see that it consists of an includes command and the path location to the SSI file. Depending on the type of server you are using, the exact markup may vary. It will also affect the file extension you use for both the SSI and the webpage file itself. The include behavior is considered a dynamic function and typically requires a file extension that supports these capabilities. If you save the file with the default .htm or .html extension, you may find that the browser won't load the SSI. In the following example, you'd have to use the extension .shtml to support SSI functionality. Later, you'll build pages using the .asp, .cfm, and .php extensions for data publishing. These extensions support SSI capabilities by default. But in some instances, you may need to save the SSI itself with a different extension.

In this exercise, you will replace the existing menu with the one stored in the SSI.

1  If necessary, open **library_test.html**.

    The file still contains the original vertical menu; to insert the SSI, you'll need to delete it.

2  Insert the cursor in the vertical menu. Click the <nav> tag selector. Press Delete.

    The entire <nav> element disappears, but don't move your cursor—it's in the perfect position to insert the SSI. Let's insert the SSI.

3  Select Insert > Server-Side Include.

4  Select **vertical-nav.html** from the **includes** folder. Click OK.

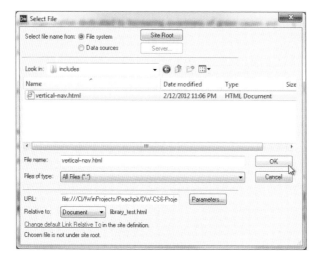

The vertical menu reappears, but there are two significant differences: The menu is not editable, and more importantly, the code for the menu is not even resident in this file.

**5** Switch to Code view. Observe the code where the menu should appear.

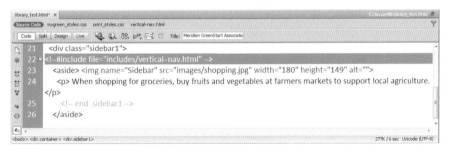

The code for the `<nav>` element has been replaced by the `include` command and the path to **vertical-nav.html**. Although the code is not present here, the menu will look and function normally on the Internet as well as in Dreamweaver.

## Invisible includes?

SSIs can be seen in Dreamweaver in Design view and in Live view. However, they may not render in a browser while it is still located on your local hard drive unless you're using a testing server (See Lesson 13, "Working with Online Data"). To test SSIs properly, you may have to upload the page to a server configured to work with dynamic content.

If you don't see the SSI in Dreamweaver, however, you may have to flip a switch in your program preferences.

**1** Press Ctrl-U/Cmd-U to edit Dreamweaver preferences. Or, choose Edit > Preferences (Windows) or Dreamweaver > Preferences (Mac) to display the Preferences dialog box.

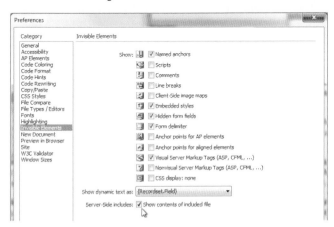

**2** From the Category list, select Invisible Elements. Select the Show Contents Of Included File option, if necessary. Click OK.

**6** Switch to Design view. Click the Live view button to preview the page. Test the functionality of the vertical menu.

The menu appears and behaves as expected.

▷ **Tip:** The name of the server-side include may need to change depending on the server model you are using. Dynamic server models (ASP, CF, or PHP) require different extension names and include commands.

**7** Select File > Save As. Name the file **library_test.shtml**.

As long as you didn't miss the additional "s" in the extension, you just created a new version of **library_test.html** and left the original file unchanged. Without the new extension, the SSI will not appear at all when it's uploaded to a web server. As it is, you'll also discover that the SSI probably can't even be tested in your primary browser.

That's because SSIs need specific server functionality to manage and load them into a browser. Testing them on your local hard drive requires that you install and run a *local web server*. Since you won't learn about testing servers until Lesson 13, you'll have to be content testing SSIs in Live view for now.

So far, you've created a server-side include and inserted it on a page in the site. In the next exercise, you'll learn how easy it is to update a file that uses an SSI.

## Updating server-side includes

Although working with templates and library items offers vast improvements in productivity, it can also be a tedious chore. Changes made must be saved and updated to all the appropriate pages, and then each newly updated page must be uploaded to the server. When the change involves hundreds of pages, the problem is compounded. When you use SSIs, on the other hand, the only file that must be changed, saved, and uploaded is the include file itself. To see this method in action, it helps to insert the SSI into more than one page.

**1** Open the file **library_copy.html**. Replace the library item holding the vertical menu with the SSI, **vertical-nav.html**, as you did in library_test.shtml.

**2** Save the file as **library_copy.shtml**.

Let's change the include file and see how Dreamweaver handles the change.

**3** Choose File > Open Recent > **vertical-nav.html**. You can also open the SSI by double-clicking its name in the Files panel.

**4** Insert the cursor at the end of the last bullet, *Green Tips*. Press Enter/Return to insert a new list item. Type **Green Club** on the new line.

You created a new bulleted item, but it won't be formatted the same way as the other menu items if you don't add a hyperlink placeholder.

**5** Select the text *Green Club* and type # in the Link field of the Property inspector to create a hyperlink placeholder.

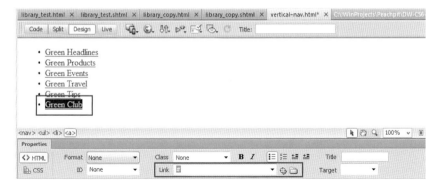

You have added a new menu item, complete with hyperlink placeholder.

**6** Click the tab for **library_test.shtml** and then the tab for **library_copy.shtml** to bring those files to the front. Observe the vertical menu in both files.

The menu has not changed yet.

**7** Click the tab for **vertical-nav.html** to bring this page to the front. Save the file.

**8** Examine the vertical menu in **library_test.shtml** and **library_copy.shtml**.

The menus have changed in both files. You should also notice one more thing: The file tabs at the top of the document window don't show an asterisk indicating that the file has changed and needs to be saved. Why? It's because the SSI is not really part of the file. So when the code was changed in **vertical-nav.html**, it had no impact on the file one way or another.

▶ **Tip:** In most cases, Dreamweaver will update the SSI instantly. If it doesn't, simply press F5 to refresh the display, or check to make sure you actually saved the SSI, as needed.

**9** Close all files.

You've learned how to create a server-side include, add it to a page, and update it. Many other webpage elements—such as logos, menus, privacy notices, and banners—can be added to your site using these easily maintained server-side includes. For small sites, templates and library items are fine; but for large sites, using SSIs instead can garner huge productivity gains. There's no need to upload dozens or even hundreds of updated pages at a time—you only need to upload one.

Dreamweaver's productivity tools—templates, library items, and server-side includes—help you build and automatically update pages quickly and easily. In the upcoming lessons, you will use the newly completed template to create files for the project site. Although choosing to use templates and the other productivity tools is a decision you should make when first creating a new site, it's never too late to use them to speed up your workflow and make site maintenance easier.

## Sorry, no SSIs for now

A server-side include is a logical and important element for any web designer. So you may be wondering why we're not adding the SSI to the project template that you just completed. The reason is simple: You won't be able to see the SSI in a browser if it's stored on your local hard drive without a testing server. So for convenience, we'll stick to the template-based components in the current workflow. However, once you have a full-fledged testing server installed and operating, feel free to permanently replace any appropriate template and library items with equivalent SSIs.

SSI in Dreamweaver

SSI without local web server

# Review questions

1  How do you create a template from an existing page?

2  Why is a template dynamic?

3  What must you add to a template to make it useful in a workflow?

4  How do you create a child page from a template?

5  What are the differences and similarities between library items and server-side includes?

6  How do you create a library item?

7  How do you create a server-side include file?

# Review answers

1  Choose File > Save as Template and enter the name of the template in the dialog box to create a .dwt file.

2  A template is dynamic because Dreamweaver maintains a connection to all pages derived from it within a site. When the template is updated, it can pass the changes to the dynamic areas of the child pages.

3  You must add editable regions to the template; otherwise, unique content can't be added to the child pages.

4  Choose File > New, and in the New Document dialog box select Pages From Templates. Locate the desired template and click Create. Or, right-click the template name in the Assets > Template category and choose New From Template.

5  Library items and server-side includes are used to store and present reusable code elements and page components. But whereas the code for library items is inserted fully in the targeted page, the code for server-side includes is inserted in the page by the server, dynamically.

6  Select the content on the page that you want to add to the library. Click the New Library Item button at the bottom of the Library category of the Assets panel, and then name the library item.

7  Open a new, blank HTML document. Enter the desired content. In Code view, remove any page elements from the code except the content you want included. Save the file in the proper format for your workflow.

# 7 WORKING WITH TEXT, LISTS, AND TABLES

## Lesson Overview

In this lesson, you'll create several webpages from your new template and work with headings, paragraphs, and other text elements to do the following:

- Enter heading and paragraph text
- Insert text from another source
- Create bulleted lists
- Create indented text
- Insert and modify tables
- Spell check your website
- Search and replace text

 This lesson will take about 2 hours and 45 minutes to complete. Before beginning, make sure you have copied the files for Lesson 7 to your hard drive as described in the "Getting Started" section at the beginning of the book. If you are starting from scratch in this lesson, use the method described in the "Jumpstart" section of "Getting Started."

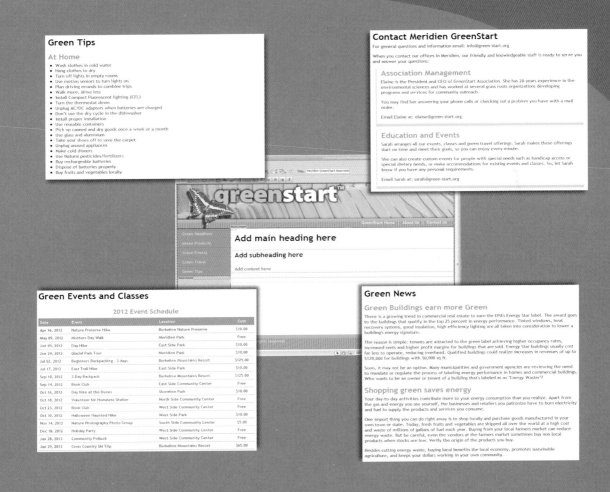

Dreamweaver provides numerous tools for creating, editing, and formatting web content, whether it's created within the program or imported from other applications.

# Previewing the completed file

To get a sense of the files you will work on in the first part of this lesson, let's preview the completed pages in a browser.

1  Launch Adobe Dreamweaver CS6, if necessary. Close any files currently open if Dreamweaver is running.

2  If necessary, press F8/Cmd-Shift-F to open the Files panel, and select DW-CS6 from the site list. Or, if you are starting from scratch in this lesson, follow the "Jumpstart" instructions in the "Getting Started" section at the beginning of the book.

3  In the Files panel, expand the lesson07 folder. If you are using the Jumpstart method, all lesson files will appear in the site root folder.

   Dreamweaver allows you to open one or more files at the same time.

4  Select **contactus_finished.html**. Press Ctrl/Cmd and select **events_finished.html**, **news_finished.html**, and **tips_finished.html**.

   By pressing Ctrl/Cmd before you click, you can select multiple non-consecutive files.

5  Right-click any of the selected files. Choose Open from the context menu.

   All four files open. Tabs at the top of the document window identify each file.

6  Click the **news_finished.html** tab to bring that file to the top.

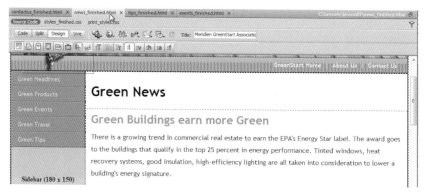

Note the headings and text elements used.

**7** Click the **tips_finished.html** tab to bring that file to the top.

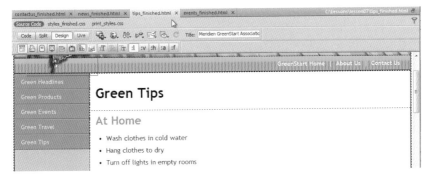

Note the bulleted list elements used.

**8** Click the **contactus_finished.html** tab to bring that file to the top.

Note that text elements are indented and formatted.

**9** Click the **events_finished.html** tab to bring that file to the top.

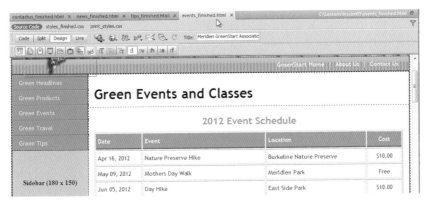

Note the two table elements used.

In each of the pages, there are a variety of elements used, including headings, paragraphs, lists, bullets, indented text, and tables. In the following exercises, you will create these pages and learn how to format each of these elements.

**10** Choose File > Close All.

# Creating and styling text

Most websites are composed of large blocks of text with a few images sprinkled in for visual interest. Dreamweaver provides a variety of means of creating, importing, and styling text to meet any need. In the following exercises, you will learn a variety of techniques for how to work with and format text.

## Importing text

In this exercise, you'll create a new page from the site template and then insert heading and paragraph text from a text document.

**1** Choose Window > Assets to display the Assets panel. In the Template category, right-click **mygreen_temp** and choose New From Template from the context menu.

A new page is created based on the site template.

**2** Save the file as **news.html** in the site root folder.

**3** In the Files panel, double-click **green_news.rtf** in the lesson07 > resources folder.

The file opens in a compatible program. The text is unformatted and features extra lines between each paragraph. These extra lines are intentional. For some reason, Dreamweaver strips out single paragraph returns from text when you copy and paste it from outside the program. Adding a second return forces Dreamweaver to honor the paragraph breaks.

This file contains four news stories. When you move the stories to the webpage, you're going to create your first semantic structures. As explained earlier, semantic web design attempts to provide a context for your web content so that it will be easier for users and web applications to find information and reuse it, as necessary. To aid in this goal, you'll move each story over to the webpage one at a time and insert them into their own individual content structures.

4   In the text editor or word processing program, insert the cursor at the beginning of the text *Green Buildings earn more Green* and select all the text up to and including *"Energy Waster"?* (The first four paragraphs.) Press Ctrl-X/ Cmd-X to cut the text.

5   Switch back to Dreamweaver. In Design view, select the placeholder heading *Add main heading here* in `<article.content>` and type **Green News** to replace it.

6   Insert the cursor in the placeholder heading *Add subheading here* and note the tag selectors at the bottom of the document window.

The heading and the paragraph text are contained in one of the new HTML5 semantic elements: `<section>`. By inserting each news story into its own `<section>` element, you'll identify them as separate stand-alone content that can be viewed independently of each other.

7   Click the `<h2>` tag selector to select the element. Holding the Shift key, click at the end of the placeholder text *Add content here.*

The heading and paragraph placeholders are selected.

8   Press Ctrl-V/Cmd-V to paste the text from the clipboard and swap out the placeholder text.

The clipboard text appears in the layout. Now you're ready to move the next story.

9   Save the file.

Using a technique you learned earlier, you will create three new `<section>` elements and then populate them with the remaining news stories.

## Alternative HTML 4 workflow

The upcoming sections describe and build an HTML5 workflow using semantic elements and structures. If you are unable to use this type of workflow and must still rely on HTML 4–compatible elements and structures, never fear. You can build your pages using an equivalent HTML 4–compatible CSS layout and simply insert your content entirely in the `<div.content>` element that appears therein, or you can substitute generic `<div>` elements in place of the semantic elements described next. You can even create a semantic structure by adding an attribute such as `class="section"` to the containing `<div>` element.

> **Tip:** When moving stories individually, cutting the text helps you keep track of which paragraphs have already been moved.

> **Tip:** When you use the clipboard to bring text into Dreamweaver from other programs, you must be in Design view if you want to honor the paragraph returns.

> **Tip:** Use the `<h2>` tag selector to select the placeholder text and the HTML tags too.

## Creating semantic structures

In this exercise, you will insert three HTML5 <section> elements to hold the remaining news stories. If you need to work in HTML 4, an alternative method would be to insert the stories into individual <div> elements and then assign them a class attribute of section. But such a technique doesn't convey the same semantic weight as the HTML5 <section> element.

1 Switch to the text editor or word processor. Select the next four paragraphs, beginning at *Shopping green saves energy* and ending at *...in your own community.* Press Ctrl-X/Cmd-X to cut the text.

2 Switch to Dreamweaver. In Design view, insert the cursor anywhere in the existing news story and click the <section> tag selector.

The entire <section> element and its contents are selected.

3 Press the Right Arrow key once to move the cursor after the closing </section> tag in the code.

▶ **Tip:** You may have to press Enter/Return twice to create the new element.

4 Press Ctrl-T/Cmd-T to access the Tag Editor. Type **<section>**, or double-click section in the Tag Editor hinting menu and press Enter/Return to create the element.

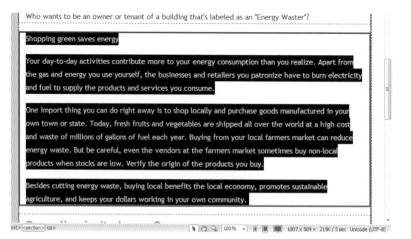

5 Press Ctrl-V/Cmd-V to paste the text from the clipboard and insert it into the new <section> element.

The second news story appears in the new <section> element.

**6** Repeat steps 1–5 to create new <section> elements for the remaining two news stories.

When you're finished you should have four <section> elements, one for each news story.

**7** Close **green_news.rtf**. Do not save any changes.

**8** Save **news.html**.

## Creating headings

In HTML, the tags <h1>, <h2>, <h3>, <h4>, <h5>, and <h6> create headings. Any browsing device, whether it is a computer, a Braille reader, or a cell phone, interprets text formatted with any of these tags as a heading. Headings are used to introduce distinct sections with helpful titles, just as they do in books, magazine articles, and term papers.

Following the semantic meaning of HTML tags, the news content begins with a heading "Green News" formatted as an <h1>. Since <h1> is the most important heading, to be semantically correct in HTML 4, only one such heading should be used per page. However, in HTML5, best practices have not been formalized yet. Some believe that we should continue the practice used in HTML 4. Others think that it should be permissible to use an <h1> in each semantic element or structure on a page; in other words, each <section>, <article>, <header>, or <footer> could have its own <h1> heading.

Until the practice is codified, let's continue to use only one <h1> element per page (as the page title). All other headings should therefore descend in order from the <h1>. Since each news story has equal importance, they all can begin with a second-level heading, or <h2>. At the moment, all the pasted text is formatted as <p> elements. Let's format the news headings as <h2> elements.

**1** Select the text *Green Buildings earn more Green*, and choose Heading 2 from the Format menu in the Property inspector or press Ctrl-2/Cmd-2.

> **Tip:** If the Format menu is not visible, select the HTML mode of the Property inspector.

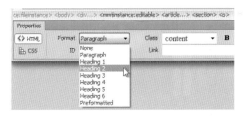

The text will be formatted as an <h2> element.

**2** Repeat step 1 with the text *Shopping green saves energy, Recycling isn't always Green*, and *Fireplace: Fun or Folly?*

All the selected text should now be formatted as <h2> elements. Let's create a custom rule for this element to set it off from the other headings.

**3**  Insert the cursor in any of the newly formatted <h2> elements. Choose Window > CSS Styles to open the CSS Styles panel, if necessary.

▶ **Tip:** A good designer carefully manages the naming and order of CSS rules. By selecting a rule in the panel before clicking the New CSS Rule icon, Dreamweaver inserts the new rule immediately after the selection. If the new rule doesn't appear in the proper location, just drag it to the desired position.

**4**  In the CSS Styles panel, select the `.content h1` rule in **mygreen_styles.css** before you click the New CSS Rule ( ) icon.

**5**  Choose Compound from the Selector Type menu. Click the Less Specific button once. Click OK.

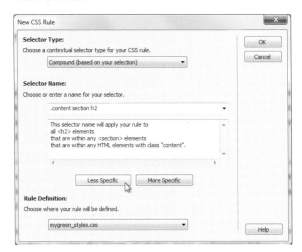

The "New CSS Rule Definition For *.content .section h2*" dialog box appears.

● **Note:** By default, each heading tag—<h1>, <h2>, <h3>, and so on—is formatted smaller than the preceding tag. This formatting reinforces the semantic importance of each tag. Although size is an obvious method of indicating hierarchy, it's not a requirement; feel free to experiment with other styling techniques, such as color, indenting, borders, and background shading, to create your own hierarchical structure.

**6**  In the Type category, enter **170%** in the Font-size field and **#090** in the Color field.

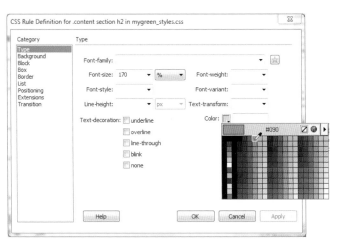

**7**  In the Box category, deselect the Same For All option in the Margin section, enter **15px** in the Top margin field, and enter **5px** in the Bottom margin field. Click OK.

**8** In the document Title field, select the placeholder text *Add Title Here.* Type **Green News** to replace the text. Press Enter/Return to complete the title.

**9** Save all files.

## Creating lists

Formatting should add meaning, organization, and clarity to your content. One method of doing this is to use the HTML list elements. Lists are the workhorses of the web because they are easier to read than blocks of dense text and also help users find information quickly. In this exercise, you will learn how to make an HTML list.

**1** Choose Window > Assets to bring the Assets panel to the front. In the Template category, right-click **mygreen_temp** and choose New From Template from the context menu.

A new page is created based on the template.

**2** Save the file as **tips.html** in the site root folder.

**3** In the document Title field, select the placeholder text *Add Title Here.* Type **Green Tips** to replace the text. Press Enter/Return to complete the title.

**4** In the Files panel, double-click **green_tips.rtf** in the lesson07 > resources folder.

The text consists of three individual lists of tips on how to save energy and money at home, at work, and in the community. As with the news file, you will insert each list into its own `<section>` element.

**5** In the text editor or word processing program, select the text beginning with *At Home* and ending with *Buy fruits and vegetables locally.* Press Ctrl-X/Cmd-X to cut the text.

**6** Switch back to Dreamweaver. In Design view, select the placeholder heading *Add main heading here* in `<article.content>` and type **Green Tips** to replace it.

**7** Select the placeholder heading *Add subheading here* and the paragraph text *Add content here.* Press Ctrl-V/Cmd-V to paste the text from the clipboard.

The text appears, creating the first list section.

**8** Switch to the text editor or word processing program; select the text beginning with *At Work* and ending with *Buy natural cleaning products*. Press Ctrl-X/Cmd-X to cut the text.

**9** Switch to Dreamweaver. In Design view, insert the cursor anywhere in the existing list of tips and click the `<section>` tag selector.

The entire `<section>` element and its contents are selected.

**10** Press the Right Arrow key once to move the cursor after the closing `</section>` tag in the code.

**11** Press Ctrl-T/Cmd-T to access the Tag Editor. Type **`<section>`**, or double-click `section` in the Tag Editor menu and press Enter/Return to create the element.

**12** Press Ctrl-V/Cmd-V to paste the text from the clipboard and insert it into the new `<section>` element.

The second list appears in the new element.

**13** Repeat steps 8–12 to create the third list, *In the community*.

All three lists now appear in their own `<section>` elements.

As we did with the titles of the news stories, let's format the headings that identify the tip categories.

**14** Select the text *At Home* and format it as a Heading 2.

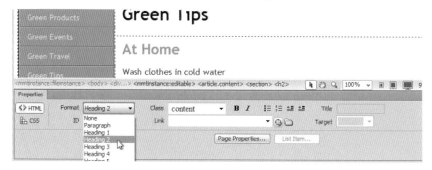

**15** Repeat step 14 with the text *At Work* and *In the Community*.

The remaining text is currently formatted entirely as <p> elements. Dreamweaver makes it easy to convert this text into an HTML list. Lists come in two flavors: ordered and unordered.

**16** Select all the <p> formatted text between the headings *At Home* and *At Work*. In the Property inspector, click the Ordered List (≣) icon.

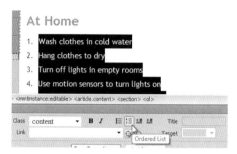

An ordered list adds numbers automatically to the entire selection. Semantically, it prioritizes each item, giving them an intrinsic value relative to one another. As you may see, this list doesn't seem to be in any particular order. Each item is more or less equal to the next one. An unordered list is another method of formatting a list when the items are in no particular order. Before you change the formatting, let's take a look at the markup.

▶ **Tip:** The easiest way to select the entire list is to use the <ol> tag selector.

**17** Switch to Split view. Observe the list markup in the Code section of the document window.

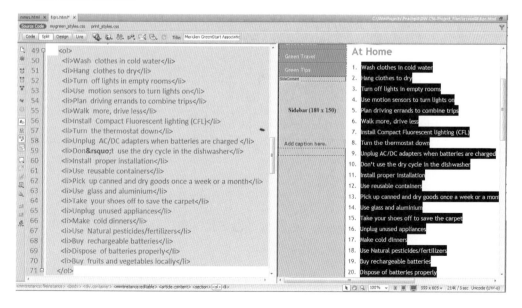

The markup consists of two elements: <ol> and <li>. Note that each line is formatted as an <li> (*list item*). The <ol> parent element begins and ends the list and designates it as an ordered list. Changing the formatting from numbers to bullets is simple and can be done in Code or Design view.

Before changing the format, ensure that the formatted list is still entirely selected.

**18** In the Property inspector, click the Unordered List (▤) icon.

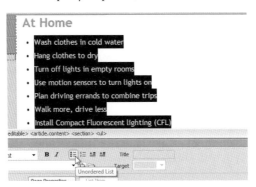

▶ **Tip:** You could also change the formatting by editing the markup manually in the Code view window. But don't forget to change both the opening and the closing parent elements.

All the items are now formatted as bullets. Observe the list markup. The only thing that has changed is the parent element. It now says <ul>, for *unordered list*.

**19** Select all the <p> formatted text between the headings *At Work* and *In the Community*. In the Property inspector, click the Unordered List (▤) icon.

**20** Repeat step 19 with all the text following the heading *In the Community*.

All three lists are now formatted with bullets.

**21** Select File > Save.

## Creating text indents

Today, many designers use the <blockquote> element as an easy way to indent headings and paragraph text. Semantically, the <blockquote> element is intended to identify whole sections of text quoted from other sources. Visually, text formatted this way will appear indented and set off from the regular paragraph text and headings. But if you want to comply with web standards, you should leave this element for its intended purpose and instead use custom CSS classes when you want to indent text, as you will in this exercise.

**1** Create a new page from the template **mygreen_temp**. Save the file as **contact_us.html** in the site root folder.

**2** In the document Title field, select the placeholder text *Add Title Here*. Type **Contact Meridien GreenStart** to replace the text. Press Enter/Return to complete the title.

**3** Switch to the Files panel and double-click **contact_us.rtf** in the lesson07 folder.

The text consists of five department sections, including headings, descriptions, and email addresses for the managing staff of GreenStart. You will insert each department into its own `<section>` element.

**4** In the text editor or word processing program, select the first two introductory paragraphs. Press Ctrl-X/Cmd-X to cut the text.

**5** Switch back to Dreamweaver. Select the placeholder heading *Add main heading here* in `<article.content>` and type **Contact Meridien GreenStart** to replace it.

**6** Press Enter/Return to insert a new paragraph. Press Ctrl-V/Cmd-V to paste the text.

The introductory text is inserted directly below the `<h1>` element. The text is not in the `<section>` element.

**7** Switch to the text editor or word processing program and select the next four paragraphs, which make up the *Association Management* section. Press Ctrl-X/Cmd-X to cut the text.

**8** Switch to Dreamweaver. In Design view, select the placeholder heading *Add subheading here* and the paragraph text *Add content here*. Press Ctrl-V/Cmd-V to paste the text from the clipboard.

**9** Select the text *Association Management* and format it as a Heading 2.

The first section is inserted.

**10** Switch to the text editor or word processing program and select the next four paragraphs, which make up the *Education and Events* section. Press Ctrl-X/Cmd-X to cut the text.

**11** Switch to Dreamweaver. Insert the cursor anywhere in the *Association Management* text and click the `<section>` tag selector.

**12** Press Ctrl-T/Cmd-T to access the Tag Editor. Type **`<section>`**, or double-click `section` in the Tag Editor menu and press Enter/Return to create the element.

**13** Press Ctrl-V/Cmd-V to paste the text from the clipboard and insert it into the new `<section>` element.

**14** Select the text *Education and Events* and format it as a Heading 2.

**15** Repeat steps 10–14 to create `<section>` elements for the remaining departments: *Transportation Analysis*, *Research and Development*, and *Information Systems*.

With all the text in place you're ready to create the indent styling. If you wanted to indent a single paragraph, you would probably create and apply a custom class to the individual `<p>` element. In this instance, you'll use the existing `<section>` elements to produce the desired graphical effect. First, let's assign a `class` attribute to the element. Since the class has not been created yet, you'll have to create it manually. This can be done in Code view or in Design view using the Tag Editor.

**16** Insert the cursor anywhere in the *Association Management* `<section>` element. Click the `<section>` tag selector. Press Ctrl-T/Cmd-T.

The Tag Editor appears, displaying the `<section>` tag. The cursor should appear at the end of the tag name.

**17** Press the spacebar to insert a space.

The Code Hinting window appears, displaying the appropriate attributes for the `<section>` element.

**18** Type **`class`** and press Enter/Return, or double-click the `class` attribute in the Code Hinting window.

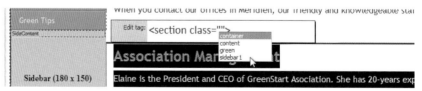

Dreamweaver automatically creates the attribute markup and provides any existing `class` or `id` attributes. Since the class doesn't exist yet, you'll type the name yourself.

**19** Type **`profile`** as the class name. Press Enter/Return to complete the attribute.

**20** Select the `<section.profile>` tag selector at the bottom of the document window. Select `.content section h2` in the CSS Styles panel. Click the New CSS Rule ( ⊞ ) icon.

**21** In the New CSS Rule dialog box, click Less Specific once to remove `.container` from the Selector Name field.

The Selector Name field should display `.content .profile`.

**22** Click OK to create the new CSS rule.

**23** Select the Box category. Deselect Same For All in the Margin section.

Enter **25px** in the Right and Left margin fields only. In the Bottom margin field only, enter **15px**.

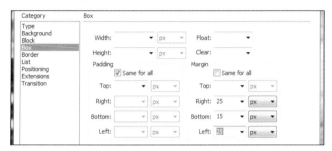

**24** In the Border category, enter the following specifications for the Bottom border fields only: **solid**, **10px**, **#CADAAF**.

**25** Enter the following specifications for the Left border fields only: **solid**, **2px**, **#CADAAF**. Click OK.

The border helps to visually group the indented text under its heading.

**26** Select each of the remaining `<section>` elements and apply `profile` from the Class field menu in the Property inspector.

Each section is indented and displays the custom border.

**27** Save all files.

# Creating and styling tables

Before the advent of CSS, HTML offered few tools to execute effective page designs. Instead, web designers resorted to using images and tables to create page layouts. Today, tables are eschewed for page design and layout purposes for several reasons. Tables are hard to create, format, and modify. They can't adapt easily to different screen sizes or types. And, certain browsing devices and screen readers don't see the comprehensive page layouts, they only see tables for what they actually are—rows and columns of data.

When CSS debuted and was promoted as the preferred method for page design, some designers came to believe that tables were bad altogether. That was a bit of an overreaction. Although tables are not good for page layout, they are very good, and necessary, for displaying many types of data, such as product lists, personnel directories, and time schedules. In the following exercises, you will learn how to create and format HTML tables.

1   Create a new page from the template **mygreen_temp**. Save the file as **events.html** in the site root folder.

2   In the document Title field, select the placeholder text *Add Title Here*. Type **Green Events and Classes** to replace the text. Press Enter/Return to complete the title.

Dreamweaver enables you to create tables from scratch, to copy and paste them from other applications, or to create them instantly from data supplied by database or spreadsheet programs.

## Creating tables from scratch

Dreamweaver makes it easy to create tables from scratch.

1   In Design view, select the placeholder heading *Add main heading here* in `<article.content>` and type **Green Events and Classes** to replace it.

2   Select the placeholder heading *Add subheading here* and the paragraph text *Add content here*. Press Delete.

▶ **Tip:** Whenever you select complete elements it's a good practice to use the tag selectors.

3   Choose Insert > Table.

The Table dialog box appears. The width and some other specifications of tables, like most HTML elements, can be controlled either by HTML attributes or by CSS. HTML-based table formatting, as you've already learned, has been deprecated, but certain HTML table attributes continue to be used. Although best practices lean heavily toward using CSS for its power and flexibility, nothing beats the down-and-dirty convenience of HTML. For example, when you enter values in this dialog box, Dreamweaver applies them via HTML attributes.

4   Enter **2** in the Rows field and **4** in the Columns field. Enter **90** in the Table
    Width field, and choose percent from the Table Width menu. Enter **0** in the
    Border thickness field. Click OK.

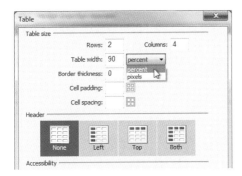

A four-column, two-row table appears below the heading. Note that it is flush to
the left edge of `<article.content>`. The table is ready to accept input.

5   Insert the cursor in the first cell of the table. Type **Date** and press Tab to move
    into the next cell in the first row.

▶ **Tip:** Pressing the Tab
key moves the cursor
to the next cell on the
right. Hold the Shift key
when pressing the Tab
key to move to the left,
or backwards, through
the table.

6   In the second cell, type **Event** and press Tab. Type **Location** and press Tab.
    Type **Cost** and press Tab to move the cursor to the first cell of the second row.

7   In the second row, type **May 1** (in cell 1), **May Day Parade** (in cell 2), **City Hall**
    (in cell 3), and **Free** (in cell 4).

    Inserting additional rows in the table is easy.

8   Press Tab to insert a new blank row in the table.

    Dreamweaver also allows you to insert multiple new rows at once.

9   Select the `<table>` tag selector at the bottom of the document window.

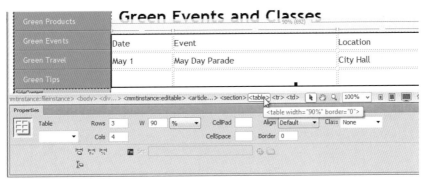

The Property inspector displays the properties of the current table, including
the total number of rows and columns.

**10** Select the number 3 in the Rows field. Type **10** and press Enter/Return to complete the change.

Dreamweaver adds seven new rows to the table. The fields in the Property inspector create HTML attributes to control various aspects of the table, including table width, the width and height of cells, text alignment, and so on.

## Copying and pasting tables

Although Dreamweaver allows you to create tables manually inside the program, you can also move tables from other HTML files or even other programs by using copy and paste.

**1** Open the Files panel, and double-click **calendar.html** in the lesson07 resources folder to open it.

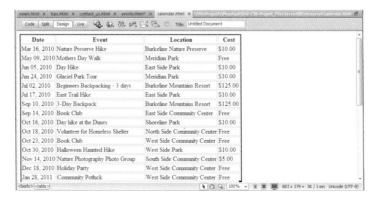

This HTML file will open in its own tab in Dreamweaver. Note the table structure—it has four columns and numerous rows.

**2** Insert the cursor in the table. Click the `<table>` tag selector. Press Ctrl-C/ Cmd-C to copy the text.

**3** Click the **events.html** tab to bring that file to the front.

**4** Insert the cursor in the table. Select the `<table>` tag selector. Press Ctrl-V/Cmd-V to paste the table.

The new table element completely replaces the existing table.

**5** Save the file.

● **Note:** Dreamweaver allows you to copy and paste tables from some other programs, like Microsoft Word. Unfortunately, it doesn't work with every program.

## Styling tables with CSS

Right now, your table aligns to the left, touching the edge of `<article.content>`, and stretches most of the way across the element. Tables can be formatted by HTML attributes or by CSS rules. HTML attributes must be applied to and edited for each table individually. As you've already learned, CSS gives you the power to control table formatting sitewide using only a handful of rules.

**1** Select the `<table>` tag selector. Select the `.content .profile` rule in the CSS Styles panel, and then click the New CSS Rule icon.

The New CSS Rule dialog box appears.

**2** Choose Compound from the Selector Type menu, if necessary. Click Less Specific once to remove `.container` from the Selector Name field. Click OK.

The CSS definition dialog box for the new `.content section table` rule appears.

Before you apply formatting to the table, you should know what other settings are already affecting the element and what ramifications new settings could have to your overall design and structure. For example, the `.content` rule sets the width of the element to 770 pixels. Other elements, such as `<h1>` and `<p>`, feature left padding of 15 pixels. If you apply widths, margins, and padding that total a number larger than 770 pixels, you could inadvertently break the careful structure of your page design.

**3** In the Type category, enter **90%** in the Font-size field.

**4** In the Box category, enter **740px** in the Width field. Enter **15px** in only the Left margin field.

● **Note:** Adding the width to the margin totals 755 pixels, 15 pixels less than the current width of `<article.content>`. Keep this in mind going forward in case other settings conflict with the table specifications.

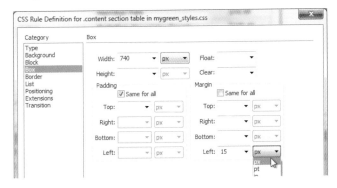

**5** In the Border category, enter the following specifications only in the Bottom border fields: **solid**, **3px**, **#060**. Click OK.

The table resizes, moves away from the left edge of `<article.content>`, and displays a dark green border at the bottom. You have applied the desired styling to specific table properties, but you can't stop there. The default formatting of the tags that make up table markup is a hodgepodge of different settings that are honored haphazardly in various browsers. You'll find that the same table can be displayed differently in every browser.

One setting that may cause trouble is the HTML-based `cellspacing` attribute, which produces a margin-like effect between individual cells. If you leave this attribute blank, some browsers will insert a small space between cells and actually split any cell borders in two. In CSS, this attribute is handled by the `border-collapse` property. If you don't want the table borders to be split inadvertently, you need to include this setting in the styling. Unfortunately, this is one of the few specifications you can't access within Dreamweaver's CSS Rule Definition dialog box.

**6** Choose Window > CSS Styles to reveal the CSS Styles panel, if necessary. Select the `.content section table` rule and observe the Properties section of the panel.

The Properties section displays the current settings for the `.content section table` rule.

● **Note:** You won't find the `border-collapse` property in the pop-up menu, so you have to type it yourself. Once you type the property name, the value menu will then populate properly with the available options.

**7** Click the Add Property link at the bottom of the list of properties. Type **border-collapse** and press Tab to move the cursor to the Value column field. Type **collapse** and press Enter/Return to complete the property.

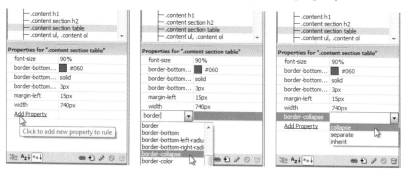

In Design view, you may not see any difference in how the tables are displayed, but don't let that dissuade you from the need for this attribute.

**8** Save all files.

The `.content section table` rule you just created will format the overall structure of every table inserted into `<article.content>` on any page using this style sheet throughout the site. But the formatting isn't complete yet. The widths of the individual columns are not controlled by the `<table>` element. To control the column widths, you need to look elsewhere.

## Styling table cells

Just as for tables, specifications for columns can be applied by HTML attributes or CSS, with similar advantages and disadvantages. Formatting for columns is applied through two elements that create the individual cells: `<th>` for *table header* and `<td>` for *table data*. The table header is a handy element that you can use to differentiate titles and header content from regular data.

It's a good idea to create a generic rule to reset the default formats of the `<th>` and `<td>` elements. Later, you will create custom rules to apply to specific columns and cells.

**1** Insert the cursor into any cell of the table. Select the `.content section table` rule before you click the New CSS Rule icon.

**2** Choose Compound from the Selector Type menu, if necessary. Click Less Specific once to remove `.container` from the Selector Name field. Edit the Selector Name to say `.content section td, .content section th` and click OK.

The simplified selector will work fine.

**3** In the Block category, choose `left` from the Text-align field menu.

**4** In the Box category, enter **5px** in all Padding fields.

**5** In the Border category, enter **solid**, **1px**, and **#090** in only the Top border fields. Click OK.

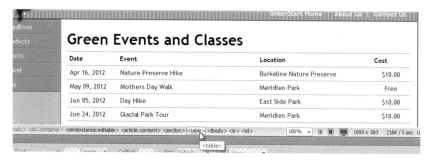

A thin green border appears above each row of the table, making the data easier to read. To see the border properly, you may need to preview the page in Live view first. Headers are usually formatted in bold to help them stand out from the normal cells. You can make them stand out even more by giving them a touch of color.

> **Note:** Remember that the order of the rules can affect the style cascade, as well as how and what styling is inherited.

**6** Select `.content section td`, `.content section th` in the CSS Styles panel. Click the New CSS Rule icon. Choose Compound from the Selector Type menu, if necessary. Type `.content section th` in the Selector Name field. Click OK.

**7** In the Type category, enter **#FFC** in the Color field.

**8** In the Background category, enter **#090** in the Background-color field. In the Border category, enter **solid**, **6px**, and **#060** in only the Bottom border fields. Click OK.

The rule is created, but it still needs to be applied. Dreamweaver makes it easy to convert the existing `<td>` elements into `<th>` elements.

**9** Insert the cursor into the first cell of the first row of the table. In the Property inspector, select the Header option. Note the tag selector.

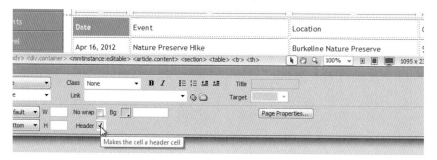

The cell is filled with green. When you click the Header checkbox, Dreamweaver automatically rewrites the markup, converting the existing `<td>` to `<th>` and thereby applying the CSS formatting. This functionality will save you lots of time over editing the code manually. You can also convert multiple cells at one time.

**10** Insert the cursor into the second cell of the first row. Drag to select the remaining cells in the first row. Or, you can select an entire row at once by positioning the cursor at the left edge of the table row and clicking when you see the black selection arrow appear.

**11** In the Property inspector, select the Header option to convert the table cells to header cells.

The whole first row is filled with green as the table cells are converted to header cells.

**12** Save all files.

## Controlling column width

Unless you specify otherwise, empty table columns will divide the available space between them equally. But once you start adding content to the cells, all bets are off—the table seems to get a mind of its own and divvies up the space in a different way. It usually awards more space to columns that contain more data.

Allowing the table to decide for itself probably won't achieve an acceptable balance, so many designers resort to HTML attributes or custom CSS classes to control the width of table columns. When you create custom styles to format column widths, one idea is to base the rule names either on the width value itself or on the content, or subject, of the column.

**1** Select the `.content section th` rule in the CSS Styles panel, and then click the New CSS Rule icon. Choose Compound from the Selector Type menu. Delete any text in the Selector Name field, and then type `.content section .w100`. Click OK.

In the new value for the selector name, the w stands for *width* and 100 indicates the value: 100 pixels.

**2** In the Box category, enter **100px** in the Width field. Click OK.

Controlling the width of a column is quite simple. Since the entire column must be the same width, you only have to apply a width specification to one cell. If cells in a column have conflicting specifications, typically the largest width wins. Let's apply a class to control the width of the Date column.

● **Note:** Rule names can't start with numerals or punctuation characters, except for a period (which indicates a class) or a hash mark (#) (which indicates an ID).

**3** Insert the cursor into the first cell of the first row of the table. Select the <th> tag selector. In the Property inspector, choose w100 from the Class menu.

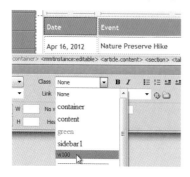

The first column resizes to a width of 100 pixels. The remaining columns automatically divvy up the available space. Column styling can also specify text alignment as well as width. Let's create a rule for the content in the Cost column.

**4** Select the `.content .w100` rule in the CSS Styles panel and click New CSS Rule. Choose Compound from the Selector Type menu. Delete any text in the Selector Name field and type `.content section .cost`. Click OK.

Obviously, this rule is intended for the Cost column. But don't add the width value to the name as you did before; that way, you can change the value in the future without worrying about changing the name (and the markup) as well.

**5** In the Block category, choose center from the Text-align field menu.

**6** In the Box category, enter **75px** in the Width field. Click OK.

Unlike with the previous example, to apply text alignment to the contents of a column, you must apply the class to every cell in the column.

**7** Click in the first cell of the Cost column and drag down to the last cell of the column to select all the cells. Or, position the cursor over the top of the column and click using the black arrow to select the entire column at once. Choose `.cost` from the Class menu in the Property inspector.

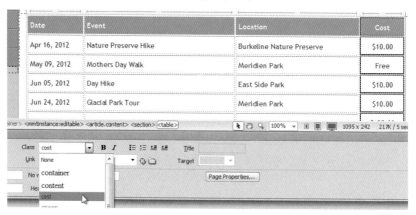

The Cost column resizes to a width of 75 pixels, and the text aligns to the center. Now if you want to change only the Cost column, you have the ability to do so.

8  Save all files.

## Inserting tables from other sources

In addition to creating tables by hand, you can also create them from data exported from databases and spreadsheets. In this exercise, you will create a table from data that was exported from Microsoft Excel to a comma-separated values (CSV) file. As with the other content models, you will first create a `<section>` element in which to insert the new table.

1  Insert the cursor anywhere in the existing table. Select the `<section>` tag selector. Press the Right Arrow key to move the cursor after the closing `</section>` tag in the code.

2  Press Ctrl-T/Cmd-T to access the Tag Editor. Type **`<section>`**, or double-click `section` in the Tag Editor menu and press Enter/Return to create the element.

   A new `<section>` element is added to the page.

3  Without moving the cursor, choose Insert > Table Objects > Import Tabular Data.

   The Import Tabular Data dialog box appears.

4  Click the Browse button and select **classes.csv** from the lesson07 > resources folder. Click Open.

   Comma should be automatically selected in the Delimiter menu.

5  In the Table Width option, select Fit to Data. Delete any values appearing in the other fields not mentioned already. As with most dialog box options in Dreamweaver, all of these fields will apply HTML attributes instead of CSS styling.

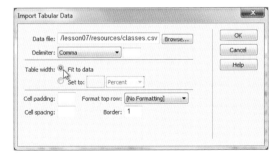

6  Click OK.

A new table—containing a class schedule—appears below the first. The new table consists of five columns with multiple rows. The first row contains header information but is still formatted as normal table cells.

**7** Select the first row of the class schedule. In the Property inspector, select the Header option.

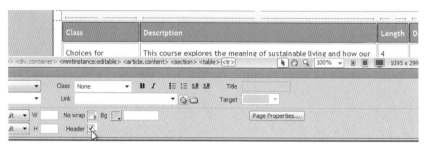

The first row appears in green with reversed text. You'll notice that the text is wrapping awkwardly in the last three columns. You will use the class `.cost` for the Cost column in the new table, but the other two will need custom classes of their own.

**8** Select the Cost column as you did in the previous exercise. In the Property inspector, choose `.cost` from the Class menu.

**9** In the CSS Styles panel, right-click the `.content section .cost` rule and choose Duplicate from the context menu.

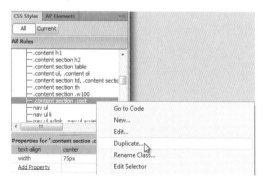

**10** Change the Selector Name field to `.content section .day` and click OK.

**11** Apply `.content section .day` to the Day column in the Classes table, as in step 8.

**12** Duplicate `.content section .day`, name the new rule `.content section .length`, and click OK. Apply it to the Length column in the Classes table.

By creating custom classes for each column, you have the means to modify each column individually. One more rule is needed to format the Class column. This column requires only a generic rule to apply a more appealing width.

**13** Right-click the `.content section .w100` rule and duplicate it. Name the new rule **`.content section .w150`** and click OK.

**14** Edit the new rule and change the Width to **150px** in the Box category. Apply the new rule only to the header cell for the Class column.

**Tip:** When applying a width value, only one cell needs to be formatted.

**15** Save all files.

## Adjusting vertical alignment

If you study the content of the Class table, you will notice that many of the cells contain paragraphs that wrap to multiple lines. When cells in a row have differing amounts of text in them, the shorter content is aligned vertically to the middle of the cell, by default. Many designers find this behavior unattractive and prefer to have the text align to the tops of the cells. As with most of the other attributes, vertical alignment can be applied by HTML attributes or CSS. To control the vertical alignment with CSS, you can add the specification to an existing rule.

| Class | Description | Length | Day | Cost |
|---|---|---|---|---|
| Choices for Sustainable Living | This course explores the meaning of sustainable living and how our choices have an impact on ecological systems. | 4 weeks | M | $40 |
| Exploring Deep Ecology | An eight-session course examining our core values and how they affect the way we view and treat the earth. | 4 weeks | F | $40 |
| Future Food | Explores food systems and their impacts on culture, society and ecological systems. | 4 weeks | Tu-Th | $80 |
| | This class explores the affect of global trade on | | | |

`<mmtinstance:editable>`  100%  1095 x 299  221K / 5 sec

**1** Double-click the `.content section th, .content section td` rule to edit it.

The `<th>` and `<td>` elements style the text stored in the table cells.

**2** In the Block category, choose **top** from the Vertical-align field menu. Click OK.

**Tip:** Some designers like to leave the text in `<th>` cells aligned to the middle or even the bottom. If you wanted to do this, you'd need to create separate rules for each element.

| Class | Description | Length | Day | Cost |
|---|---|---|---|---|
| Choices for Sustainable Living | This course explores the meaning of sustainable living and how our choices have an impact on ecological systems. | 4 weeks | M | $40 |
| Exploring Deep Ecology | An eight-session course examining our core values and how they affect the way we view and treat the earth. | 4 weeks | F | $40 |
| Future Food | Explores food systems and their impacts on culture, society and ecological systems. | 4 weeks | Tu-Th | $80 |
| The Impact of | This class explores the affect of global trade on | 6 weeks | Tu | $60 |

`<mmtinstance:editable>`  100%  1095 x 299  221K / 5 sec

All the text in both tables now aligns to the top of the cells.

**3** Save all files.

## Adding and formatting <caption> elements

The two tables you inserted on the page contain different information but don't feature any differentiating labels or titles. To help users distinguish between the two sets of data, let's add a title to each and a bit of extra spacing. The <caption> element was designed to identify the content of HTML tables. This element is inserted as a child of the <table> element.

1  Insert the cursor in the first table. Select the <table> tag selector. Switch to Code view.

   By selecting the table in Design view, Dreamweaver automatically highlights the code in Code view, making it easier to find.

2  Locate the opening <table> tag. Insert the cursor directly after this tag. Type <caption> or select it from the code-hinting menu when it appears.

3  Type **2012-13 Event Schedule**, and then type **</** to close the element.

4  Switch to Design view.

   The caption is complete and inserted as a child element of the table.

5  Repeat steps 1 and 2 for the second table. Type **2012-13 Class Schedule**, and then type **</** to close the element.

6  Switch to Design view.

   The captions are relatively small, and they're lost against the color and formatting of the table. Let's beef them up a bit with a custom CSS rule.

7  Insert the cursor in either caption. Click the New CSS Rule icon.

8  Choose Compound from the Selector Type menu, if necessary. Click Less Specific once to remove **.container** from the Selector Name field. Click OK.

9 In the Type category, enter **160%** in the Font-size field. Enter **1.2em** in the Line-height field. Choose `bold` from the Font-weight field menu. Enter **#090** in the Color field.

10 In the Box category, enter **20px** only in the Top margin field.

11 Enter **10px** only in the Bottom padding field. Click OK.

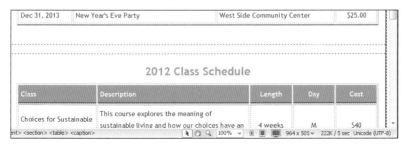

12 Save all files.

13 Examine your work using Live view or a browser.

Formatting the tables and the captions with CSS has made them much easier to read and understand. Feel free to experiment with the size and placement of the caption and specification settings that affect the tables. In Lesson 13, "Working with Online Data," you will learn how to use tables to create dynamic web content.

# Spell checking webpages

It's important to ensure that the content you post to the web is error free. Dreamweaver includes a robust spell checker capable of identifying commonly mis-spelled words and creating a custom dictionary for nonstandard terms.

1 Click the **contact_us.html** tab to bring that document to the front, or open it from the site root folder.

2 Insert the cursor at the beginning of the main heading *Contact Meridien GreenStart* in `<article.content>`. Choose Commands > Check Spelling.

Spell-checking starts wherever the cursor has been inserted. If the cursor is located lower on the page, you will have to restart the spell check at least once to examine the entire page.

3 The Check Spelling dialog box highlights the word *Meridien*, which is the name of the fictional city where the association is located. You could click Add To Personal to insert the word into your custom dictionary, but for now

click Ignore All, which will skip over other occurrences of the name during this check.

4 Dreamweaver highlights the word *GreenStart*, which is the name of the association. Click Ignore All again.

In most cases, you would add the name and location of your own company or association to the Dreamweaver dictionary.

5 Dreamweaver highlights the word *email*. The word is listed as *e-mail* in the dictionary. If your company uses the hyphenated spelling, go ahead and click Change; otherwise, click Ignore All again.

6 Dreamweaver highlights the domain for the email address *info@green-start.org*. Click Ignore All. Click Ignore All again when it stops on the name of the town (*Meridien*).

7 Dreamweaver highlights the word *Asociation*, which is missing an *s*. To correct the spelling, locate the correctly spelled word (Association) in the Suggestions list and double-click it.

8 The next word the spell check stops on is *grassroots*, which is in the dictionary as two words. In this case, the word is being used as a compound adjective made from two separate words. If you look it up, many dictionaries will show it with a hyphen between the two words. To make this type of change, add the hyphen in the Change To field so that the correction reads *grass-roots* and click Change.

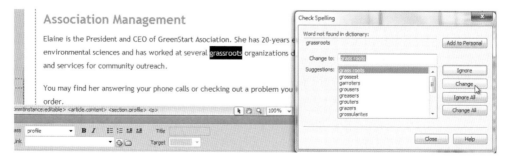

**9** Continue the spell check to the end. Correct any misspelled words and ignore proper names, as necessary. If a dialog prompts you to start the check from the beginning, click Yes.

**10** Save the file.

# Finding and replacing text

The ability to find and replace text is one of Dreamweaver's most powerful features. Unlike other programs, Dreamweaver can find almost anything, anywhere in your site, including text, code, and any type of white space that can be created in the program. You can search the entire markup, or you can limit the search to just the rendered text in Design view or to just the underlying tags. Advanced users can enlist powerful pattern-matching algorithms called *regular expressions* to perform the most sophisticated find-and-replace operations. And then Dreamweaver takes it one step further by allowing you to replace the targeted text or code with similar amounts of text, code, and white space.

In this exercise, you'll learn some important techniques for using the Find And Replace feature.

**1** Click the **events.html** tab to bring that file to the front, or open the file from the site root folder.

There are several ways to identify the text or code you want to find. One way is simply to type it in the field manually. In the Events table, the name *Meridien* was spelled incorrectly as *Meridian*. Since *Meridian* is an actual word, the spell checker won't flag it as an error and give you the opportunity to correct it. So, you'll use find and replace to make the change instead.

**2** Switch to Design view, if necessary. Insert the cursor in the heading *Green Events and Classes*. Choose Edit > Find And Replace.

The Find And Replace dialog box appears. The Find field is empty.

**3** Type **Meridian** in the Find field. Type **Meridien** in the Replace field. Choose Current Document from the Find In menu, and choose Text from the Search menu.

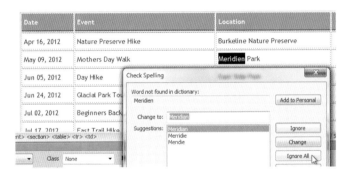

**4** Click Find Next.

Dreamweaver finds the first occurrence of *Meridian*.

**5** Click Replace.

Dreamweaver replaces the first instance of *Meridian* and immediately searches for the next instance. You can continue to replace the words one at a time, or you can choose to replace all occurrences.

**6** Click Replace All.

If you replace the words one at a time, Dreamweaver inserts a one-line notice at the bottom of the dialog box that tells you how many items were found and how many were replaced. When you click Replace All, Dreamweaver closes the Find And Replace dialog box and opens the Search report panel, which lists all the changes made.

**7** Right-click the Search report tab and select Close Tab Group from the context menu.

Another method for targeting text and code is to select it *before* activating the command. This method can be used in either Design or Code view.

**8** In Design view, locate and select the first occurrence of the text *Burkeline Mountains Resort* in the Location column of the Events table. Choose Edit > Find And Replace.

The Find And Replace dialog box appears. The selected text is automatically entered into the Find field by Dreamweaver. This technique is even more powerful when used in Code view.

**9** Close the Find And Replace dialog box. Switch to Code view.

**10** With the cursor still inserted in the text *Burkeline Mountains Resort*, click the `<tr>` tag selector at the bottom of the document window.

**11** Choose Edit > Find And Replace. The Find And Replace dialog box appears.

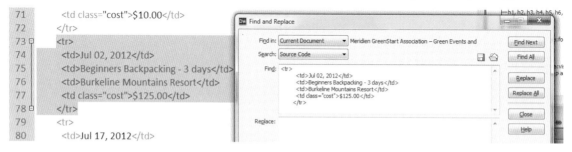

Observe the Find field. The selected code is automatically entered into the Find field by Dreamweaver, including the line breaks and white space. The reason this is so amazing is that there's no way to enter this type of markup in the dialog manually.

**12** Select the code in the Find field. Press Delete to remove it. Type `<tr>` and press Enter/Return to insert the line break. Observe what happens.

Pressing Enter/Return did not insert a line break; instead, it activated the Find command, which finds the first occurrence of the `<tr>` element. In fact, you can't manually insert any type of line break within the dialog.

You probably don't think this is much of a problem, since you've already seen that Dreamweaver inserts text or code when it's selected first. Unfortunately, the method used in step 8 doesn't work with large amounts of text or code.

**13** Close the Find And Replace dialog box. Click the `<table>` tag selector.

The entire markup for the table is selected.

**14** Choose Edit > Find And Replace. Observe the Find field.

This time Dreamweaver did not transfer the selected code into the Find field. To get larger amounts of text or code into the Find field, and to enter large amounts of replacement text and code, you need to use copy and paste.

**15** Close the Find And Replace dialog box. Select the table, if necessary. Press Ctrl-C/Cmd-C to copy the markup.

## Superpowerfindelicious!

Note the options in the Find In and Search menus. The power and flexibility of Dreamweaver shines brightest here. The Find And Replace command can search in selected text, the current document, all open documents, in a specific folder, in selected files of the site, or the entire current local site. But as if those options weren't enough, Dreamweaver also allows you to target the search to the source code, text, advanced text, or even a specific tag.

 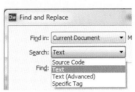

**16** Press Ctrl-F/Cmd-F to activate the Find And Replace command. Insert the cursor in the Find field, and press Ctrl-V/Cmd-V to paste the markup.

The entire `<table>` selection is pasted into the Find field.

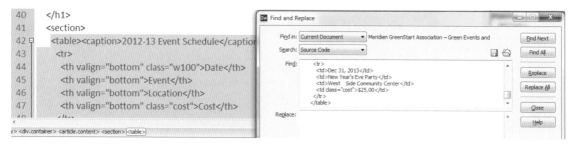

**17** Insert the cursor into the Replace field, and press Ctrl-V/Cmd-V.

The entire selection is pasted into the Replace field. Obviously, the two fields contain identical markup, but it illustrates how easy it would be to change or replace large amounts of code.

**18** Close the Find And Replace dialog box. Save all files.

In this lesson you created four new pages and learned how to import text from other sources. You formatted text as headings and lists, and then styled it using CSS. You inserted and formatted tables, and added captions to each one. And you reviewed and corrected text using Dreamweaver's spell check and find and replace tools.

# Review questions

1 How do you format text to be an HTML heading?

2 Explain how to turn paragraph text into an ordered list and then an unordered list.

3 Describe two methods for inserting HTML tables into a webpage.

4 What element controls the width of a table column?

5 Describe three ways to insert content in the Find field.


# Review answers

1 Use the Format field menu in the Property inspector to apply HTML heading formatting.

2 Highlight the text with the cursor, and click the Ordered List button in the Property inspector. Then click the Unordered List button to change the numbered formatting to bullets.

3 You can copy and paste a table from another HTML file or a compatible program. Or, you can insert a table by importing the data from a delimited file.

4 The width of a table column is controlled by the widest <th> or <td> element that creates the individual table cell.

5 You can type text into the field; you can select text before you open the dialog box and then allow Dreamweaver to insert the selected text; or you can copy the text or code and then paste it into the field.

# 8 WORKING WITH IMAGES

## Lesson Overview

In this lesson, you'll learn how to work with images to include them in your webpages in the following ways:

- Inserting an image

- Using Bridge to import Photoshop or Fireworks files

- Using Photoshop Smart Objects

- Copying and pasting an image from Photoshop and Fireworks

This lesson will take about 55 minutes to complete. Before beginning, make sure you have copied the files for Lesson 8 to your hard drive as described in the "Getting Started" section at the beginning of the book. If you are starting from scratch in this lesson, use the method described in the "Jumpstart" section of "Getting Started."

Dreamweaver provides many ways to insert and adjust graphics, both within the program and in tandem with other Creative Suite tools such as Adobe Bridge, Adobe Fireworks, and Adobe Photoshop.

# Reviewing web image basics

The web is not as much a place as it is an experience. And essential to that experience are images and graphics—both still and animated—that populate most websites. In the computer world, graphics fall into two main categories: *vector* and *raster*.

Vector graphics excel in line art, drawings, and logo art. Raster technology works better for storing photographic images.

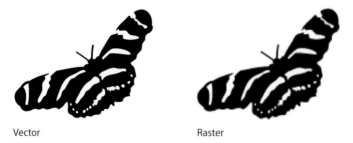

Vector                                      Raster

## Vector graphics

Vector graphics are created by math. They act like discrete objects, allowing you to reposition and resize them as many times as you want without affecting or diminishing their output quality. The best application of vector art is wherever geometric shapes and text are used to create artistic effects. For example, most company logos are built from vector shapes.

Vector graphics are typically stored in the AI, EPS, PICT, or WMF file formats. Unfortunately, most web browsers don't support these formats. The format that is supported is SVG, which stands for *Scalable Vector Graphic*. The simplest way for you to get started with SVG would be to create a graphic in your favorite vector-drawing program—like Adobe Illustrator or CorelDRAW—and then export it to this format. If you are good at programming, you may want to try creating SVG graphics using Extensible Markup Language (XML). To find out more about creating SVG graphics yourself, check out www.w3schools.com/svg.

## Raster graphics

Although SVG has definite advantages, web designers primarily use raster-based images in their web designs. Raster images are built from *pixels*, which stands for *picture elements*. Pixels have three basic characteristics:

- They are perfectly square in shape.
- They are all the same size.
- They display only one color at a time.

Raster-based images are usually composed of thousands, even millions, of different pixels arranged in rows and columns, in patterns that create the illusion of an actual photo, painting, or drawing. It's an illusion, because there is no real photo on the screen, just a bunch of pixels that fool your eyes into seeing an image. And as the quality of the image increases the more realistic the illusion becomes. Raster-image quality is based on three factors: resolution, size, and color.

Raster images are built of thousands or even millions of pixels that produce the illusion of a photograph.

## Resolution

Resolution is the most well known of the factors affecting raster image quality. It is the expression of image quality measured in the number of pixels that fit in one inch (ppi). The more pixels you can fit in one inch, the more detail you can depict in the image. But better quality comes at a price. An unfortunate byproduct of higher resolution is larger file size. That's because each pixel must be stored as bytes of information within the image file—information that has real overhead in computer terms. More pixels mean more information, which means larger files.

Resolution has a dramatic effect on image output. The web image on the left looks fine in the browser but doesn't have enough quality for printing.

72 ppi

300 ppi

Although these two images share the identical resolution and color depth, you can see how image dimensions can affect file size.

Luckily, web images only have to be optimized to look best on computer screens, which are based mostly on a resolution of 72 ppi. This is low compared to other applications—like printing, where 300 dpi is considered the lowest acceptable quality. The lower resolution of the computer screen is an important factor in keeping most web image files down to a reasonable size for downloading from the Internet. Because webpages are intended for viewing and not printing, the pictures don't need to have a resolution higher than 72 ppi.

### Size

Size refers to the vertical and horizontal dimensions of the image. As image size increases, more pixels are required to create it, and therefore the file becomes larger. Since graphics take more time to download than HTML code, many designers in recent years have replaced graphical components with CSS formatting to speed up the web experience for their visitors. But if you need or want to use images, a method to ensure snappy downloads is to keep image size small. Even today, with the proliferation of high-speed Internet service, you won't find too many websites that depend on full-page graphics.

500KB

1.6MB

### Color

Color refers to the color space, or *palette*, that describes each image. Most computer screens display only a fraction of the colors that the human eye can see. And different computers and applications display varying levels of color, expressed by the term *bit depth*. Monochrome, or 1-bit color, is the smallest color space, displaying only black and white, with no shades of gray. Monochrome is used mostly for line-art illustrations, for blueprints, and to reproduce handwriting.

The 4-bit color space describes up to 16 colors. Additional colors can be simulated by a process called *dithering*, where the available colors are interspersed and juxtaposed to create an illusion of more color. This color space was created for the first color computer systems and game consoles. Because of its limitations, this palette is seldom used today.

The 8-bit palette offers up to 256 colors or 256 shades of gray. This is the basic color system of all computers, mobile phones, game systems, and handheld devices. This color space also includes what is called the *web-safe* color palette. Web-safe refers to a subset of 8-bit colors that are supported on both Macintosh and Windows computers. Most computers, game consoles, and handheld devices now support higher color palettes, but 8-bit is the fallback for all web-compatible devices.

Today, some cell phones and handheld games support the 16-bit color space. This palette is called *high color* and sports a grand total of 65,000 colors. Although this sounds like a lot, 16-bit color is not considered good enough for most graphic design purposes or professional printing.

The highest color space is 24-bit color, which is called *true color*. This system generates up to 16.7 million colors. It is the gold standard for graphic design and professional printing. Several years ago a new color space was added to the mix: 32-bit color. It doesn't offer any additional colors, but it provides an additional eight bits of data for an attribute called *alpha transparency*.

Alpha transparency enables you to designate parts of an image or graphic as fully or even partially transparent. This trick allows you to create graphics that seem to have rounded corners or curves and can eliminate the white bounding box typical of raster graphics.

24-bit color

8-bit color

4-bit color

Here you can see a dramatic comparison of three color spaces and what the total number of available colors means to image quality.

As with size and resolution, color depth can dramatically affect image file size. With all other aspects being equal, an 8-bit image is over seven times larger than a monochrome image. And the 24-bit version is over three times larger than the 8-bit image. The key to effective use of images on a website is finding the balance of resolution, size, and color to achieve the desired optimal quality.

## Raster image file formats

Raster images can be stored in a multitude of file formats, but web designers have to be concerned with only three: GIF, JPEG, and PNG. These three formats are optimized for the Internet and compatible with most browsers. However, they are not equal in capability.

### GIF

GIF (graphic interchange format) was one of the first raster image file formats designed specifically for the web. It has changed only a little in the last 20 years. GIF supports a maximum of 256 colors (8-bit palette) and 72 ppi, so it's used mainly for web interfaces—buttons and graphical borders and such. But it does have several interesting features that keep it pertinent for today's web designers: index transparency and support for simple animation.

### JPEG

JPEG, also written JPG, is named for the Joint Photographic Experts Group that created the image standard back in 1992 as a direct reaction to the limitations of the GIF file format. JPEG is a powerful format that supports unlimited resolution, image dimensions, and color depth. Because of this, most digital cameras use JPEG as their default file type for image storage. It's also the reason most designers use JPEG on their websites for images that must be displayed in high quality.

This may sound odd to you since high quality—as described earlier—usually means large file size. Large files take longer to download to your browser. So, why is the format so popular on the web? JPEG's claim to fame comes from its patented user-selectable image compression algorithm that can reduce file size as much as 95 percent. JPEG images are compressed each time they are saved and then decompressed before they are opened and displayed.

Unfortunately, there's a downside to all this compression. Too much compression damages image quality. This type of compression is called *lossy*, because it loses quality each time. In fact, it can damage an image so much that the image can be rendered useless. Each time designers save a JPEG image, they face a trade-off between image quality and file size.

Here you see the effects of different amounts of compression on the file size and quality of an image.

Low quality
High compression
130K

Medium quality
Medium compression
150K

High quality
Low compression
260K

## PNG

PNG (Portable Network Graphic) was developed in 1995 because of a looming patent dispute involving the GIF format. At the time, it looked as if designers and developers would have to pay a royalty for using the .gif file extension. Although that issue blew over, PNG has found many adherents and a home on the Internet because of its capabilities.

PNG combines many of the features of GIF and JPEG and then adds a few of its own. For example, it offers support for unlimited resolution, 32-bit color, and full alpha and index transparency. It also provides lossless compression, which means you can save an image in PNG format and not worry about losing any quality each time you open and save the file. That's the good news.

The bad news is that although the format has been around for over 15 years, its features—such as alpha transparency—are not fully supported in older browsers.

# Previewing the completed file

To get a sense of the files you will work on in this lesson, let's preview the completed pages in the browser.

1  Launch Adobe Dreamweaver CS6.

2  If necessary, press Ctrl-Shift-F/Cmd-Shift-F to open the Files panel, and select DW-CS6 from the site list.

3  In the Files panel, expand the lesson08 folder.

4  Open the **contactus_finished.html** and **news_finished.html** files from the lesson08 folder, and preview the pages in your primary browser.

The pages include several images, as well as a Photoshop Smart Object image.

5  Close your browser and return to Dreamweaver.

# Inserting an image

**Note:** If you are starting from scratch in this chapter, use the Jumpstart instructions in the "Getting Started" section at the beginning of the book.

Images are key components of any webpage, both for developing visual interest and for telling stories. Dreamweaver provides numerous ways to populate your pages with images, using built-in commands and even using copy and paste. One method is to insert the image using Dreamweaver's built-in tools.

1   In the Files panel, open the **contact_us.html** file from the site root folder (this is the file you completed in Lesson 7, "Working with Text, Lists, and Tables").

    An image placeholder appears in `<div.sidebar1>` to indicate where an image should be inserted.

2   Double-click the image placeholder labeled *Sidebar (180 x 150).*

    The Select Image Source dialog box appears.

3   Select **biking.jpg** from the site images folder. Click OK/Open.

    The image appears in the sidebar.

In the best of all worlds, your images will always appear at the place and size you specified on your pages. But frequently, images will not display as desired. This can be caused by numerous situations, such as incompatible devices or file types, as well as server and browser errors. Some users may have disabilities that prevent them from "seeing" the images altogether. What can you do when your images won't display or can't be seen? HTML provides an *Alternate text* (`alt`) attribute just for those situations. When the images do not appear or can't be seen, the alternate text will be displayed instead or can be accessed by assistive devices.

In most cases, Dreamweaver will prompt you for the Alt text each time you insert a new image from scratch. When replacing an image placeholder, however, you'll have to do it manually.

**4** Insert the cursor in the Alt field in the Property inspector, type **Bike to work to save gas**, and press Enter/Return to the complete the entry.

**5** To give your image a caption, select the placeholder text *Add caption here* and type **We practice what we preach, here's Lin biking to work through Lakefront Park.**

You've successfully inserted an image using one technique, but Dreamweaver offers other techniques too. You'll now add an image to the page using the Assets panel.

**6** Insert the cursor at the beginning of the first paragraph under the heading *Association Management* in `<section.profile>`. The cursor should be inserted before the name *Elaine.*

**7** Choose Window > Assets to display the Assets panel, if necessary. Click the Images category (🖼) icon to display a list of all images stored within the site.

**8** Locate and select **elaine.jpg** in the list.

A preview of **elaine.jpg** appears in the Assets panel. The panel lists the image's name, dimensions in pixels, and file type, as well as its directory path.

**9** Note the dimensions of the image: 150 pixels by 150 pixels.

**10** At the bottom of the panel, click the Insert button.

The image appears at the current cursor location.

> **Tip:** Dreamweaver also allows you to drag the image icon from the Assets panel to the page.

> **Note:** The Images window shows all images stored anywhere in the defined site—even ones outside the site's default images folder—so you may see listings for images stored in the lesson subfolders too.

> **Warning:** If more than one file with the same name appears in the Assets panel, make sure you select the image stored in the default images folder.

**11** In the Alternate text field in the Image Tag Accessibility Attributes dialog box, type **Elaine, Meridien GreenStart President and CEO** and click OK.

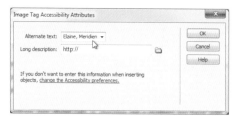

**12** Choose File > Save.

You inserted Elaine's picture in the text, but it doesn't look very nice at its current position. In the next exercise, you will adjust the image position using a CSS class.

## Adjusting image positions with CSS classes

The <img> element is an inline element by default. That's why you can insert images inline into paragraphs and other elements. When the image is taller than the font size, the image will increase the vertical space for the line in which it appears. In the past you could adjust its position using HTML attributes or CSS, but the HTML-based attributes have been deprecated from the language as well as from Dreamweaver CS6. Now you must rely completely on CSS-based techniques.

If you want all the images to align in a certain fashion, you can create a custom rule for the <img> tag to apply specific styling. In this instance, we want the employee photos to alternate from right to left going down the page, so you'll create a custom class to provide options for left and right alignment.

**1** If necessary, open **contact_us.html**.

**2** Select the New CSS Rule icon in the CSS Styles panel.

**3** In the New CSS Rule dialog box, choose Class from the Selector Type menu.

**4** Name the rule flt_rgt and click OK to create the rule.

The name is short for "float right," hinting at what command you're going to use to style the images.

**5** In the Box category, choose Right from the Float menu. In the Left margin field, enter **10px** and click OK.

You can apply the class from the Property inspector.

**6** In the layout, select the image **elaine.jpg**. From the Class menu in the Property inspector, select flt_rgt.

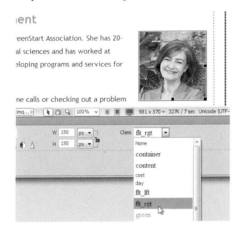

The image moves to the right side of the section element, and the text wraps around on the left. The margin setting keeps the text from touching the edge of the image itself. You will create a similar rule to align images to the left in the next exercise.

# Working with the Insert panel

The Insert panel duplicates key menu commands and has a number of options that make inserting images and other code elements both quick and easy.

**1** Insert the cursor at the beginning of the first paragraph under the heading *Education and Events*, before the name *Sarah*.

**2** Choose Window > Insert to display the Insert panel, if necessary.

● **Note:** If you don't see the Insert panel docked on the right side of the screen, it may appear as a toolbar at the top of the document window—as it does in the Classic workspace, for example.

**3** In the Insert panel, choose the Common category.

Click to open the Images button.

The button drop-down menu offers seven options: Image, Image Placeholder, Rollover Image, Fireworks HTML, Draw Rectangular Hotspot, Draw Oval Hotspot, and Draw Polygon Hotspot. A *hotspot* is basically a hyperlink enabled by a user-defined area drawn on an image.

**4** From the pop-up menu, choose Image.

The Select Image Source dialog box appears.

**5** Select **sarah.jpg** from the default images directory and note the dimensions of the image: 150 pixels by 150 pixels. Click OK/Choose.

**6** In the Image Tag Accessibility Attributes dialog box, type **Sarah, GreenStart Events Coordinator** in the Alternate text field and click OK.

**7** Select the New CSS Rule icon in the CSS Styles panel.

**8** In the New CSS Rule dialog box, choose Class from the Selector Type menu.

**9** Name the rule flt_lft, and click OK to create the rule.

The name is short for "float left."

**10** In the Box category, choose Left from the Float menu. In the Right margin field, enter **10px** and click OK.

**11** Apply the flt_left class to this image.

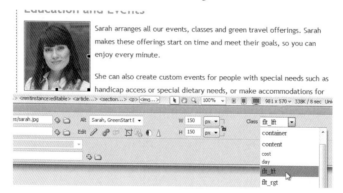

The image drops down into the paragraph on the left side, with the text wrapping to the right.

**12** Save the file.

Another way to insert images in your webpage is by using Adobe Bridge.

# Using Adobe Bridge to insert images

Adobe Bridge CS6 is an essential tool for web designers that can quickly browse directories of images and other supported assets, as well as manage and tag files with keywords and labels. Bridge is fully integrated with Dreamweaver: You can launch it from within Dreamweaver and either drag images directly from Bridge into your layouts or use specific commands.

1  Insert the cursor at the beginning of the first paragraph under the heading *Transportation Analysis*, before the name *Eric*.

2  Choose File > Browse in Bridge.

   Adobe Bridge launches. The interface in Bridge can be set up to your liking and saved as a custom workspace. For most operations, you can use the Essentials workspace, as shown.

3  Click the Folders tab to bring the Folders panel to the top. If necessary, choose Window > Folders Panel. Navigate to the folder designated as your default site images folder on your hard drive. Observe the names and types of files displayed in the folder.

   Bridge displays a thumbnail image of each file in the folder. Bridge can display thumbnails for all types of graphic files, including AI, BMP, EPS, GIF, JPG, PDF, PNG, SVG, and TIFF, among others.

**4** Click **eric.png**. Observe the Preview and Metadata panels. Note the dimensions, resolution, and color space of the image.

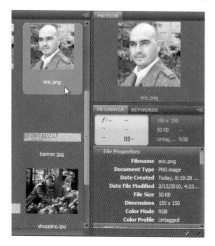

The Preview panel displays a high-quality preview of the selected image.

Bridge also has capabilities for helping you locate and isolate specific types of files.

**5** Choose Window > Filter Panel to display the panel if it's not visible.

The Filter panel displays a default set of data criteria—such as file type, ratings, keywords, date created, and so forth—that are then populated automatically by the contents of a particular folder. You can filter the contents to these criteria by clicking one or more of these items.

**6** In the Filter panel, expand the File Type criterion. Select the JPEG File criterion.

A check mark appears beside the JPEG File criterion. The PNG file you selected earlier is no longer visible. The Content panel in the center of Adobe Bridge displays only JPEG files.

**7** In the File Type criteria, select GIF Image.

A check mark appears beside the GIF Image criterion. The Content panel now displays only GIF and JPEG files. Other file types are being hidden by Bridge but still exist in the folder. You can use Bridge to insert one of these files into Dreamweaver or another Creative Suite application.

**8** Select **eric.jpg** in the Content panel. Note the dimensions in the Metadata panel: 150 pixels by 150 pixels. Choose File > Place > In Dreamweaver.

Your computer switches back to Dreamweaver automatically. The Image Tag Accessibility Attributes dialog box appears.

**9** In the Image Tag Accessibility Attributes dialog box, type **Eric, Transportation Research Coordinator** in the Alternate text field, and click OK.

The **eric.jpg** image appears in the Dreamweaver layout at the last position of the cursor.

**10** Apply the `flt_rgt` class to this image.

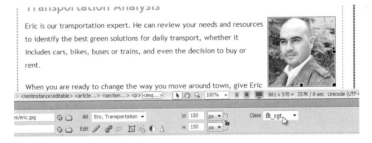

**11** Save the file.

Dreamweaver is not limited to the file types GIF, JPEG, and PNG; it can work with other file types too. In the next exercise, you will learn how to insert a Photoshop document (PSD) into a webpage.

# Inserting non-web file types

Although most browsers will display only the web-compliant image formats described earlier, Dreamweaver allows you to choose from many different formats—the program will then automatically convert the file to a compatible format on the fly.

1   Insert the cursor at the beginning of the first paragraph under the heading *Research and Development*, before the name *Lin*.

2   Choose Insert > Image. Navigate to the **resources** folder in the lesson08 folder. Select **lin.psd**.

Notice that the Dreamweaver dialog box doesn't offer a preview or any image specifications for the PSD file. It would be difficult or impossible using this dialog box to identify and select images saved in this format. If you're familiar with the names of the files you want to use, you could still select them from this dialog box—otherwise, this is an ideal application for Adobe Bridge.

3   Click Cancel. Switch to or launch Adobe Bridge. Navigate to the resources folder in the lesson08 folder. Observe the images in the resources folder.

The folder contains two images: a PSD and a TIFF. Note that Bridge previews the file contents and provides important metadata for each image.

4   Click **lin.psd** and select File > Place > Place in Dreamweaver.

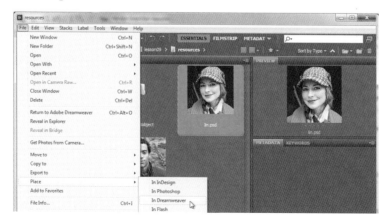

The image appears in the layout, and the Image Optimization dialog box opens—it acts as an intermediary that allows you to specify how and to what format the image will be converted.

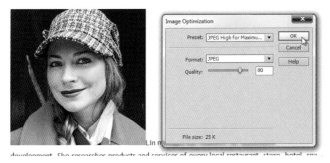

5   Observe the options in the Preset and Format menus.

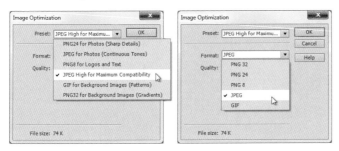

The presets allow you to select predetermined options that have a proven track record for web-based images. The Format drop-down menu allows you to specify your own settings from among five options: GIF, JPEG, PNG 8, PNG 24, and PNG 32.

6   Choose JPEG High For Maximum Compatibility from the Presets menu. Note the Quality setting.

This Quality setting produces a high-quality image with a moderate amount of compression. If you lower the Quality setting, you automatically increase the compression level and reduce the file size; increase the Quality setting for the opposite effect. The secret to effective design is to select a good balance between quality and compression. The default setting for the JPEG High preset is 80; this should be sufficient for our purposes.

7   Click OK to convert the image.

The Save Web Image dialog box appears with the name *lin* entered in the Save As field. Dreamweaver will add the .jpg extension to the file automatically and save the file to the default site images folder.

8   Click Save.

The Image Tag Accessibility Attributes dialog box appears.

**Note:** When an image has to be converted this way, Dreamweaver usually saves the converted image into the default site images folder. This is not the case when the images inserted are web-compatible. So before you insert an image, you should be aware of its current location in the site and move it to the proper location, if necessary.

**9** Enter **Lin, Research and Development Coordinator** in the Alternate text field. Click OK.

The image appears in Dreamweaver at the cursor position. The image has been resampled to 72 ppi but still appears at its original dimensions, which are larger than the other images in the layout. You can resize the image in the Property inspector.

**10** In the Property inspector, select the Toggle Size Constrain (🔒) icon and change the Width field to **150px**.

The change to the image size is only temporary at the moment, as indicated by the Reset (⊘) and Commit (✔) icons.

**11** Click the Commit (✔) icon.

The image resizes to 150 by 150 pixels.

**12** Apply the flt_lft class to this image. Save the file.

The image now appears likes the other images in the layout, but there's still something different about it. An icon appears in the upper-left corner that identifies this image as a Photoshop Smart Object.

# Working with Photoshop Smart Objects

Unlike other images, Smart Objects maintain a connection to the original Photoshop (PSD) file. If the PSD file is altered in any manner and then saved, Dreamweaver will identify those changes and provide the means to update the web image used in the layout.

● **Note:** Dreamweaver and Photoshop can work with the existing quality of an image only. If your initial image quality is unacceptable, you may not be able to fix it in Photoshop. You will have to re-create the image or pick another.

1   If necessary, open **contact_us.html**. Scroll down to the image **lin.jpg** in the *Research and Development* section. Observe the icon in the upper-left corner of the image.

The icon indicates that the image is a Smart Object. The circular green arrows indicate that the original image is unchanged. If you want to edit or optimize the image, you can simply right-click the image and select the appropriate option from the context menu.

To make substantive changes to the image, you will have to open it in Photoshop. (If you don't have Photoshop installed, copy lesson08 > resources > smartobject > **lin.psd** into the lesson08 > resources folder to replace the original image, and then skip to step 6.) In this exercise, you will edit the image background of the image using Photoshop.

2   Right-click **lin.jpg**. Choose Edit Original With > Photoshop from the context menu.

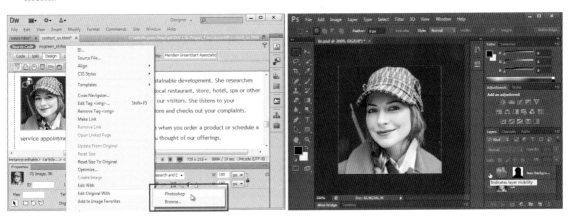

Photoshop launches—if it is installed on your computer—and loads the file.

**3** In Photoshop, choose Window > Layers to display the Layers panel, if necessary. Observe the names and states of any existing layers.

The image has two layers: Lin and New Background. New Background is turned off.

**4** Click the eye () icon for the New Background layer to display its contents.

The background of the image changes to show a scene from a park.

**5** Save the Photoshop file.

**6** Switch back to Dreamweaver.

Lin manages our research for sustain
products and services of every local
business that we recommend to our
comments on our recommendations

You can expect to hear from Lin wh

In a moment or two, the Smart Object icon in the upper-left corner changes to indicate that the original image has been changed. The icon appears only within Dreamweaver itself; visitors see the normal image in the browser. You don't have to update the image at this time, and you can leave the out-of-date image in the layout for as long as you want. Dreamweaver will continue to monitor its status as long as it's in the layout. But for this exercise, let's update the image.

**7** Right-click the image and choose Update From Original from the context menu.

This Smart Object and any other instances of it change to reflect the new background.

Lin manages our research for sustain
products and services of every local
business that we recommend to our
comments on our recommendations

You can expect to hear from Lin wh

**8** Save the file.

As you can see, Smart Objects have advantages over a typical image workflow. For images that are changed or updated frequently, using a Smart Object can simplify updates to the website in the future.

## Copying and pasting images from Photoshop and Fireworks

As you build your website, you will need to edit and optimize many images before you use them in your site. Adobe Fireworks and Adobe Photoshop are both excellent programs for performing these tasks. A common workflow is to manually export the optimized GIF, JPEG, or PNG to the default images folder in your website when you're finished working on it. But sometimes it's faster to simply copy images and paste them directly into your layout. Whether you're working with Fireworks or Photoshop, the steps are nearly identical and the result is the same; in this exercise, feel free to use whichever program you are most familiar with.

1 Launch Adobe Fireworks or Adobe Photoshop, if necessary. Open **matthew.tif** from the lesson08 > resources folder. Observe the Layers panel.

   The image has only one layer. In Fireworks, you can select multiple layers and copy and paste them into Dreamweaver. In Photoshop, either you will have to merge or flatten layers before you copy and paste them or you will have to use the command Edit > Copy Merged to copy images with multiple active layers.

2 Press Ctrl-A/Cmd-A to select the entire image. Press Ctrl-C/Cmd-C to copy the image.

3 Switch to Dreamweaver. Scroll down to the section *Information Systems* in **contact_us.html**. Insert the cursor at the beginning of the first paragraph in this section, before the name *Matthew*.

4 Press Ctrl-V/Cmd-V to paste the image from the clipboard.

   The image appears in the layout, and the Image Optimization dialog box opens.

5   Select the preset PNG24 for Photos (Sharp Details), and select PNG 24 from the Format menu. Click OK.

The Save Image dialog box appears.

6   Name the image **matthew.png**, and select the default site images folder, if necessary. Click Save.

The Image Description (Alt text) dialog box appears.

7   Enter **Matthew, Information Systems Manager** in the Image Description (Alt text) field. Click OK.

The **matthew.png** image appears in the layout. As in the earlier exercise, the PNG image is larger than the other images.

● **Note:** Raster images can be scaled down in size without losing quality, but the opposite is not true. Unless a graphic has a resolution higher than 72 ppi, it may not be possible to scale it larger without noticeable degradation.

8   In the Property inspector, change the size to **150px** by **150px**. Click the Commit (✔) icon to apply the change permanently.

9   Apply the class flt_rgt to **matthew.png**.

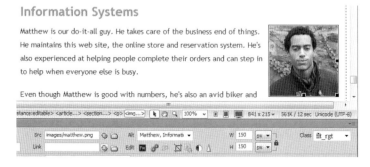

The image appears in the layout at the same size as the other images and aligned to the right. Although this image came from Fireworks or Photoshop, it's not "smart" like a Photoshop Smart Object and can't be updated automatically. It does, however, keep track of the location of the original image if you want to edit it later.

● **Note:** The Edit Original With option may not be available to users who do not have Photoshop or Fireworks installed.

10  In the layout, right-click the **matthew.png** image and choose Edit Original With > Browse from the context menu.

**11** Navigate to and select the program Fireworks or Photoshop on your hard drive. Click Open.

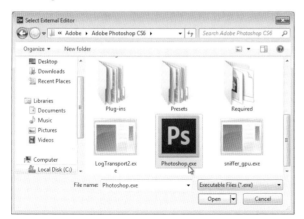

▶ **Tip:** The executable program file is usually stored in the Program Files folder in Windows and in the Applications folder on a Macintosh.

The program launches and displays the original TIFF file. You can make changes to the image and copy and paste it into Dreamweaver by repeating steps 2 through 9. Although there's no way to automatically replace the image, as with Smart Objects, there's a more efficient way than using copy and paste. Photoshop users should skip to step 13.

**12** In Fireworks: Choose File > Image Preview. In the Options mode, select PNG 24 from the Format menu. In the File mode, change the Width and Height fields to **150px**. Click Export.

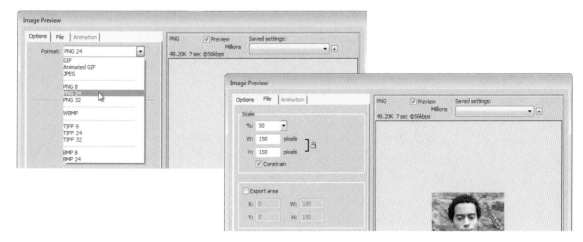

The Image Preview dialog box allows you to specify the export size of the image. Fireworks will remember the specifications you select in this dialog box when you save and close the file. Fireworks users can skip to step 15.

**13** In Photoshop: Choose File > Save For Web. Choose PNG-24 from the Preset menu. Change the Image Size Width field to **150px**. Click Save.

The Save For Web dialog box appears.

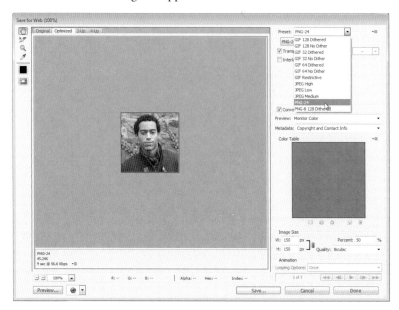

▶ **Tip:** Clicking the name inserts the existing filename in the dialog box field and avoids any spelling or typing errors, which is vital for Unix-based web servers.

● **Note:** Although Dreamweaver automatically reloads any modified file most browsers won't. You will have to refresh the browser display before you see any changes.

**14** Navigate to the default site images folder and click to select the existing **matthew.png** file.

The name *matthew.png* appears in the Filename field of the dialog box.

**15** Click Export/Save.

**16** Switch back to Dreamweaver. Scroll down to view **matthew.png** in the *Information Systems* section.

No further action is needed to update the image in the layout, because you saved the new image over the original file. As long as the filename hasn't changed, Dreamweaver isn't concerned and no other action is necessary. This method saves you several steps and avoids any potential typing errors.

**17** Save the file.

Copy and paste is just one of the handy methods for inserting images. Dreamweaver also allows you to drag images into your layout.

# Inserting images by drag and drop

Most of the programs in the Creative Suite offer drag-and-drop capabilities and Dreamweaver is no exception.

1 Open the **news.html** file you created in the last lesson from the site root folder.

2 Choose Window > Assets to display the Assets panel, if necessary. For this exercise, the panel should be docked. Select Window > Workspace Layout > Reset Designer to restore the default panel configuration, if necessary.

3 Click the Images icon in the Assets panel.

4 Drag **city.jpg** from the panel to the beginning of the first paragraph under the heading *Green Buildings earn more Green*.

▶ **Tip:** If you don't see specific image files listed in the Assets panel, click the Refresh (**C**) icon to reload site images.

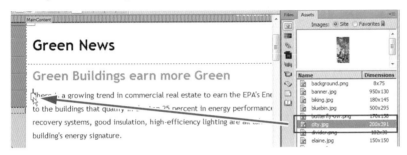

The Image Tag Accessibility Attributes dialog box appears.

5 In the Alternate text field, enter **Green buildings are top earners** and click OK.

6 Apply the class `flt_lft` to the image. Save the file.

▶ **Tip:** Dreamweaver also allows you to drag the image from Bridge to the page.

It takes a steady hand and a little practice to perfect your drag-and-drop technique, but it's a good way to get images into your layout quickly.

# Optimizing images with the Property inspector

Optimized web images try to balance image dimensions and quality against file size. Sometimes you may need to optimize graphics that have already been placed on the page. Dreamweaver has built-in features that can help you achieve the smallest possible file size while preserving image quality. In this exercise, you'll use tools in Dreamweaver to scale, optimize, and crop an image for the web:

1 Insert the cursor at the beginning of the first paragraph under the heading *Shopping green saves energy*. Choose Insert > Image. Select **farmersmarket.png** from the site images folder and click OK/Choose.

**2** In the Alternate text field, enter **Buy local to save energy** and click OK.

**3** Apply the class flt_rgt to the image.

The image is too large and could use some cropping. To save time, you can use tools in Dreamweaver to fix the image composition.

**4** If necessary, choose Window > Properties to display the Property inspector.

Whenever an image is selected, image-editing options appear in the lower-right corner of the Property inspector. The buttons here allow you to edit the image in Fireworks or Photoshop or to adjust various settings in place. See the sidebar "Dreamweaver's graphic tools" for an explanation of each button.

There are two ways to reduce the dimensions of an image in Dreamweaver. The first method changes the size of the image temporarily by imposing user-defined dimensions.

**5** Select **farmersmarket.png**. In the Property inspector, select the Toggle Size Constrain (🔒) icon and change the image width to **300px**.

The height automatically conforms to the new width. Dreamweaver indicates that the new size is not permanent by displaying the current specifications in bold and the Reset (⊘) and Commit (✔) icons.

**6** Click the Reset (⊘) icon.

The image returns to its original size. The image can also be resized interactively.

▶ **Tip:** As you scale the image, the Property inspector gives a real-time display of the image dimensions.

**7** Drag the lower-right corner to scale the image down to a width of 350 pixels. If you hold down the Shift key as you start scaling, the height will change proportionately; otherwise, select the Toggle Size Constrain (🔒) icon when you're finished to enforce proportionate scaling.

The Reset (⊘) and Commit (✔) icons appear in the Property inspector.

**8** Click the Commit (✔) icon.

A dialog box appears that indicates the change will be permanent.

**9** Click OK.

Dreamweaver can also crop images within the program.

**10** Click the Crop ( ⊠ ) icon in the Property inspector.

A dialog box appears that indicates that the action will permanently change the image. Click OK. Crop handles appear on the image.

**11** Crop the image to a width and height of 300 pixels.

**12** Press Enter/Return to finalize the change.

**13** Save the file.

## Bonus exercise: completing the news page

The news page still needs a couple of images and a caption for the sidebar. Take a few minutes and apply some of the skills you have learned in this lesson to complete the page.

**1** Using any of the techniques you have learned in this lesson, replace the sidebar image placeholder with **sprinkler.jpg**. Use the following Alt text: **Check watering restrictions in your area**.

**2** Add the following caption to the sidebar: **The Meridien city council will address summer watering restrictions at the next council meeting.**

**3** In the article *Recycling isn't always Green*, insert the **recycling.jpg** image with the Alt text **Learn the pros and cons of recycling**. Apply the class flt_lft.

**4** Save all files.

In this lesson, you learned how to insert images and Smart Objects into a Dreamweaver page, work with Adobe Bridge, copy and paste from Fireworks and Photoshop, and use the Property inspector to edit images.

There are numerous ways to create and edit images for the web. The methods examined in this lesson show but a few of them and are not meant to recommend or endorse one method over another. Feel free to use whatever methods and work-flow you desire based on your own situation and expertise.

# Dreamweaver's graphic tools

All of Dreamweaver's graphic tools are accessible from the Property inspector when an image is selected. Here are the seven tools:

**Edit**—Opens the selected image in the defined external graphics editor. You can assign a graphics-editing program to any given file type in the File Types/ Editors category of the Preferences dialog box. The button's image changes according to the program chosen. For example, if Fireworks is the designated editor for the image type, a Fireworks ( **Fw** ) icon is shown; if Photoshop is the editor, you'll see a Photoshop ( **Ps** ) icon.

**Edit Image Settings**—Opens the image optimization dialog box, allowing you to apply user-defined optimization specifications to the selected image.

**Update From Original**—Updates the placed Smart Object to match any changes to the original source file.

**Crop**—Permanently removes unwanted portions of an image. When the Crop tool is enabled, a bounding box with a series of control handles appears within the selected image. You can adjust the bounding box size by dragging the handles. When the box outlines the desired portion of the image, double-click the graphic to apply the cropping.

**Resample**—Permanently resizes an image. The Resample tool is active only when an image has been resized.

**Brightness And Contrast**—Offers user-selectable adjustments to an image's brightness and contrast. A dialog box presents two sliders—for brightness and contrast—that can be adjusted independently. A live preview is available so that you can evaluate adjustments before committing to them.

**Sharpen**—Affects the enhancement of image details by raising or lowering the contrast of pixels on a scale from 0 to 10. As with the Brightness And Contrast tool, Sharpen offers a real-time preview.

You can undo most graphics operations by choosing Edit > Undo until the containing document is closed or you quit Dreamweaver.

# Review questions

1 What are the three factors that determine raster image quality?

2 What file formats are specifically designed for use on the web?

3 Describe at least two methods for inserting an image into a webpage using Dreamweaver.

4 True or false: All graphics have to be optimized outside of Dreamweaver.

5 What is the advantage of using a Photoshop Smart Object over copying and pasting an image from Photoshop?


# Review answers

1 Raster image quality is determined by resolution, image dimensions, and color depth.

2 The compatible image formats for the web are GIF, JPEG, and PNG.

3 One method to insert an image into a webpage using Dreamweaver is to use the Insert panel. Another method is to drag the graphic file into the layout from the Assets panel. Images can be copied and pasted from Photoshop and Fireworks. Images can also be inserted from Adobe Bridge.

4 False. Images can be optimized even after they are inserted into Dreamweaver by using the Property inspector. Optimization can include rescaling, changing format, or fine-tuning format settings.

5 A Smart Object can be used multiple times in different places on a site, and each instance of the Smart Object can be assigned individual settings. All copies remain connected to the original image. If the original is updated, all the connected images are immediately updated as well. When you copy and paste all or part of a Photoshop file, however, you get a single image that can have only one set of values applied to it.

# 9 WORKING WITH NAVIGATION

## Lesson Overview

In this lesson, you'll apply several kinds of links to page elements by doing the following:

- Creating a text link to a page within the same site

- Creating a link to a page on another website

- Creating an email link

- Creating an image-based link

- Creating a Spry navigation menu

 This lesson will take about 2 hours to complete. Before beginning, make sure you have copied the files for Lesson 9 to your hard drive as described in the "Getting Started" section at the beginning of the book. If you are starting from scratch in this lesson, use the method described in the "Jumpstart" section of "Getting Started."

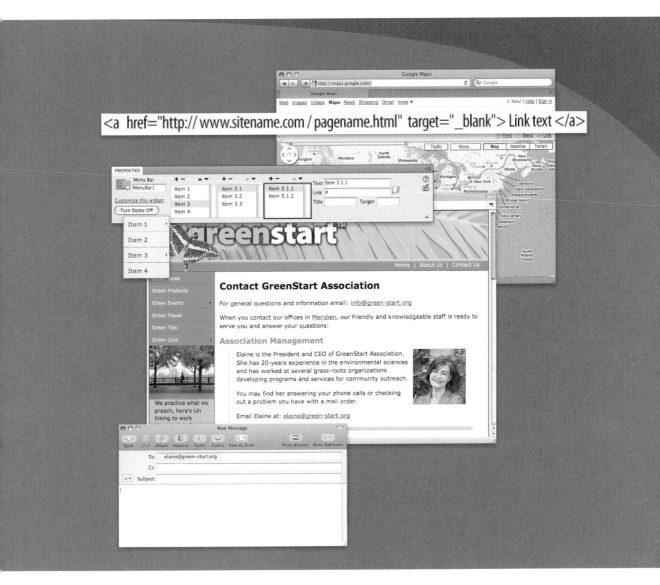

Dreamweaver can create and edit many types of links—from text-based links to image-based links—and does so with ease and flexibility.

# Hyperlink basics

The World Wide Web, and the Internet in general, would be a far different place without the hyperlink. Without hyperlinks, HTML would simply be "ML" for *markup language*. The *hypertext* in the name refers to the functionality of the hyperlink. So what is a hyperlink?

A hyperlink, or *link*, is an HTML-based reference to a resource that is available on the Internet or within your own computer. The resource can be anything that can be stored on and displayed by a computer, such as a webpage, image, movie, sound file, and so on. A hyperlink creates an interactive behavior specified by HTML and CSS, or the programming language you're using, and is enabled by a browser or other application.

An HTML hyperlink consists of the anchor <a> element and one or more attributes.

## Internal and external hyperlinks

The simplest hyperlink is one that takes the user to another part of the same document or to another document stored in the same folder or hard drive. This type is called an *internal* hyperlink. An *external* hyperlink is designed to take the user to a document or resource outside your hard drive, website, or web host.

Internal and external hyperlinks may work differently, but they both have one thing in common: Both are enabled in HTML by the <a> anchor element. This element designates the *address* of the destination, or *target*, of the hyperlink and can then specify how it functions using several attributes. You will learn how to create and modify the <a> element in the exercises that follow.

## Relative vs. absolute hyperlinks

The hyperlink address can be written in two different ways. When you refer to a target by where it is stored in relation to the current document, it is called a *relative* link. This is like telling someone that you live next door to the blue house. If someone were driving down your street and saw the blue house, they would know where you live. But it really doesn't tell them how to get to your house or even to your neighborhood. A relative link frequently will consist of the resource name and perhaps the folder it is stored within, such as **logo.jpg** or **images/logo.jpg**.

Sometimes, you need to spell out precisely where a resource is located. In those instances, you need an *absolute* hyperlink. This is like telling someone you live at 123 Main Street in Meridien. This is typically how you you refer to resources outside your website. An absolute link includes the entire URL of the target and may even include a filename—such as http://forums.adobe.com/index.jspa—or just a folder within the site.

There are advantages and disadvantages to both types of links. Relative hyperlinks are faster and easier to write, but they may not work if the document containing them is saved in a different folder or location in the website. Absolute links always work no matter where the containing document is saved, but they can fail if the targets are moved or renamed. A simple rule that most web designers follow is to use relative links for resources within a site and absolute links for resources outside the site. Then, it's important that you test all links before deploying the page or site.

# Previewing the completed file

To see the final version of the file you will work on in this lesson, let's preview the completed page in the browser.

1 Launch Adobe Dreamweaver CS6.

2 If necessary, press F8/Cmd-Shift-F to open the Files panel, and select DW-CS6 from the site list.

3 In the Files panel, expand the lesson09 folder.

4 Right-click **aboutus_finished.html** in the Files panel, choose Preview In Browser, and select your preferred browser to preview the file.

The file **aboutus_finished.html** appears in your default browser. This page features only internal links in both the horizontal and vertical menus.

▶ **Tip:** Firefox and Internet Explorer usually display the hyperlink destination in a thin strip in the lower-left corner of the screen, called the status bar.

▶ **Tip:** If you don't see the status bar in Firefox, choose View > Status Bar to turn it on. In Internet Explorer, choose View > Toolbars > Status Bar to turn it on.

**5** Position the cursor over the *Contact Us* link in the horizontal menu. Observe the browser to see if it's displaying the link's destination anywhere on the screen.

Typically, the browser shows the link destination in the status bar.

**6** In the horizontal navigation menu, click the *Contact Us* link.

The browser loads the Contact Us page, replacing the About Us page. The new page includes internal, external, and email links.

**7** Position the cursor over the *Meridien* link in the main content area. Observe the status bar.

The status bar displays the link http://maps.google.com.

**8** Click the *Meridien* link.

A new browser window appears and loads Google Maps. The link is intended to show the visitor where the Meridien GreenStart offices are located. You can even include address details or the company name in this link so that Google can load the exact map and directions, if desired.

Note that the browser opened a separate window or document tab when you clicked the link. This is a good behavior to use when directing visitors to resources outside your site. Since the link opens in a separate window, your own site is still open and ready to use. It's especially helpful if your visitors are unfamiliar with your site and may not know how to get back to it once they click away.

**9**  Close the Google Maps window.

The GreenStart Contact Us page is still open. Note that each employee has an email link.

**10**  Click an email link for one of the employees.

The default mail application will launch on your computer. If you have not set up this application to send and receive mail, the program will usually start a wizard to help you set up this functionality. If the email program is set up, a new message window will appear with the email address of the employee automatically entered in the To field.

**11**  Close the new message window and exit the email program.

**12**  Switch back to the browser. Position the cursor over the vertical menu. Hover over each of the buttons and examine the behavior of the menu.

The menu looks similar to the one you created in Lesson 4, "Creating a Page Layout," and Lesson 5, "Working with Cascading Style Sheets," but there's a new behavior that didn't exist before: Some of the buttons have submenus.

**13**  Hover on the *Green Events* link, and then click the submenu link *Class Schedule*.

The browser loads the Green Events page and automatically jumps down to the table containing the class schedule. As you can see, hyperlinks not only can target a specific page, they can target a specific item on the page to help visitors move quickly up and down long pages.

**14**  Click the *Return to Top* link that appears above the class schedule.

The browser jumps back to the top of the page.

**15**  Close the browser and switch to Dreamweaver.

## Creating internal hyperlinks

Dreamweaver makes it easy to create hyperlinks of all types. In this exercise, you'll create text-based links to pages in the same site using a variety of methods.

**1**  In the Files panel, double-click the **about_us.html** file in the site root folder to open it. Or, if you are starting from scratch in this lesson, follow the "Jumpstart" instructions in the "Getting Started" section at the beginning of the book.

**2**  In the horizontal menu, position the cursor over the text *Home* in the horizontal menu.

> **Note:** Many web visitors don't use email programs installed on their computers. They use web-based services like AOL, Gmail, Hotmail, and so on. For these types of visitors, email links like the one you tested won't work. To learn how to receive information from visitors without relying on client-based email, see Lesson 12, "Working with Forms."

> **Note:** If you're using the method described in the "Jumpstart" section of "Getting Started," preexisting files may display the lesson number, such as mygreen_temp_09.dwt.

The horizontal menu was not added to an editable region in Lesson 6, "Working with Templates," so it's considered part of the template and is locked. To add a hyperlink to this menu item, you'll have to open the template.

**Tip:** When editing or removing an existing hyperlink, you don't need to select the entire link; you can just insert the cursor anywhere in the link text. Dreamweaver assumes you wish to change the entire link by default.

**3** Choose Window > Assets. In the Assets panel, click the Template (▣) icon. Right-click **mygreen_temp** in the list and choose Edit from the context menu.

**4** In the horizontal menu, select the *Home* text.

The horizontal menu is editable in the template.

**5** If necessary, choose Window > Properties to open the Property inspector. Examine the contents of the Link field in the Property inspector.

To create links, the HTML tab must be selected in the Property inspector. The Link field shows a hyperlink placeholder (#). The home page doesn't exist yet. But links can be created by manually typing the name of the file or resource.

**Note:** The link won't have the typical hyperlink appearance because of the special formatting you applied to this menu in Lesson 5.

**6** Select the hash mark (#) in the Link field. Type **../index.html** and press Enter/Return to complete the link.

You've created your first text-based hyperlink. Since the template is saved in a subfolder, you need to add the path element ../ notation to the filename so that the link properly resolves once the template pages are updated. The ../ notation tells the browser or operating system to look in the parent directory of the current folder. Dreamweaver will rewrite the link when the template is applied to a page, depending on where the containing page is saved.

If the file already exists, Dreamweaver also offers interactive ways to create links.

**7** In the horizontal menu, select the text *About Us*.

**8** Click the Browse For File ( 📁 ) icon, adjacent to the Link field. When the Select File dialog box opens, select **about_us.html** from the site root folder. Make sure that the Relative To menu is set to Document. Click OK/Choose.

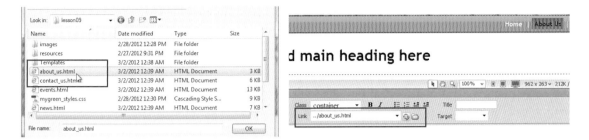

The hyperlink placeholder is replaced by the text `../about_us.html`. Now let's try a more visual approach.

**9** In the horizontal menu, select the *Contact Us* text.

**10** Click the Files tab to bring the panel to the top, or choose Window > Files.

**11** In the Property inspector, drag the Point To File (⊕) icon—next to the Link field—to **contact_us.html** in the site root folder displayed in the Files panel.

**Note:** You can select any range of text to create a link, from one character to an entire paragraph or more; Dreamweaver will add the necessary markup to the selection.

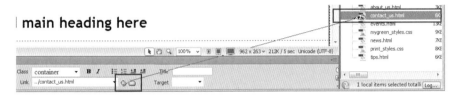

Dreamweaver enters the filename and any necessary path information into the Link field. To apply the links to all the pages formatted by this template, just save the page.

**12** Choose File > Save.

The Update Template Files dialog box appears. You can choose to update pages now or wait until later. You can even update the template files manually, if desired.

**13** Click Update.

**Tip:** If a folder in the Files panel contains a page you want to link to but the folder is not open, drag the Point To File icon over the folder and hold it in place to expand that folder so that you can point to the desired file.

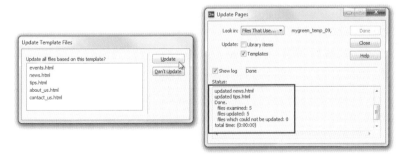

**Tip:** If you don't see the update report, select the Show Log option.

Dreamweaver updates all pages created from the template. The Update Pages dialog box appears and displays a report listing the pages that were updated.

14 Close the Update Pages dialog box. Close **mygreen_temp.dwt**.

Note the asterisk in the document tab for **about_us.html**. This indicates that the page has changed but has not been saved.

15 Save **about_us.html** and preview it in the default browser. Position the cursor over the text *About Us* and *Contact Us*.

When the template was saved, it updated the locked regions of the page, adding the hyperlinks.

16 Click the *Contact Us* link.

The Contact Us page loads to replace the About Us page in the browser.

17 Click the *About Us* link.

The About Us page loads to replace the Contact Us page. The links were added even to pages that weren't open at the time.

18 Close the browser and switch to Dreamweaver.

You learned three methods for creating hyperlinks with the Property inspector: typing the link manually, using the Browse For File function, and using the Point To File tool.

## Creating an image-based link

Links can also be applied to images. Image-based links work like any other hyperlink and can direct users to internal or external resources. In this exercise, you will create and format an image-based link that will direct users to the organization's About Us page.

1 Open the Assets panel and click the Template (▤) icon. Double-click **mygreen_temp** to open it.

2 Select the butterfly image at the top of the page. In the Property inspector, click the Browse For File icon next to the Link field.

3 Select **about_us.html** in the site root folder. Click OK/Choose.

The text *about_us.html* appears in the Link field.

4 In the Alt field of the Property inspector, replace the existing text with **Click to learn about Meridien GreenStart** and press Enter/Return.

The Alt text will appear whenever the picture doesn't load or if the user is using an assistive device to access the webpage.

5  Save the template. Update all child pages.

   The Update Pages dialog box appears, reporting how many pages were updated.

6  Close the Update Pages dialog box. Open **contact_us.html**, if necessary, and preview it in the default browser. Position the cursor over the butterfly image. Test the image link.

   Clicking the image loads **about_us.html** in the browser.

7  Switch back to Dreamweaver. Close the template file.

## Creating an external link

The pages you linked to in the previous exercise were stored within the current site. You can also link to any page—or other resource—stored on the web if you know the full web address, or URL. In this exercise, you'll apply an external link to existing text.

1  Click the document tab for **contact_us.html** to bring it to the top, or open it from the site root folder.

2  In the second paragraph <p> element in the *MainContent* region, select the word *Meridien*.

   You'll link this text to the Google Maps site. If you don't know the URL of a particular site, there's a simple trick to obtain it.

3  Launch your favorite browser. In the URL field, type **google.com** and press Enter/Return. Or, in the search field, type **Google Maps** and press Enter/Return. Locate the link for Google Maps in the search report and click it.

   Google Maps will appear in the browser window.

▶ **Tip:** For this trick, you can use any search engine.

● **Note:** In some browsers you can type the search phrase directly in the URL field.

● **Note:** Normally an image formatted with a hyperlink would display a blue border, similar to the blue underscore that text links get. But the predefined CSS that came with the layout includes an img rule, which sets this default border to None.

**4** Select the entire URL that appears at the top of the document window. Press Ctrl-C/Cmd-C to copy this link.

**5** Switch to Dreamweaver. In the Property inspector, insert the cursor in the Link field, press Ctrl-V/Cmd-V to paste the link, and press Enter/Return.

The text displays the standard formatting for a hyperlink.

**6** Save the file and preview it in the default browser. Test the link.

When you click the link, the browser takes you to the opening page of Google Maps, assuming you have a connection to the Internet. But there was a problem: Clicking the link replaced the Contact Us page in the browser; it didn't open a new window as in the earlier example. To make the browser open a new window, you need to add a simple HTML attribute to the link.

**7** Switch to Dreamweaver. Insert the cursor in the *Meridien* link text, if necessary.

**8** Choose _blank from the Target field menu.

**9** Save the file and preview the page in the default browser. Test the link.

This time a new, separate window opens for Google Maps.

**10** Close the browser windows and switch back to Dreamweaver.

As you can see, Dreamweaver makes it easy to create links to internal or external resources.

# Setting up email links

Another type of link is the email link, but instead of taking the visitor to another page it opens the visitor's email program instead. It can create an automatic, pre-addressed email message from your visitors for customer feedback, product orders, or other important communications. The code for an email link is slightly different from the normal hyperlink and—as you probably guessed already—Dreamweaver can create the proper code for you automatically.

**1** If necessary, open **contact_us.html**.

**2** Select Elaine's email address (elaine@green-start.org) and press Ctrl-C/Cmd-C to copy the text.

**3** Choose Insert > Email link.

The Email Link dialog box appears. The selected text is automatically entered into the Text field.

**4** Insert the cursor in the Email field and press Ctrl-V/Cmd-V to paste the email address.

> **Tip:** If the text is selected before you access the dialog box, Dreamweaver will enter the text in the field for you automatically.

**5** Click OK. Examine the Link field in the Property inspector.

Dreamweaver inserted the email address into the Link field and did one more thing. As you can see, it also entered the notation `mailto:` in front of the address. This text changes the link to an email link that will automatically launch the visitor's default email program.

6  Save the file and preview it in the default browser. Test the email link.

The default email program launches and creates an email message. If there is no default email program, your computer's operating system will launch an available email program or ask you to identify one.

7  Close any open email program, related dialog boxes, or wizards. Switch to Dreamweaver.

## Client-based vs. server-side functions

The email link you just created relies on software installed on the visitor's computer, such as Outlook or Apple Mail. Such applications are referred to as *client-based*, or *client-side*, functionality. The email link won't work, however, if a user sends his or her mail via an Internet application—such as Hotmail or Gmail—and doesn't have a desktop email application installed and set up to send and receive email.

Another detraction is that open email links like this can be picked up easily by spambots that roam the Internet. If you want to ensure that you'll get feedback from every user who wants to send it, you should instead rely on functionality supplied by your server. Web-based applications for capturing and passing data are referred to as *server-side* functionality. Using server-side scripts and proprietary languages—such as ASP, ColdFusion, and PHP—it's relatively easy to capture data and return it by email or even insert it directly into a hosted database. You'll learn some of these techniques in Lesson 12, "Working with Forms," and Lesson 14, "Building Dynamic Pages with Data."

## Targeting page elements

As you add more content on a page, it gets longer and more difficult to navigate. Typically, when you click a link to a page, the browser window displays the page starting at the very top. Whenever possible, it's a good idea to provide convenient methods for users to link to a specific point on a page.

In HTML 4.01, there are two methods for targeting specific content or page structures: One uses a *named anchor* and the other an ID attribute. However, the named anchor has been deprecated in HTML5 in favor of IDs. That doesn't mean named anchors will suddenly cease to function the day HTML5 is adopted, but you should start practicing now. In this exercise, you'll work only with ID attributes.

1  Open **events.html**.

2  Scroll down to the table that contains the class schedule.

When users move down this far on the page, the navigation menus are out of sight and unusable. The farther they read down the page, the farther they are from the primary navigation. Before users can navigate to another page, they have to use the browser scroll bars or the mouse scroll wheel to get back to the top of the page. Adding a link to take users back to the top can vastly improve their experience on your site. Let's call this type of link an internal *targeted* link.

Internal targeted links have two parts: the link itself and the target element. It doesn't matter which one you create first.

3  Insert the cursor in the Class table. Select the `<table>` tag selector. Press the Left Arrow key to move the cursor before the opening `<table>` tag.

4  Type **Return to Top** and select the text. In the Property inspector, choose Paragraph from the Format menu.

The text is inserted between the two tables and is formatted as a `<p>` element. Let's center the text.

5  In the CSS panel, click the New CSS Rule icon.

6  Choose Class from the Selector Type menu. In the Selector Name field, type **ctr**. Click OK.

7  In the Block category, choose Center from the Text-align field menu. Click OK.

8  Select the tag selector for the paragraph element *Return to Top*. In the Property inspector Class menu, choose `ctr`.

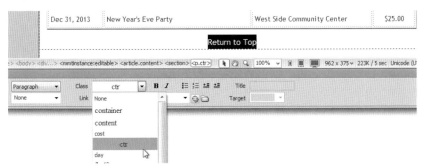

The text *Return to Top* is aligned to the center. The tag selector now says `<p.ctr>`.

**Tip:** In some browsers you need only to type the hash mark (#) to enable this function. The browser will jump to the top of the page whenever an unnamed anchor is referenced. Unfortunately, other browsers will ignore them altogether, so it's important to use a target element as well.

**9** In the Link field, type **#top** and press Enter/Return. Save all files.

By using #top, you have created a link to a target within the current page. When users click the *Return to Top* link, the browser window will jump to the position of the target. This target doesn't exist yet. For this link to work properly, you need to insert the destination as high on the page as possible.

**10** Scroll to the top of **events.html**. Position the cursor over the header element.

The mouse icon indicates that this part of the page (and its related code) is uneditable because the header and horizontal navigation menu are based on the site template. It's important to put the target at the very top, or a portion of the page may be obscured when the browser jumps to it. Since the top of the page is part of an *un*editable region, the best solution is to add the target directly to the template.

## Creating a link destination using an ID

By adding a unique ID to the template, you will be able to access it automatically throughout the site wherever you want to add a link back to the top of a page.

**1** Open the Assets panel. Click the Template category (▤) icon. Double-click **mygreen_temp** to open it.

**2** Click the tag selector for <header>. In the Property inspector, type **top** in the ID field, and press Enter/Return to complete the ID.

The tag selector changes to <header#top>; otherwise, there's no visible difference in the page. The big difference is in how the page reacts to the internal hyperlink.

**3** Save the file and update all template pages. Close the template.

**4** Switch to or open **events.html**, if necessary. Save the file and preview it in the default browser.

**5** Scroll down to the Class table. Click the *Return to Top* link.

The browser jumps back to the top of the page.

Now that the ID has been inserted in every page of the site by the template, you can copy the *Return to Top* link and paste it wherever you want to add this functionality.

**6** Switch to Dreamweaver. Insert the cursor in the *Return to Top* link. Select the `<p.ctr>` tag selector. Press Ctrl-C/Cmd-C.

**7** Scroll down to the bottom of **events.html**. Insert the cursor in the Class table, and select the `<table>` tag selector. Press the Right Arrow key to move the cursor after the closing `</table>` tag. Press Ctrl-V/Cmd-V.

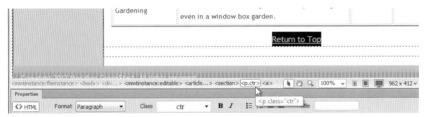

The `<p.ctr>` element and link appear at the bottom of the page.

**8** Save the file and preview it in the browser. Test both *Return to Top* links.

Both links can be used to jump back to the top of the document. In the next exercise, you'll learn how to use element attributes as link targets.

## Adding an ID to an HTML table

Named anchors can be used anywhere you want to create a link. But you don't need to add the extra code if there's a handy element nearby that you can add an ID attribute to.

**1** If necessary, open **events.html**. Insert the cursor anywhere in the Events table and select the `<table>` tag selector.

The Property inspector displays the attributes of the Events table.

**2** Open the ID field menu in the Property inspector.

Dreamweaver will display any ID defined by the CSS but currently unused within the page. There are no IDs displayed in the menu that can be applied to the table, but it's easy to create a new one.

> **Note:** An ID can be applied to any HTML element. They don't have to be referenced in the style sheet at all.

**Note:** When creating IDs, remember that they have to be unique names. IDs are case sensitive, so look out for typos.

**3** Insert the cursor in the ID field. Type **calendar** and press Enter/Return.

The tag selector now displays `<table#calendar>`. Since IDs are unique identifiers, they can be used for targeting specific content on a page. Don't forget to create an ID for the Class table too.

**4** Select the Class table, as in step 1. Insert the cursor in the ID field. Type **classes** and press Enter/Return.

The tag selector now displays `<table#classes>`. You'll learn how to link to these IDs in the next exercise.

**5** Save the file.

## Inserting Spry menu bars

The existing vertical menu is currently targeting pages within the site. It's a good start, but it could be better. In the example at the beginning of this lesson, the menu in the finished page enabled you to navigate directly to specific content in the site. These links were displayed as a submenu in the vertical menu.

Although your current menu doesn't have this functionality, you could add it to the existing code yourself if you were handy with JavaScript and CSS. But why go to all that bother when Dreamweaver offers everything you need in a prebuilt widget? A widget performs a specific set of functions in a browser, enabled by programming that combines HTML code, CSS, and JavaScript—otherwise known as Ajax and Adobe's Spry framework.

To create the menu and behavior you experienced earlier, you will have to replace the existing vertical menu with one of Dreamweaver's Spry widgets. Spry menu bars are an easy and powerful way to insert advanced functionality in your site without having to perform all the coding by hand. Since the vertical menu is stored in an uneditable region, you need to open the site template to replace it.

**1** In the Assets panel, double-click **mygreen_temp** in the Templates category to open the file. If you are using the Jumpstart method, the filename for the template will include the lesson number, such as **mygreen_temp_09**.

# Learning about Ajax and Spry

The early Internet was dominated by sites and applications that simply re-created existing products and services online. Web 2.0 ushered in a new era in Internet usability and interactivity. The concept behind Web 2.0 was to break down the existing barriers between customer and service or product, to make the online experience seamless.

The prime technology driving Web 2.0 is known as Ajax, which stands for Asynchronous JavaScript and XML. If you've ever scrolled through a Google Map or browsed a photo collection on Flickr, you've experienced what Ajax can do.

The key term in the Ajax acronym is *asynchronous*, which means "not at the same time." Normally, viewing pages on the web is a very linear process: You load a page and the browser displays it and everything remains unchanged until you reload the page or load a new page. In other words, if you don't reload the entire page, you can't change any of the information on the page.

Ajax throws out those old rules. Using JavaScript and XML data, Ajax-driven pages can actually update data on the fly without reloading the whole page. This makes the user experience much smoother and more interactive. Data can change at any time, either when it's updated on the server or when prompted by the user.

Most implementations of Ajax require an advanced knowledge of JavaScript and a great deal of hand coding. To ease the learning curve, Adobe has developed the Spry framework, which integrates Ajax seamlessly with Dreamweaver CS6. There are four sets of Spry tools:

- **Spry data**—Incorporates HTML or XML data into any webpage and allows for the interactive display of data. You will work with a Spry data set in Lesson 13, "Working with Online Data."

- **Spry effects**—Extend the Dreamweaver behavior library with advanced functionality to interactively affect page elements. Spry effects include the ability to fade, reveal, slide, highlight, and shake targeted page components.

- **Spry form widgets**—Combine form elements, such as text fields and lists, with JavaScript validation functions and user-friendly error messages. You will work with Spry form widgets in Lesson 12, "Working with Forms."

- **Spry layout widgets**—Provide a series of sophisticated layout controls, including tabbed and accordion panels. In Lesson 10, "Adding Interactivity," you will work with Spry Accordion widgets.

Visit Adobe Labs at http://labs.adobe.com/technologies/spry if you'd like to peek under the hood and learn more about Spry and how it works.

**2** Insert the cursor in the vertical menu, and click the <nav> tag selector. Press Delete.

**3** Select Insert > Spry > Spry Menu Bar.

**4** In the Spry Menu Bar dialog box, select Vertical, and click OK.

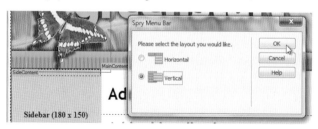

A new vertical menu appears in the sidebar. Note the blue bar that appears directly above the menu displaying the name Spry Menu Bar: MenuBar1. The menu features four items and a default set of CSS formatting. You will adjust the width and appearance of the menu in the next exercise. Dreamweaver provides special formatting capabilities geared toward Spry widgets.

**5** Click the blue bar above the Spry menu.

The Property inspector displays a special interface you can use to add, delete, and modify links within the menu.

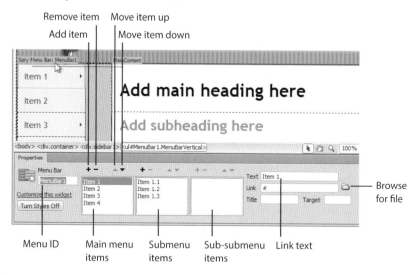

**6** Before customizing the menu bar, choose File > Save. If Dreamweaver asks you about copying dependent files, click OK.

Dreamweaver inserts into your site root folder a folder called SpryAssets, which will contain necessary components for any Spry widget. Custom CSS and JavaScript files needed for the menu bar will also be added to this folder. When files are added to the folder, Dreamweaver will automatically link the template to them.

The Spry menu bar can be modified directly within the Property inspector.

**7** In the first column of the Property inspector, click Item 1 to select it. In the Text field, select the *Item 1* text. Type **Green News** to replace it, and press Enter/ Return to complete the change.

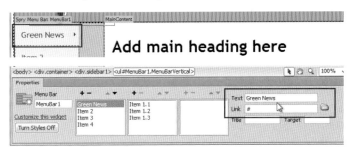

The text *Green News* appears in the first menu item on the screen and in the Property inspector. The Property inspector also provides the means to add the hyperlink to the item.

**8** In the Property inspector, click the Browse ( ) icon.

**9** Select **news.html** in the site root folder. Click OK/Choose.

The text *../news.html* is entered in the field. Dreamweaver inserted the notation *../* into the link because the file you are working in at the moment is stored in a sub-folder of the site root folder. Remember to add this notation to any links you create manually.

Note that the Green News button features three sub-items in the Property inspector. Note the triangle icon on the button in the menu. This graphic indicates to the user that the button contains a submenu. Dreamweaver makes it easy to add or delete sub-items.

10 Click Item 1.1 to select it. Click the Remove Item (−) icon above the column to delete the sub-item.

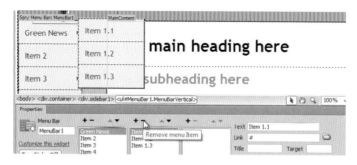

Item 1.1 is removed from the list.

11 Delete Item 1.2 and Item 1.3.

When the last sub-item is removed, Dreamweaver automatically removes the submenu icon from the Green News button.

12 Select Item 2 and change the text field to read **Green Products**.

There is no Products page to link to yet, but this doesn't stop you from entering the filename in the Link field manually.

13 Select the hash mark (#) and type **../products.html** in the Link field. Press Enter/Return to complete the change.

14 Select Item 3. Change the Text field to read **Green Events** and link the item to **events.html** in the site root folder.

▶ **Warning:** Whenever you manually type hyperlink names and path information, keep track of the exact spelling and other details you use. When the target file is created later, make sure it matches. Typos and even differences in case can cause links to fail.

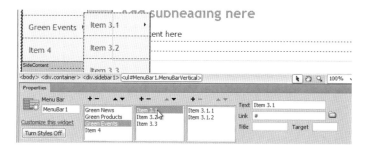

Note that the Green Events button features three sub-items and two sub-sub-items. You'll use the submenu to link to the Events and Class tables.

**15** Select Item 3.1 and change the Text field to read **Events Calendar**. In the Link field, browse and select **events.html** from the site root folder.

The link at the moment will merely open and display the page starting at the very top as normal. To target the Events table, you need to add the ID you created earlier to the link code.

**16** In the Link field, insert the cursor at the end of the filename **events.html**. Type **#calendar** and press Enter/Return.

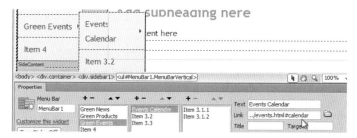

The text now reads `../events.html#calendar` in the Link field. Note that the Events Calendar item features two sub-items of its own.

**17** Select and delete Item 3.1.1 and Item 3.1.2 in the Property inspector.

**18** Change Item 3.2 to read **Class Schedule**, and enter **../events.html#classes** in the Link field.

Before you test the link functionality, let's finish the rest of the menu.

**19** Delete Item 3.3.

**20** Change Item 4 to **Green Travel**, and enter **../travel.html** in the Link field.

You have re-created four of the five items from the original menu, but there's still one missing. The Property inspector makes it simple to add new menu items.

**21** Click the Add Item (✚) icon above the first column to add a new item.

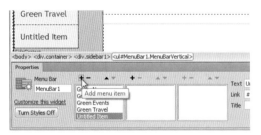

A new *Untitled Item* appears at the bottom of the list.

**22** Replace the text *Untitled Item* with **Green Tips** and link the item to **tips.html** in the site root folder.

**23** Save the file. Update all child files.

**24** Save all files. Open and preview **events.html** in the browser. Check out the menu behavior and test the sub-item links to Events Calendar and Class Schedule.

**Note:** Notice that the sub-item isn't wide enough to display the link text on one line. You will adjust the width of the sub-item in an upcoming exercise.

The menu behavior is similar to that of the menu you tested at the beginning of this lesson. When you hover over the *Green Events* item, a submenu pops open showing you links to the events calendar and class schedule. When the link is clicked, the browser jumps down to each table automatically.

**25** Switch back to Dreamweaver.

The completed Spry menu appears in the sidebar. In the next exercise, you'll learn how to modify this menu by hand.

## Modifying Spry menus directly

Although it may look like magic, Spry components are built with everyday HTML and CSS, with a little JavaScript to spice it up a bit. Most widgets can be modified directly in Code or Design view, if desired. Don't be afraid to dive into the code and create or edit the menu by hand.

**1** Switch to or open the site template, if necessary. Insert the cursor into the Spry menu. Click the tag selector `<ul#MenuBar1.MenuBarVertical>` to display the Spry menu interface in the Property inspector.

**2** In the Property inspector, click the Turn Styles Off button.

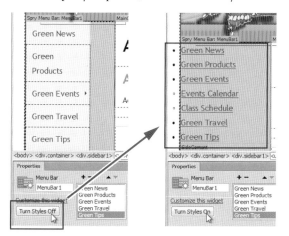

In Design view, you see that the list is displayed without CSS formatting. Note that parts of the list are formatted differently, correlating to the main and sub-item levels of the menu. Some may find it easier to work in the document window instead of in the Property inspector. The menu can now be edited just as any other HTML list. It's a simple matter now to add a new link.

**3** Insert the cursor at the end of the bulleted text *Green Tips*, and press Enter/Return to insert a new line.

The new line is formatted as a list item. Let's add a link to a tentative new page in the site.

**4** Type **Green Club** and select the text.

The text is part of the list, but it's not a hyperlink yet.

**5** In the Link field of the Property inspector, type # and press Enter/Return to create a link placeholder.

You can even add sub-items using this method. Since the club is for members only, let's add a login page as a sub-item.

**6** Insert the cursor at the end of the text *Green Club*. Press Enter/Return to insert a new line. Type **Member Login** and select the text. In the Link field of the Property inspector, enter #.

Note that it is formatted identically to the main level items.

**7** In the Property inspector, click the Blockquote button to indent the text.

Although it's hard to see in this view, the Member Login item has actually been indented. But the difference between the list items is very subtle and takes the form of a different type of bullet character. If you study the tag selectors and examine the bullets carefully, you'll see that *Member Login* is formatted in the same way as the sub-items *Events Calendar* and *Class Schedule*.

▶ **Tip:** If you don't see the Turn Styles On button, insert the cursor anywhere in the Spry-based menu and click the blue bar above it to select it again.

**8** Click the tag selector <ul#MenuBar1.MenuBarVertical> to display the Spry menu interface in the Property inspector. Click the Turn Styles On button to return to the styled appearance.

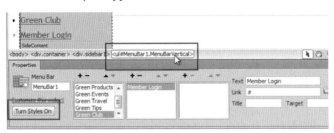

When you turn the formatting back on, you may notice that the Green Club item doesn't show the submenu icon, as Green Events does.

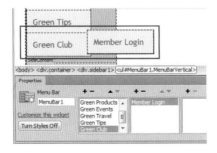

**9** Insert the cursor in the Green Club item. Examine the tag selector.

The tag selector shows <a> for a normal hyperlink element.

**10** Insert the cursor in the Green Events item. Examine the tag selector.

The tag selector shows `<a.MenuBarItemSubmenu>`. Because you didn't use the Spry interface to add the sub-item, Dreamweaver didn't apply a needed class to the Green Club parent element. This class applies CSS formatting for the submenu, including the submenu icon. You can apply the class using the Property inspector.

**11** Insert the cursor in the Green Club item. Select the `<a>` tag selector. Choose MenuBarItemSubmenu from the Class menu.

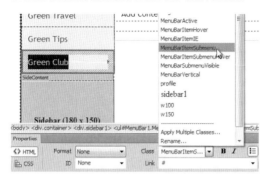

The button is properly formatted now and displays the submenu icon. As you can see, the Spry interface offers several advantages over hand coding.

**12** Save the file.

Whenever Dreamweaver saves a document containing Spry components, it inserts the dependent CSS and JavaScript files in the SpryAssets folder for you automatically. If you delete a component and the dependent files are no longer needed, Dreamweaver deletes any link reference to them from the document code. The Spry interface and automatic file management are two more reasons why you'll want to use Dreamweaver in any HTML-based workflows.

## Customizing the appearance of the Spry menu bar

As you can see, the Spry menu bar offers a way to quickly and easily create a sophisticated, professional-looking menu. Styling a Spry component is no different than styling the original HTML menu it replaced. You'll need to modify the width and styling of this menu to make it conform to the layout and the site color scheme. It's important to remember that Spry elements are normally styled by their own CSS files.

1 Open the site template, if necessary. Open the CSS Styles panel and scroll to the bottom of the list of style sheets.

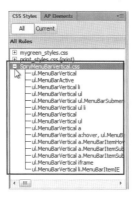

A new style sheet—**SpryMenuBarVertical.css**—has been added by Dreamweaver.

2 Expand the **SpryMenuBarVertical.css** style sheet.

This style sheet includes the formatting instructions for the Spry vertical menu. You should feel confident enough by now in your CSS skills to modify the style sheet without any help. Feel free to try, or simply follow these instructions.

3 Insert the cursor in the Green News item in the Spry menu. Press Ctrl-Alt-N/ Cmd-Opt-N to open the Code Navigator, or click the Code Navigator (✸) icon when it appears.

The Code Navigator window appears, listing the style sheets and rules that format this item.

4 Examine the list of CSS rules that format this item. Pay special attention to the rules in **SpryMenuBarVertical.css**.

5 Using the cursor, hover over each rule in this style sheet until you identify the properties you'll need to modify.

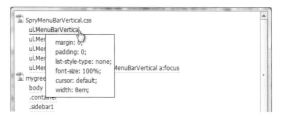

You're looking for rules that specifically apply to width, color, and hyperlink behavior. The ul.MenuBarVertical rule sets the width of the menu.

**6** In the CSS Styles panel, click the `ul.MenuBarVertical` rule and examine its properties.

This rule sets the width of the `<ul>` element to 8 ems. Since the current site is based on a fixed-width layout, these settings should be changed to match. The new vertical menu is part of the sidebar element, which was originally set to a width of 180 pixels.

● **Note:** Whenever you set the width of a container using absolute measurements, like pixels or points, you should anticipate that the container, and your layout, may break when visitors override your chosen settings to enlarge the text. Fortunately, most modern browsers now magnify the webpage rather than simply enlarging the text.

# Em or ex? It's all relative

An em is a relative measurement system used in graphic design, based on the width of the capital letter *M* in the current default font for the site. An ex is a measurement based on the size of the lowercase *x*. Designers use ems and exes when they want to format a text container to preserve certain line breaks. A container width specified in ems will scale along with the text as it gets larger. A container set to a fixed width won't scale as the text gets larger; to fit, the text has to wrap to additional lines.

> Four score and seven years ago our fathers brought forth, up on this continent, a new nation, conceived in Liberty, and dedicated to the proposition that all men are created equal.

> Four score and seven years ago our fathers brought forth, up on this continent, a new nation, conceived in Liberty, and dedicated to the proposition that all men are created equal.

Fixed-width containers: text reflows

> Four score and seven years ago our fathers brought forth, up on this continent, a new nation, conceived in Liberty, and dedicated to the proposition that all men are created equal.

> Four score and seven years ago our fathers brought forth, up on this continent, a new nation, conceived in Liberty, and dedicated to the proposition that all men are created equal.

Em-width containers: no reflow

That's because the em measurement is based on the size of the font and not on an arbitrary pixel or other fixed measurement. This means that if the user chooses to override your chosen font size in the browser, any web structure based on ems or exes will scale up or down proportionally to adapt to the new font size. That way, line breaks will be preserved and text-based menus won't break or reflow as the text enlarges, as they will in designs using pixels or fixed measurements.

Width set in pixels: text wraps

Width set in ems: everything scales

**7** Change the width value to **180px**.

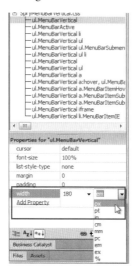

Note that the width of the menu doesn't change. The `ul.MenuBarVertical` rule establishes the maximum size of the menu, but because `<ul>` is not a block-level element, the width of the menu is actually controlled by a different rule. Only one other rule specifies a width setting for the first-level items— namely, `ul.MenuBarVertical li`.

**8** In the CSS Styles panel, select `ul.MenuBarVertical li` and change the width to **180px** in the Properties section.

The Spry menu assumes the full width of `<div.sidebar1>`, matching the size of the previous vertical menu you replaced. In this case, everything seems to be working fine, but that doesn't mean it always will. Replacing existing structures in a web template can be dangerous. The new element can conflict with the existing layout and possibly break it, as it did in Lesson 4 "Creating a Page Layout." Keep an eye on the sizes of the other elements within your layout. Remember that there is an overall wrapper or container element that has a fixed size—in this case, 950 pixels. A border, margin, or padding setting could have an unexpected interaction that might upset your carefully created layout.

For example, did you notice that there are two ul.MenuBarVertical rules in the style sheet? One adds a 1-pixel border on the menu that is unnecessary in this layout design. Let's delete it.

9   Select the second ul.MenuBarVertical rule, which contains the following specifications: 1px solid #CCC. In the CSS Styles panel, click the Delete ( 🗑 ) icon to remove the extraneous rule.

The second ul.MenuBarVertical rule has only one property—the border specification—and can be deleted without affecting the rest of the layout. Let's continue to format the Spry menu to conform to the site design theme.

10  Double-click the ul.MenuBarVertical a rule to edit it.

11  In the Type category, enter **#FFC** in the Color field and **90%** in the Font-size field. In the Background category, change the Background-color field to **#090**. In the Box category, change all Padding fields to **0.5em**.

12  In the Border category, enter **solid**, **1px**, **#0C0** for the Top border fields. Enter **solid**, **1px**, **#060** for the Right border fields. Enter **solid**, **1px**, **#060** for the Bottom border fields. Enter **solid**, **1px**, **#0C0** for the Left border fields. Click OK.

Watch for any problems resulting from adding the 1-pixel border to each menu item. It may break the layout. If it does, you'll need to adjust the width of one of the page's structural elements to compensate.

13  Save the template and update all child pages. Select File > Save All to save all open files. Click the Live view button. Position the cursor over each of the Spry menu items and observe the behavior.

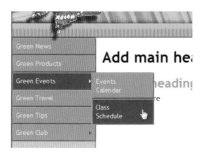

The menu is nearly finished. The initial state of the menu looks good, but the a:hover state of the hyperlinks doesn't conform to the site color scheme. To investigate the situation, you can access the Code Navigator even in Live view.

**14** While hovering over the menu item, right-click the Spry menu. Choose Code Navigator from the context menu. Identify any rules affecting the a:hover state of the menu hyperlinks.

There are two rules that apply both text and background colors to the a:hover state.

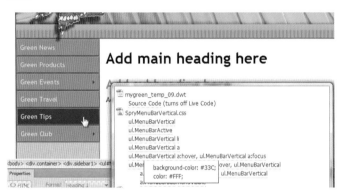

**15** Click the Live view button to turn it off.

**16** In the CSS Styles panel, click the ul.MenuBarVertical a:hover, ul.MenuBarVertical a:focus rule. In the Properties section, change the Color value to **#FFC** and the Background-color value to **#060**.

**17** In the CSS Styles panel, click the ul.MenuBarVertical a.MenuBarItemHover, ul.MenuBarVertical a.MenuBarItemSubmenuHover, ul.MenuBarVertical a.MenuBarSubmenuVisible rule. In the Properties section, change the Color value to **#FFC** and the Background-color value to **#060**. Click OK.

**18** Save all files. Test the menu behavior in Live view or the default browser.

The color and behavior matches the menu you tested at the beginning of the lesson. But the sub-items would look better on one line. How would you correct this problem? Here are two obvious fixes: shorten the text or make the button wider.

## Editing CSS using the Code Navigator

The Code Navigator isn't just a tool for examining CSS code; it can also help you to edit it.

**1** Insert the cursor in the Spry menu. Click the blue bar above the vertical menu to access the Spry menu interface in the Property inspector. Select the item Green Events in the first column of the interface. Select the item Events Calendar in the second column.

The sub-items for the Green Events button appear in the Spry interface and in the Design view document window.

► **Tip:** The sub-items will remain displayed as long as the Events or Class sub-items are selected in the Property inspector. To hide the sub-item menu, select any parent element.

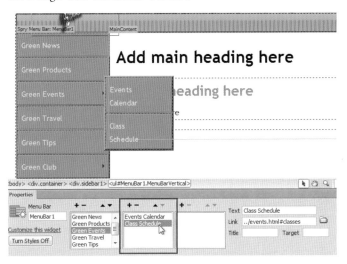

**2** In Design view, insert the cursor in the sub-item Events Calendar. Press Ctrl-Alt-N/Cmd-Opt-N to activate the Code Navigator. Examine the rules to find the one that formats the width of the sub-items.

As with the level-1 items, there are two rules that apply the width to the sub-items `ul.MenuBarVertical ul` and `ul.MenuBarVertical ul li`.

**3** In the Code Navigator window, click the `ul.MenuBarVertical ul` rule.

Dreamweaver switches to Split view automatically, loads **SpryMenuBarVertical.css** in the code half, and automatically positions the screen at the line in the file for `ul.MenuBarVertical ul`.

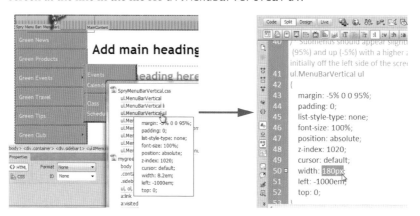

**4** Change the Width value to **180px**.

**5** Use the Code Navigator as in steps 2 through 3 to access the `ul.MenuBarVertical ul li` rule. Change the Width value to **180px**.

**6** Save the file. Update all child pages.

You may need to refresh the Design view window to see the results of the changes.

**7** Click the Refresh Design view ( **C** ) icon or press F5.

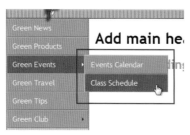

The sub-items are wider now, allowing the link text to fit on one line, as desired. But you may notice that there is a 1-pixel gray border on the submenu. The gray border doesn't fit with the site theme. A darker green border would be more appropriate. As with the base menu, there is a duplicate rule that applies only the gray border.

**8** Change the border color in the second `ul.MenuBarVertical ul` rule to **#060**.

**9** Save the file. Update all child pages and refresh the Design view display.

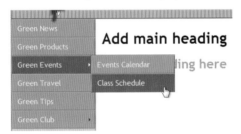

The Spry menu is complete and styled properly.

**10** Close the template.

If you don't need to troubleshoot the template components themselves, you should be able to make most of your future changes to the CSS directly from any normal site page. Since the CSS files are external to the template, changes can be made without the template being open, even to items within the uneditable regions of each page.

# Checking your page

Dreamweaver will automatically check your page for browser compatibility, accessibility, and broken links. In this exercise, you'll check your links and learn what you can do in case of a browser compatibility problem.

**1** If necessary, open **contact_us.html**.

**Tip:** You can also check links for the entire website by selecting Check Links For Entire Current Local Site from the Check Links (  ) icon or by choosing Site > Check Links Sitewide.

2   Choose File > Check Page > Links.

A Link Checker panel opens. The Link Checker panel reports a broken link to **index.html** and to the other links you created for nonexistent pages. You'll make these pages later, so there's no need to worry about fixing this broken link now. The Link Checker will also find broken links to external sites, should you have any.

3   Right-click the Link Checker tab and choose Close Panel Group.

4   Choose File > Check Page > Browser Compatibility.

The Browser Compatibility report panel opens, listing any identified compatibility problems along with the file that contains the error and a description of it. No issues were detected, but if there had been, you could click the Check Adobe.com link in the lower-right corner of the panel to receive more information about the issue directly from Adobe.

5   Double-click the Browser Compatibility tab to collapse it.

You've made big changes to the appearance of the pages in this lesson by adding a Spry menu bar and by creating links to specific positions on a page, to email, and to an external site. You also created a link that uses an image as the clickable item and re-created the main navigation menu using a Spry menu bar. Finally, you checked your page for broken links and browser compatibility.

# Review questions

1 Describe two ways to insert a link into a page.

2 What information is required to create a link to an external webpage?

3 What's the difference between standard page links and email links?

4 What are the benefits of using Spry menu bars?

5 How can you check to see if your links will work properly?

# Review answers

1 Select text or a graphic, and then in the Property inspector, select the Browse For File icon next to the Link field and navigate to the desired page. A second method is to drag the Point To File icon to a file within the Files panel.

2 Link to an external page by typing or copying and pasting the full web address (a fully formed URL) in the Link field of the Property inspector.

3 A standard page link opens a new page or moves the view to a position somewhere on the page. An email link opens a blank email message window if the visitor has an email application installed.

4 All the work of setting up the style rules to make a list appear like a horizontal or vertical menu bar has been done for you, and so has the work of writing the JavaScript to make pop-up submenus function.

5 Run the Link Checker to test links on each page or sitewide.

# 10 ADDING INTERACTIVITY

## Lesson Overview

In this lesson, you'll add Web 2.0 functionality to your webpages by doing the following:

- Using Dreamweaver behaviors to create an image rollover effect

- Inserting a Spry Accordion widget

 This lesson will take about 1 hour to complete. Before beginning, make sure you have copied the files for Lesson 10 to your hard drive as described in the "Getting Started" section at the beginning of the book. If you are starting from scratch in this lesson, use the method described in the "Jumpstart" section of "Getting Started."

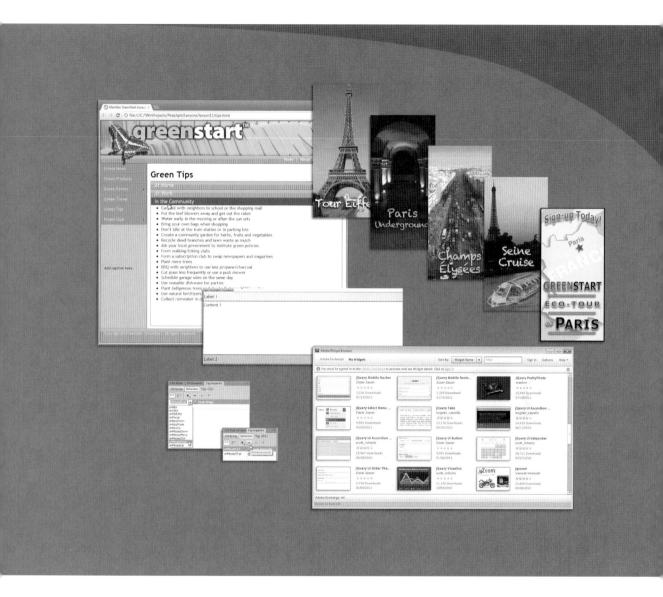

Dreamweaver can create sophisticated interactive
effects with behaviors and accordion panels using
Adobe's Spry framework.

# Learning about Dreamweaver behaviors

The term Web 2.0 was coined to describe a major change in the user experience on the Internet from mostly static pages, featuring text, graphics, and simple links, to a new paradigm of dynamic webpages filled with video, animation, and interactive content. Dreamweaver has always led the industry in providing a variety of tools to drive this movement, from its tried-and-true collection of JavaScript behaviors and Spry widgets to the latest support for jQuery Mobile and even PhoneGap. In this lesson, we'll explore two of these capabilities: Dreamweaver behaviors and Spry Accordions.

A Dreamweaver *behavior* is predefined JavaScript code that performs an action—such as opening a browser window or showing or hiding a page element—when it is triggered by an event, such as a mouse click. Applying a behavior is a three-step process:

1. Create or select the page element that you want to trigger the behavior.

2. Choose the behavior to apply.

3. Specify the settings or parameters of the behavior.

**Note:** To access the Behaviors panel and menu, you must have a file open.

The triggering element often involves a hyperlink applied to a range of text or to an image. In some cases, the behavior is not intended to load a new page, so it will employ a dummy link enabled by the hash (#) sign, similar to ones that you used in Lesson 9, "Working with Navigation." The Swap Image behavior you will use in this lesson does not require a link to function, but keep this in mind when you work with other behaviors.

Dreamweaver offers more than 20 built-in behaviors, all accessed from the Tag inspector (Window > Tag Inspector). Hundreds of other useful behaviors can be downloaded from the Internet for free or a small fee. Many are available from the online Dreamweaver Exchange, which you can access by clicking the Add Behavior (✚￬) icon in the Tag inspector and choosing Get More Behaviors from the pop-up menu. When the Adobe Marketplace & Exchange site loads in the browser, click the link to Dreamweaver for a full list of plug-ins and behaviors.

The Adobe Marketplace & Exchange offers tons of resources for web designers and developers, including both free and paid add-ons to Dreamweaver and other Creative Suite applications.

The following are some of the types of functionality available to you using the built-in Dreamweaver behaviors:

• Opening a browser window

• Swapping one image for another to create what is called a *rollover effect*

• Fading images or page areas in and out

• Growing or shrinking graphics

- Displaying pop-up messages

- Changing the text or other HTML content within a given area

- Showing or hiding sections of the page

- Calling a custom-defined JavaScript function

Not all behaviors are available all the time. Certain behaviors become available only in the presence and selection of certain page elements, such as images or links. For example, you can't use the Swap Image behavior unless an image is present.

Each behavior invokes its own unique dialog box that provides relevant options and specifications. For instance, the dialog box for the Open Browser Window behavior enables you to open a new browser window, set its width, height, and other attributes, and set the URL of the displayed resource. After the behavior is defined, it is listed in the Tag inspector with its chosen triggering action. As with other behaviors, these specifications can be modified at any time.

Behaviors are extremely flexible, and multiple behaviors can be applied to the same trigger. For example, you could swap one image for another and change the text of the accompanying image caption—and do it all with one click. While some effects may appear to happen simultaneously, behaviors are actually triggered in sequence. When multiple behaviors are applied, you can choose the order in which the behaviors are processed.

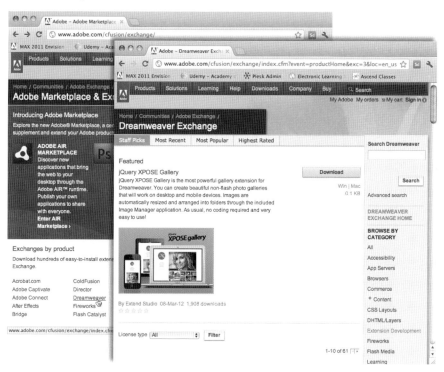

# Previewing the completed file

● **Note:** If you are starting from scratch in this exercise, see the "Jumpstart" instructions in the "Getting Started" section at the beginning of the book. Then, follow the steps in this exercise.

● **Note:** The Image Tag Accessibility Attributes dialog box doesn't appear automatically when you insert an image this way. To add Alt text to this image, use the Alt field in the Property inspector.

In the first part of this lesson, you'll create a new page for GreenStart's travel services. Let's preview the completed page in the browser.

1   Launch Adobe Dreamweaver CS6.

2   If necessary, press F8/Shift-Cmd-F to open the Files panel, and choose DW-CS6 from the site list.

3   In the Files panel, expand the lesson10 folder. Right-click **travel_finished.html**, choose Preview In Browser from the context menu, and select your primary browser.

    The page includes Dreamweaver behaviors.

4   If Microsoft Internet Explorer is your primary browser, a message may appear above the browser window indicating that JavaScript is prevented from running. If so, click Allow Blocked Content.

5   Position the cursor over the heading *Tour Eiffel*. Observe the image to the right of the text.

    The existing image swaps for one of the Eiffel Tower.

6   Move the pointer to the heading *Paris Underground*. Observe the image to the right of the text.

As the pointer moves off the heading *Tour Eiffel*, the image reverts to the Eco-Tour ad. Then, as the pointer moves over the heading *Paris Underground*, the ad image swaps for one of underground Paris.

7  Pass the pointer over each of the headings and observe the image behavior.

The image alternates between the Eco-Tour ad and images of each of the cities. This effect is the Swap Image behavior.

8  When you're finished, close the browser window and return to Dreamweaver.

In the next exercise, you will learn how to work with Dreamweaver behaviors.

## Working with Dreamweaver behaviors

Adding Dreamweaver behaviors to your layout is a simple point-and-click operation. But before you can add the behaviors, you have to create the travel page.

1  Open the Assets panel and click the Template category icon. Right-click the site template and choose New From Template from the context menu.

A new document window opens based on the template.

2  Save the new document as **travel.html**.

3  Double-click the image placeholder in the sidebar. Navigate to the site images folder. Select **train.jpg** and click OK/Choose.

The train image appears in the sidebar.

4  In the Property inspector Alt field, enter **Electric trains are green** and press Enter/Return.

5  Open the Files panel and expand the lesson10 > resources folder. Double-click the **travel-caption.txt** file.

The caption text opens in Dreamweaver.

6  Press Ctrl-A/Cmd-A to select all the text. Press Ctrl-C/Cmd-C to copy the text. Close **travel-caption.txt**.

7  Select the caption placeholder in the sidebar. Press Ctrl-V/Cmd-V to paste the new caption text.

8  In the Files panel in the resources folder, double-click **travel-text.html**.

The **travel-text.html** file contains a table and text for the travel page. Note that the text and table are unformatted.

9  In Design view, press Ctrl-A/Cmd-A to select all the text along with the table. Press Ctrl-C/Cmd-C to copy the content. Close **travel-text.html**.

10  Select the main heading placeholder *Add main heading here* in **travel.html**. Type **Green Travel** to replace the text.

**11** Select the heading placeholder *Add subheading here* and type **Eco-Touring** to replace it.

**12** Select the <p> tag selector for the text *Add content here*. Press Ctrl-V/Cmd-V to paste the travel text.

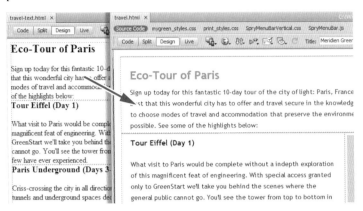

The content from **travel-text.html** appears. It assumes the default formatting for text and tables applied by the style sheet you created in Lesson 7, "Working with Text, Lists, and Tables."

Let's insert the Eco-Tour ad, which will be the base image for the Swap Image behavior.

**13** Double-click the SideAd image placeholder. Navigate to the site images folder and select **ecotour.png**. Click OK/Choose.

The placeholder is replaced by the Eco-Tour ad. But before you can apply the Swap Image behavior, you have to identify the image you want to swap. You do this by giving the image an ID.

**14** If necessary, select **ecotour.png** in the layout. Select the existing ID SideAd in the Property inspector. Type **ecotour** and press Enter/Return. Enter the text **Eco-Tour of Paris** in the Alt field.

**Tip:** Although it takes more time, it's a good practice to give all your images unique IDs.

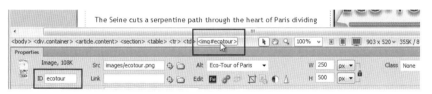

**15** Save the file.

Next, you will create a Swap Image behavior for **ecotour.jpg**.

## Applying a behavior

As described earlier, many behaviors are context sensitive, based on the elements or structure present. A Swap Image behavior can be applied to any document text element.

**1** Choose Window > Behaviors to open the Tag inspector.

**2** Insert the cursor in the *Tour Eiffel* text and select the <h3> tag selector.

**3** Click the Add Behavior (➕) icon. Choose Swap Image from the behavior list.

**Note:** Users of previous versions of Dreamweaver may be looking for the Behaviors panel. It's now called the Tag inspector.

The Swap Image dialog box appears, listing any images on the page that are available for this behavior. This behavior can replace one or more of these images at a time.

**4** Select the item image "ecotour" and click Browse.

**5** In the Select Image Source dialog box, select **tower.jpg** from the site images folder. Click OK/Choose.

**6** In the Swap Image dialog box, select the Preload Images option, if necessary, and click OK.

**Note:** The Preload Images option forces the browser to download all images necessary for the behavior before the page loads. That way, when the user clicks the trigger, the image swap will occur without any lags or glitches.

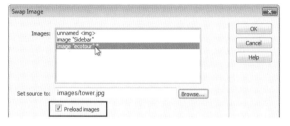

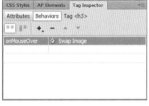

A Swap Image behavior is added to the Tag inspector with an attribute of onMouseOver. Attributes can be changed, if desired, using the Tag inspector.

7 Click the onMouseOver attribute to open the pop-up menu and examine the options.

The menu provides a list of trigger events, most of which are self-explanatory. For now, however, leave the attribute as onMouseOver.

8 Save the file and click Live view to test the behavior. Position the cursor over the *Tour Eiffel* text.

When the cursor passes over the text, the Eco-Tour ad is replaced by the image of the Eiffel Tower. But there is a small problem. When the cursor moves away from the text, the original image doesn't return. The reason is simple: you didn't tell it to. To bring back the original image, you have to add another command—Swap Image Restore—to the same element.

## Applying a Swap Image Restore behavior

In some instances, a specific action requires more than one behavior. To bring back the Eco-Tour ad once the mouse moves off the trigger, you have to add a restore function.

1 Return to Design view. Insert the cursor in the *Tour Eiffel* heading and examine the Tag inspector.

The inspector displays the currently assigned behavior. You don't need to select the element completely; Dreamweaver assumes you want to modify the entire trigger.

2 Click the Add Behavior (**+**▾) icon and choose Swap Image Restore from the pop-up menu. Click OK in the Swap Image Restore dialog box to complete the command.

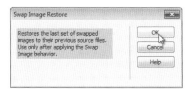

The Swap Image Restore behavior appears in the Tag inspector with an attribute of `onMouseOut`.

3  Switch to Code view and examine the markup for the *Tour Eiffel* text.

```
‹h3 onMouseOver="MM_swapImage('ecotour','','images/tower.jpg',1)" onMouseOut="MM_swapImgRestore()">
```

The trigger events—`onMouseOver` and `onMouseOut`—were added as attributes to the `<h3>` element. The rest of the JavaScript code was inserted in the document's `<head>` section.

4  Save the file and click Live view to test the behavior. Test the text trigger *Tour Eiffel*.

When the pointer passes over the text, the Eco-Tour image is replaced by the one of the Eiffel Tower and then reappears when the pointer is withdrawn. The behavior functions as desired, but there's nothing visibly "different" about the text to indicate that something magical will happen if the user rolls the pointer over the heading. Since most Internet users are familiar with the interactivity provided by hyperlinks, applying a link placeholder on the heading will encourage the visitor to explore the effect.

## Removing applied behaviors

Before you can apply a behavior to a hyperlink, you need to remove the current Swap Image and Swap Image Restore behaviors.

1  Open the Tag inspector, if necessary. Insert the cursor in the *Tour Eiffel* text.

    The Tag inspector displays the two applied events. It doesn't matter which one you delete first.

2  Select the Swap Image event. In the Tag inspector, click the Remove Event (−) icon. Select the Swap Image Restore event. In the Tag inspector, click the Remove Event icon.

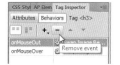

    Both events are removed. Dreamweaver will also remove any unneeded JavaScript code.

3  Save the file and check the text in Live view again.

The text no longer triggers the Swap Image behavior. To reapply the behavior, you need to add a link or link placeholder to the heading.

## Adding behaviors to hyperlinks

Behaviors can be added to hyperlinks, even if the link doesn't load a new document. For this exercise, you'll add a link placeholder to the heading to support the desired behavior.

1 Select the text *Tour Eiffel* within the <h3> element. In the Property inspector Link field, type # and press Enter/Return to create the link placeholder.

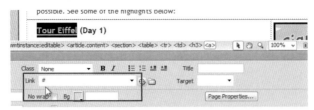

The text displays with the default hyperlink styling.

2 Insert the cursor in the link. In the Tag inspector, click the Add Behavior icon and choose Swap Image from the pop-up menu.

As long as the cursor is still inserted anywhere in the link, the behavior will be applied to the entire link markup.

3 In the Swap Image dialog box, select the item `image "ecotour"`. Browse and select **tower.jpg** from the site images folder. Click OK/Choose.

4 In the Swap Image dialog box, select the Preload Images and Restore Images `onMouseOut` options, if necessary, and click OK.

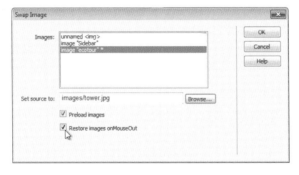

The Swap Image event appears in the Tag inspector along with a Swap Image Restore event. Since the behavior was applied all at once, Dreamweaver provides the restore functionality as a productivity enhancement.

5 Select and apply a link (#) placeholder to the *Paris Underground* text. Apply the Swap Image behavior to the link. Select the image **underground.jpg** from the site images folder.

6 Repeat step 5 for the *Seine River Dinner Cruise* text. Select the image **cruise.jpg**.

7 Repeat step 5 for the *Champs Élysées* text. Select the image **champs.jpg**.

The swap image behaviors are now complete, but the text and link appearance don't match the site color scheme. Let's create custom CSS rules to format them accordingly. You will create two rules: one for the heading element and another for the link itself.

**8** Insert the cursor in any of the rollover links. In the CSS Styles panel, select the `.content section h2` rule in the **mygreen_styles.css** style sheet. Click the New CSS Rule icon.

**9** If necessary, select Compound from the Selector Type menu. In the rule Name field, enter `.content section h3` and click OK to create the rule.

**10** In the Box category, enter the following specifications:
Top-margin: **0px**
Bottom-margin: **5px**

**11** Click OK to complete the rule.

**12** Create a new CSS rule named `.content section h3 a` and enter the following specifications:
Font-size: **140%**
Color: **#090**

**13** Click OK to complete the rule.

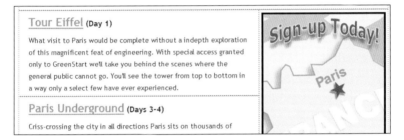

The headings are now styled to match the site theme.

**14** Save the file and test the behaviors in Live view.

The Swap Image behavior works successfully on all links.

**15** Close **travel.html**.

In addition to eye-catching effects, Dreamweaver also provides structural components—such as Spry widgets—that conserve space and add more interactive flair to your website.

# Working with Spry Accordion widgets

The Spry Accordion widget allows you to organize a lot of content into a compact space. In the Accordion widget, the tabs are stacked and when opened, they expand vertically rather than side by side. When you click a tab, the panel slides open with a smooth action. The panels are set to a specific height, and if the content is taller or wider than the panel itself, scroll bars appear automatically. Let's preview the completed layout.

**Note:** If you are starting from scratch in this exercise, see the "Jumpstart" instructions in the "Getting Started" section at the beginning of the book. Then, follow the steps in this exercise.

1   In the Files panel, select **tips_finished.html** from the lesson10 folder and preview it in your primary browser.

The page content is divided among three panels using the Spry Accordion widget.

2   Click each panel in turn to open and close them.

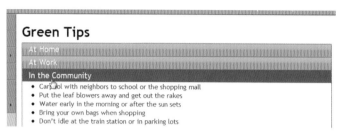

3   Close your browser and return to Dreamweaver.

## Inserting a Spry Accordion widget

In this exercise, you'll incorporate a Spry Accordion widget into your layout.

1   Open **tips.html**.

The page consists of three bulleted lists separated by <h2> headings. Let's start by inserting a Spry Accordion before the first <h2>.

2   Insert the cursor in the heading *At Home* and select the <h2> tag selector. Press the Left Arrow key once to move the cursor before the opening <h2> tag.

3   In the Spry category of the Insert panel, click the Spry Accordion button.

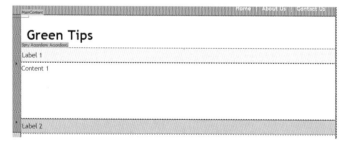

Dreamweaver inserts the Spry Accordion widget element. The initial element is a two-panel Accordion widget that appears with the top panel open. As with the Spry menu bar you created in Lesson 9, "Working with Navigation," a blue tab appears above the new object—this one with the title *Spry Accordion: Accordion1*.

4   Select the placeholder text *Label 1* and type **At Home** to replace the text.

Scroll down and insert the cursor into the <h2> heading *At Home* and select the <h2> tag selector. Press Delete.

5 Insert the cursor in the first bullet, *Wash clothes in cold water*, and select the `<ul>` tag selector. Press Ctrl-X/Cmd-X to cut the whole list.

6 Select the text *Content 1* in the top Accordion widget panel. Press Ctrl-V/Cmd-V to paste the bulleted list.

In Design view, you may see only part of the content you added, because scrolling isn't active in Design view.

7 To see or edit all the content, right-click the content window and choose Element View > Full from the context menu.

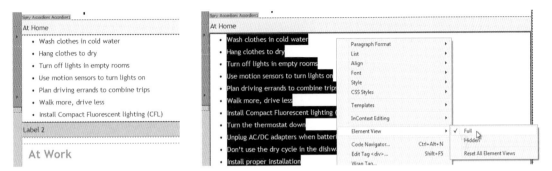

The entire list of tips appears.

8 Right-click the content window and choose Element View > Hidden from the context menu to reset the size of the panel.

9 Delete the `<h2>` heading *At Work*. Select and cut the subsequent `<ul>` element containing the "Work" tips.

10 Position the cursor over the bar displaying the text *Label 2*. Click the eye (👁) icon to open panel 2, if necessary.

11 Select the text *Label 2* and type **At Work**.

12 Select the text *Content 2* and paste the `<ul>` element.

Two of the panels are complete, but you need to insert a new panel to complete the Spry Accordion widget.

## Adding additional panels

You can add panels to or remove panels from the Spry Accordion widget using the Property inspector.

1 Select the blue tab above Accordion1 in the document window.

The Property inspector displays settings for the Accordion widget.

**2** In the Property inspector, click the Add Panel icon.

A new panel is added to the Accordion widget.

**3** In the document window, delete the <h2> heading *In the Community*. Select and cut the subsequent <ul> element containing the "Community" tips.

**4** Change the text *Label 3* to read **In the Community** and paste the <ul> text into the new content area.

**5** Save the file. Click OK in any additional dialog boxes for Spry-dependent files.

You created a Spry Accordion and added content and additional panels. Although the content added in this exercise was already on the page, you can enter and edit content directly in the content panels, if desired. You could also copy material from other sources, such as Microsoft Word, TextEdit, and Notepad, among others. In the next exercise, you'll customize the CSS for the Spry Accordion.

## Customizing a Spry Accordion

Like other widgets, a Spry Accordion is formatted by its own CSS file. In this exercise, you will modify the component and adapt its default styling to the website color theme. Let's start by tracking down the rules that format the horizontal tabs.

**1** Insert the cursor into the tab labeled *At Home* and examine the names and order of the tag selectors.

The tabs are formatted by the `.AccordionPanelTab` class.

**2** In the CSS Styles panel, expand the **SpryAccordion.css** style sheet. Double-click `.AccordionPanelTab` to edit it.

**3** Enter the following specifications for the `.AccordionPanelTab` rule:
Font-size: **120%**
Color: **#FFC**
Background-color: **#090**
Background-image: **background.png**
Background-repeat: **repeat-x**
Left Padding: **15px**
Top Border Color: **#060**
Bottom Border Color: **#090**

**4** Save all files and preview the document in Live view. Test and examine the Accordion behavior.

The horizontal tabs display a hover behavior. The text turns gray, but when combined with the background image the result is an effect that's not very eye catching. Let's change the text color to provide some contrast and remove the background image altogether.

**5** Return to Design view. Examine the Accordion style sheet to find the rule that applies a hover behavior.

Two rules apply a hover effect. One applies when the panel is closed (`.AccordionPanelTabHover`) and one when it is open (`.AccordionPanelOpen .AccordionPanelTabHover`).

**6** Double-click `.AccordionPanelTabHover` to edit it.

**7** Enter the following specifications for the `.AccordionPanelTabHover` rule:
Color: **#FFC**
Background-color: **#060**
Background-image: **none**

**8** Repeat step 7 with the `.AccordionPanelOpen .AccordionPanelTabHover` rule.

**9** Save all files and test the hover behavior again.

The tabs drop the background graphic and become darker.

Note the two rules containing the word *focused* at the bottom of the Accordion style sheet. This is a hyperlink behavior identical to hover, except that it's activated when the visitor uses the Tab key or arrow keys instead of the mouse to navigate around the page. These rules may interfere with your hover formatting, so it's a good idea to give them the same settings.

**10** Edit the `.AccordionFocused .AccordionPanelTab` and `.AccordionFocused .AccordionPanelOpen .AccordionPanelTab` rules. Enter the following specifications:
Color: **#FFC**
Background-color: **#060**
Background-image: **none**

When open, the panels are not tall enough to display all the bullets in a list at once. You can adjust the height of the panels within the CSS, too.

11 Insert the cursor into the bullet list and examine the names and order of the tag selectors.

The panel content region is formatted by the `.AccordionPanelContent` class.

12 Select the `.AccordionPanelContent` rule in the CSS Styles panel. In the panel Property section, change the Height value to **450px**.

The new height setting allows all the content to be visible. For a final touch, let's move the Spry Accordion in from both sides to keep it from touching the edges of the content window.

13 Edit the `.Accordion` rule. Enter the following specifications:
Left-margin: **15px**
Right-margin: **15px**

14 Save all files and test the document in the default browser.

You've successfully applied formatting to the Accordion widget so it matches the website color scheme and adjusted the component height to allow more content to display. The Accordion is just one of the 16 Spry widgets and components offered by Dreamweaver that allow you to incorporate advanced functionality into your website while requiring little or no programming skill. All can be accessed via either the Insert menu or panel. In upcoming lessons, you will learn how to use more of Dreamweaver's built-in Spry components.

Dozens more widgets are available from the Adobe Exchange. You could search for and install these manually, but Adobe has made it unbelievably easy by providing its own Widget Browser. This Air-enabled app can be downloaded from http://tinyurl.com/widgets-browser.

Once installed, the Widget Browser makes it simple to check out available widgets and use them with Dreamweaver.

## Review questions

1   What is a benefit of using Dreamweaver behaviors?

2   What three steps must be used to create a Dreamweaver behavior?

3   What's the purpose of assigning an ID to an image before applying a behavior?

4   What does a Spry Accordion widget do?

5   How do you add new panels to a Spry Accordion widget?

## Review answers

1   Dreamweaver behaviors add interactive functionality to a webpage quickly and easily.

2   To create a Dreamweaver behavior, you need to create or select a trigger element, select a desired behavior, and specify the parameters.

3   The ID makes it easier to select the specific image during the process of applying a behavior.

4   A Spry Accordion includes two or more collapsible panels that hide and reveal content in a compact area of the page.

5   Select the panel in the document window and click the Add Panel icon in the Spry interface of the Property inspector.

# 11 WORKING WITH WEB ANIMATION AND VIDEO

## Lesson Overview

In this lesson, you'll learn how to incorporate web-compatible animation and video components into your webpage and do the following:

- Insert Flash-based animation

- Insert web-compatible animation

- Insert Flash-based video

- Insert web-compatible video

 This lesson will take about 35 minutes to complete. Before beginning, make sure you have copied the files for Lesson 11 to your hard drive as described in the "Getting Started" section at the beginning of the book. If you are starting from scratch in this lesson, use the method described in the "Jumpstart" section of "Getting Started."

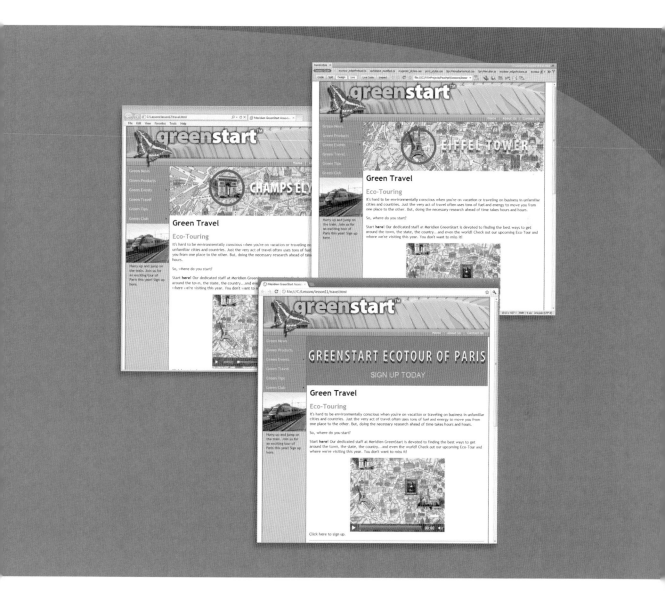

Dreamweaver allows you to integrate
HTML5-compatible animation and video.

# Understanding web animation and video

The web can provide a variety of experiences to the average user. One second, you are downloading and reading a best-selling novel. Next, you're listening to your favorite radio station or performing artist. Then, you're watching live television coverage or a feature-length movie. Before Adobe Flash, animation and video were hard to incorporate on websites. Much of this content was provided in various formats using a hodgepodge of applications, plug-ins, and coder-decoders (codecs) that could transfer data across the Internet to your computer and browser, often with enormous difficulties and incompatibilities. Frequently, a format that worked in one browser was incompatible with another. Applications that worked in Windows didn't work on the Mac. Most formats required their own proprietary players or plug-ins.

For a time, Adobe Flash brought order to this chaos. It provided a single platform for creating both animation and video. Flash started as an animation program and changed the web for all time. A few years ago, it revolutionized the industry again by making it a simple task to add video to a site. By inserting a video into Flash and saving the file as a SWF or FLV file, web designers and developers were able to take advantage of the almost universal distribution of the Flash Player—installed on over 90 percent of all desktop computers. No more worries over formats and codecs—Flash Player took care of all that.

Unfortunately, that run of success and popularity came to an abrupt end with the release of the iPhone in 2007. Apple decided that the Flash Player, for all its benefits and capabilities, was too difficult to support in its new mobile operating system (iOS). With Apple leading the way, other phone and tablet manufacturers announced that they too would drop support for Flash in future products.

The wishes of its critics aside, Flash is not dead. It's still unmatched for its multimedia power and functionality. The Flash Player—the application required to play Flash's SWF and FLV files—still enjoys one of the widest installed bases of any browser plug-in. But today, all bets are off when it comes to animation and video. The techniques for creating web-based media are being reinvented. As you may have guessed, this trend away from Flash is ringing in a new era of chaos on the web media front. Half a dozen or more codecs are competing to become the "be-all end-all" format for video distribution and playback for the web.

The only ray of sunshine in this morass is that HTML5 was developed with built-in support for both animation and video. Great strides have already been made to replace much of the capability of Flash-based animation using native HTML5 and CSS3 functionality. The status of video is not as clear. So far, a single standard has not yet emerged, which means that to support all the popular desktop and mobile browsers, you will have to produce several different video files. In this lesson, you will learn how to incorporate different types of web animation and video into your site.

# Previewing the completed file

To see what you will work on in this lesson, preview the completed page in the browser. This is the travel page of the travel site you assembled in the previous lesson.

1   Launch Adobe Dreamweaver CS6.

2   If necessary, press Ctrl-Shift-F/Cmd-Shift-F to open the Files panel, and choose DW-CS6 from the site list.

3   In the Files panel, expand the lesson11 folder.

4   Select the **travel_finished.html** file and preview it in your primary browser.

The page includes two media elements: the banner animation at the top of the MainContent region and the video inserted in the sidebar. Depending on what browser you view the page in, the video may be generated from one of four different formats: MP4, WebM, Ogg, or Flash Video.

5   Note that the banner ad plays once, when the page loads completely.

6   To view the video, move your pointer over the video in the sidebar and click the Play button that appears.

Depending on the video format that your browser supports, you may notice that the controls fade if you move your cursor away from the video, but that they return once your cursor is positioned over the video again.

7  When you're finished previewing the media, close your browser and return to Dreamweaver.

## Adding web animation to a page

● **Note:** If you are starting from scratch in this exercise, see the "Jumpstart" instructions in the "Getting Started" section at the beginning of the book.

In this exercise, you'll insert an HTML5-based banner animation into the MainContent area of your webpage. Creating original web animations is beyond the scope of this book, so check out the e-book *Introduction to Adobe Edge Preview 6* (Peachpit, 2012) to learn how to create these types of items and much more. Let's start by opening the file containing the sample animation.

1  Open **ecotour.html** from the ecotour folder.

When you first open this file, you may not see any visible content; Dreamweaver's Design view can't preview Edge animation.

## Introducing Adobe Edge

Edge is a new program developed by Adobe—not to replace Flash, but to create web animation and interactive content natively, using HTML5, CSS3, and JavaScript. At the time of this writing, the program is in beta testing and available for free download from the Adobe Labs website: www.labs.adobe.com. The exact cost and date of the release of the first complete version of this product was not finalized at the time of this printing, but even as a beta program, Edge is already a usable tool with amazing capabilities. In fact, the animation used in this lesson was built in Edge.

**2** Select Code view.

You may be surprised by how little code appears in the document. Most of the animation is actually enabled and stored in files linked externally. To get the animation working in your own site, you have to move only two blocks of code.

**3** Select and copy the code starting with `<!--Adobe Edge Runtime-->` and ending with `<!--Adobe Edge Runtime End-->` (lines 6–8). Note the location of code within the structure of the current file.

```
3    <head>
4        <meta http-equiv='Content-Type' content='text/html; charset=utf-8'>
5        <title>Untitled</title>
6    <!--Adobe Edge Runtime-->
7        <script type="text/javascript" charset="utf-8" src="ecotour_edgePreload.js"></script>
8    <!--Adobe Edge Runtime End-->
9
10   </head>
```

This code appears directly after the `<title>`...`</title>` element and links to a JavaScript file that loads all the components of the animation. The link targets a file in the site root folder. At the moment, that file doesn't reside there; you will move it and the other necessary components later in the lesson.

**4** Open **travel.html** from the site root folder. Or, if you are starting from scratch in this exercise, see the "Jumpstart" instructions in the "Getting Started" section at the beginning of the book.

The banner needs to be inserted outside any text elements.

**5** Select Code view, if necessary. Locate the closing `</title>` element. Insert the cursor at the end of the element.

**6** Press Enter/Return to create a new line. Press Ctrl-V/Cmd-V to paste the code.

Now you need to insert the `stage` element.

**7** Switch to **ecotour.html**.

**8** In Code view, insert the cursor into the `<div id="Stage" class="EDGE-10410789"> </div>` element. Select the `<div#stage>` tag selector.

**9** Press Ctrl-C/Cmd-C to copy the element.

**10** Switch to **travel.html**.

The `stage` element must be inserted outside any text element.

**11** Insert the cursor in the *Green Travel* heading text and select the `<h1>` tag selector. Press the Left Arrow key to move the cursor outside the `<h1>` element.

**12** In Code view, press Ctrl-V/Cmd-V to paste the `stage` element code. Save all files.

```
80    <!-- InstanceBeginEditable name="MainContent" -->
81    <article class="content">
82    <div id="Stage" class="EDGE-10410789">
83    </div> <h1>Green Travel</h1>
84    <section>
```

You are nearly finished, but before the animation will play, you have to move some other files into the site root folder.

**13** If necessary, open the Files panel by selecting Window > Files.

● **Note:** Some of the JavaScript files are needed to make this specific animation function, while the others support any Edge animation inserted in your site.

**14** In the Files panel, click the Expand (⊞) button. Display the contents of the `ecotour` folder.

The folder contains two subfolders, three JavaScript files, one .html file, and one .edge file. For the animation to function properly, you must move the two folders and all three JavaScript files to the site root folder. The .html and .edge files are not needed.

**15** Select the `eco_images` and `edge_includes` folders and the JavaScript (.js) files. Press Ctrl-C/Cmd-C to copy the components.

**16** In the Files panel, select the site root folder. Press Ctrl-V/Cmd-V to paste the files and folders.

**17** Select Live view.

The banner animation plays automatically in Live view once the code is processed, but there is an undesirable gap between the animation and the horizontal navigation menu. To identify the cause of the gap, you can use the Code Navigator.

**18** Position the cursor over the banner animation. Right-click, and select Code Navigator from the Context menu.

The Code Navigator window appears, listing all CSS rules that affect the banner animation.

**19** Working up from the bottom, identify the rule that is creating the gap.

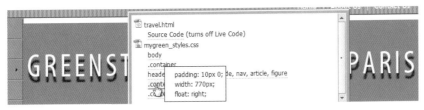

The .content rule applies 10 pixels of padding to div.content.

**20** In the CSS panel, select the .content rule. In the Properties section of the panel, change Top Padding from 10px to **0px**.

**21** Save all files. Refresh the Live view display.

The banner animation fits flush to the top of the content section of the page. Congratulations, you've successfully incorporated an HTML5- and CSS3-based animation on your page.

# Adding web video to a page

Implementing HTML5-compatible video in your site is a bit more involved than it was when you only had to insert a single Flash-based file. Unfortunately, there's no single video format that's supported by all browsers in use today. To make sure your video content plays everywhere, you'll have to supply several different formats. At the moment, Dreamweaver doesn't provide a built-in technique, so you'll have to do all the coding yourself. In this exercise, you will learn one popular method for inserting HTML5-compatible video on a page in your site.

**1** If necessary, open **travel.html**.

You will insert the video in the MainContent section of the page.

**2** Insert the cursor in the paragraph *Click here to sign up*. Click the <p> tag selector. Press the Left Arrow key to move the insertion point before the opening <p> tag.

**3** Switch to Code view. Type the following code:
```
<video width="400" height="300" controls="controls"></video>
```

```
    upcoming Eco-Tour and where we're visiting this year. You don't want to miss it!</p>
89    <video width="400" height="300" controls="controls"></video>
90    <p>Click here to sign up.</p>
```

This line creates the video element. Note that there is no reference for the actual video files. You could add a src attribute within this element to call a video file, but then you would be able to add only one filename. To call more than one video, you will use the new HTML5 <source> element.

**4** Insert the cursor between the opening and closing <video> </video> tags.

**5** Press Enter/Return to create a new line. Enter **<source src="** on the new line.

When you enter src=" Dreamweaver will prompt you to browse for a file.

**6** Click to activate the Browse command. Navigate to the movies folder and select the **paris.mp4** file. Click OK/Choose.

MP4, also known as MPEG-4, is a video format based on Apple's QuickTime standard. It is supported natively by iOS devices. Many experts advise loading MP4 files first—otherwise, iOS devices may ignore the video element altogether.

**7** Complete the element thusly: **<source src="movies/paris.mp4" type="video/mp4" />**

The next format you will load is WebM, which is an open-source, royalty-free video format sponsored by Google. It is compatible with Firefox 4, Chrome 6, Opera 10.6, and Internet Exporer 9 and later browsers.

**8** Press Enter/Return to create a new line.
Enter **<source src="movies/paris.webm" type="video/webm" />** on the new line.

To round out our HTML5 video selections, the next format you'll load is a lossy, open-source multimedia format: Ogg. It is designed for the distribution of multimedia content free of copyright and other media restrictions.

**Tip:** You are using the FLV video as alternate content for the HTML5 video. In the same respect, you can insert an FLV video and use the HTML5 <video> element and the <source> references as the alternate content. That way, if the browser or device doesn't support Flash, the HTML5 video appears instead.

**9** Press Enter/Return to create a new line.
Enter **<source src="movies/paris.theora.ogv" type="video/ogg" />** on the new line.

```
89    <video width="400px" height="300" controls="controls">
90      <source src="movies/paris.mp4" type="video/mp4"/>
91      <source  src="movies/paris.webm"  type="video/webm"/>
92      <source src="movies/paris.theora.ogv" type="video/ogg" /></video>
93    <p>Click here to sign up.</p>
```

These three formats should support all the modern desktop and mobile browsers. But to support older software and devices, it may be necessary to use a stalwart old friend: Flash video. By adding it last, we're ensuring that only browsers that don't support the other three formats will load the Flash content. Although Flash is being abandoned by many, Dreamweaver still provides support for inserting both FLV and SWF files.

**10** Press Enter/Return to create a new line. Choose Insert > Media > FLV.

**11** When the Insert FLV dialog box appears, make sure the Video Type pop-up menu is set to Progressive Download Video.

**12** Click Browse and navigate to the movies folder in the site root folder. Choose **paris.flv** and click OK/Choose.

To allow the user to start, stop, and rewind the video, you'll want to add controls. Be sure to pick controls that are no wider than the video itself.

**13** From the Skin pop-up menu, choose Corona Skin 3.

At 400 pixels in width, any of the available controls will work with this video. The video controls will automatically appear and disappear when the visitor moves their cursor over the video.

**14** Click the Detect Size button to enter the Width and Height of the video automatically, or manually enter Width: **400** and Height: **300**. Select the Constrain and Auto Rewind options. Click OK.

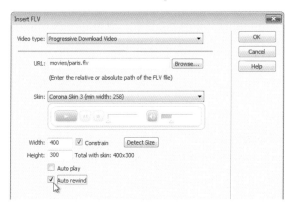

Dreamweaver inserts a placeholder in the layout, which can be customized somewhat with the Property inspector. FLV files cannot be previewed within Design view and must be viewed in Live view or a browser.

**15** Save the file.

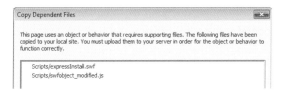

Note: The Travel page now contains two notices prompting users to sign up for the Eco-Tour. In Lesson 12, "Working with Forms," you will create a new page with the sign-up form and link this text to it.

When you save the file, the Copy Dependent Files dialog box may appear, displaying a message explaining that the dependent files **expressInstall.swf** and **swfobject_modified.js** will be placed into a new Scripts folder. These files are essential for running an FLV file in the browser and must be uploaded to your web server to support Flash functionality. If this dialog box appears, click OK.

Note: The Copy Dependent Files dialog box may not appear for users following the jumpstart method in this lesson. The files already exist in your site folder, and Dreamweaver doesn't need to copy them.

**16** Switch to Design view.

If you use the <video> element without an FLV, Dreamweaver won't generate a preview of the video content. Fortunately, it will generate a placeholder for the FLV component. The actual video files will appear only in compatible browsers. The placeholder appears in the layout flush to the left side of <div.content>. Let's center it.

**17** Click the FLV placeholder. Select the <video> tag selector. In the CSS Styles panel, click the New CSS Rule icon.

The <video> tag is an inline element by default. By assigning it the block property, you can control how the video aligns on the page and relates to other block elements.

**18** Create a new CSS rule named **.content section video** and enter the following specifications:
Display: **block**
Margin-right: **auto**
Margin-left: **auto**

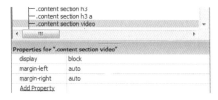

▶ **Tip:** Create custom classes as necessary to control the placement of individual elements.

This rule centers all <video> elements inserted in <div.content>. But the element also includes an FLV component, which doesn't use the <video> tag—it uses the <object> tag. To make sure the FLV content is centered, let's create a rule for that tag, too.

**19** In the CSS Styles panel, right-click the .content video rule and select Edit > Duplicate from the context menu.

**20** Change the rule name to **.content section object** and click OK to create the rule.

Now all <video> and <object> elements will be centered.

**21** Preview the page in Live view, or preview the page in a browser. If the video controls are not visible, move your cursor over the still image to display them. Click the Play button to view the movie.

● **Note:** Some versions of Microsoft Internet Explorer may block active content until you give the browser permission to run it. If you don't have Flash Player, or if it's not the current version, you may be asked to download the latest version.

Dreamweaver

Chrome

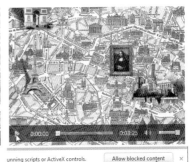

Internet Explorer

Depending on where you preview the page, you will see one of the four video formats. For example, in Live view you will see the FLV-based video. The controls will appear differently depending on what format is displayed. There is no sound in this movie, but the controls will still include a speaker button to adjust the volume or mute the sound.

**22** When you're finished, switch back to Design view.

You've embedded three HTML5-compatible videos and an FLV fallback, which should give you support for most browsers and devices that can access the Internet. But you've used only one possible technique for supporting this evolving standard. To learn more about HTML5 video and how to implement it, check out the following links:

http://tinyurl.com/video-1-HTML5

http://tinyurl.com/video-2-HTML5

http://tinyurl.com/video-3-HTML5

# Review questions

1 What advantage does HTML5 have over HTML 4 regarding web-based media?

2 What programming language created the HTML5-compatible animation used in this lesson?

3 True or false: To support all web browsers, you can select a single video format.

4 What video format is recommended to support older browsers?

5 What role do "dependent files" play in the operation of an FLV file?

# Review answers

1 HTML5 has built-in support for web animation and video.

2 The animation used in this lesson was created by Adobe Edge natively using HTML5, CSS3, and JavaScript.

3 False. A single format has not emerged that is supported by every browser. Developers recommend incorporating four video formats to support the majority of browsers: MP4, WebM, Ogg, and FLV.

4 FLV (Flash video) is recommended as the fallback format for older browsers because of the widespread installation of the Flash Player.

5 Dependent files provide essential functionality on the Internet for playing Flash components and must be uploaded to your server along with the relevant HTML and video.

# 12 WORKING WITH FORMS

## Lesson Overview

In this lesson, you'll create forms for your webpage and do the following:

- Insert a form
- Include text fields
- Work with Spry Form widgets
- Insert radio buttons
- Insert checkboxes
- Insert list menus
- Add form buttons
- Incorporate field sets and legends
- Create an email solution for processing data
- Style your form with CSS

This lesson will take about 2 hours to complete. Before beginning, make sure you have copied the files for Lesson 12 to your hard drive as described in the "Getting Started" section at the beginning of the book. If you are starting from scratch in this lesson, use the method described in the "Jumpstart" section of "Getting Started."

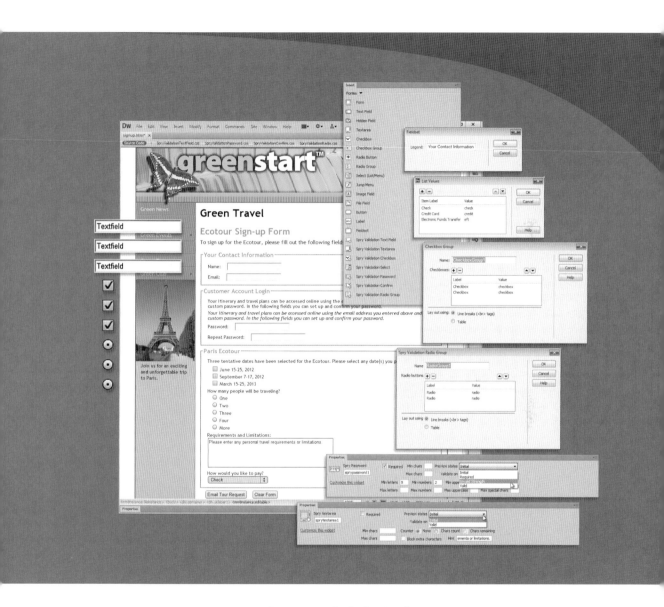

For many people, the first time they encounter interactivity on the web is when they fill out a form. Forms
are an essential tool on the modern Internet, allowing
you to capture important information and feedback.

# Previewing the completed file

To understand the project you will work on in this lesson, you can preview the completed Paris Ecotour page in the browser.

**1**  Launch Dreamweaver CS6.

**2**  If necessary, open the Files panel and select DW-CS6 from the site list. Expand the lesson12 folder.

**3**  Select **signup_finished.html** and preview it in your primary browser.

The page includes several form elements. Try them out to observe their behaviors.

**4**  Click in the Name field and type a name. Press Tab.

The name appears in the data field.

**5**  Click in the Email field and press Tab without entering an email address.

A Spry Form widget provides validation for this field and displays an error message if the field is left empty.

**6**  In the Email field, type **jdoe@mycompany** and press Tab.

Because you left off the *.com*, the Spry Form widget displays an error message prompting you to correct the entry.

**7**  At the end of the *jdoe@mycompany* entry, type **.com** and press Tab.

Now that the entry represents a complete email address, the error message disappears.

**8**  In the Password field, type **mypassword** and press Tab.

An error message appears, saying that the password entered doesn't meet the minimum requirements specified.

9   In the Password field, type **mypassword12** and press Tab.

10  In the Repeat Password field, type **mypass12** and press Tab.

The Spry Validation Confirm widget detects that the two passwords do not match and displays an error message.

11  In the Repeat Password field, type **mypassword12** and press Tab.

12  Select one or more options to indicate when you plan to travel.

13  Use the radio buttons to choose a number of travelers.

14  Click in the Restrictions And Limitations field. Type **I prefer window seats** and press Tab.

If this form were loaded on your web server, you would normally click the Email Tour Request button to submit the form. A thank-you page like the one pictured below would take the place of the signup page.

15  When you're finished, close all browser windows and return to Dreamweaver.

Before you construct your own form with its various form elements, let's take a look at how forms work.

# Learning about forms

Forms, on paper or on the web, are tools for gathering information. In both cases, the information is entered into interactive form elements, or *fields*, to make it easier to find and understand. Forms should be clearly delineated.

Paper forms often use a separate page or graphical borders to distinguish them, while web forms use the <form> tag and other specific HTML elements to designate and collect the data.

Online forms have decided advantages over paper forms because the user enters the data in a way that can then be automatically transferred into spreadsheets or databases, reducing the labor costs and error rates associated with paper forms.

Web-based forms are composed of one or more HTML elements, each used for a specific purpose:

- **Text field**—Permits the entry of text and digits up to a specific number of characters. Text fields designated as password fields mask or obscure characters as they are typed.

- **Text area**—Identical to text fields but intended for larger amounts of text, such as multiple sentences or paragraphs.

- **Radio button**—A graphical element that permits users to select one option from a group of choices. Only one item in each group can be chosen. The selection of a new item in the group deselects any currently selected item. Once one item is selected, it can't be deselected unless the form is reset or another item is selected.

- **Checkbox**—A graphical element that permits users to indicate a yes or no selection. Checkboxes can be grouped together; however, unlike radio buttons, they allow multiple items to be chosen within the group. Also unlike radio buttons, checkboxes can be deselected if desired.

- **List/menu**—Displays entries in a pop-up menu format. Lists (also called select lists) may enforce the selection of a single element or allow the choice of multiple items.

- **Hidden**—A predefined data field that conveys information to the form-processing mechanism and is unseen by the user. Hidden form elements are used extensively in dynamic page applications. Hidden data may contain information passed from a previous page on your site or default data that you do not want the user to see before submitting, such as the actual date or time the form is submitted.

- **Button**—Submits the form or performs some other single-purpose interaction, such as clearing or printing the form.

Paper forms, when completed, are mailed or passed along for processing, usually in a highly manual process. Web forms are usually electronically mailed or processed. The <form> tag includes an *action* attribute, and the value of the action attribute is triggered when the form is submitted. Often, the action is the web address for another page or server-side script that processes the form.

# Adding a form to a page

For this exercise, you will create a new page for signing up participants for the Paris Ecotour described in the travel page completed in Lesson 11, "Working with Web Animation and Video."

**Note:** If you are starting from scratch in this exercise, see the "Jumpstart" instructions in the "Getting Started" section at the beginning of the book. Then, follow the steps in this exercise.

1  Open the Assets panel and click the Template category icon. Right-click **mygreen_temp** and choose New From Template from the context menu.

2  Save the file as **signup.html** in the site root folder.

3  In the MainContent region, select the placeholder heading *Add main heading here* and type **Green Travel** to replace the text.

4  In the MainContent region, select the placeholder heading *Add subheading heading here* and type **Ecotour Sign-up Form** to replace the text.

5  Select the placeholder paragraph *Add content here.* Type **To sign up for the Ecotour, please fill out the following fields:** and press Enter/Return to create a new paragraph.

   All form fields must be contained within a `<form>` element, so it's typically best to add it to the page before inserting any field elements. Any field inserted outside the `<form>` element will be ignored when the form is submitted and processed.

6  Open the Insert panel and select Forms from the category list. In the Forms category, click the Form ( ) icon.

   Dreamweaver inserts the `<form>` element at the insertion point, which is indicated visually by a red dashed line. Forms should always feature a unique ID. If you don't create your own, Dreamweaver will add one.

**Note:** If you try to insert a form element without a `<form>` tag, Dreamweaver will prompt you to add one.

7  If necessary, select the `<form>` tag selector. Insert the cursor in the Form ID field of the Property inspector. Type **ecotour** and press Enter/Return to create a custom ID.

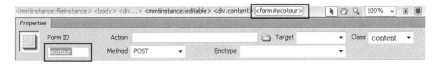

   The `<form#ecotour>` element extends left and right to the edges of `<div.content>`.

# One tag to control them all

Text fields, checkboxes, radio buttons, list menus, and text areas have at least one thing in common: They are all created using the HTML `<input>` tag. Just change the `type` attribute and/or one or more other settings, and you can convert a checkbox into a radio button, a text field, or a list menu. No other HTML element is so flexible and powerful. As you insert form fields in this lesson, feel free to peek in the code to see how this magic is accomplished.

You may see something like the following examples:

Textfield    `<input type="text" name="color" id="color" />`

☑    `<input type="checkbox" name="color" id="color" value="red" />`

◉    `<input type="radio" name="color" id="color" value="red" />`

8   Open the CSS Styles panel, if necessary. Select the `.content` rule in the **mygreen_styles.css** style sheet. In the CSS Styles panel, click the New CSS Rule (🗗) icon.

9   Choose Compound and name the new rule `.content section #ecotour`. Click OK.

10  In the Box category, enter **15 px** only in the Left and Right margin fields. Click OK.

A new rule—`.content section #ecotour`—will appear in the CSS Styles panel. The red outline of the form indents 15 pixels away from the left and right edges of MainContent.

11  Save all files.

You created a form; next, you'll insert some form fields.

## Inserting text form elements

Text fields are the workhorses of all the form elements. Text fields are the basic vehicles for gathering unstructured text and numeric data, and it's hard to imagine a form without them. In fact, many forms are composed exclusively of text-input fields.

In the upcoming exercises, you'll insert basic text fields, Spry text fields, password text fields, password-confirmation text fields, and text areas. Before you can start, however, confirm that Dreamweaver is configured to add form elements in their most accessible manner.

## Setting preferences for accessible forms

Accessibility technologies place special requirements on form elements. Assistive technology devices, such as screen readers, require precise code that allows them to correctly read forms and individual form elements. Dreamweaver provides an option that outputs form code in the proper format. These preferences may be set as the default configuration; if so, merely confirm that the options for accessible forms are set.

1   Choose Edit > Preferences (Windows) or Dreamweaver > Preferences (Mac).

2   When the Preferences dialog box appears, select the Accessibility category.

3   In the Accessibility category, make sure that the Form Objects option is selected. Click OK.

# HTML5 field fun

As with the semantic page elements we've been using, HTML5 also offers over a dozen very interesting new form elements, field types, and attributes, too. New elements like `<datalist>` and `<keygen>` and field types like date, time, email, telephone, and so on will allow for better data input control and validation capabilities. In other words, the field itself will know what type of data is supposed to be entered, and it will provide features to validate and flag incorrect entries.

Unfortunately, HTML5 fields and their amazing features are not fully supported by some major browsers, cell phones, and mobile devices. Because of the vital role data fields play in collecting information, we can't recommend the general use of these fields just yet. Feel free to experiment with them, but for this lesson we'll stick to the tried and true HTML field types. If you do use these field types and they are not supported natively by the browsing app, in most cases they will behave just like regular text fields. However, on some cell phones and mobile devices, HTML5 fields or attributes may not function at all.

To learn more about the new field types, check out **tinyurl.com/HTML5-input**.

As you'll see in the following exercises, when accessibility for form objects is enabled, a dialog box appears before the form element is inserted. This dialog box has a number of options for including a form element label, as well as other special attributes. You'll learn more about these attributes later.

## Using text fields

Text fields accept alphanumeric characters—letters and numbers. Unless otherwise specified, a text field can display around 20 characters. If you type more characters than will fit, the text will scroll within the field. To show more or fewer characters on the screen, set a specific field size in the Width field in the Property inspector. Although there's no built-in limit to the amount of text you can enter into a text field element, you're more likely to run into limits imposed by your target data application.

Spreadsheet and database fields frequently limit the amount of data that can be entered. If you enter too much data into a field and submit it, the data application usually just ignores, or dumps, whatever exceeds its maximum capacity. To prevent this from happening, you can restrict HTML text fields to a specific number of characters by using the Max Chars attribute field in the Property inspector.

1 If necessary, open **signup.html** from the site root folder.

2 Insert the cursor in the red form outline.

The tag selector should display <form#ecotour>.

3 In the Forms category of the Insert panel, click the Text Field (☐) icon.

The Input Tag Accessibility Attributes dialog box appears. The dialog box enables you to designate specific attributes and markup for the <input> element. When a form field is inserted, Dreamweaver makes it easy to define some of these options immediately.

For example, the most important attribute is id, because it gives the field a unique name that assists in processing the form data later. If you don't give each form field a unique ID, Dreamweaver will create generic ones for you, like *textfield*, *textfield2*, *textfield3*, and so on. Since generic IDs will be difficult to work with, it's important to create descriptive custom names yourself.

4 In the ID field, type **name** and press Tab.

Text fields can also include HTML markup for a descriptive label that will appear in the webpage. Such markup is optional, and if you select the No Label Tag option in the dialog box, Dreamweaver will leave off the <label> markup entirely.

On the other hand, if you wish to use the <label> element, Dreamweaver inserts the HTML markup for you and provides two methods for inserting it: by wrapping the label around the text field element, or by inserting it as a separate element that uses a "for" attribute. Although the attribute is not visible to the average user, it allows you to identify the fields for visitors with visual disabilities. In these cases, the "for" option provides the most flexibility for form design, while still complying with Section 508 disabilities regulations.

5   In the Label field, type **Name:** and press Tab.

The ID is in lowercase, because it appears only in the code. The label is capitalized because it actually displays in the form, before or after the text field element.

6   Select the Attach Label Tag Using 'for' Attribute option. Select the Before Form Item option, if necessary. Click OK.

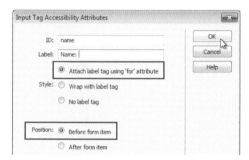

When the Attach Label Tag Using 'for' Attribute option is selected, Dreamweaver inserts code like this:

```
<label for="name">Name:</label><input type="text" id="name" />
```

This code arrangement allows for maximum flexibility in your form design. For example, you can keep the two elements on the same line, put them on two lines, or format each separately using CSS. In some instances you may use a table to create your form layout. Using a separate label element allows you to place each item in separate cells and columns of the table.

7   Save the file.

The first of your form objects is now in place. Inserting other standard text fields is a similar operation. In the next exercise, you'll add a Spry Validation Text Field, which is a specialized version of the text field that has been customized with Ajax functionality.

## Including Spry Validation Text Fields

In Lesson 10, "Adding Interactivity," you learned about the Adobe Spry framework for Ajax and worked with the Spry Accordion panel. Dreamweaver also includes a range of Spry objects for forms. Each Spry Form widget combines form elements with sophisticated JavaScript to create easy-to-use form fields with built-in *validation*.

Validation is the process of verifying that appropriate data has been entered into a form element. This maintains the integrity and quality of the data entered into the form and passed to your data application. For example, if a site visitor enters an incomplete or invalid email address into an email text field, the form data becomes worthless. Validation can ensure that all required fields are completed before the form can be submitted. That way, a customer can't accidentally submit a form if they forget to fill in their payment information or other critical data.

Spry Form widgets are available for a variety of tasks, including text fields, text areas, checkboxes, passwords and password confirmation, radio groups, and select lists. Each widget works basically the same way: You insert the widget and then specify its properties using a Spry interface in the Property inspector.

In this exercise, you'll insert a Spry Validation Text Field to make sure that the user submits a properly structured email address.

1   If necessary, open **signup.html**.

2   Insert the cursor at the end of the Name text field inserted in the previous exercise and press Shift-Enter/Shift-Return to insert a forced line break.

▶ **Tip:** Press Tab to move quickly from field to field.

3   In the Forms category of the Insert panel, click the Spry Validation Text Field (⊥) icon.

The Input Tag Accessibility Attributes dialog box appears.

4   In the ID field, type **email**. In the Label field, type **Email:** and then select the Attach Label Tag Using 'for' Attribute option. Select the Before Form Item option. Click OK.

5   Save the file. If Dreamweaver alerts you of the external JavaScript files used, click OK.

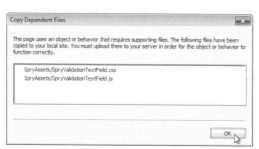

Once the element is inserted on the page, you can customize its Spry functionality.

6   If the blue Spry TextField tab isn't visible, position your mouse pointer over the Email text field and wait until it appears. Click the tab to select the element. If necessary, open the Property inspector.

The Property inspector displays attributes and settings for a generic Spry text field. Note that the Preview States menu displays the text *Initial*.

**7** In the Property inspector, choose **Email Address** from the Type pop-up menu.

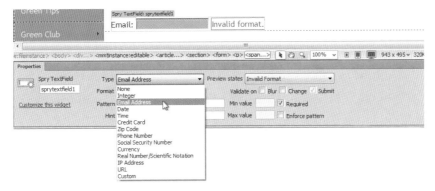

Note that the Preview States menu now displays *Invalid Format* and the warning text appears to the right of the field.

The Email Address field type checks to see that the entry contains an @ character followed by a domain name. Examine the available triggers in the Property inspector. The Blur option is a trigger activated when a user tabs from one field to the next in a form. The Change option activates when data is entered or altered in the field. The Submit option is activated when the form is processed by the browser and the web application.

**Note:** When a field is required, the user must complete it before the form will submit.

**8** In the Property inspector, select Validate On Blur and make sure that the Required option is selected.

By default, all validations occur when the form is submitted, but as in the Email field, you can add triggers to check validation sooner. This type of interactivity provides a more immediate response and a better user experience. The user doesn't have to wait until they are finished filling out the entire form before being notified that they missed a field or entered incorrect data. Dreamweaver makes it easy to customize the error messages using the Spry interface in the Property inspector.

**9** From the Preview States menu, choose Required.

The warning text *A value is required* appears to the right of the Spry Email field. Let's make the warning a bit less cryptic.

**10** Select the text *A value is required* and type **An email address is required.**

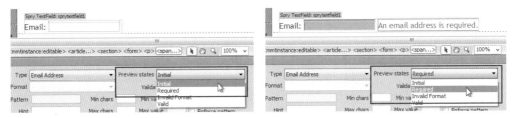

This message will appear when an invalid email address is entered in the field.

**11** From the Preview States menu, choose Invalid Format.

The warning text *Invalid format* appears to the right of the Spry Email field.

**12** Select the text *Invalid format* and type **Please enter a valid email address.**

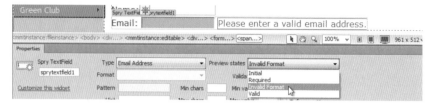

**13** Save the file.

## Creating a field set

One way to make forms more user friendly is to organize fields into logical group-ings, called field sets. The HTML `<fieldset>` element was designed for this pur-pose and even features a helpful description element called *legend*.

**1** If necessary, open **signup.html**.

**2** Insert the cursor in the Email label. Click the blue tab to select the Spry text field. Press the Right Arrow key to move the cursor after the Spry component. Press Enter/Return to create a new paragraph.

**3** Insert the cursor into the Name label and select the `<label>` tag selector. Hold the Shift key, and click at the end of the Email text field to select both fields and their associated markup.

Selecting the relevant code can be a bit tricky in Design view. To make sure you are selecting everything you need, switch to Code view or Split view.

**4** Ensure that you've selected this entire code block.

```
51      <form id="ecotour" name="ecotour" method="post" action="">
52      <label for="name">Name:</label>
53      <input type="text" name="name" id="name" />
54      <br />
55      <span id="sprytextfield1">
56      <label for="email">Email:</label>
57      <input type="text" name="email" id="email" />
58      <span class="textfieldRequiredMsg">PleasePlease</span><span class="textfieldInvalidFormatMsg">Please
        enter a valid email address.</span></span>
59      <p> </p>
60      </form>
```

**5** In the Forms category of the Insert panel, click the Fieldset (⬚) icon.

The selected code is inserted into a `<fieldset>` element.

**6** In the Legend field, type **Your Contact Information** and click OK.

**7** Switch to Design view.

The field set is not rendered accurately in Design view; however, it does clearly display the legend.

8   Save all files and preview the page in Live view.

The field set neatly encloses the two fields in a labeled container.

9   Switch back to Design view.

In the next exercise, you'll create password and password confirmation fields.

## Creating password text fields

The password field is a common sight on the web. Normally, a text field displays the characters entered into it, but this wouldn't be desirable for a password field. Instead, password fields mask the characters as they're typed, displaying a series of asterisks or bullets, depending on the browser. Designed as a security measure, it prevents a casual passerby from observing your password as you type.

1   Insert the cursor anywhere in the field set you just created, and select the `<fieldset>` tag selector. Press the Right Arrow key to move the cursor after the element. Press Enter/Return to create a new paragraph.

2   Type the following text:

    **Your itinerary and travel plans can be accessed online using the email address you entered above and a custom password. In the following fields you can set up and confirm your password.**

3   Press Enter/Return to create a new paragraph. Type **Your password must contain at least 8 characters, at least two of them numbers, such as "password12".** Select the paragraph and click the *I* button in the Property inspector to apply the `<em>` tag.

4   Press Enter/Return to create a new paragraph. In the Forms category of the Insert panel, click the Spry Validation Password ( ) icon.

    The Input Tag Accessibility Attributes dialog box appears.

5   In the ID field, type **password**. In the Label field, type **Password:** and select the Attach Label Tag Using 'for' Attribute and the Before Form Item options. Click OK.

6   Click the blue Spry Password tab.

    The Property inspector displays the settings and attributes for the Spry Password field.

**Note:** If you don't want the default error message to show in your design window, in the Property inspector, choose Initial from the Preview States menu.

**7** Select the Required and Validate On Blur options. In the Min Letters field, enter **8**. In the Min Numbers field, enter **2**.

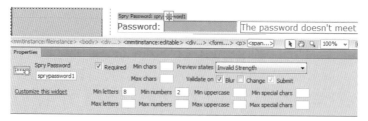

**8** Click the blue Spry Password tab. Press the Right Arrow key to move the cursor after the Password field. Then, press Shift-Enter/Shift-Return to create a line break after the Password field.

**9** In the Forms category of the Insert panel, click the Spry Validation Confirm ( ) icon to create a password confirmation text field.

The Input Tag Accessibility Attributes dialog box appears.

**10** In the ID field, type **confirm_pw**. In the Label field, type **Repeat Password**. Select the Attach Label Tag Using 'for' Attribute and the Before Form Item options. Click OK.

▶ **Tip:** Although you may not need to use Code view or Split view to help you select the desired code this time, don't hesitate to use these valuable tools whenever necessary.

**11** Click the blue Spry Confirm tab. Select the Required and Validate On Blur options. From the Validate Against pop-up menu, choose **"password" in form "ecotour."**

The instructions created in steps 2 and 3 and the two Spry Validation fields can be enclosed in their own field set at this point.

**12** Select the instructional paragraphs and the two Spry fields.

**13** In the Insert panel, click the Fieldset button. In the Legend field, type **Customer Account Login** and click OK.

Note that the text is indented but the fieldset is flush to the edge of the content element. The text indent is being applied by one of the preexisting CSS rules from the original CSS layout. You'll correct this inconsistency and apply additional styling by creating a custom CSS style sheet just for forms at the end of the lesson.

**Ecotour Sign-up Form**

To sign up for the Ecotour, please fill out the

Your Contact Information

Name:

Email:

Customer Account Login

Your itinerary and travel plans can be accessed o password. In the following fields you can set up a *Your password must contain at least 8 characters*

Password:

Repeat Password:

**14** Save all files.

The Copy Dependent Files dialog box appears indicating that specific Spry assets are being copied to your site folder. This dialog box will appear whenever you save a file after adding a new type of Spry-based form component.

**15** Click OK to close the Copy Dependent Files dialog box.

The password field you added allows a website user to create a password that complies to the rules you set. The password-confirm field requires that the password be retyped in exactly the same manner. Since the password is screened when entered, this will help website users to detect typos so they don't unintentionally submit a password that is not what they intended.

# Inserting checkboxes

Checkboxes provide a series of options that can be chosen in any combination. Like text fields, each checkbox has a unique ID and value attributes. Dreamweaver provides two methods for adding checkboxes to your page. You can either insert each checkbox individually or insert an entire group at once. You can also choose between normal HTML checkboxes and ones powered by Spry. The Spry checkboxes allow you to add customized error messages and other functionality. In this exercise, you will insert a checkbox group.

**1** If necessary, open **signup.html**.

**2** Insert the cursor in the Customer Account Login field set and select the `<fieldset>` tag selector. Press the Right Arrow key to move the cursor outside the element. Press Enter/Return to insert new paragraph.

**3** Type **Three tentative dates have been selected for the Ecotour. Please select any date(s) you prefer:** in the field.

**4** Press Enter/Return to insert a new paragraph.

**5** In the Forms category of the Insert panel, click the Checkbox Group ( ) icon.

The Checkbox Group dialog box appears, displaying two predefined options.

**6** Change the Name field to **tourdate**.

Note that the dialog box offers two columns: Label and Value. Unlike text fields, checkboxes provide predefined options where the label can be different from the value actually submitted. This method offers several advantages over user-fillable fields.

First, the predefined options can deliver specific desired values that may not make any sense to the user. For example, the label can display the name of a product, while the value can pass along the stock-keeping unit, or SKU, number. Secondly, checkboxes and other predefined fields greatly reduce user-entry errors common in many forms.

▶ **Tip:** Press Tab to move quickly between labels and values to fill out the entire list.

**7** In the Checkbox Group dialog box, click the Add (+) button next to the word *Checkboxes* to create a third item in the list.

**8** Enter the following values in the Checkbox Group dialog box:

Label 1: **June 15-25, 2012**　　　　Value 1: **tour1**
Label 2: **September 7-17, 2012**　　Value 2: **tour2**
Label 3: **March 15-25, 2013**　　　Value 3: **tour3**

● **Note:** Labels for checkboxes and radio buttons appear after the element, by default.

**9** For the Lay Out Using option, select Line Breaks (<br> Tags). Click OK.

The checkbox group appears in the document below the text typed in step 3. Using the checkbox group eliminates the need to enter any settings in the Property inspector. A quick glance at the code reveals the advantages of using the checkbox group.

**10** Insert the cursor in any of the checkbox labels and switch to Split view. Examine the code for the related `<input>` element.

```
<label><input type="checkbox" name="tourdate" value="tour1" id="tourdate_0">June 15-25, 2012</label><br>
<label><input type="checkbox" name="tourdate" value="tour2" id="tourdate_1">September 7-17, 2012</label><br>
<label><input type="checkbox" name="tourdate" value="tour3" id="tourdate_2">March 15-25, 2013</label><br>
```

Each checkbox in the group displays the `name="tourdate"` attribute. Note that the `id` attributes have been automatically incremented as `tourdate_0`, `tourdate_1`, and `tourdate_2`. By using the checkbox group feature, Dreamweaver has saved you time by automating the process of adding multiple checkbox elements.

**11** Save all files.

You've created a group of checkboxes. More than one checkbox can be selected in a group. In the next exercise, you will learn how to work with radio buttons.

# Creating radio buttons

Sometimes you want users to select one option from an array of choices. The element of choice in that case is the radio button. Radio buttons differ from checkboxes in two ways. When a radio button is selected, it can't be deselected, except by clicking one of the other buttons in the group. Then, when you click one radio button, any other option in the same group is deselected automatically.

The enabling mechanism behind this behavior is simple but effective. Unlike other form elements, each radio button does not have a unique name and ID; rather, all radio buttons in a group have the same name *and* ID. Radio buttons are differentiated by instead giving each distinctive *values*.

As with checkboxes, you can add radio buttons to your page using two methods. You can insert each radio button individually, or you can insert an entire group at once. You can also choose between normal HTML radio buttons and ones powered by Spry. If you choose HTML radio buttons, you'll be totally responsible for inserting and naming each manually. If you choose the Spry Validation Radio Group, Dreamweaver will take care of all the naming logistics, as well as the associated JavaScript and CSS files needed for the customized error messages and styling. In this exercise, you'll insert the Spry Validation Radio Group.

**1** If necessary, open **signup.html** and switch to Design view.

**2** Insert the cursor in the last checkbox label. Select the <p> tag selector and press the Right Arrow key to move the cursor after the element. Press Enter/Return to insert a new paragraph.

**3** Type **How many people will be traveling?** Press Shift-Enter/Shift-Return to insert a line break.

**4** In the Insert panel, click the Spry Validation Radio Group (⊟) icon.

**5** Change the Name field to **travelers**.

**6** Click the Add (+) button for Radio Buttons three times to create a total of five radio buttons.

As with checkboxes, you can enter values that are different than the labels.

⬤ **Note:** Checkboxes and radio buttons use identical code markup. To convert a radio button to a checkbox, simply give each item a unique name. To change a checkbox to a radio button, give each item the same name but unique values.

Tip: If you want to re-order the radio buttons in this dialog box, use the up arrow and down arrow buttons.

**7** Enter the following values in the Spry Validation Radio Group dialog box:

Label 1: **One**      Value 1: **1**

Label 2: **Two**      Value 2: **2**

Label 3: **Three**    Value 3: **3**

Label 4: **Four**     Value 4: **4**

Label 5: **More**     Value 5: **contact**

**8** From the Lay Out Using options, choose Line Breaks (<br> Tags). Click OK.

The Spry Radio Group appears below the text entered in step 3.

**9** If necessary, click the blue tab to select the Spry Radio Group widget. In the Property inspector, select the Required option.

**10** From the Preview States menu, choose Required. Examine the Spry error text.

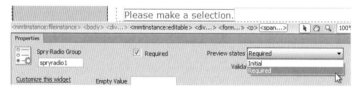

Let's customize the generic error text.

**11** Select the Spry error text *Please make a selection.* Type **Please choose the number of travelers.**

Please choose the number of travelers.

**12** Save all files.

You've created a set of radio buttons. By using the Spry Validation Radio Group interface, you easily made this element a required form field and customized the error text. If the user does not select one of the radio buttons, the error message will appear when the form is submitted.

# Incorporating text areas

Every now and then, you may want to give users an opportunity to enter a larger amount of information. Text areas provide a vehicle to enable this goal. Text areas permit multiple-line entry and word wrapping. If the entered text exceeds the physical space of the text area on the page, scroll bars automatically appear. Dreamweaver offers both HTML and Spry text area components. The Spry-based text area component allows you to include a customized user prompt, so we'll use it in this exercise.

1   If necessary, open **signup.html** and switch to Design view.

2   Click the blue tab to select the Spry radio group. Select the <p> tag selector and press the Right Arrow key to move the cursor after the element. Press Enter/ Return to create a new paragraph.

3   In the Forms category of the Insert panel, click the Spry Validation Textarea (⬛) icon.

    The Input Tag Accessibility Attributes dialog box appears.

4   In the ID field, type **requirements**. In the Label field, type **Requirements and Limitations:**. If necessary, select the Attach Label Tag Using 'for' Attribute and Before Form Item options. Click OK.

The comment text area appears, displaying inline with the label—which doesn't look very attractive. So, let's move the text area to its own line.

5   Insert the cursor in the text area label *Requirements and Limitations*. Select the <label> tag selector and press the Right Arrow key. Press Shift-Enter/Shift-Return to create a line break.

    The text area label *Requirements and Limitations* is sufficiently vague that it requires a bit more description to generate the desired response. In an HTML-based text area, you can insert some default text, or an *initial value,* to request the proper data.

    Basically, it works this way: You enter text in the Init Val field of the Property inspector and save the page. When the browser renders the form, the entered text appears automatically in the text area.

    Unfortunately, the text in the Init Val field will be passed to the data application if the user doesn't enter his or her own response. This behavior can clog your database with lots of repetitive and useless data. Since many users won't have special travel requirements, this field will be skipped over frequently. That's where the Spry Validation Text Area comes in. It provides a different technique (one that doesn't pass unwanted data) to supply the initial value.

6 Click the blue tab to select the Spry Text Area. In the Property inspector Hint field, type **Please enter any personal travel requirements or limitations.**

When the website user begins to type in this field, the initial value or the hint text will disappear automatically, but since the hint text is not stored in the field itself, it can't be passed to your data application.

The Spry Text Area is formatted as a required field by default. Since this will be an optional field, you need to deselect this checkbox.

7 Click the Required option to deselect it.

The default text area is quite small and should have more space.

▶ **Warning:** Design view doesn't render text fields accurately. Always test the widths in Live view or a browser.

8 Click the text area to select it. In the Property inspector Char Width field, enter **60** and press Enter/Return.

9 Save all files.

The text area you added allows the website user to type comments that aren't limited to a single line or checkbox. Another important form element also allows you to present multiple choices to the visitor, but in a more compact space.

## Working with lists

List and menu form elements offer a flexible method for presenting multiple options in two different formats. When displayed as a menu, the element functions like radio buttons. When displayed as a list, the element behaves like checkboxes. In this exercise, you'll insert a menu element with three options.

1 If necessary, open **signup.html** and switch to Design view.

2 Select the Spry Text Area. Select the <p> tag selector that contains it, and press the Right Arrow key to move the cursor after the element. Press Enter/Return.

**3** Type **How would you like to pay?** and press Shift-Enter/Shift-Return.

**4** In the Insert panel, click the Select (List/Menu) (📰) icon.

The Input Tag Accessibility Attributes dialog box appears.

**5** In the ID field, type **payment**. Leave the Label field empty. Select the No Label Tag option. Click OK.

There is no need for a label tag, because the text in the form element serves as label text for this form element.

An empty menu element appears in the document. Now you're ready to add the list entries. Dreamweaver provides a separate dialog box for this task, accessible from the Property inspector.

**6** In the Property inspector, click the List Values button.

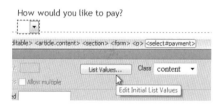

▶ **Tip:** Lists don't have to be in alphabetical order, but it makes the options easier to read and find, especially in longer lists.

The List Values dialog box appears. Note that the first label field is selected automatically.

**7** In the first Label field, type **Check**. In the first Value field, type **check**. For the second label, type **Credit Card**. For the second value, type **credit**. For the third label, type **Electronic Funds Transfer**. For the third value, type **eft**. Click OK.

The options appear in the Initially Selected field of the Property inspector. Once the list menu is complete, you can select the item that's displayed by default.

**Tip:** One strategy favored by some developers is to select your most preferred option to display by default. In other words, if you like the convenience and security offered by credit cards, the credit card option should be the option pre-selected by default.

**Note:** In some browsers, to select multiple options you first have to hold the Ctrl/Cmd key. If this is the case with your menu, you should add instructions that explain how to make multiple selections.

8 In the Property inspector, from the Initially Selected list, select Credit Card. If necessary, in the Type area, select the Menu option.

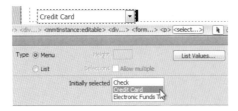

When the List/Menu element is formatted as a Menu, multiple selections are not allowed. To allow multiple selections, change the attribute to List, and then select the Allow Multiple option.

Let's enclose the last four components in their own field set.

9 Select the intro paragraph and the last four components you created using the appropriate tag selector and keyboard and mouse actions. In the Insert panel, click the Fieldset button. Name the new field set **Paris Ecotour**.

10 Save all files.

Menus can contain numerous choices—like all 50 states—and so they provide a powerful tool to the website designer and developer while requiring only a tiny amount of space on the webpage itself. Using a database connection, the list options can also be populated dynamically and even updated instantly as new entries are made by administrators or other users.

Your form is almost complete—the last step is to add a button to submit the entered information for processing.

## Adding a Submit button

Every form needs a control to invoke the dynamic process, or *action*, desired. This job typically falls to the Submit button, which, when clicked, sends the entire form for processing. By default, buttons inserted by Dreamweaver are set to Submit, although they can also be assigned the options Reset or None. Although many buttons used on the Internet feature the text *Submit*, it's not required and may not clearly reflect what action will be performed.

1 Insert the cursor in any form element in the last field set, and select the `<fieldset>` tag selector.

You'll insert the Submit button outside the last field set.

2 Press the Right Arrow key to move the cursor after the selected field set. Then press Enter/Return to create a new paragraph for the button.

**3** In the Insert panel, click the Button () icon.

The Input Tag Accessibility Attributes dialog box appears.

**4** In the ID field, type **submit**. If necessary, select the No Label Tag checkbox. Click OK.

The Submit button appears in the document at the bottom of the form. The Property inspector displays the settings specific to this element. Note that the Button Name and Value fields show the text *submit* and that the Action radio button for Submit Form is selected. Let's change the text in the button to better reflect what's going to happen.

**5** In the Property inspector, change the Value field to **Email Tour Request**.

Some users may change their minds while filling out a form and want to start over or clear the form. In this case, you need to add a Reset button to the form, too.

**6** Insert the cursor after the Submit button. Press Ctrl-Shift-Spacebar/Cmd-Shift-Spacebar to insert a non-breaking space.

## Tabbing tantrums

When filling out forms online, have you ever pressed the Tab key to move from one form field to the next and nothing happened? Or, worse yet, the focus moved to some other field in an unexpected order? The ability to tab through forms is a default process that you should support on your website. It may even be required, in some cases, under Section 508 accessibility mandates.

Tabbing to the various form fields you have created should happen automatically, but some browsers may not support every field type automatically. So, to enforce the tabbing order, you can add a tabindex attribute to each field, like this:

```
<input type="text" name="name" id="name" tabindex="1" />
<input type="text" name="address" id="add1" tabindex="2" />
```

When inserting certain form fields, you may notice a Tab Index field in the dialog box. Enter the desired tab order number here. If the field isn't available, you can insert the attribute manually in Code view. By inserting this code attribute into each form element, you will codify the tabbing order and make your form more accessible to all users, as well as comply with web standards.

**7** Repeat steps 2 through 5 to create a Reset button. In the ID field, type **reset**. In the Value field, type **Clear Form** and select the Reset Form option.

**8** Save the file.

The form elements are all in place and ready to be accessed and filled in, but the form itself won't be complete until you add an action to specify how the data will be processed. Typical actions include sending the data by email, passing it to another webpage, or inserting it into a web-hosted database. In the next exercise, you will apply an action and create the supporting code to email the form data.

## Specifying a form action

As described in the exercise "Setting up email links" in Lesson 9, "Working with Navigation," sending email is not as simple as inserting the `mailto` command into the Action field and adding your email address. Many of your web visitors don't use email programs installed on their computers; they use web-hosted systems like AOL, Gmail, and Hotmail. To guarantee that you receive the form responses, you need to use a server-based application like the one you'll create in this exercise. The first step is to set the form action that passes the data to generate the email.

**Note:** In this exercise, we're using PHP-based code to generate the email form. To set up the action for ASP or ColdFusion coding, you simply add the appropriate extension (.asp or .cf) for the target application.

**1** If necessary, open **signup.html**.

**2** Insert the cursor anywhere in the form, and select the `<form#ecotour>` tag selector.

The Property inspector displays the settings and specifications for the form.

**3** In the Property inspector Action field, type **email_form.php**. If necessary, from the Method field menu, select POST.

**4** Save all files.

HTML provides two built-in methods—GET and POST—for processing form data. The GET method transfers data by appending it to the URL. You see this method used most in search engines, like Google and Yahoo. The next time you conduct a web search, examine the URL on the results page and you will see your search term tucked away somewhere after the domain name, usually bracketed by special characters. There are a couple of disadvantages to using the GET method. First, the search term is visible in the URL, which means other people can see what you're searching for and will also be able to retrieve your search from the browser cache. Second, URLs have a maximum size of a little over 2000 characters (including the filename and path information), which limits the total amount of data you can pass.

The POST method doesn't use the URL. Instead it passes the data behind the scenes and places no limits concerning the amount of data. The POST method doesn't cache the data, so no one can recover sensitive information, like your credit card or driver's license numbers, from the browser history. This method is used by most high-end data applications and online stores. The only disadvantage to using the POST method is that you can't see how the data is being passed to the next page—as you can using GET—which helps when you are troubleshooting application errors.

By selecting POST in step 3, the data the user entered into the form in **signup.html** will be passed to the **email_form.php** file when you click the Email Tour Request (submit) button. As with most hyperlinks, the process loads the new page in the window and resets **signup.html**, deleting the user data from the form. If you navigate back to that page using the site menus, or hyperlinks, the form will be blank. In some instances, you can reload the form page with the data by clicking the Back button in the browser. However, security-conscious developers sometimes add code to their form pages that deletes form data automatically when the page is submitted to prevent this very situation. But no matter how you set up your form, closing the browser will delete the data irrevocably from the local computer.

# Emailing form data

The **email_form.php** file targeted by the form action doesn't exist, so you need to create it from scratch. Although the GreenStart template is an HTML file, you can use it to create a PHP-based form mailer.

1  Open the Assets panel. Select the Template category. Right-click **mygreen_temp** and choose New From Template from the context menu.

2  Save the page as **email_form.php**.

The file extension .php is used for dynamic pages that use the server-based scripting language PHP. The extension informs the browser that the page needs to be processed differently than basic HTML. Some browsers may ignore ASP, ColdFusion, and PHP scripting if the files don't use the appropriate extensions.

3  Select the text *Add main heading here*. Type **Green Travel** to replace the selected text.

> **Warning:** Typing code is tedious and exacting work. PHP—like all scripting languages, such as ASP, ColdFusion, JavaScript, and so on—is not as forgiving of errors as HTML is. While a webpage may function and display in the browser with a broken or incomplete code element, in many cases a PHP script will fail completely if you miss even a single needed character or punctuation mark. So type carefully.

**4** Select the text *Add subheading here.* Type **Thanks for signing up for the Paris Ecotour!** to replace the selected text.

**5** Select the text *Add content here.* Type **A Meridien GreenStart representative will contact you soon to set up your Paris Ecotour. Thanks for your interest in GreenStart and Ecotour!**

**6** Switch to Code view.

The page currently is identical to the HTML-based template and has no PHP markup. The scripting that will process the data and generate the server-based email will be inserted before all other code on the page, even before the <DOCTYPE> declaration that starts the HTML code.

**7** Insert the cursor at the beginning of line 1 in Code view. Type **<?php** and press Enter/Return to create a new paragraph.

```
1   <?php
2   <!DOCTYPE html PUBLIC "-//W3C//DTD XHTML 1.0 Transitional//EN"
```

Dreamweaver's Code Hinting feature starts to help you to enter the code, but you'll quickly realize that this feature doesn't support PHP as it does HTML and JavaScript, so if you like to hand-code PHP, you'll be on your own.

● **Note:** This email address is for the fictitious GreenStart Association. For your own website, insert an email address supported by your server.

**8** Type **$to = "info@green-start.org";** and press Enter/Return to create a new line.

The dollar sign ($) declares a variable in PHP. A variable is a piece of data that will be created within the code or received from another source, such as your form. In this case, the $to variable is declaring the email address to which all the form data will be sent. If you want to experiment with PHP, feel free to substitute the sample address with your own personal email.

**9** Type **$subject = "Paris Ecotour Sign Up Form";** and press Enter/Return to create a new line.

```
1   <?php
2   $to = "info@green-start.org";
3   $subject = "Paris Ecotour Sign Up Form";
4   <!DOCTYPE HTML>
```

This line creates the variable for the email subject. A $subject variable is required in the PHP code, but it can be left blank (" "), although subjects help you organize and filter emails quickly.

**10** Type **$message** = and press Enter/Return to create a new line.

This variable begins the body of the email. The next code elements you enter will list all the form fields you wish to collect, as well as a bit of structural trickery to make the email easier to read. Although you can list the fields in any order you want (and more than once), in this exercise you will type them in the same order they are in the form. If you recall, the first field in the sign-up form was Name.

**11** Type **"Customer name: " . $_POST['name'] . "\r\n" .**

The first part of this entry is part of the "trickery" we just mentioned. The text **"Customer name: "** has nothing to do with the form. You are adding it to the email simply to identify the raw customer data that's being inserted by the **$_POST['name']** variable. The period (.) character concatenates, or combines, the text and the data variable into one string. The code element **"\r\n"** inserts a new paragraph after the customer name. Insert this code after each form variable to put each piece of data on its own line.

**12** Complete the email body by typing the following code. Insert spaces after the colon (:) to indent the variable statements so that they align to the same position. (Some lines will get more spaces than others.)

```
"Email:            " . $_POST['email'] . "\r\n" .
"Password:         " . $_POST['password'] . "\r\n" . "\r\n" .
"Requested tour:   " . $_POST['tourdate_0'] . "\r\n" .
"Requested tour:   " . $_POST['tourdate_1'] . "\r\n" .
"Requested tour:   " . $_POST['tourdate_2'] . "\r\n" .
"Total travelers:  " . $_POST['travelers'] . "\r\n" . "\r\n" .
"Restrictions:     " . $_POST['restrictions'] . "\r\n" . "\r\n" .
"Payment type:     " . $_POST['payment'];
```

When you are finished, the code should look like the following figure.

```
4   $message =
5   "Customer name: " . $_POST['name'] . "\r\n" .
6   "Email:          " . $_POST['email'] . "\r\n" .
7   "Password:       " . $_POST['password'] . "\r\n" . "\r\n" .
8   "Requested tour: " . $_POST['tourdate_0'] . "\r\n" .
9   "Requested tour: " . $_POST['tourdate_1'] . "\r\n" .
10  "Requested tour: " . $_POST['tourdate_2'] . "\r\n" .
11  "Total travelers: " . $_POST['travelers'] . "\r\n" . "\r\n" .
12  "Restrictions:    " . $_POST['restrictions'] . "\r\n" . "\r\n" .
13  "Payment type:   " . $_POST['payment'];
14  <!DOCTYPE HTML>
```

Adding spaces before the variables should align the form data when inserted into the message, making the email neater and easier to read. Note that certain lines show code for two paragraph returns (**"\r\n" . "\r\n" .**). Putting extra lines between specific data elements can help make the email easier to read.

**13** Press Enter/Return. Type `$from = $_POST['email'];` and press Enter/Return.

This code creates a variable that will be used to populate the From email address using the information the customer entered in the form.

**14** Type `$headers = "From: $from" . "\r\n";` and press Enter/Return.

This line creates the email "From" header using the variable from step 13.

**15** Type `$headers = "Bcc: lin@green-start.org" . "\r\n";` and press Enter/Return.

This line is optional. It generates a blind carbon copy of the email to Lin, the transportation expert at GreenStart. Feel free to customize the code by adding your own email here or the email of a coworker.

**16** Type `mail($to,$subject,$message,$headers);` and press Enter/Return.

This line creates the email and sends it using a PHP-enabled server.

● **Note:** This email address is for the fictitious GreenStart Association. For your own website, insert an email address supported by your server.

● **Note:** This code will work only on a PHP-enabled web server. It may not function on a local web server. Specific commands may not be supported by your server type. It's a good idea to check with your Internet host provider to obtain a list of the code items supported by your server.

# Supporting other scripting languages

The server-based functionality you just created is also available in every major scripting language. Although Dreamweaver doesn't provide this functionality out of the box, frequently you can find the exact code structure you need through a quick search of the Internet. Just type the phrase *form data to email* or *web form mail* and you'll get thousands of options. Add your favorite scripting language to the search phrase (like *form data to email+ASP*) to target or narrow the results.

Here are a few examples:

- **ASP:** tinyurl.com/asp-formmailer
- **ColdFusion:** tinyurl.com/cf-formmailer
- **PHP:** tinyurl.com/php-formmailer

You may also find these books good resources:

- *Adobe Dreamweaver CS5 with PHP: Training from the Source*, David Powers (Adobe Press, 2010)
- *Adobe Dreamweaver CS3 with ASP, ColdFusion, and PHP: Training from the Source*, Jeffrey Bardzell and Bob Flynn (Adobe Press, 2007)
- *Build Your Own Database Driven Web Site, 4th Edition*, Kevin Yank (SitePoint Pty Ltd., 2009)

**17** Type **?>** to close and complete the PHP form email function.

**18** Press Enter/Return to insert one last paragraph return. Save all files.

```
12  "Restrictions:       " . $_POST['restrictions'] . "\r\n" . "\r\n" .
13  "Payment type:    " . $_POST['payment'];
14  $from = $_POST['email'];
15  $headers = "From: $from" . "\r\n";
16  $headers = "Bcc: lin@green-start.org" . "\r\n";
17  mail($to,$subject,$message,$headers);
18  ?>
19  <!DOCTYPE HTML>
```

# Styling forms

Although the form and the email application you've been working on in this lesson are now functional, it's mostly *un*styled. Good styling can enhance form readability and comprehension and can make forms easier to use. In the following exercise, you'll style the form by creating a new custom style sheet.

**1** If necessary, open or switch to **signup.html**.

**2** Open the CSS Styles panel.

You'll create a new style sheet just for forms; that way, it can be attached to this and other form pages but not to the entire site. Separating the CSS rules for forms from the master style sheet limits the amount of code that must be downloaded and creates a more efficient site overall. Less code means faster downloads and a better user experience.

**3** At the bottom of the CSS Styles panel, click the Attach Style Sheet (⊜) icon.

The Attach External Style Sheet dialog box appears.

**4** In the File/URL field, type **forms.css**. Select the options Add as: Link and Media: Screen. Click OK.

Dreamweaver alerts you that the named style sheet does not exist.

**5** Click Yes to link to the new style sheet.

6   Insert the cursor in the legend text *Your Contact Information*. Click the New CSS Rule icon.

The New CSS Rule dialog box appears.

7   At the bottom of the dialog box, select the **forms.css** style sheet from the pop-up menu. This tells Dreamweaver to define your new rule in the **forms.css** file. Choose Compound from the Selector Type menu. Edit the Selector Name to read `.content section legend`. Click OK.

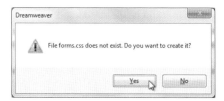

Dreamweaver asks if you want to create the **forms.css** style sheet.

8   Click Yes to create the style sheet.

9   Enter the following specifications for the `.content section legend` rule:
Font-size: **110%**
Font-weight: **bold**
Color: **#090**

10  Create a new CSS rule in **forms.css** named `.content section fieldset`.

11  Enter the following specifications for the `.content section fieldset` rule:
Padding: **5px**
Borders: **solid**, **2px**, and **#090**

12  Save all files.

**13** Preview the page in the primary browser.

Ecotour Sign-up Form

To sign up for the Ecotour, please fill out the following fields:

┌─ Your Contact Information ─────────────────────────────────────
│  Name: [                    ]
│
│  Email: [                    ]
└────────────────────────────────────────────────────────────────

┌─ Customer Account Login ───────────────────────────────────────
│  Your itinerary and travel plans can be accessed online using the email address you entered above
│  and a custom password. In the following fields you can set up and confirm your password.
│
│  *Your itinerary and travel plans can be accessed online using the email address you entered*
│  *above and a custom password. In the following fields you can set up and confirm your*
│  *password.*
│
│  Password: [                    ]
│
│  Repeat Password: [                    ]
└────────────────────────────────────────────────────────────────

┌─ Paris Ecotour ────────────────────────────────────────────────
│  Three tentative dates have been selected for the Ecotour. Please select any date(s) you prefer:
│
│  ☐ June 15-25, 2012
│  ☐ September 7-17, 2012
│  ☐ March 15-25, 2013
└────────────────────────────────────────────────────────────────

In this lesson, you built a user-fillable form with a variety of HTML and Spry form elements. You created and attached a custom style sheet to liven up its appearance. In the browser, you will be able to test all the form fields. When you click the Email Tour Request button, the form data will be passed to the **email_form.php** file. If the page is previewed in a PHP-enabled system, an email will be generated and sent to the email address targeted in the PHP code.

At the moment, this form simply collects the data and processes it as a standard, text-based email. The recipient still has to access and further process the data manually. To take this process to the next level of automation, you can use Dreamweaver to modify **signup.html** so that it will insert the information directly into a web-hosted database.

● **Note:** Unless all files are uploaded to a PHP-compatible testing server, you will probably receive an error message if you try to submit this page. That's because the code you created is designed to work on the fictitious GreenStart website running a PHP server. For your own website, insert email addresses supported by your server and modify the code as necessary.

# Review questions

1 What is the purpose of the `<form>` tag?

2 What does selecting the Attach Label Tag Using 'for' Attribute option do?

3 What advantages do the Spry Form widgets have over standard form objects?

4 What's the difference between a standard text field and a text area?

5 What's the main difference between radio buttons and checkboxes?

6 How do you specify that separate radio buttons belong to a group?

7 What is the purpose of the `<fieldset>` element?

# Review answers

1 The `<form>` tag wraps around all the form elements and includes an action attribute that defines the file or script to handle the form processing.

2 It connects the `<label>` tag to the form element, which has a matching ID value.

3 Spry Form widgets make it easier to create form elements. They include built-in validation to ensure that the data submitted is properly formatted and, if required, completed.

4 A standard text field is intended for short character strings, whereas a text area can hold multiple paragraphs.

5 Radio buttons only allow for mutually exclusive choices, whereas checkboxes permit the user to select as many items as desired.

6 All radio buttons with the same name will be in the same radio button group.

7 A `<fieldset>` element is used to group related form fields together with an accompanying `<legend>` element that identifies the group. It helps to organize a form and clarify the purpose of the various form fields.

# 13 WORKING WITH ONLINE DATA

## Lesson Overview

In this lesson, you will learn how to work with information stored in tables and databases to do the following:

- Create dynamic content based on HTML tables and XML data sets

- Select a server model

- Set up a testing server

- Connect to a data source

This lesson will take about 90 minutes to complete, plus an additional 30–45 minutes to create a local web server, if needed. Before beginning, make sure you have copied the files for Lesson 13 to your hard drive as described in the "Getting Started" section at the beginning of the book. If you are starting from scratch in this lesson, use the method described in the "Jumpstart" section of "Getting Started."

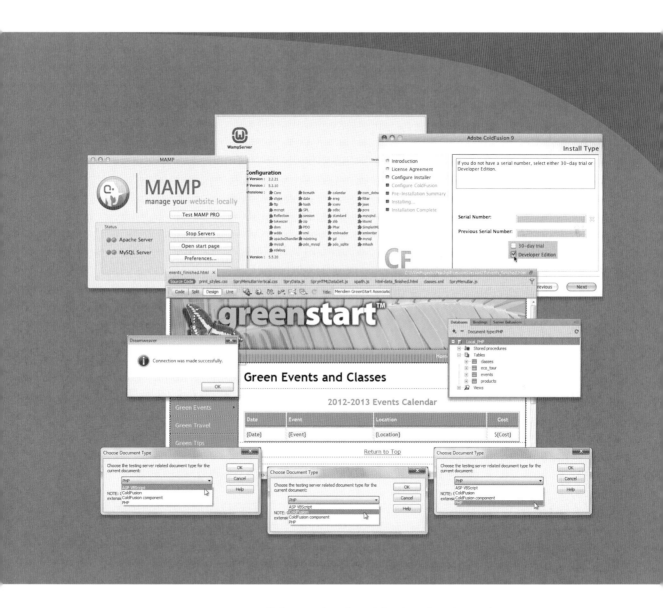

By its very nature, the web is a dynamic environment. Get the most out of your website by connecting it to live data using Spry, ASP, ColdFusion, or PHP.

# Working with dynamic content

Except for a few interactive Spry components and a little HTML5-compatible animation and video, the pages you have built in this training have been mostly static, like text and pictures on paper. Yet the web is a dynamic environment. The live connection to the Internet makes the delivery of text, pictures, animation, and video only a click away.

Many of the most popular websites today supply content through two-way interactions with their visitors. This "query and response" method of content delivery can't be accomplished by HTML alone. It requires scripting and a variety of server-based applications that are supported by languages like Ajax, ASP, ColdFusion, JavaScript, and PHP, among others. This technique also requires information stored on the Internet, usually in the form of a table or database.

Until a few years ago, HTML tables were static containers. But now the lowly table has been liberated through the intervention of Asynchronous JavaScript and XML (Ajax). Dreamweaver can easily harness all the power of Ajax through Adobe's Spry framework and some surprisingly powerful widgets. At the moment, you may lack the ability to develop more sophisticated applications, but there's no longer any excuse for putting static tables on your website.

# Previewing the completed file

● **Note:** If you are starting from scratch in this lesson, see the "Jumpstart" instructions in the "Getting Started" section at the beginning of the book.

To see what Ajax can do for HTML-based tables, let's preview the completed file.

1  Launch Dreamweaver, if necessary. Open **events_finished.html** in the lesson13 folder, and examine the Events Calendar and Class Schedule tables.

## Green Events and Classes

### 2012-2013 Events Calendar

| Date | Event | Location | Cost |
|------|-------|----------|------|
| {Date} | {Event} | {Location} | ${Cost} |

Return to Top

### 2012-2013 Class Schedule

| Class | Description | Length | Day | Cost |
|-------|-------------|--------|-----|------|
| {Class} | {Description} | {Length} | {Day} | ${Cost} |

Return to Top

Both tables consist of two rows: a header row and a data row. Note the placeholder text in the second row of each table, such as {Date} and {Event}. These are components of Spry widgets that generate table data dynamically.

2  Preview the page in Live view.

## Green Events and Classes

2012-2013 Events Calendar

| Date | Event | Location | Cost |
|------|-------|----------|------|
| Mar 16, 2012 | Nature Preserve Hike | Burkeline Nature Preserve | $10 |
| May 09, 2012 | Mothers Day Walk | Meridien Park | $0 |
| Jun 05, 2012 | Day Hike | East Side Park | $10 |
| Jun 24, 2012 | Glacial Park Tour | Meridien Park | $10 |
| Jul 02, 2012 | Beginners Backpacking - 3 days | Burkeline Mountains Resort | $125 |
| Jul 17, 2012 | East Trail Hike | East Side Park | $10 |
| Sep 10, 2012 | 3-Day Backpack | Burkeline Mountains Resort | $125 |
| Sep 14, 2012 | Book Club | East Side Community Center | $0 |
| Oct 16, 2012 | Day hike at the Dunes | Shoreline Park | $10 |
| Oct 18, 2012 | Volunteer for Homeless Shelter | North Side Community Center | $0 |

The placeholders are replaced by data from external sources. Additional rows are generated automatically. Note that the text in the Events table is sorted by date.

3  Click the header cell for each column.

The data in the table sorts based on the data in the column.

4  Move the cursor over each row in the table.

As the cursor passes over each row, it changes color momentarily.

5  Click any row in the table, and then move the cursor away from that row.

The selected row changes color completely and remains highlighted as the cursor moves away.

6  Repeat steps 3–5 for the Class table.

The Class table exhibits the same behaviors as the Events table. The functionality for sorting tables interactively and creating the *hover* and *select* effects are all produced by Ajax scripting.

In the next exercise, you'll learn how to tap into the power of Ajax by using Spry to liberate data stored in HTML tables and XML files, and you will produce these same effects.

# Using HTML and XML data

Before you can display data on your webpages, you'll need to establish a proper data source. In years past, this meant working with proprietary programming languages like ASP, ColdFusion, and PHP. These are powerful languages that are still used in thousands of websites today, and you'll learn more about them later in this lesson. But Ajax has revolutionized the role of data within many sites. As powerful as they are, the traditional languages can display data changes only after they reload the entire page. On the other hand, Ajax can update data in real time.

This capability is enabled through the use of HTML and XML data sets and JavaScript. In HTML, the data is stored in tables. XML (Extensible Markup Language) data is stored in a plain-text file using a standardized specification for marking up text. In the following exercises, you'll work with both HTML and XML data sets.

HTML (left) and XML (right) store information in different ways, but both are accessible to Dreamweaver.

```
264  <tr>
265  <td>Choices for Sustainable Living</td>
266  <td>This course explores the meaning of sustainable living
     and how our choices have an impact on ecological systems.
     </td>
267  <td class="length">4 weeks</td>
268  <td class="day">M</td>
269  <td class="cost">$40 </td>
270  </tr>
271  <tr>
272  <td>Exploring Deep Ecology</td>
273  <td>An eight-session course examining our core values and
     how they affect the way we view and treat the earth.</td>
274  <td class="length">4 weeks</td>
275  <td class="day">F</td>
276  <td class="cost">$40 </td>
277  </tr>
278  <tr>
```

```
3   <classes>
4   <Class>Choices for Sustainable Living</Class>
5   <Description>This course explores the meaning of
    sustainable living and how our choices have an impact on
    ecological systems.</Description>
6   <Length>4 weeks</Length>
7   <Day>M</Day>
8   <Cost>40</Cost>
9   </classes>
10  <classes>
11  <Class>Exploring Deep Ecology</Class>
12  <Description>An eight-session course examining our core
    values and how they affect the way we view and treat the
    earth.</Description>
13  <Length>4 weeks</Length>
14  <Day>F</Day>
15  <Cost>40</Cost>
16  </classes>
```

## Working with HTML data

**Tip:** HTML tables can be created quickly and easily from spreadsheet and database files. See Lesson 7, "Working with Text, Lists and Tables."

Until the advent of Ajax, data stored in HTML tables was static and unusable by the rest of the website. In other words, the data in a table on page A could not be used by page B unless you copied and pasted part or all of the data onto that page, too. The problem with this workflow is obvious. Once you paste the data onto multiple pages, you have to constantly update every page manually when the data changes, creating a lot more work and possibilities for error. Using the Adobe Spry framework, Dreamweaver can now tap into HTML table-based data in a new, dynamic way.

1  If necessary, launch Dreamweaver and switch to Design view. Open **events.html** from the site root folder.

   This page contains two HTML-based tables filled with data. At the moment, the data is static, but by using Ajax via the Spry framework you'll be able to tap into this data for a variety of purposes. The first step is to move the table into a separate document.

**2** Insert the cursor into the Events table and select the `<table#calendar>` tag selector. Press Ctrl-X/Cmd-X to cut the table.

**3** Select File > New. Choose Blank Page > HTML > <none>. Click OK/Create.

A new, blank document is created.

**4** If necessary, insert the cursor in the Design view window. Press Ctrl-V/Cmd-V to paste the table. Insert a new, empty paragraph after the table.

▶ **Tip:** If you copy the table in Design view, you must paste it in Design view.

Before a table can be used as a Spry data set, it must have a unique ID.

**5** Insert the cursor into the table. Examine the tag selectors.

The tag selector displays `<table#calendar>`.

**6** Select the `<table#calendar>` tag selector and examine the Property inspector.

Note that the ID field displays the text *calendar*. You applied IDs to both tables in Lesson 9, "Working with Navigation," and the ID was preserved when you copied and pasted the table into this file.

● **Note:** You may notice that none of the attached style sheets contain a #calendar rule. Although IDs are frequently used to create styling, no CSS rule has to be created to use the ID for this purpose.

**7** Save the file as **html-data.html** in the site root folder.

There's no limit to how many tables one file can hold, but don't go crazy; files containing lots of tables can take longer to download from the Internet and can detract from a user's overall experience.

**8** Click the **events.html** document tab to bring it to the front. Repeat step 2 to cut the Class table. Switch to **html-data.html**. Paste the Class table in the empty paragraph below the Events table.

● **Note:** The order of the tables does not affect how you can use them.

**9** Save and close the file.

**10** If necessary, click the tab for **events.html** to bring that document to the front. Insert the cursor at the end of the *Green Events and Classes* heading and press Enter/Return to create a new, empty paragraph.

**11** Open the Insert panel. Choose Spry from the Category menu. Click the Spry Data Set button.

The Spry Data Set dialog box appears.

**12** In the Select Data Type menu, choose HTML.

In the Data Set Name field, enter **ds_events**.

In the Detect field menu, choose Tables.

Click Browse and, from the site root folder, select **html-data.html**. Click Open/Choose.

A preview of the data sources in **html-data.html** appears in the Data Preview window.

**13** In the Data Containers menu in the upper right, choose Calendar. Click the Next button at the bottom of the dialog box.

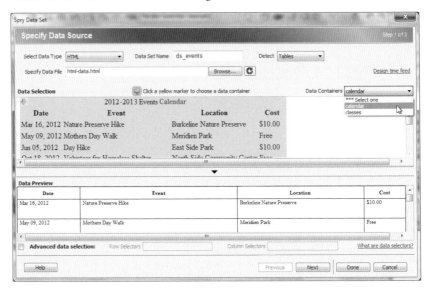

The Spry Data Set dialog box now displays a window to set data options. In this window you can identify specific types of data, such as text (string), numbers, dates, and HTML code. Identifying the data type is important if you want to sort data by certain values, such as by dates or cost, or use the data for other special purposes.

## Spry data types

The proper data type is necessary for sorting operations. The available data types are:

- string—Alphanumeric data
- number—Numeric data only
- date—A full date, such as 1/1/2011 or January 1, 2011 or Jan 1, 2011
- html—Marked-up text, such as the lists in this example

**14** In the Column Name menu, choose Date. In the Type menu, choose string.

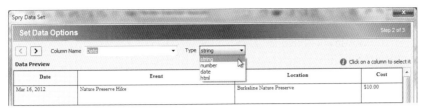

Note that the Use First Row As Header option is selected. If you use a table that doesn't contain a header row, this option should be deselected.

**15** In the Sort Column field, choose Date. Examine the order of the data in the Data Preview window.

Note that the column sorts incorrectly, based on the spelling of the month. You can correct this problem by changing its data type.

**16** Click the first row of the Date column. In the Type menu, choose date.

The column is now sorted correctly, based on the event date.

For Spry applications, dates can be entered in two basic formats: by spelling out the month, day, and year—typically January (or Jan) 1, 2011—or by standard numeric notation, such as 1/1/2011. However, the Spry Data Set dialog box will not recognize dates written like this: 1-1-2011.

**17** Click the first row in the Event column. In the Type menu, choose string. Select the Location column. In the Type menu, choose string.

Now it's time to assign the data type to the Cost column. You may notice that the Cost column of the Events table contains numeric and non-numeric characters. If a field contains characters other than those accepted by that type of data, you should choose string from the Type menu. For this example, you will assign the number type. This will cause an error at first, but you will adjust the data later to compensate.

**18** Select the Cost column. In the Type menu, choose number. Click Next.

The Spry Data Set dialog box now displays the insert options for the data set.

**19** Click the Set Up button beside the Insert Table option.

The Spry Data Set–Insert Table dialog box appears. This dialog box allows you to specify what data will be displayed and how it will appear. Feel free to experiment by removing or changing the order of the data columns, and by specifying whether they are *sortable* or not.

**Note:** Choosing **number** as the Type for the Cost column will cause an error when the data is rendered, because the column currently contains non-numeric data. Before you can test the file successfully, you will have to remove the dollar sign ($) and any other non-numeric characters.

**20** Select the Sort Column When Header Is Clicked check box, if necessary.

In the Odd Row Class field, enter **odd**.

In the Even Row Class field, enter **even**.

In the Hover Class field, enter **rowhover**.

In the Select Class field, enter **rowselect**. Click OK.

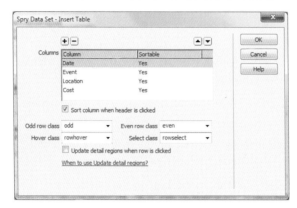

This dialog box assigns CSS classes to style the table interactively, powered by JavaScript. These classes don't exist yet; if they did, you could select them from the menus. You will create them in the next exercise.

**21** Click Done.

A two-row Spry data table placeholder is inserted in the layout. Some of the formatting on the placeholder should match the default table styling you created in Lesson 7, "Working with Text, Lists, and Tables." The Spry component is nearly complete, but it still needs custom CSS rules for the classes you assigned in step 20.

## Styling Spry tables

The odd/even, hover, and select effects are styled using CSS rules invoked by JavaScript. These rules don't exist yet. You will also have to reapply some of the table styles you created in Lesson 7.

**1** In the CSS Styles panel, select the last rule in **mygreen_styles.css**. Click the New CSS Rule icon in the CSS Styles panel.

The new rule will be inserted at the end of the style sheet.

**2** In the Selector Type menu, choose Class. In the Selector Name field, enter **odd**. Click OK.

**3** In Background-color, enter **#FFC** and click OK.

**4** Create a new CSS class for **even**. Assign it a background color of **#CFC**.

**5** Create a new CSS class for **rowhover**. Assign it a background color of **#9C6**.

**6** Create a new CSS class for **rowselect**. In the Type category Color field, enter **#FFF**. Assign it a background color of **#990**.

**7** Save all files.

A dialog box may appear indicating that files are being added to the SpryAssets folder to enable the Spry functionality. Before you test the Spry functionality, let's reapply the styling for the Date and Cost columns.

**8** If necessary, click OK.

**9** Insert the cursor in the header for the Date column. Select the `<th>` tag selector. From the Class menu in the Property inspector, choose w100.

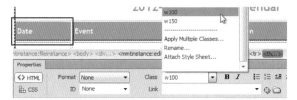

**10** Select the cells in both rows of the Cost column. From the Class menu, choose cost.

In Lesson 9, "Working with Navigation," you added ID attributes to both tables to create hyperlink destinations. You need to add those attributes to your new Spry tables.

**11** Select the `<table>` tag selector. In the Property inspector ID field, enter **calendar** and press Enter/Return.

The last step is to re-create the table caption. Tag selectors can help you locate specific markup when you work in Code view.

**12** Insert the cursor in the table. Click the `<table#calendar>` tag selector. Switch to Code view. Insert the cursor directly after the opening table tag. Type `<caption>2012-2013 Events Calendar</caption>`.

**13** Switch to Design view. Save all files.

**14** Preview the page in Live view and test the table behaviors.

When you click the header fields, the table sorts based on the data content. When you move the cursor over the rows, they change color. When you click any individual data row, the color of the row changes completely and the text appears in white.

## 2012-2013 Events Calendar

| Date | Event | Location | Cost |
|------|-------|----------|------|
| Mar 16, 2012 | Nature Preserve Hike | Burkeline Nature Preserve | NaN |
| May 09, 2012 | Mothers Day Walk | Meridien Park | NaN |
| Jun 05, 2012 | Day Hike | East Side Park | NaN |

The only problem seems to be coming from the Cost column, which is displaying an error message: NaN, which stands for "Not a Number." The original table was not designed for this use, and the data contains non-numeric characters. You'll have to remove these characters from the data table to complete the component.

## Updating HTML data

You can correct the data table manually, or you can use Dreamweaver's Find/Replace command.

**1** Open **html-data.html** from the site root folder. Select the dollar sign ($) in the first row of the Events table. Press Ctrl-F/Cmd-F.

The Find and Replace dialog box appears. The dollar sign ($) is entered in the Find field automatically.

**2** Confirm that the Find In: Current Document and Search: Text options are selected. Leave the Replace field empty and click Replace.

The selected dollar sign is removed and Dreamweaver automatically selects the next dollar sign in the file.

**3** Continue to click Replace to remove the dollar signs one at a time, or click Replace All to remove them all at once.

Clicking Replace All will close the Find and Replace dialog box. To perform the next step you will have to press Ctrl-F/Cmd-F to re-open the Find and Replace dialog box.

4   Replace the text *Free* with the number **0** (zero). Replace the word *Donation* with the number **0** (zero).

5   Close the Find and Replace dialog box. Save and close **html-data.html**.

6   Click the tab for **events.html** to bring it to the front. If necessary, preview the page in Live view.

Now that you have removed the non-numeric characters, the HTML-based data displays properly. But users may be confused by prices appearing without dollar signs. Although the dollar sign is incompatible in the data file, there's a simple trick that will allow you to use it in the final display.

7   Switch back to Design view. Insert the cursor before the data placeholder {cost}. Type **$**.

The placeholder now appears as ${cost}.

8   Preview the document in Live view.

By adding the dollar sign before the data placeholder, Dreamweaver clones it automatically for each data row. You can use this method for all sorts of introductory characters and text.

9   Save all files.

Spry data sets can also be based on XML data.

## Working with XML data

XML is a markup language closely related to HTML. They both use the same tag-based method for marking up text. The reason XML is called *extensible* is because you create your own tag names (unlike HTML).

The language was invented directly in response to HTML's limitations in dealing with data in web applications. The simplest way to explain their different roles is this: HTML was designed to *display* data; XML was designed to *define* it.

In XML, data elements are placed between opening and closing tag pairs, like this:

<company>Meridien GreenStart</company>

XML can be written by hand or it can be exported from a number of data applications, such as MS Access, MS Excel, FileMaker Pro, and large-scale databases like Oracle and SQL Server. Non-proprietary databases—such as MySQL—are very popular on the web and are also compatible with XML. You will learn about other types of web-based database applications later in this lesson.

Spry data sets can use XML data and HTML data tables interchangeably.

1 If necessary, open **events.html**. In Design view, insert a new paragraph after the first *Return to Top* hyperlink.

The XML-based data set must be inserted outside the `<div>` element containing the HTML data set. Nested Spry data sets are not allowed in Dreamweaver.

2 In the Insert panel, click the Spry Data Set button.

The Spry Data Set dialog box appears.

3 From the Select Data Type menu, choose XML. In the Data Set Name field, enter **ds_classes**. Browse and select **classes.xml** from the lesson13 > resources folder.

The Specify Data Source dialog box appears displaying the structure of the XML data. The window shows a list of the XML tags, or *elements*, contained within the file. The first tag is `<dataroot>`, which is the root, or main parent, element that contains all data. The next element is `<classes>`, and you can tell from how the other tags are indented that it is the parent of the remaining elements. The plus (+) sign on the element indicates that the file contains two or more classes.

4 Select the `classes` tag and note the Data Preview window. Click Next.

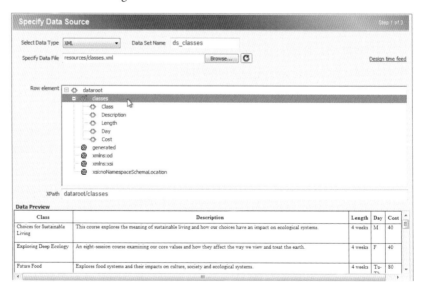

The Set Data Options screen appears.

5 For the data type for the first four columns, choose string. For the data type for the Cost column, choose number. In the Sort Column menu, choose Class.

This file doesn't contain date data; the entire contents can be treated as text or numbers.

**6**  Click Next. For the Insert Table option, click Set Up.

**7**  Make sure the Sort Column When Header Is Clicked check box is selected.
In the Odd Row Class field, enter or select **odd**.
In the Even Row Class field, enter or select **even**.
In the Hover Class field, enter or select **rowhover**.
In the Select Class field, enter or select **rowselect**. Click OK.

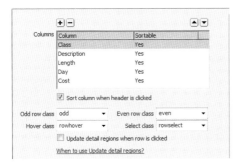

Selecting the class names from the menus can prevent you from typing the names incorrectly. Since the CSS classes already exist, the new table should be ready to function.

**8**  Click Done.

The XML-based Spry table is inserted in the page, complete with data placeholders. Before previewing it, let's add the original caption.

**9**  Insert the cursor into the XML-based Spry table. Click the `<table>` tag selector. Switch to Code view and add the following code after the opening `<table>` tag:

```
<caption>2012-2013 Class Schedule</caption>
```

**10**  Save all files and preview the page in Live view.

Both tables display the appropriate data and behave just like the sample you previewed at the beginning of the lesson.

Spry data sets provide a powerful option for importing and displaying HTML and XML source materials dynamically, but it's not a perfect solution. Although Ajax makes the data *display* dynamic, the data *files* are anything but. For one thing, there's no native method for updating HTML and XML data that changes quickly, like sports scores and weather forecasts.

Instead, developers store data in traditional databases and then, using custom scripting, generate HTML and XML data files periodically or interactively upon a user request. This type of hybrid system brings together the benefits of both techniques, and many sites are following this model today. Although many sites have switched over to Ajax completely, quite a few are still using ASP, ColdFusion, and PHP. In upcoming exercises, you'll explore how some of these powerful tools and capabilities work.

# Choosing a server model

If you decide to build dynamic web applications, one of the first steps you have to make before you write a single line of code is to choose the server model you'll use for your site. Many factors go into this decision, including the purpose of the site, the type of applications you wish to develop, the cost of the server model, and even the type of database you wish to use. In some cases, the choice of database will select the server; in others, the reverse will be true.

For example, the MS Access database favors the ASP server model, which runs on Windows Server operating systems. On the other hand, the MySQL database, which is typically combined with either ColdFusion or PHP, runs equally well on all servers. Here's a quick overview of the major server models that you should keep in mind while you are making your choice:

**ASP** (Active Server Pages) is a Microsoft technology that runs natively in Windows. Dreamweaver provides server behaviors for ASP in Visual Basic (VBScript) but not in JavaScript. While some think it's difficult to learn and use, it's included for free with Microsoft's Internet Information Services (IIS), which means that all Windows users can immediately create applications with little extra setup. Also available is ASP.NET, the successor to ASP, developed to correct some of ASP's limitations and increase the speed and power of the resulting web applications. Dreamweaver no longer provides server behaviors for ASP JavaScript and ASP.NET, although you will still be able to hand-code and test these pages in the program.

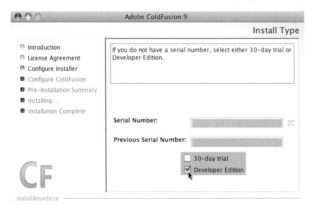

**ColdFusion** is an Adobe server technology that uses a tag-based syntax that some feel is easier to learn and use than ASP or PHP. For many processes, ColdFusion requires fewer lines of code, which provides advantages during development and deployment of web applications. Unlike the other server technologies described here, ColdFusion is not free, although some feel that the productivity gains are worth the extra cost. ColdFusion can run on Windows, Linux/Unix, and Macintosh servers. To get a head start, you can download and install the free Developer's

Edition of ColdFusion, which enables you to build a fully workable dynamic site locally, before you upload it to the Internet.

**PHP** (PHP Hypertext Processor), originally known as Personal Home Page, is now one of the most popular languages used on the web. It is free and works well with a variety of databases and other services. It offers a similar level of difficulty as ASP, but because of its popularity there are plenty of resources available to obtain code examples as well as support, which is also free, for the most part.

# Configuring a local web server

There are two ways to test dynamic pages. You can upload them to your web host and test them live on the Internet, or you can test the files *before* you upload them on your own personal computer. While nothing beats the authenticity of the actual Internet servers that will host your site, a local server offers advantages of both speed and security. It also allows you to work offline, without a live connection to the Internet.

Before you can test any of the dynamic webpages that you will build in the next lesson, you must install the applications and components needed for a local web server. This process is tedious and prone to error. It consists of numerous critical steps for loading and configuring all aspects of your chosen environment. As such, it is outside the scope of this book. Luckily, there are many sources both in print and online that can assist you in this endeavor. Here are a few:

In Print:

- *Adobe Dreamweaver CS3 with ASP, ColdFusion, and PHP: Training from the Source*, Jeffrey Bardzell and Bob Flynn (Adobe Press, 2007)

Online:

- ASP and IIS—tinyurl.com/setup-asp *or* tinyurl.com/IIS-setup
- ColdFusion— tinyurl.com/setup-ColdFusion
- PHP— tinyurl.com/setup-apachephp

The specific examples shown in the following exercises are based on the Windows/ Macintosh Apache MySQL PHP (WAMP/MAMP) web servers, so this may be your obvious choice. Download WAMP at tinyurl.com/WAMP-setup. Download MAMP at tinyurl.com/MAMP-setup. Another Windows-based web server, called XAMPP, is also available and is referenced in several of the links provided in this lesson. To download and try out this server, go to tinyurl.com/XAMPP-server.

Although the exercises were created for the WAMP/MAMP environments, it's possible to install and use an ASP or ColdFusion server, as well. Unfortunately, there won't be any help within the exercises to adapt the instructions to those servers. You'll be on your own.

# Setting up a testing server

**Note:** Internet-based servers usually require authentication using a user name and password, which you should obtain in advance from your server administrator.

To preview and test dynamic pages, you need to connect to a *testing server* in Dreamweaver. "Local web server" and "testing server" sound similar, but they are not the same. A testing server is simply a connection to a web hosting server—either local or on the Internet—where dynamic functions can be "tested." You can use your own local web server, which you should have installed at this point, or you may use the actual web server where you intend to upload your final website.

When you choose to test a particular page, Dreamweaver copies the necessary files to the testing server and then loads the document in a browser or in Live view. The testing server is configured in Dreamweaver's Site Setup dialog box.

1  Select Site > Manage Sites.

2  Select DW-CS6 from the Manage Sites dialog box. Click Edit.

3  Select the Servers category.

If you have an existing server configured, you can click the check box under the Testing column in the server list to identify it as your testing server. For the purpose of the following exercises, the instructions assume you have chosen and configured PHP/MySQL as your server model and will use an Apache local web server to test pages on your computer.

**Note:** The WAMP/ MAMP servers are free, easy to set up, and compatible with both Windows and Mac OS X computers.

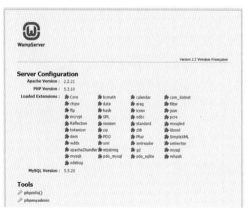
Windows

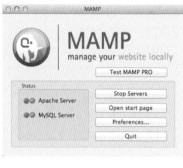
Macintosh

**Note:** Your computer will treat the local web server as if it's a live web server and all sites located within it as if they're on the Internet.

4  Click the Add New Server button at the bottom of the server list.

5  Name the server **PHP-Test**. From the Connect Using menu, choose Local/ Network.

6  Click the Browse button to the right of the Server Folder field.
In Windows, navigate to **C:\wamp\www**.
In OS X, navigate to **Applications/MAMP/htdocs**.

**7** Create a new folder and name it **DWCS6-Test**. If necessary, double-click the new folder to open it. Click Select/Choose.

For Windows users, the path will be **C:\wamp\www\DWCS6-Test**.
For Mac users, the Server Folder field displays the path **Applications/MAMP/ htdocs/DWCS6-Test**.

▶ **Tip:** If you are using your actual web server as your testing server, enter the URL of your website here. For example, http://www.green-start.org.

**8** Enter the path to the testing site in the Web URL field.

For the WAMP PHP, the default URL will probably be **http://localhost/ DWCS6-Test**.
For the MAMP PHP, the default URL will probably be **http://Localhost:8888/ DWCS6-Test**.
For other types of server models, the URL will be different. Enter the URL appropriate for your server. Without the correct URL, the page will not load correctly in your local server.

**9** Click the Advanced button.

The dialog box displays the Advanced configuration options.

**10** From the Server Model menu, choose PHP MySQL.

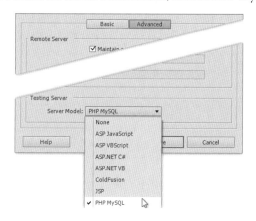

**11** Click Save.

**12** Select the Testing option in the Servers category to enable the testing server.

▶ **Tip:** Windows servers are not case sensitive, so the capitalization of your file and folder names is not critical. Linux/ Unix servers are case sensitive. It's a good idea to write down file and folder names or use only lowercase characters to prevent server errors when loading test pages and content.

● **Note:** In PHP and ColdFusion servers, you may have to include the port number in the URL to enable the connection.

● **Note:** While you can define and configure multiple servers in the CS6 Site Setup dialog box, only one testing server and one remote server may be active at a time. You do not have to use the same server for both.

**13** Click Save to dismiss the Site Setup dialog box. Dreamweaver will probably prompt you to rebuild the cache. Click OK.

**14** Click Done to close the Manage Sites dialog box.

Your testing server for PHP is now configured. Although the server is intended for one specific language, other scripting languages may still be supported, depending on your server setup. As you may have noticed from the menu in step 10, Dreamweaver supports all the major server models. The importance of what server model you select can't be overstated. Changing server models once you start to build pages would require you to scrap all your work and start over.

# Building database applications

One item ties all of these applications together. They all require a database of some sort. Database applications come in two basic categories: stand-alone and server-based. Stand-alone applications like MS Access and Apple FileMaker Pro are usually accessible by one user at a time in a desktop environment. In some cases, multiple users can be allowed to access the data, but the total number of simultaneous users is typically small. Server-based databases—like IBM DB2, Oracle, and SQL Server—are much more robust and can easily host thousands of simultaneous requests for information. But with this power comes a hefty price tag. Between these two tiers exists a popular alternative: MySQL, which offers server-based capabilities at a great price—free. A more robust *enterprise* version of MySQL is also available, but it's not free. Check it out at www.mysql.com/products/enterprise/.

For the purposes of creating dynamic applications on the Internet, both types of databases can be used effectively. Which one you will use depends primarily on the type of data, how much of it you need to store, how many users will access the data at any particular time, and cost. If you expect the number of simultaneous users to be from 1 to 1000, then a stand-alone database application may work for you. If you're trying to build the next Amazon.com, then you need to focus exclusively on server-based applications.

Luckily for the purposes of this lesson, Dreamweaver interfaces with stand-alone and server-based databases in an almost identical fashion.

## Database design basics

A database is similar to a spreadsheet. Data is stored in a series of columns and rows called a *table*, much like the ones you created using HTML and Spry. Spreadsheets typically supply the names of the columns and rows for you, using letters (A, B, C) for the columns and numbers (1, 2, 3) for the rows. Databases differ in this area by requiring you to supply the column, or *field*, names. Rows, or *records*, are usually delineated with unique numbers or IDs. Some databases refer to these as *unique keys*, *primary keys*, or just *keys*. The key allows you or your data application to retrieve a specific record or set of records.

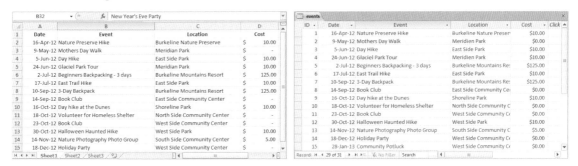

Simple databases store all the information being gathered in a single table, usually called a *flat* file. Using a single table for everything often leads to the duplication of data when certain types of information are entered multiple times, as when you take new orders from repeat customers. For example, a customer's name, address, and phone number must be entered in the same table each time they place an order. This type of redundant data bloats the size of the database unnecessarily and can cause errors over time. For example, an order may be shipped to an address listed in a previous order.

Spreadsheets (left) and databases (right) have common roots and can perform similar tasks.

One way to prevent duplication is to separate certain types of data into their own tables and then link the various tables together. This process of linking multiple tables creates what is called a *relational* database and makes for a much more efficient system.

Relational databases typically store the *customer* and *product* information as separate functions, and then bring them together in an *orders* table that keeps track of what products are ordered by each customer. That way, if any changes need to be made to a customer or product record, it only has to be made in one place, where it will instantly update all other instances. All the popular databases in use today support these types of relationships.

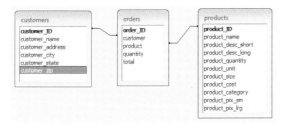

Relational databases store information in separate tables and connect them together in logical relationships. This prevents data duplication and makes the database function more efficiently.

An online database is typically stored within a subfolder of the target website, where it can be accessed by any page on the site. Databases can provide a variety of different types of information—from product descriptions and pricing, to customer names and addresses, to complete site editorial content. While some databases are configured to be read-only, where data is served in only one direction, most online databases are capable of both serving and capturing data, providing the utmost power and flexibility.

The design and construction of a web-compatible database is a complex topic that must consider a host of parameters well beyond the scope of this book. You can obtain much of the information regarding this topic online from a variety of resources. Unfortunately, much of it is written by and for IT or computer professionals and not readily accessible to the average web designer or computer user. If possible, try starting with stand-alone database applications like MS Access or Apple FileMaker Pro to get some valuable experience first. Designing and editing a relational database in these applications is usually straightforward and much easier to learn and do. You will find that there are inexpensive utilities available that can convert database files from the stand-alone applications into fully functional MySQL databases for a lot less time and effort (and frustration) than it would take to build one from scratch.

● **Note:** In some situations, the database will be stored within your own site. In others, the database may be hosted by the server itself and stored in a location to which you may not have access. Check with your IS/IT manager or your hosting provider for specific details about your configuration.

For the purposes of the upcoming exercises, we have supplied a complete MySQL database containing multiple data tables in the **mysql > greendata** folder on the disc accompanying this book. You will need to copy the **greendata** folder to the proper location on your local web server or on your remote host first before you will be able to access this data. For the WAMP server running in Windows, the folder may be something like **wamp > bin > mysql5.5.20 > data > mysql**. In Mac OS X, the folder may be **MAMP > db > mysql**. Check the help or support files that are provided with your own server version to obtain the correct location. The database folder must be copied properly or it will simply not function.

## Connecting to a database

Once your database is created, properly copied/uploaded, and configured, you need to connect each dynamic page to it before the data can be accessed. Each server model features specific methods for connecting to a database. For our exercises, we will concentrate on MySQL/PHP using the WAMP/MAMP environment, as noted earlier.

### Connecting to MySQL

In a PHP/MySQL environment, database connections are handled by custom scripts or by configuration files located on your hard drive or on the server. These scripts and configuration files handle the connection and any required user authentication.

There are numerous ways to write the code for these items, depending on the server model and specific database, so it's best to consult your server administrator or support staff to obtain the proper syntax. Many times, Dreamweaver can help you create the needed files and write the necessary code. In this exercise, you will connect to a MySQL database on a PHP server model.

1   Before attempting to complete this exercise, you first have to install and configure the necessary files and components for a PHP server and MySQL database. The master Lessons folder on the disc that came with this book contains a MySQL folder holding the **greendata** database intended for the following exercises. Copy this database folder to the testing server as required under your PHP/MySQL server installation. Once they are installed and configured properly, make sure both are launched and running before proceeding to the next step.

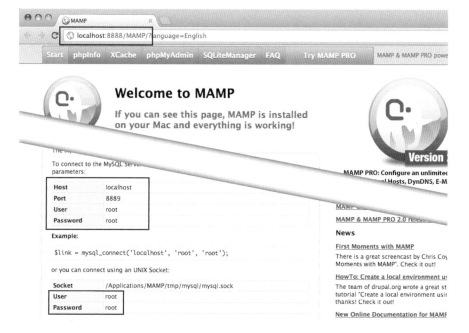

Here is a sample start page for a MAMP installation in Mac OS X. The URL of this start page displays the port for the MAMP Apache server: 8888; the page displays the port for the MySQL database server: 8889. Note the host name, ports, and other configuration settings in your own start page. You will need these specifications to connect to your servers and databases if you're using Mac OS X.

▶ **Tip:** In Windows, the **greendata** database folder located on the CD-ROM typically would be copied to the **wamp > bin > mysql5.5.20 > data > mysql** folder; in OS X, it would be copied to the **MAMP > db > mysql** folder. However, your installation may be different.

2   If necessary, define and configure a testing server in Dreamweaver for PHP/MySQL as described earlier in this lesson.

The PHP/MySQL configuration should point to the folder on your hard drive that will eventually hold your web content on the testing server. In Windows, it's typically named **www**; on the Mac, it's called **htdocs**. However, the name on your server may be different.

**Note:** It's possible that another local web server may already be installed and running on your computer. In most cases, WAMP and MAMP will not run properly (or at all) until you shut down or uninstall any existing server.

**3** Launch the server.

**4** Create a new page based on the site template.

MySQL databases can be used by all major server models. In this exercise, you'll use PHP.

**5** Save the page into the root folder as **products.php**.

**6** If necessary, select Window > Databases to open the Databases panel.

In the Databases panel, check to see if the plus (**+.**) icon is selectable or grayed out. If the icon is grayed out, you will not be able to connect this page to the database. Just adding the extension .php to the file name may not be sufficient to allow you to activate the dynamic functionality of the local web server. See the sidebar "Extension tension" in this lesson. Otherwise, proceed to step 7.

**Note:** In our example using WAMP in Windows, there is no password. Just dismiss any dialog boxes warning you about the password.

**7** Click the plus (**+.**) icon in the Databases panel and choose MySQL Connection.

The MySQL Connection dialog box opens.

**8** In the Connection Name field, enter **Local_PHP**.
Enter your server name (usually **localhost**), your user name, and your password.

In Windows, the **greendata** database should have a user name of **root** and no password. On the Macintosh under MAMP, the user name will be **root** and a password of **root**.

**Note:** On the Macintosh, you will probably need to include the port number in the MySQL server field, like: localhost:8888 for the connection to work properly.

**9** If the connection information is correct, you should be able to choose the **greendata** database by clicking the Select button in the dialog box.

Windows

OSX

# Extension tension

When you try to save a new document, Dreamweaver will often add the .html extension by default. The .html extension is fine for standard webpages but not for dynamic pages using ASP, ColdFusion, or PHP functionality. If you use the wrong extension, you won't be able to connect to your data source or run other types of programming. Adding the extension manually may work, but there's a way to force Dreamweaver to add the correct one for your server model automatically.

1   Make sure you have a site definition and a testing server created for the desired server model.

2   Create a new document from the site template.

3   Before you save, open the Server Behaviors panel.

4   Click the *document type* link that appears in the panel.

5   When the Choose Document Type dialog box opens, choose PHP or other appropriate document type from the pop-up menu and click OK.

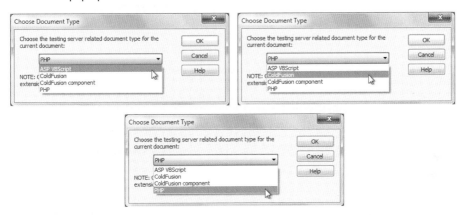

6   Select File > Save.

When the Save As dialog box appears, Dreamweaver will prompt you for a name for the new document and will have added the appropriate extension automatically.

**Tip:** If you receive an error message after this step, check if the WAMP/MAMP server is running. If it is, check that you have the correct user name and password for the database.

**10** Click Test.

If everything is working properly, Dreamweaver reports a successful connection to the database.

**11** Click OK. Examine the Databases panel.

The Databases panel displays the name of your database connection.

**12** Expand the database listing.

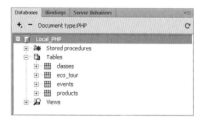

The listing displays the stored procedures, tables, and views contained within the database.

**13** Save all files.

In this lesson, you learned how to work with HTML and XML data. Then, you learned about other types of database applications and selected a server model, configured a testing server, and created a database connection. You have developed the foundation for a dynamic website using PHP. In the next lesson, you will use this environment to build dynamic pages. Believe it or not, if you get the local web server and MySQL database installed and running properly, you will have accomplished the hardest part of setting up your dynamic website workflow.

# Review questions

1  What advantage does Ajax/Spry have over traditional data applications?

2  True or false: XML is a method for storing data in a plain-text file for use in web applications.

3  What is a server model?

4  What is a testing server?

5  You have a file that is compatible with your server model (.asp, .cfm, or .php), but your database doesn't appear in the Databases panel. How can you make the connection appear in the panel again?

6  True or false: The MySQL database can be used only on Linux/Unix and Mac OS X server platforms.

# Review answers

1  Ajax/Spry applications don't have to reload an entire page; they can update data in real time.

2  True. XML is similar to HTML and is used to identify data.

3  A server model is the basic environment used to build dynamic web applications. It also encompasses specific programming languages and scripting models, such as ASP, ColdFusion, and PHP.

4  A testing server is where dynamic pages are tested using a compatible server model. It is set up in the Site Setup dialog box.

5  Examine the Databases panel and the displayed steps for connecting to your data source. Complete any steps that are not checked. The data source should then be displayed again.

6  False. MySQL can be used on any web server.

# 14

# BUILDING DYNAMIC PAGES WITH DATA

## Lesson Overview

In this lesson, you will learn how to dynamically create webpage content using information stored in tables and databases to do the following:

- Create a recordset from online data

- Insert data on a webpage dynamically

- Create a master/detail page set

- Create a dynamic link from the master page to the detail page

 This lesson will take about 2 hours to complete. Before beginning, make sure you have copied the files for Lesson 14 to your hard drive as described in the "Getting Started" section at the beginning of the book. If you are starting from scratch in this lesson, before beginning you must first complete portions of Lesson 13 detailing the installation of a local web server, setup of the MySQL database, and connection to the **greendata** database provided on the disc that came with this book. Then use the method described in the "Jumpstart" section of "Getting Started." Macintosh users should target the lesson14 Mac folder.

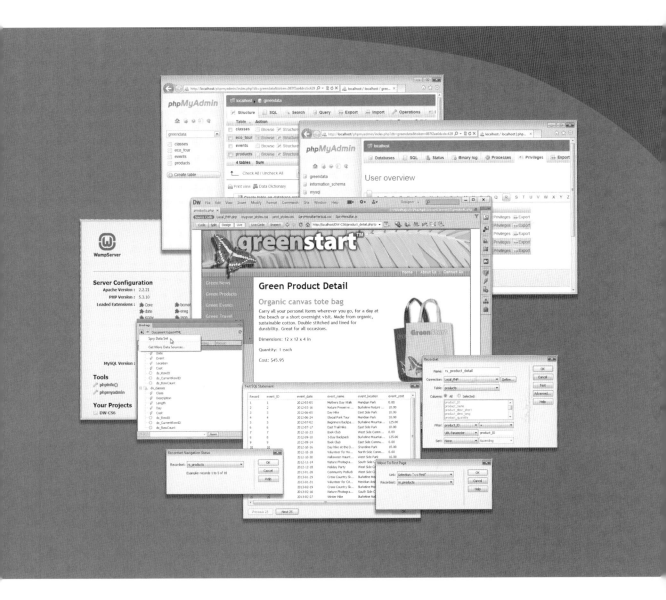

Dreamweaver has built-in features that help you build rich, dynamic, data-driven webpages using simple point-and-click tools.

# Building pages with PHP

**Note:** The default files in the lesson14 folder should work fine for Windows users. For Mac users, a custom lesson14 folder is supplied on the DVD provided with the book.

**Warning:** Developing dynamic applications is an exacting chore that can fail for the simplest reasons. Misplacing even a semicolon or period can cause an error. Read and follow every step in this lesson carefully.

**Warning:** This exercise can be completed only if you have successfully configured a testing server and connected to the **greendata** database as you were instructed in Lesson 13.

In Lesson 13, "Working with Online Data," you learned how to select a server model, set up a testing server, and connect to an online database. Dreamweaver makes it easy to access this data to create dynamic content.

## Creating a recordset

The following exercises assume you have already completed Lesson 13 successfully and have established a live connection to your database. The next step in the process of generating dynamic content is to create a recordset. A recordset is an array of information pulled from one or more tables in your database in response to a question posed by code in the webpage. The code that asks the question is written in Structured Query Language (SQL).

The question, or *query*, can be as simple as "Show me all the events in the Events table" or as complex as "Show me the events in the table that occur after May 1st and cost less than $10 in descending alphabetical order by name." This query can be hardwired into the page so it always shows the same results. Frequently, the query itself is also dynamic—created by the user by clicking checkboxes or radio buttons, choosing from menus, or typing into a text field (as you do on Google and Yahoo).

Like ASP, ColdFusion, and PHP, SQL is a robust language with its own terms, structure, and syntax. Dreamweaver can help you write most of the statements you'll ever need, but to perform complex data routines you may need to hire a professional consultant or learn some SQL yourself. Adobe provides a good SQL primer at tinyurl.com/sql-primer, or you can check out tinyurl.com/sql-tutorial for the SQL tutorial offered by W3Schools.

In this exercise, you'll re-create the 2012 events calendar dynamically by using a table from your current database connection.

1  Open **events.html** from the site root folder.

   The file contains two tables of two rows each, complete with Spry data sets and placeholders. Instead of starting from scratch, you can use most of the existing components for the PHP-based workflow.

2  Examine the Databases panel. If necessary, select Window > Databases to open the panel.

   The Local_PHP database connection you created in Lesson 13 is not visible. If you open the Connection menu in the Bindings panel, you will see only a Spry Data Set option. At the moment, you couldn't create a database connection even if you wanted to. That's because the Events page uses the extension .html, which is compatible only with the dynamic server model Ajax (Spry). To get the page ready to support the desired database connection, you have to choose the proper document type.

**3** Click the link that appears in Databases panel item #2: "Choose a document type."

The Choose Document Type dialog box appears.

**4** Select PHP from the pull-down menu and click OK.

Dreamweaver changes the extension of the file to .php. The database connection Local_PHP, which was defined in Lesson 13, should now appear in the panel. It should appear automatically whenever you are working with a PHP-based page.

▶ **Tip:** If the database connection still does not appear after saving the file with the extension .php, complete any steps suggested within the Databases panel. Sometimes, closing and opening the file may fix the problem.

**5** Save the file as **events.php**.

Each server model may use one or more specific extensions. For example, ASP uses the extensions .asp and .aspx. ColdFusion uses the extensions .cfm, .cfml, and .cfc. Always use the extension appropriate for your server model and application.

**6** Display the Bindings panel. Click the plus (**+**) icon at the top of the Bindings panel. Choose Recordset (Query) from the pop-up menu.

▶ **Tip:** If you connected successfully to the database in Lesson 13, you can simply copy the Connection folder from that lesson to replace the one in the current site root.

The Recordset dialog box appears. The current database connection should appear in the Connection menu, by default. If you have more than one database connection, you will have to select the desired database from this menu first.

**7** Select the Local_PHP connection from the Connection menu and click the Simple button, if necessary.

By selecting options within this dialog box, Dreamweaver enables you to write basic SQL statements without having to know a single line of the SQL language. The Advanced version of the Recordset dialog box permits you to create more-complex SQL statements.

▶ **Tip:** If the **greendata** database still doesn't appear in the Databases panel at all, you may need to click the Define button and enter your login information again. See "Connecting to a database" in Lesson 13.

**8** In the Name field, enter **rs_events**.

This field creates the name of the recordset that will be referenced in the query.

**9** From the Table menu, choose events.

This selection identifies the table from which the data will be retrieved.

**10** If necessary, click the All option in the Columns section.

This option indicates that you want to retrieve data from all columns, or fields, in the table. By default, the query will return all events from the data table.

**11** Click the Test button.

If everything works properly, the Test SQL Statement dialog box will appear displaying the results from the query you just constructed. If you don't see any data or if an error message appears, it could mean that the table has no records that meet your search criteria or that you have to troubleshoot your database, database connection, or testing server configuration.

In this case, the test window is showing all records in the Events table, even events that may have passed already. But who wants to see events that have already passed? No problem; one of the advantages of using a database and a dynamic PHP workflow is that you can filter out data that isn't relevant to the user or query. For example, let's set up the recordset to show only dates in the future.

**12** Click OK to close the Test SQL Statement dialog box and return to the Recordset dialog box.

**13** In the Filter section, in the left column choose event_date.

Choose >= in the right column.

Choose Entered Value in the next row.

Then, enter the current date in the format **'yyyy-m-d'** in the open field. Be sure to add single quotes around the date.

The Filter section refines the search by targeting specific data and excluding others. The options you entered are requesting a list of events from the table that take place today or in the future. Events scheduled prior to today's date will be ignored and should not appear in the results.

**14** In the Sort section, choose event_date and Ascending from the appropriate menus.

● **Note:** In the MySQL database, the year is entered first.

● **Note:** The table contains dates up to 2013-3-27. If the date you enter is after that day, your recordset will be empty.

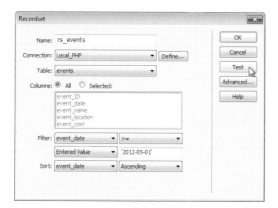

The Sort section allows you to display data in ascending or descending alphanumeric order.

**15** Click the Test button.

The Test SQL Statement dialog box appears again. Depending on what date you entered in the filter, some events may not appear in the displayed recordset.

**16** Click OK to close the Test SQL Statement dialog box and return to the Recordset dialog box. Click the Advanced button.

The Recordset dialog box provides advanced options for creating an SQL statement. You should notice that the SQL statement you created is displayed in the SQL field of the dialog box. If you already know how to write SQL statements, you can enter them directly into this field. Note the sections in the dialog box that are devoted to variables and database items. These built-in point-and-click productivity enhancements help to speed up the process of writing statements by hand by giving you quick access to your data resources and specific SQL commands.

**Note:** Many times you can copy and paste SQL statements from other programs (such as Microsoft Access) into this dialog and they will work just fine.

Note the date text displayed in the SQL window. This is the date you entered in step 13. Entering a date in this fashion is fine if the date doesn't change. The problem here is that you want the table to show only current and future events. By tomorrow, the filter you created will be invalid. Instead, you need to enter a special SQL function that will always remain valid.

**17** Select and delete the date and the quotes around it.

**18** Type **now()** in the SQL window to replace the deleted text.

The now() function obtains the current time and date from the server to use for the data filter. The manually entered date is no longer needed.

**19** Click the Test button.

The Test SQL Statement dialog box appears displaying the query result. It should look identical to the test you performed in step 15.

**20** Click OK to complete the recordset.

Recordset (rs_events) appears in the Bindings panel.

**21** Expand Recordset (rs_events) and examine the items displayed.

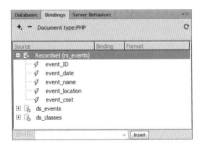

The recordset contains items for all five data columns in the Events table.

**22** Save all files.

You are now ready to create a dynamic webpage. In the next exercise, you will learn how to display data generated by a recordset.

## Displaying data from a database

Now that you have all the cogs installed, the only thing left to do is put the machinery into action. As with most of the other steps, displaying data in Dreamweaver is a simple point-and-click process.

**1** If necessary, open **events.php**.

The file's extension should be compatible with your server model now, and it should feature the database connection and recordset you created previously. But the page also displays two Spry-based recordsets. You're not going to use the Spry data but that doesn't mean you have to start completely from scratch. To preclude any conflicts let's reuse the table element itself, but discard the Spry data sets and support code.

**2** Insert the cursor in the *Events* table placeholder. Select the tag selector for the `<table>` placeholder. Press Ctrl-X/Cmd-X to cut the table.

The Spry table was contained in a `<div>` element that contains a reference to the Spry data set and is no longer needed. If you haven't moved your cursor, the `<div>` element is still displayed in the tag selector. Spry elements exhibit an orange tinge in the tag selector display.

**3** Select the `<div>` tag selector. Press Delete.

Before we re-insert the table, let's remove the Spry data sets too.

**4** In the Bindings panel, select the **ds_events** data set. Click the minus (−) icon at the top of the panel to remove the data set. Dismiss any dialog boxes that may appear when deleting the data set.

**5** Remove the **ds_classes** data set. Dismiss any dialog boxes that may appear when deleting the data set.

Insert the cursor in the first *Return to Top* link. Click the `<p>` tag selector, and press the Left Arrow key once to move the cursor to the correct position for the Events table.

**6** Press Ctrl-V/Cmd-V to paste the Events table placeholder.

The table placeholder appears below the heading. However, it still contains Spry code residue that should also be deleted.

**7** Insert the cursor in the table header row. Switch to Code view and examine the header row elements.

```
103    <tr>
104      <th class="w100" spry:sort="Date">Date</th>
105      <th spry:sort="Event">Event</th>
106      <th spry:sort="Location">Location</th>
107      <th class="cost" spry:sort="Cost">Cost</th>
108    </tr>
109    <tr spry:repeat="ds_events" spry:odd="odd" spry:even="even" spry:hover="rowhover" spry:select="rowselect">
110      <td>{Date}</td>
```

Each of the `<th>` elements contains a `spry:sort="..."` attribute.

**8** Delete the `spry:sort="..."` attributes from each of the `<th>` elements, as well as other Spry attributes elsewhere in the table, such as `spry:repeat`, `spry:odd`, `spry:even`, and so on. But be careful not to delete any `class="..."` attributes.

All Spry references in the Events table are gone.

**9** Switch to Design view and save all files.

Converting the Spry data placeholders to PHP placeholders for the current workflow is a simple process.

**10** In the table, select the `{Date}` placeholder.

**11** Open the Bindings panel, if necessary. Expand the **rs_events** recordset.

**12** In the Bindings panel, select the event_date field. Click the Insert button at the bottom of the Bindings panel.

A new `{rs_events.event_date}` placeholder appears in the table cell, replacing the Spry placeholder.

**13** Replace `{Event}` with **event_name**.

**14** Replace `{Location}` with **event_location**.

**15** Replace `{Cost}` with **event_cost**.

Be sure not to delete the dollar sign before the placeholder.

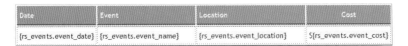

**16** Save all files.

When working on dynamic pages, it's essential to test the functionality frequently. But unlike the Spry data structure using PHP, certain files must be uploaded to the testing server before you can preview the current dynamic layout.

## Staging files on the testing server

You won't be able to test this file in Live view or in a browser until you upload the page as well as other specific files that connect the page to the database to the local testing server. So which files need to be uploaded? Luckily, Dreamweaver will handle the logistics for you.

**1**  Select Live view.

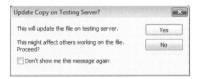

Dreamweaver prompts you to update the file on the testing server.

**2**  Click Yes to update the file on the testing server.

Dreamweaver should prompt you to upload dependent files. If this is the first time you have tested this file, click Yes. This will upload whatever files are needed to display this page properly. Once the dependent files are uploaded, there's probably no need to upload the dependent files again unless you make changes to this page or the dependent files.

**3**  Click Yes to upload dependent files.

| Date | Event | Location | Cost |
|------|-------|----------|------|
| 2012-06-05 | Day Hike | East Side Park | $10.00 |

The table displays one row of data. To display more data, you have to add a *repeat region* behavior.

## Adding a repeat region

Data placeholders can display only one record at a time. To see more than one record, you have to wrap the placeholders in a server behavior called a *repeat region*.

**1**  Switch to Design view. Position the cursor at the beginning of the data row of the table, and select the entire row. Select the `<tr>` tag selector.

The entire row is selected.

**Note:**  You won't be able to test this page until you have successfully installed and configured a local testing server for PHP and MySQL. See Lesson 13 for more details.

**Tip:**  If Dreamweaver didn't prompt you to upload dependent files, you'll have to select the options "Prompt on Get operations" and "Prompt on Put operations" under the Site category of the Dreamweaver Preferences dialog box.

**2** Select Window > Server Behaviors. In the Server Behaviors panel, click the plus (**+.**) icon, and choose Repeat Region from the pop-up menu.

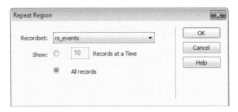

The Repeat Region dialog box appears. The Recordset menu displays rs_events as the current recordset. By default, the behavior will display ten records at a time. You can specify a different number or display all the records at once.

When you choose to display fewer than all the records you will also have to create a *record paging* behavior to permit the user to view the remaining data. For this table, let's keep things simple and display all the records at once.

**3** Select the All Records option. Click OK.

| Date | Event | Location | Cost |
|------|-------|----------|------|
| Repeat | | | |
| {rs_events.event_date} | {rs_events.event_name} | {rs_events.event_location} | ${rs_events.event_cost} |

A gray tab displaying the word *Repeat* appears above the data row of the table.

**4** Save all files. Preview the page in Live view.

### 2012-2013 Events Schedule

| Date | Event | Location | Cost |
|------|-------|----------|------|
| 2012-06-05 | Day Hike | East Side Park | $10.00 |
| 2012-06-24 | Glacial Park Tour | Meridian Park | $10.00 |
| 2012-07-02 | Beginners Backpacking - 3 days | Burkeline Mountains Resort | $125.00 |
| 2012-07-17 | East Trail Hike | East Side Park | $10.00 |
| 2012-10-23 | Book Club | West Side Community Center | $0.00 |
| 2012-09-10 | 3-Day Backpack | Burkeline Mountains Resort | $125.00 |

The table displays all the upcoming events from today's date into the future. But better yet, as each day passes, events will be removed from the display automatically because their date no longer meets the requirements of the query filter.

# Creating a dynamic table for classes and seminars

Before you move on to the next exercise, use the skills and understanding you have learned so far to rebuild the Spry table for the classes and seminars. The steps to re-create this table are simple and straightforward.

1 Create a recordset that returns data from all fields of the Class table in the database. Unlike the events recordset, there's no need to filter or sort the class data by date. You can sort by class_name if you would like the events to be listed in alphabetical order.

**Note:** Except for the date filtering, the steps needed to replace the remaining Spry Class table with a PHP equivalent are identical to the ones described in this exercise. If you have the time, put your new skills to the test and try replacing the remaining Spry widget on your own.

**Note:** You may need to click the Simple button to return to the simple Recordset dialog box.

2 Select the Spry table and press Ctrl-X/Cmd-X. Delete the Spry `<div>` element and paste the table back into the layout at the same position.

3 Clean up any residual Spry code left in the table.

4 Insert data placeholders from the new recordset into the appropriate data row cells.

5 Apply a repeat region server behavior on the data row for rs_classes.

6 Test the results in Live view.

### 2012-2013 Class Schedule

| Class | Description | Length | Day | Cost |
|---|---|---|---|---|
| Choices for Sustainable Living | This course explores the meaning of sustainable living and how our choices have an impact on ecological systems. | 4 weeks | M | $40.00 |
| Exploring Deep Ecology | An eight-session course examining our core values and how they affect the way we view and treat the earth. | 4 weeks | F | $40.00 |
| Future Food | Explores food systems and their impacts on culture, society and ecological systems. | 4 weeks | Tu-Th | $80.00 |

7 Save all files.

Displaying data dynamically is a huge improvement over static lists and tables. Allowing users to interact with data engages them in the process in a way that can't be done otherwise. These exercises have given you only a small glimpse of what you can achieve with dynamic webpages. In the next exercise, you will build one of the most common dynamic applications: a master/detail page set.

It's a scenario common to many websites: A page displays a *master* list of several products or events; you click the one that interests you most; then the website loads a new page with specific *details* about the selected item. But what you didn't see, or notice, is how the master page passed your request to the detail page.

# Creating a master/detail page set

The master/detail page set is one of the most frequently used applications on data-driven websites. By adding a hyperlink to the displayed data, you allow visitors to navigate to a new page that will display information specific to the selected item. Master/detail page sets can be created in any server environment, including ASP, ColdFusion, PHP, and Spry. The steps and procedures are similar for each server model, but some are easier to implement than others.

## Creating the master page

● **Note:** Before you attempt this exercise, you must create the **products.php** file and connect it to your database as described in Lesson 13.

In this exercise, you will create a master/detail page set using your existing database connection.

1  Launch Dreamweaver, if necessary, and open **products.php**.

You'll use this page as the master.

2  Select the text *Add main heading here.* Type **Green Products** to replace the text.

3  Select the text *Add subheading here.* Type **GreenStart offers only the best in green products** to replace the text.

4  Select the text *Add content here.* Type **Click on any product link you wish to learn more about**.

Let's create a <div> element to hold the product information.

5  Click the <p> tag selector. Press the Right Arrow key to move the cursor outside the <p> element.

6  Select Insert > Layout Objects > Div Tag.

The Insert Div Tag dialog box appears.

7  In the Class field, enter **productmaster** and click OK to create the element.

The <div> element appears with sample placeholder text. Next you should create a recordset to display all the product data.

8  Open the Databases panel and ensure that the Local_PHP connection is still available.

▷ **Tip:** If the database connection is missing, follow any steps described in the Databases panel window to create a valid connection.

9  Open the Bindings panel. Click the plus (**+▾**) icon and choose Recordset (Query).

10 Enter the following specifications for the new recordset:
Name: **rs_products**
Connection: **Local_PHP**
Table: **products**
Filter: **None**
Sort: **product_category** and **Ascending**

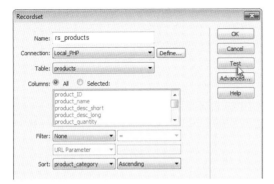

11 Click Test to see if your query produces a valid data set.

The Test SQL Statement dialog box displays product data from the **greendata** database.

12 Click OK in all dialog boxes to create the recordset and return to the document window.

The rs_products recordset appears in the Bindings panel.

There's no restriction on how you use the data fields in the recordset. You can insert them once, multiple times, or not at all. They can also be displayed in any order on the page.

13 Select the placeholder text in the <div> element you created in step 7.

14 In the Bindings panel, select the product_name field. Click Insert.

The text {rs_products:product_name} replaces the placeholder text in <div.productmaster>.

15 Format {rs_products:product_name} as a Heading 3. Insert a new paragraph after the placeholder.

**16** In the next line, insert the **product_desc_short** field.

● **Note:** Before previewing the data, make sure you upload all the dependent files to the testing server.

**17** Save all files. Preview the page in Live view. If prompted to Put Dependent Files, choose Yes.

## Green Products

GreenStart offers only the best in green products

Click on any product you wish to learn more about

{rs_products.product_name}
{rs_products.product_desc_short}

## Green Products

GreenStart offers only the best in green products

Click on any product you wish to learn more about

**Organic canvas tote bag**
Spacious tote for personal items. Made from organic, sustainable canvas.

If your testing server is properly configured, Dreamweaver will display the selected two fields of the first record of the database in the document window. But dynamic content isn't limited to text; you can display images dynamically too.

## Displaying images dynamically

What would a product page be without pictures of the products? Adding images to the product description is no more difficult than inserting text. In this exercise, you'll learn how to insert dynamic images into your layout.

**1** If necessary, open **products.php**. Select Design view.

**2** Insert the cursor at the beginning of the placeholder {rs_products:product_name} in <div.productmaster>. Press Enter/Return to insert a new paragraph before the placeholder.

The empty paragraph is formatted as an <h3> element.

**3** Insert the cursor in the new paragraph. In the HTML mode of the Property inspector, select Paragraph from the Format menu.

**4** Select Insert > Image.

The Select Image Source dialog box appears. Normally, you would select the desired image and simply click OK. But to insert a dynamic image, there are a few extra steps involved.

**5** Click the Data Sources option in the dialog box.

The dialog box changes from a file browser to a display of the data fields from the rs_products recordset.

**6** Select the product_pix_sm field.

The URL field in the dialog box displays a complex piece of code that will insert a picture based on the filename stored in the database field—in this case, product_pix_sm. But the field contains only the filename of the picture, not the path.

Since folder names and file locations can change over time, it doesn't make sense to insert path information into a database field. Instead, you can simply build the image path statement in the dynamic code at the time you need it. That way, if you move pictures from one folder to another on the site, you only have to make one small edit in the code to adapt to the change.

If you look at the Files panel, you will find that the images named in the database are located in the **products** folder.

7   Insert the cursor at the beginning of the URL field. In the field, type **products/** and click OK.

By inserting the folder name into the URL field, Dreamweaver will append the text *products/* to the image name to pull the desired image from that subfolder of your site, like this: **products/1-lrg.jpg**.

8   In the Image Tag Accessibility Attributes dialog box, select <empty> from the Alternate Text field menu. Click OK.

9   Save all files and preview the page in Live view.

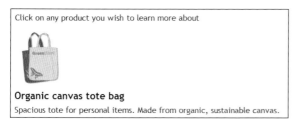

The small image of the sample product appears on the screen along with the text. Now that you have one product displayed successfully, it's a simple matter to show multiple data items, as you did with the Events and Class tables earlier.

## Displaying multiple items

To display more than one record, you need to add a repeat region as you did before. Although there's no table row (as there is in the previous example), you can assign the behavior to the `<div.productmaster>` element instead.

1   Switch back to Design view and select the `<div.productmaster>` tag selector.

2   Open the Server Behaviors panel.

3   Click the plus (**+.**) icon and choose Repeat Region.

4   In the Repeat Region dialog box, enter the following specifications:
    Recordset: **rs_products**
    Show: **6** Records at a Time
    Click OK.

A gray tab displaying the word *Repeat* appears above `<div.productmaster>`.

5   Save all files. Preview the page in Live view. Click Yes to update the page on the testing server. Click Yes to upload dependent files.

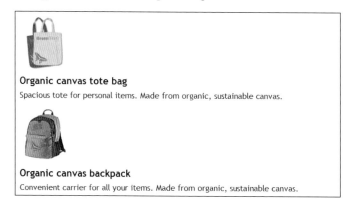

Dreamweaver now displays six records from the Products table. `<div.productmaster>` defaults to 100 percent of the width of the main content area, so the records stack one atop the other. Later you'll style `<div.productmaster>` to use the screen more effectively, but for the moment, we'll make sure the visitors will be able to view all the products in the database. The first six records display by default; to display the next set of six records, you have to add a paging behavior.

# Creating a record paging behavior

Paging controls are usually inserted outside the repeat region so that they appear only once per page. In this exercise, you will create a record paging behavior for the rs_products recordset.

1   Click the Repeat tab to select the repeat region. Press the Right Arrow key to move the cursor after the code for the `<div>` element and the repeat region.

    The paging controls can be inserted as text or as graphical elements on the page. Frequently, tables are used to control their presentation.

2   Insert a table with the following specifications:
    Rows: **2**
    Columns: **4**
    Width: **600 pixels**
    Border thickness: **0**
    Cell padding: **0**
    Cell spacing: **0**

    The width is set at 600 pixels, but the table will automatically conform to dimensions set by existing CSS rules created in Lesson 7. You will override these styles later in this lesson. To enable this level of precision control, you'll have to apply a unique ID to this table.

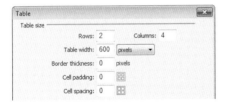

3   In the Table ID field, enter **master_paging**.

4   Select all the cells in the first row. In the W field of the Property inspector, enter **25%**.

5   Enter the following text in the first row of the table:
    Cell 1: << **First**
    Cell 2: < **Previous**
    Cell 3: **Next** >
    Cell 4: **Last** >>

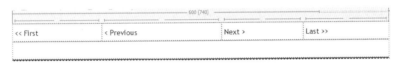

The angle brackets provide a visual cue to the user for the results of the paging behavior.

**6** Select the text << *First*. Select Insert > Data Objects > Recordset Paging > Move To First Page.

The Move To First Page dialog box appears. The Link field displays Selection: "<< First", and the Recordset field menu displays rs_products.

**7** Click OK.

A dynamic hyperlink behavior is applied to the text that will load the first six records of the Products table.

**8** Apply the following paging behaviors to the other text:
< Previous: Move To Previous Page
Next >: Move To Next Page
Last >>: Move To Last Page

**9** Save all files. Preview the page in Live view.

The first six records appear. If you click the paging controls, nothing happens. To invoke the paging controls, you have to use a modifier key.

**10** Hold down the Ctrl/Cmd key and click the *Next* paging link.

Live view loads the next six records.

**11** Hold down the Ctrl/Cmd key and click the *Last* paging link.

Live view loads the last set of records.

**12** Test the *Previous* and *First* paging links.

You have created a set of record paging links that allow visitors to display recordsets in batches designated by the repeat behavior. But there's a small problem. When the page is displaying the first set of records, there are no "previous" records. Likewise, when the last set of records is displayed, there are no "next" records. Leaving these links on the page would be confusing for the visitor. As you have probably already guessed, Dreamweaver provides a tailor-made behavior for such situations.

## Hiding unneeded paging controls

*Visibility* is a common property that can be controlled by HTML and CSS. It's relatively easy to set an element's visibility and then invoke a behavior or scripted action to change it for a specific purpose. In this exercise, you will apply a dynamic server behavior that will modify the paging link's visibility based on the results of the recordset. In effect, it will hide the controls when their role is invalid.

1   Return to Design view. Insert the cursor in the << *First* link and select the <a> tag selector.

**Note:** Make sure you don't select the <td> element. Hiding the entire cell will cause the remaining cells to expand across the content area.

To hide all traces of the link, you have to select all the markup for the record paging element. The Show behavior can be accessed from the Insert menu or from the Server Behaviors panel.

2   In the Server Behaviors panel, click the plus (**+▾**) icon and select Show Region > Show If Not First Page.

The Show If Not First Page dialog box appears displaying rs_products in the Recordset menu.

3   Click OK.

A gray tab displaying the words *Show If* appears above the *First* link.

4   Select the < *Previous* link, as in step 1. Apply the Show If Not First Page server behavior.

5   Select the *Next* > link and then the *Last* >> link, and apply to each the Show If Not Last Page server behavior.

6   Save all files and preview the page in Live view.

The first six records are displayed. Examine the paging links. The *Previous* and *First* links don't appear.

7   Hold down the Ctrl/Cmd key and click the *Last* link.

The last set of records is displayed. Note that the *Next* and *Last* links are no longer displayed. The Show Region behaviors will automatically hide and display the paging links based on whether the page shows the first or last set of records, or somewhere in between. Dreamweaver offers over two dozen pre-built server behaviors that allow you to customize all aspects of the records display.

## Displaying the record count

When you have lots of records to view, it's easy to lose track of what record you're looking at, so it's a good idea to give the user a status report. In this exercise, you'll insert a behavior that will display the total number of records and pages in the set.

1   Switch to Design view. Select all four cells in the second row of <table#master_paging>. Right-click the selection and choose Table > Merge Cells from the context menu.

**2** Click in the merged cell. Select Insert > Data Objects > Display Record Count > Recordset Navigation Status.

The Recordset Navigation Status dialog box appears.

**3** If necessary, select the rs_products recordset. Click OK.

A complete block of code and placeholder text is inserted into the second row.

**4** Save all files and preview the page in Live view.

| | Next > | Last >> |
| --- | --- | --- |
| Records 1 to 6 of 28 | | |

The status report displays the text *Records 1 to 6 of 28*.

**5** Hold down the Ctrl/Cmd key and click the *Next* link. Examine the status report.

The status report displays the text *Records 7 to 12 of 28*.

**6** Switch back to Design view.

The page is nearly complete, but before you create the detail page and the behaviors that are needed to connect the two pages, let's add a bit of style to the product display.

## Styling dynamic data

Adding style and flair to dynamic data is no different than styling static pages. In this exercise, you will create CSS rules to format the text and structure of your dynamic data. Let's start by changing the way the products are arranged on the page. The following styling will allow the products to be arranged side by side in neat rows.

**1** Open **products.php** and switch to Design view, if necessary.

**2** Open the CSS Styles panel. Select the last rule in the **mygreen_styles.css** style sheet.

**3** Create a CSS rule named `.content section .productmaster` and apply the following styling:

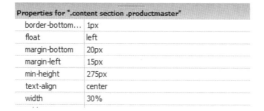

4  Create a rule named `.content section .productmaster h3` and apply the following styling:

| Properties for ".content section .productmaster h3" | |
|---|---|
| line-height | 1.1em |
| margin-bottom | 5px |
| margin-left | 0px |
| margin-right | 0px |
| margin-top | 10px |
| padding | 0px |

5  Create a rule named `.content section .productmaster h3 a, .content section .productmaster h3 a:visited` and apply the following styling:

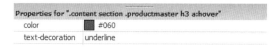

| Properties for ".content section .productmaster h3 a ,.content section .productmaster h3 a:visited" | |
|---|---|
| color | ▮ #090 |
| font-size | 120% |
| line-height | 1.2em |
| text-decoration | none |

6  Create a rule named `.content section .productmaster h3 a:hover` and apply the following styling:

| Properties for ".content section .productmaster h3 a:hover" | |
|---|---|
| color | ▮ #060 |
| text-decoration | underline |

7  Create a rule named `.content section .productmaster p` and apply the following styling:

| Properties for ".content section .productmaster p" | |
|---|---|
| margin-bottom | 5px |
| margin-left | 0px |
| margin-right | 0px |
| margin-top | 0px |
| padding | 0px |

8  Create a rule named `.content section #master_paging` and apply the following styling:

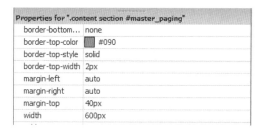

| Properties for ".content section #master_paging" | |
|---|---|
| border-bottom... | none |
| border-top-color | ▮ #090 |
| border-top-style | solid |
| border-top-width | 2px |
| margin-left | auto |
| margin-right | auto |
| margin-top | 40px |
| width | 600px |

**9** Create a rule named `.content section #master_paging td` and apply the following styling:

| Properties for ".content section #master_paging td" | |
| --- | --- |
| border-bottom... | none |
| border-left-style | none |
| border-right-style | none |
| border-top-style | none |
| text-align | center |

**10** Create a rule named `.content section #master_paging a, .content section #master_paging a:visited` and apply the following styling:

| Properties for ".content section #master_paging a , .content section #master_paging a:visited" | |
| --- | --- |
| color | ■ #060 |
| font-weight | bold |
| text-decoration | none |

**11** Create a rule named `.content section #master_paging a:hover` and apply the following styling:

| Properties for ".content section #master_paging a:hover" | |
| --- | --- |
| color | ☐ #0C0 |
| font-weight | bold |
| text-decoration | none |

**12** Save all files. Preview the page in Live view.

The new styling displays the products side by side in two convenient rows—taking up less space and permitting the user to see more products without scrolling. The paging controls enable the user to flip through the whole catalog simply by clicking. In the next exercise, you will learn how to add a special hyperlink to the master elements that will load a detailed view of a specific product.

## Inserting a go-to-detail-page behavior

By keeping the product picture and descriptions small on the master page, you allow the customer to browse quickly through your entire catalog. The more products you can show comfortably in one place, the more likely it is that the customer will find something that interests them. Then, usually they want to learn more about one product. That's where the detail page comes in. In this exercise, you'll insert a special behavior in the dynamic placeholders that will load a detail page for any item clicked on the master page.

**1** Open **products.php** and switch to Design view, if necessary.

A dynamic link can be added to text or pictures to take the user to a detail page. Although ASP provides a custom behavior for this purpose, you have to create this link yourself in ColdFusion and PHP.

**2** Select the image placeholder in `<div.productmaster>`.

A dynamic link is added using the Link dialog box.

**3** Click the Browse icon next to the Link field in the Property inspector.

**4** When the Select File dialog box opens, click the Data Sources button.

**5** Select the product_ID field.

When you select product_ID, the following code is inserted in the URL field:

```php
<?php echo $row_rs_products['product_ID']; ?>
```

**6** Insert the cursor at the beginning of the text in the URL field.

**7** Type **product_detail.php?product_ID=** and click OK.

The code you entered will pass the product_ID of the selected element to the detail page, where it should then be displayed.

**8** Save all files.

Before you can test the functionality, you first need to create the detail page.

# Creating a detail page

The detail page is almost identical to the master page in construction. Both create a recordset and display placeholders for specific fields. The major difference lies in that the master page can display all the records, while the detail page will show only one. In this exercise, you will create a detail page so that it will show information about only the product selected by the user.

▶ **Tip:** If you're not using PHP, add the extension appropriate for your server model.

1   Create a new page based on the site template. Save it as **product_detail.php**.

2   If the Databases panel doesn't display your current data connection, click the *document type* link and choose PHP or the appropriate server model for your workflow.

3   In the Bindings panel, create a new recordset named **rs_product_detail**.

The Recordset dialog box appears. The previous recordsets you have created have shown all the records in a table. For a detail page you have to create a filter to show only the record selected by the user on the master page.

4   Enter the following specifications in the Recordset dialog box:

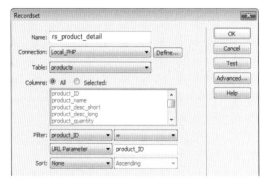

5   Click Test.

A dialog box appears requesting a test value. You have to enter a value that would be pertinent to the specific field, such as the SKU or ISBN number of the product. In this case, the values in the current Products table are simple digits from 1 to 28.

**6** Enter **1** in the field and click OK.

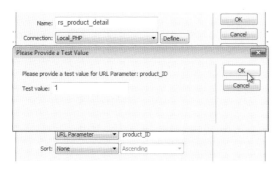

The Test SQL Statement dialog box appears displaying one record.

**7** Click OK in all dialog boxes to return to Design view.

Now you're ready to build the detail page data display.

**8** Select the text *Add main heading here*. Type **Green Product Detail** to replace the placeholder text.

**9** Select the text *Add subheading here*. In the Bindings panel, select the product_name field. Click the Insert button.

**10** Select the text *Add content here*. Insert the **product_desc_long** field.

**11** Create a new paragraph. Type **Dimensions:** in the new paragraph. Press the spacebar and insert the **product_size** field.

**12** Create a new paragraph. Type **Quantity:** in the new paragraph.
Press the spacebar and insert the **product_quantity** field.
Press Ctrl-Shift-spacebar/Cmd-Shift-spacebar to insert a non-breaking space.
Insert the **product_unit** field.

**13** Create a new paragraph. Type **Cost: $** in the new paragraph.
Press the spacebar and insert the **product_cost** field.

**14** Insert the cursor at the beginning of the placeholder {rs_product_detail. product_name}. Select Insert > Image.

**15** Click the Data Sources button. Select the **product_pix_lrg** field.
Insert the cursor at the beginning of the Code field, then type **products/** and click OK.

**16** In the Image Tag Accessibility Attributes dialog box, select <empty> from the Alternate Text field menu. Click OK.

**17** Select the new image placeholder. From the Class menu, choose flt_rgt. In the Width and Height fields, enter **300**.

**18** Save all files.

Before you upload the pages to the remote site, you should test the go-to-detail-page behavior locally.

**19** Open the Products page. Preview the page in Live view. Hold down Ctrl/Cmd and click one of the product names or pictures.

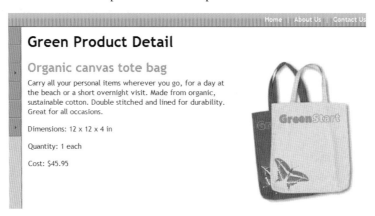

Live view loads the selected product data into **product_detail.php**.

You have completed the rudimentary steps for building a full-fledged online store. The design and construction of an online store, shopping cart, and payment gateway is complex and well beyond the scope of this book.

Prebuilt shopping cart and store solutions are available for all server models supported by Dreamweaver. They vary in cost and complexity to suit any need and budget. Some of the most economical solutions are offered by Google, Yahoo, and PayPal, among others, and they even simplify the method of receiving electronic payments by credit card and bank transfer.

In this lesson, you have created dynamic pages using live data. You've generated page content from an online database and built a complete master/detail page set. But after all that, you've barely looked under the hood of what Dreamweaver can do with dynamic data.

# Review questions

**1** What is a recordset?

**2** Why would you need to use a repeat region?

**3** What is a master/detail page set?

**4** For what purpose would you use record paging behavior?

**5** How can you hide paging controls when there are no more records to display?

# Review answers

**1** A recordset is an array of information pulled from one or more tables in a database by a query created in Dreamweaver.

**2** A repeat region allows the data application to display more than one record at a time.

**3** The master/detail page set is a common feature of data-driven websites. The master page displays multiple records and provides dynamic links within each record, which allows you to load specific information about the selected item on the detail page.

**4** A record paging behavior is used to load the results of a recordset when only a limited number of records are displayed at one time.

**5** Select the paging control link and apply a "Show" behavior pertinent to the recordset.

# 15 PUBLISHING TO THE WEB

## Lesson Overview

In this lesson, you'll publish your website to the Internet and do the following:

- Define a remote site
- Put files on the web
- Cloak files and folders
- Update out-of-date links sitewide
- Get pages from the web

 This lesson will take about 1 hour and 10 minutes to complete. Before beginning, make sure you have copied the files for Lesson 15 to your hard drive as described in the "Getting Started" section at the beginning of the book. If you are starting from scratch in this lesson, use the method described in the "Jumpstart" section of "Getting Started."

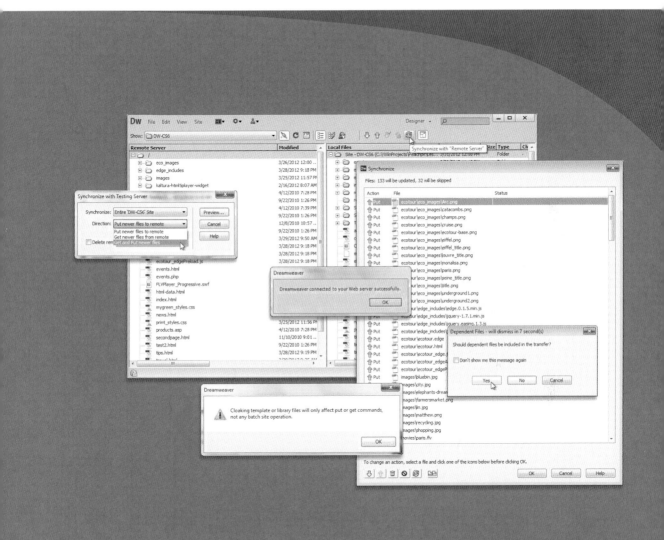

The goal of all the preceding lessons is to design, develop, and build pages for a remote website. But Dreamweaver doesn't abandon you there. It also provides powerful tools to upload and maintain any size website over time.

# Defining a remote site

Dreamweaver's workflow is based on a two-site system. One site is in a folder on your computer's hard drive and is known as the *local site*. All work in the previous lessons has been performed on your local site. The second site, called the *remote site*, is established in a folder on a web server, typically running on another computer, and is connected to the Internet and publicly available. In large companies, the remote site is often available only to employees via a network-based *intranet*. Such sites provide information and applications to support corporate programs and products.

Dreamweaver supports several methods for connecting to a remote site:

- FTP (File Transfer Protocol)—The standard method for connecting to hosted websites.

- SFTP (Secure File Transfer Protocol)—A new protocol that provides a method to connect to hosted websites in a more secure manner to preclude unauthorized access or interception of online content.

- FTP over SSL/TLS (implicit encryption)—A secure FTP method that requires all clients of the FTPS server be aware that SSL is to be used on the session. It is incompatible with non-FTPS-aware clients.

- FTP over SSL/TLS (explicit encryption)— A legacy-compatible, secure FTP method where FTPS-aware clients can invoke security with an FTPS-aware server without breaking overall FTP functionality with non-FTPS-aware clients.

- Local/Network—A local or network connection is most frequently used with an intermediate web server, called a *staging server*. Files from the staging server are eventually published to an Internet-connected web server.

- WebDav (Web Distributed Authoring and Versioning)—A web-based system also known to Windows users as Web Folders and to Mac users as iDisk.

- RDS (Remote Development Services)—Developed by Adobe for ColdFusion and primarily used when working with ColdFusion-based sites.

● **Note:** If you are starting from scratch in this lesson, use the "Jumpstart" instructions in the "Getting Started" section at the beginning of the book.

The FTP engine was completely rebuilt in CS6. Dreamweaver now can upload larger files faster and more efficiently, allowing you to return to work more quickly. In the next exercises, you'll set up a remote site using the two most common methods: FTP and Local/Network.

## Setting up a remote FTP site

The vast majority of web developers rely on FTP to publish and maintain their sites. FTP is a well-established protocol, and many variations of the protocol are used on the web—most of which are supported by Dreamweaver.

**1** Launch Adobe Dreamweaver CS6.

**2**  Choose Site > Manage Sites.

**3**  When the Manage Sites dialog box appears, you will see a list of all the sites that you may have defined. If more than one is displayed, make sure that the current site, DW-CS6, is chosen. Choose Edit.

**4**  In the Site Setup For DW-CS6 dialog box, click the Servers category.

The Site Setup dialog box allows you to set up multiple servers, so you can test several types of installations, if desired.

**5**  Click the Add New Server icon. In the Server Name field, enter **GreenStart Server**.

**6**  From the Connect Using pop-up menu, choose FTP.

**7**  In the FTP Address field, type the URL or IP (Internet Protocol) address of your FTP server.

If you contract a third-party service as a web host, you will be assigned an FTP address. This address may come in the form of an IP address, such as 192.168.1.000. Enter this number into the field exactly as it was sent to you. Frequently, the FTP address will be the name of your site, such as ftp.green-start.org. Dreamweaver doesn't require you to enter the "ftp" into the field.

**8**  In the Username field, enter your FTP user name. In the Password field, enter your FTP password.

Password fields are usually case-sensitive, and so may be the Username field; be sure you enter them correctly.

**9**  In the Root Directory field, type the name of the folder that contains documents publicly accessible to the web, if any.

Some web hosts provide FTP access to a root-level folder that might contain non-public folders—such as cgi-bin, which is used to store Common Gateway Interface (CGI) or binary scripts—as well as a public folder. In these cases, type the public folder name—such as *public*, *public_html*, *www*, or *wwwroot*—in the Root Directory field. In many web host configurations, the FTP address is the same as the public folder, and the Root Directory field should be left blank.

> **Warning:** To complete the following exercise, you must have a remote server already established. Remote servers can be hosted by your own company or contracted from a third-party web-hosting service.

> **Note:** If you do not have a web hosting service, you may use the local web server you set up for Lessons 13 and 14 to test these features.

> **Tip:** Check with your web hosting service or IS/IT manager to obtain the root directory name, if any.

**10** Select the Save option if you don't want to re-enter your user name and password every time Dreamweaver connects to your site.

**11** Click Test to verify that your FTP connection works properly.

Dreamweaver displays an alert to notify you that the connection was successful or unsuccessful.

**12** Click OK to dismiss the alert.

If you received an error message, your web server may require additional configuration options.

**13** Click the More Options icon to reveal additional server options.

Consult the instructions from your hosting company to select the appropriate options for your specific FTP server. The options are:

**Use Passive FTP**—Allows your computer to connect to the host computer and bypass a firewall restraint.

**Use IPV6 Transfer Mode**—Enables connection to IPV6-based servers, which use the most recent version of the Internet transfer protocol.

**Use Proxy**—Identifies a secondary proxy host connection as defined in your Dreamweaver preferences.

**Use FTP Performance Optimization**—Optimizes the FTP connection. Deselect if Dreamweaver can't connect to your server.

**Use Alternative FTP Move Method**—Provides an additional method to resolve FTP conflicts, especially when rollbacks are enabled or when moving files.

# Troubleshooting your FTP connection

Connecting to your remote site can be frustrating the first time you attempt it. There are numerous pitfalls you can experience, many of which are out of your control. Here are a few steps you can take if you run into this problem:

- If you can't connect to your FTP server, double-check your user name and password and re-enter them carefully. (This is the most common error.)
- Select Use Passive FTP and test the connection again.
- If you still can't connect to your FTP server, deselect the Use FTP Performance Optimization option, click OK, and click Test again.
- If none of these steps enable you to connect to your remote site, check with your IS/IT manager or your remote site administrator.

Once you establish a working connection, you may need to configure some advanced options.

**14** Click the Advanced button. Select among the following options for working with your remote site:

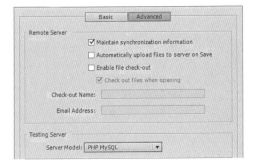

**Maintain Synchronization Information**—Automatically notes which files have been changed on the local and remote sites so that they can be easily synchronized. This feature helps you keep track of your changes and can be helpful if you change multiple pages before you upload. You may want to use cloaking with this feature. You'll learn about cloaking in an upcoming exercise. This feature is usually selected by default.

**Automatically Upload Files To Server On Save**—Transfers files from the local to the remote site when they are saved. This option can become annoying if you save often and aren't yet ready for a page to go public.

**Enable File Check-Out**—Starts the check-in/check-out system for collaborative website building in a workgroup environment. If you choose this option, you'll need to enter a user name for check-out purposes and, optionally, an email address. If you're working by yourself, you do not need to select file check-out.

It is acceptable to leave any or all of these options unselected, but for the purposes of this lesson, enable the Maintain Synchronization Information option.

**15** Click to save the settings in all open dialog boxes.

A dialog box appears, informing you that the cache will be re-created because you changed the site settings.

**16** Click OK to build the cache. When Dreamweaver finishes updating the cache, click Done to close the Manage Sites dialog box.

You have established a connection to your remote server. If you don't currently have a remote server, you can substitute a local testing server instead as your remote server.

## Establishing a remote site on a local or network web server

If your company or organization uses a staging server as a "middleman" between web designers and the live website, it's likely that you'll need to connect to your remote site through a local or network web server. You can also use this type of connection to connect to the testing server you installed and configured for Lesson 13, "Working with Online Data."

**1** Launch Adobe Dreamweaver CS6.

**2** Choose Site > Manage Sites.

**3** When the Manage Sites dialog box appears, make sure that the current site, DW-CS6, is chosen. Click Edit.

**4** In the Site Setup For DW-CS6 dialog box, select the Servers category.

If you installed and configured a testing server in Lesson 13, it will be displayed in the server list. A check mark will appear under the Testing column. To use this server as the remote server, you simply select the Remote option.

▶ **Warning:** To complete the following exercise, you must have already installed and configured a local web server.

● **Note:** If you are starting from scratch in this lesson, use the "Jumpstart" instructions in the "Getting Started" section at the beginning of the book.

**5** If you have a testing server already set up in the dialog box, select the Remote option.

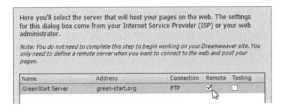

If you haven't set up a testing server yet, you will need to first install and configure a local web server. For detailed information about installing and configuring a local web server, see Lesson 13 or check out the following links:

- Apache/ColdFusion—http://tinyurl.com/setup-coldfusion
- Apache/PHP— http://tinyurl.com/setup-apachephp
- IIS/ASP— http://tinyurl.com/setup-asp

Once you set up the local web server, you can use it to upload the completed files and test your remote site. In most cases, your local web server will not be accessible from the Internet or be able to host the actual website.

**6** Click the Add New Server (✚) icon. In the Server Name field, enter **GreenStart Local**.

**7** From the Connect Using pop-up menu, choose Local/Network.

**8** In the Server Folder field, click the Browse ( 📂 ) icon. Select the local web server's HTML folder, such as C:\wamp\www\DW-CS6.

**9** In the Web URL field, enter the appropriate URL for your local web server, such as http://localhost:8888/DW-CS6 or http://localhost/DW-CS6.

*Note: The paths you enter here are contingent on how you installed your local web server and may not be the same as the ones displayed.*

Windows

Mac OS X

**10** Click the Advanced button, and, as with the actual web server, select the appropriate options for working with your remote site: Maintain Synchronization Information, Automatically Upload Files To Server On Save, and/or Enable File Check-Out.

Although it is acceptable to leave all three of these options unselected, for the purposes of this lesson select the Maintain Synchronization Information option.

**11** If you'd like to use the local web server as the testing server too, select the server model in the Advanced section of the dialog box.

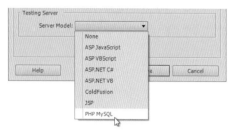

**12** Click Save to complete the remote server setup.

**13** In the Site Setup For DW-CS6 dialog box, select Remote. If you desire to use the local server as a testing server too, select Testing. Click Save.

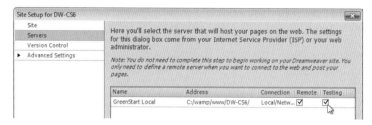

**14** In the Manage Sites dialog box, click Done. If necessary, click OK to rebuild the cache.

Only one remote and one testing server can be active at one time. One server can be used for both roles, if desired. Before you upload files for the remote site, you may need to *cloak* certain folders and files in the local site.

## Cloaking folders and files

Not all the files in your site root folder may need to be transferred to the remote server. For example, there's no point in filling the remote site with files that won't be accessed or will remain inaccessible to the website user. You may actually pay more for hosting based on how much disk space your site occupies. If you selected Maintain Synchronization Information for a remote site using FTP or a network server, you may want to *cloak* some of your local materials to prevent them from being uploaded. Cloaking is a feature of Dreamweaver that allows you to designate certain folders and files that will not be uploaded to or synchronized with the remote site.

Folders you don't want to upload include Templates and Library folders. Some other non-web-compatible file types used to create your site, like Photoshop (.psd), Flash (.fla), or MS Word (.doc) files, also don't need to be on the remote server. Although cloaked files will not upload or synchronize automatically, you may still upload them manually, if desired.

**Note:** If you are starting from scratch in this lesson, use the "Jumpstart" instructions in the "Getting Started" section at the beginning of the book.

The cloaking process begins in the Site Setup dialog box.

1  Choose Site > Manage Sites.

2  Select DW-CS6 in the site list, and click Edit.

3  Expand the Advanced Settings category. In the Cloaking category, select the Enable Cloaking and Cloak Files Ending With options.

The field below the check boxes should display the extensions .fla and .psd.

4  Insert the cursor after .psd and insert a space. Type **.doc .txt .rtf**.

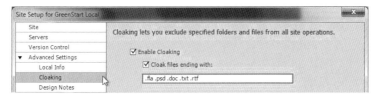

Be sure to insert a space between each extension. Because these file types don't contain any desired web content, adding their extensions here will prevent Dreamweaver from uploading and synchronizing these file types automatically.

5  Click Save. Dreamweaver may prompt you to update the cache. Click OK to update the cache. Then, click Done to close the Manage Sites dialog box.

You can also cloak specific files or folders manually.

6  Open the Files panel and click the Expand button to fill the workspace. If you are using the Jumpstart method, skip steps 7 and 8. You should not have any lesson folders in your workflow.

Note all the lesson folders. These folders contain a great deal of duplicative content that is unnecessary on the remote site.

7  Right-click the lesson01 folder. From the context menu, select Cloaking > Cloak.

8  Repeat step 7 for each of the remaining lesson folders.

Templates and Library folders are not needed on the remote site because your webpages do not reference these assets in any way. But if you work in a team environment, it may be handy to upload and synchronize these folders so that each team member has up-to-date versions of each on their own computers. For this exercise, let's assume you work alone.

**9** Apply cloaking to the Templates folder.

**Note:** Server-side includes (SSIs) must be uploaded to the server for them to function.

A dialog box appears, warning that "Cloaking template or library files will only affect put or get commands, not any batch site operation."

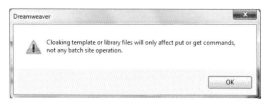

**10** Click OK.

**11** Repeat steps 9 and 10 to cloak the Library folder.

Using the Site Setup dialog box and the Cloaking context menu, you cloaked file types, folders, and files. The synchronization process will ignore cloaked items.

# Wrapping things up

Over the last 14 lessons, you have built an entire website from scratch, including dynamic applications and interactive content, but there are a few loose strings you need to tie up. Before you publish your site, you'll need to create one important file and make some crucial updates to your site navigation.

## Creating a home page

The file you need to create is one that is essential to every site: a home page. The home page is usually the first page that most users will see on your site. It is the page that loads automatically when a user enters the domain name for your site into the browser window. Since the page loads automatically, there are a few restrictions on the name and extension that you can use.

Basically, the name and extension depend on the hosting server and the type of applications running on the home page, if any. In most cases, the home page will simply be named *index*. But *default*, *start*, and *iisstart* are also used.

As you learned earlier, extensions identify the specific types of programming languages used within a page. A normal HTML home page will use an extension of .htm or .html. Extensions like .asp, .cfm, and .php, among others, are required if the home page contains any dynamic applications specific to that server model. You may still use one of these extensions—if they are compatible with your server model—even if the page contains no dynamic applications or content. Be careful—in some instances, using the wrong extension may prevent the page from loading altogether. Whenever you're in doubt, use .html, because it's supported in all environments.

The specific home page name or names honored by the server are normally configured by the server administrator and can be changed, if desired. Most servers are configured to honor several names and a variety of extensions. Check with your IS/IT manager or web server support team to ascertain the recommended name and extension for your home page.

1 Create a new file from the site template. Save the file as **index.html**. Or, use a filename and extension compatible with your server model.

2 Open lesson15 > resources > home.html.

3 Insert the cursor anywhere in the content. Select the `<article>` tag selector. Copy all the content and replace the `<article>` element in the MainContent region of the home page you created in step 1. Apply the class `.content` to the new `<article>` element.

4 In the sidebar, replace the image placeholder with **bike2work.jpg**.

5 Replace the caption placeholder with the following text: **GreenStart has launched a new program to encourage Meridien residents to leave their cars at home and bike to work. Sign up and tell a friend.**

6 Edit the page title to read **Meridien GreenStart Association – Welcome to Meridien GreenStart**.

Note the hyperlink placeholders in the MainContent region.

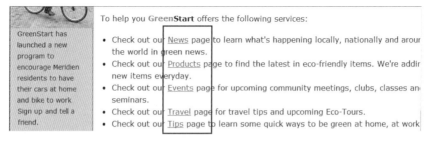

7 Insert the cursor in the *News* link. In the Property inspector, browse and connect the link to **news.html**.

**8**  Repeat step 7 with each link. Connect the links to the appropriate pages in your site root folder.

**9**  Save and close all files.

The home page is complete. Let's assume you want to upload the site at its current state of completion even though some pages have yet to be created. This happens in the course of any site development. Pages are added and deleted over time; missing pages will be completed and uploaded at a later date.

In this scenario, you have created pages for all but two links in your current navigation system: *Green Club* and *Member Login*. Development on the membership and login pages has been postponed for a short time, and the links must be removed. Additionally, a few of the existing links in the vertical menu are currently targeting pages that have been renamed—specifically the *Products* and *Events* pages. Before you can upload the site to a live server, you should update the out-of-date links and remove the dead ones.

▶ **Warning:** There are several versions of this item in the lesson folders, be sure to open the correct one for your workflow.

## Updating links

All the out-of-date links are contained in the vertical menu, which is currently part of the site template. You can update the entire site by editing the template and saving the changes.

**1**  Open the site template.

This template should control all your current site pages.

**2**  Insert the cursor in the *Green Products* link. The page is linked to **products.html**, which doesn't exist. In the Property inspector Link field, browse to the site root folder, and select **products.php**, which you created in Lesson 14, "Building Dynamic Pages with Data."

**3**  Insert the cursor in the *Green Events* link. Link to the new dynamic *Events* page you created in Lesson 14. Use the Property inspector for the Spry menu bar to update the links for *2012-2013 Events Calendar* and *2012-2013 Class Schedule*. Change the .html extension to .php.

**4**  Insert the cursor in the *Green Club* link. Click the `<li>` tag selector and press Delete.

By deleting the parent element, both the *Green Club* and *Member Login* links are removed. You can re-create these links at a later date, if and when these pages are developed.

● **Note:** The vertical menu is still a Spry-based component, so you can use the built-in menu interface to make any changes, if desired. To access the interface, click the tag selector for `<ul.MenuBar1. MenuBarVertical>`.

▶ **Tip:** Instead of rebuilding the entire link for the calendar and class schedule, simply change the extension of the filename **events.html** to match your current version.

## Prelaunch checklist

Take this opportunity to review all your site pages before publishing them to see if they are ready for prime time. In an actual workflow, you should perform most or all of the following actions, which you learned in previous lessons, before uploading a single page:

- Site-wide browser-compatibility check (Lesson 4, "Creating a Page Layout")
- Site-wide spell check (Lesson 7, "Working with Text, Lists, and Tables")
- Site-wide link check (Lesson 9, "Working with Navigation")

Fix any problems you find, and then proceed to the next exercise.

**5** Save the template. Dreamweaver will prompt you to update the site. Click Update.

The Update Pages dialog box appears, reporting what pages were and were not updated. If you do not see the report, click the Show Log option.

**6** Click the Close button. Close the template.

The vertical navigation menu has been updated throughout the site, and your pages are now ready to upload—almost.

## Sidebar sideline

As you've built the pages for your site, you've concentrated mostly on the main content and applications and ignored the sidebar content on some pages. These pages were never finished. Since these exercises were intended for training purposes only, there's no need to complete these pages. However, if your design sensibilities prevent you from leaving these pages in their current state of incompleteness, take a few minutes to finish them now. Some suggestions are offered below, but feel free to take any creative license you desire to complete the sidebar content. The images pictured are available in the default site images folder.

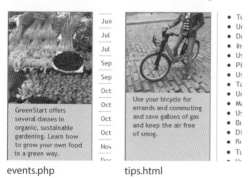

events.php          tips.html

# Putting your site online

For the most part, the local site and the remote site are mirror images, containing the same HTML files, images, and assets in identical folder structures. When you transfer a webpage from your local site to your remote site, you are publishing, or *putting*, that page. If you *put* a file stored in a folder on your local site, Dreamweaver transfers the file to the equivalent folder on the remote site. It will even automatically create the remote folder, if necessary.

Using Dreamweaver, you can publish anything—from one file to a complete site—in a single operation. When you publish a webpage, by default Dreamweaver asks if you would also like to put the *dependent* files, too. Dependent files are the images, CSS, Flash movies, JavaScript files, server-side includes, and all other files necessary to complete the page. Dreamweaver also automatically puts all the dependent files in the proper remote folders, matching their locations on your local site. If a folder doesn't exist on the remote server, Dreamweaver will create it. The same is true when you download files.

> **Warning:** Dreamweaver does a good job trying to identify all the dependent files in a particular workflow. In some cases, it may miss files crucial to a dynamic or extended process. It is imperative that you do your homework to identify these files and make sure they are uploaded.

You can upload one file at a time or the entire site at once.

1 Open the Files panel and click the Expand (⊞) icon, if necessary.

2 Click the Connect To Remote Server (⚇) icon to connect to the remote site.

If your remote site is properly configured, the Files panel will connect to the site and display its contents on the left half of the Files panel. When you first upload files, the remote site may be empty or mostly empty. If you're using your testing server for your remote site, you may see the Connections folder and perhaps one or more files that were tested in Lesson 14. If you are connecting to your Internet host, specific files and folders may appear that were created by the hosting company. Do not delete these items unless you check to see whether they are essential to the operation of the server or your own applications.

3 In the local file list, select **index.html**. On the Document toolbar, click the Put (⬆) icon.

By default, Dreamweaver will prompt you to upload dependent files. If a dependent file already exists on the server and your changes did not affect it, you can click No. Otherwise, for new files or files that have had any changes you should click Yes. Dreamweaver will then upload images, CSS, JavaScript, server-side includes (SSIs), and other dependent files needed to properly render the selected HTML file.

● **Note:** If Dreamweaver doesn't prompt you to upload dependent files, this option may be turned off. To turn this feature on, access the option in the Site category of the Dreamweaver Preferences panel.

You can also upload multiple files or the entire site.

**4** Right-click the site root folder for the local site. From the context menu, choose Put.

A dialog box appears, asking you to confirm that you want to upload the entire site.

**5** Click OK.

Dreamweaver re-creates your local site structure on the remote server. Note that none of the cloaked lesson folders were uploaded. Dreamweaver will automatically ignore all cloaked items when putting a folder or an entire site. If desired, you can manually select and upload individually cloaked items.

▶ **Warning:** Among the pages you are uploading are several that may incorporate dynamic content using ASP, ColdFusion, or PHP. The database and support files that are required for these applications that are not stored within your site structure may not be uploaded during this operation. You will probably have to locate and upload these files and folders manually. In any case, be aware that additional configuration on the remote server and database will be required before these dynamic applications will function properly.

**6** Right-click the Templates folder and choose Put.

Dreamweaver prompts you to upload dependent files for the Templates folder.

**7** Click Yes to upload dependent files.

The Templates folder is uploaded to the remote server. Note that the remote Templates folder displays a red slash indicating that it is cloaked, too. At times, you will want to cloak local and remote folders to prevent these files from being replaced or accidentally overwritten. A file that is cloaked will not be uploaded or downloaded automatically. You will have to select any specific files and perform the action manually.

The opposite of the Put command is *Get*. The Get command downloads any selected file or folder to the local site. You can *get* any file from the remote site by selecting it in the Remote or Local pane and clicking the Get (⇩) icon. Alternatively, you can drag the file from the Remote pane to the Local pane.

● **Note:** A file that is uploaded or downloaded will automatically overwrite the file at the destination.

● **Note:** Dynamic pages created earlier may not display properly to a remote site until the database connections are configured properly. Be sure your configuration is complete before testing these pages.

● **Note:** When accessing Put and Get, it doesn't matter whether you use the Local or Remote pane of the Files panel. Put always uploads to Remote; Get always downloads to Local.

**8** Use a browser to connect to the remote site on your network server or the Internet. Type the appropriate address in the URL field—depending on whether you are connecting to the local web server or the actual Internet site—such as http://localhost/DW-CS6 or http://www.green-start.org.

The GreenStart site should appear in the browser. Click to test the hyperlinks to view each of the completed pages for the site. Once the site is uploaded, it is an easy task to keep it up to date. As files change, you can upload them one at a time or synchronize the whole site with the remote server. Synchronization is especially important in workgroup environments where files are changed and uploaded by several individuals.

## Synchronizing local and remote sites

Synchronization in Dreamweaver is used to keep the files on your server and your local computer up to date. It's an essential tool when you work from multiple locations or with one or more coworkers. Used properly, it can prevent you from accidentally uploading or working on out-of-date files.

At the moment, the local and remote sites are identical. To better illustrate the capabilities of synchronization, let's make a change to one of the site pages.

**1** Open **about_us.html**.

**2** In the main heading, select the text *Green* in the name GreenStart. Apply the CSS `.green` class to this text.

**3** Apply the CSS `.green` class to each occurrence of the word *green* anywhere on the page.

**4** Save and close the page.

**5** Open and expand the Files panel. Click the Synchronize (🔁) icon in the Document toolbar.

The Synchronize Files dialog box appears.

● **Note:** Jumpstart users will see the name of the current site folder in the field menu.

**6** From the Synchronize menu, choose the option Entire 'DW-CS6' Site. From the Direction menu, choose the Get And Put Newer Files option.

Choose specific options in this dialog box that meet your needs and workflow.

# Synchronization options

During synchronization, you can choose to accept the suggested action or override it by selecting one of the other options in the dialog box. Options can be applied to one or more files at a time.

Get—Downloads the selected file(s) from remote site.

Put—Uploads the selected file(s) to remote site.

Delete—Deletes the selected file(s).

Ignore—Ignores the selected file(s) during synchronization.

Synchronized—Identifies the selected file(s) as already synchronized.

Compare—Uses a third-party utility to compare the local and remote versions of a selected file.

**7** Click Preview.

The Synchronize dialog box appears, reporting what files have changed and whether you need to get or put them. Since you just uploaded the entire site, only the file **about_us.html** should appear in the list, which indicates that Dreamweaver wants to put it to the remote site.

**8** Click OK to put the file.

If other people access and update files on your site, remember to run synchronization *before* you work on any files to be certain you are working on the most current versions of each file in your site.

In this lesson, you set up your site to connect to a remote server and uploaded files to that remote site. You also cloaked files and folders and then synchronized the local and remote sites.

Congratulations! You've designed, developed, and built an entire website and uploaded it to your remote server. By finishing all the exercises in this book, you have gained experience in all aspects of website design and development. Now you are ready to build and publish a site of your own. Good luck!

# Review questions

1 What is a remote site?

2 Name two types of file transfer protocols supported in Dreamweaver.

3 How can you configure Dreamweaver so that it does not synchronize certain files in your site root folder with the server?

4 True or false: You have to manually publish every file and associated image, JavaScript file, and server-side include that are linked to pages in your site.

5 What service does synchronization perform?

# Review answers

1  A remote site is a mirror image of your local site; the remote site is stored on a web server connected to the Internet.

2  FTP (File Transfer Protocol) and Local/Network are the two most commonly used file transfer methods. Other file transfer methods supported in Dreamweaver include Secure FTP, WebDav, and RDS.

3  Cloak the files or folders for which you do not want to maintain synchronization.

4  False. Dreamweaver will automatically transfer dependent files, if desired, including embedded or referenced images, CSS style sheets, and other linked content.

5  Synchronization automatically scans local and remote sites, comparing files on both to identify the most current version of each. It creates a report window to suggest which files to get or put to bring both sites up to date, and then it will perform the update.

# Appendix  TinyURLs

| PAGE | TINY URL | FULL URL |
|------|----------|----------|
| **Lesson 4** | | |
| 85 | http://tinyurl.com/html-differences | http://www.w3.org/TR/html5-diff/ |
| 85 | http://tinyurl.com/html-differences-1 | http://www.htmlgoodies.com/html5/tutorials/ Web-Developer-Basics-Differences-Between-HTML4-And- HTML5-3921271.htm#fbid=ZkdgDbQj8IJ |
| 85 | http://tinyurl.com/html-differences-2 | http://en.wikipedia.org/wiki/HTML5 |
| **Lesson 10** | | |
| 284 | http://tinyurl.com/widgets-browser | http://labs.adobe.com/technologies/widgetbrowser/ |
| **Lesson 11** | | |
| 297 | http://tinyurl.com/video-1-HTML5 | http://www.w3schools.com/html5/html5_video.asp |
| 297 | http://tinyurl.com/video-2-HTML5 | http://www.808.dk/?code-html-5-video |
| 297 | http://tinyurl.com/video-3-HTML5 | http://www.htmlgoodies.com/html5/client/ how-to-embed-video-using-html5.html#fbid=ZkdgDbQj8IJ |
| **Lesson 12** | | |
| 307 | http://tinyurl.com/HTML5-input | http://w3schools.com/html5/html5_form_input_types.asp |
| 328 | http://tinyurl.com/asp-formmailer | http://www.devarticles.com/c/a/ASP/ Sending-Email-From-a-Form-in-ASP/ |
| 328 | http://tinyurl.com/cf-formmailer | http://www.quackit.com/coldfusion/tutorial/coldfusion_mail.cfm |
| 328 | http://tinyurl.com/php-formmailer | http://www.html-form-guide.com/email-form/ php-form-to-email.html |
| **Lesson 13** | | |
| 349 | http://tinyurl.com/setup-asp | http://www.adobe.com/devnet/dreamweaver/articles/ setup_asp.edu.html?PID=4166869 |
| 349 | http://tinyurl.com/IIS-setup | http://learn.iis.net/page.aspx/28/ installing-iis-on-windows-vista-and-windows-7 |

| PAGE | TINY URL | FULL URL |
|---|---|---|
| 349 | http://tinyurl.com/setup-ColdFusion | http://www.adobe.com/devnet/dreamweaver/articles/setup_cf.edu.html?PID=4166869 |
| 349 | http://tinyurl.com/setup-apachephp | http://www.adobe.com/devnet/dreamweaver/articles/setup_php.edu.html?PID=4166869 |
| 349 | http://tinyurl.com/WAMP-setup | http://www.wampserver.com/en/ |
| 349 | http://tinyurl.com/MAMP-setup | http://www.mamp.info/en/index.html |
| 349 | http://tinyurl.com/XAMPP-server | http://www.apachefriends.org/en/xampp.html |

**Lesson 14**

| | | |
|---|---|---|
| 362 | http://tinyurl.com/sql-primer | http://www.adobe.com/devnet/dreamweaver/articles/sql_primer.edu.html?PID=4166869 |
| 362 | http://tinyurl.com/sql-tutorial | http://www.w3schools.com/sql/default.asp |

**Lesson 15**

| | | |
|---|---|---|
| 395 | http://tinyurl.com/setup-asp | http://www.adobe.com/devnet/dreamweaver/articles/setup_asp.edu.html?PID=4166869 |

# INDEX

<!--...--> (HTML comments), 30, 107
< > (angle brackets), 21
/* and */ (CSS comments), 52, 109

## A

<a> (anchor) tags, 30
  hyperlinks, 234
  pseudoclasses, 123
a:active pseudoclass, 123–127
absolute hyperlinks, 234–235
Access databases, 348
accessibility preferences, forms, 307–308
action attributes, 304
Adams, Cameron, 68
Adobe and Ajax's Spry framework
  Spry accordion widgets, 279–280
    customizing, 282–284
    inserting, 280–281
    panels, adding, 281–282
  Spry data, 249
    date, 340
    html, 340
    HTML table-based data, 338–344
    number, 340
    string, 340
  Spry effects, 249
  Spry form widgets, 249
    checkboxes, 315–317
    lists/menus, 320–322
    passwords, 313–315
    radio buttons, 317–318
    text areas, 319–320
    text fields, 309–315

  Spry layout widgets, 249
  Spry menu bars, 248–254
    customizing, 257–263
    modifying, 254–257
Adobe Bridge insertions
  by dragging and dropping, 227
  of images, 215–217
  of non-web file types, 218
Adobe Business Catalyst, 78
*Adobe Dreamweaver CS3 with ASP,*
*  ColdFusion, and PHP: Training*
*  from the Source,* 328
*Adobe Dreamweaver CS5 with PHP:*
*  Training from the Source,* 328
Adobe Edge, 290–292
Adobe Fireworks
  copying/pasting images from, 223–226
  website mockups, 77–78
Adobe Flash
  lack of support for, 74
  web animation, 288–289
  web video, 288–289, 294–297
Adobe Illustrator
  vector graphics, 204
  website mockups, 77–78
Adobe Omniture, 73
Adobe Photoshop
  copying/pasting images from, 223–226
  inserting Smart Objects, 221–223
  PSD (Photoshop Document) file format, 218, 221
  website mockups, 77–78
a:hover pseudoclass, 123–127, 125
AI file format, 204, 215

## J

JavaScript. *See also* Ajax
    calling functions with behaviors, 271
    code hinting, 27
    Dreamweaver support, 4
Johnson, David, 68
JPEG (Joint Photographic Experts Group) file
        format
    Adobe Bridge, 215–216, 219
    Adobe Photoshop and Fireworks, 223
    basics, 208
jQuery Mobile, 270

## K

keyboard shortcuts, 14–15
<keygen> tags, 307

## L

<label> tags, 308
<li> (list) tags, 31, 96, 178
library items. *See also* SSIs; templates
    basics, 152
    creating, 152–156
    *versus* server-side includes, 164
    updating, 156–157
<link /> (document-external resource) tags, 31
linked formatting, 46
lists/menus
    formatting, 175–178
    forms, 304, 306
        Spry widgets, 320–322
    interactive menus, 122–125
        visual effects, 127–128
    tags
        <li> (list), 31, 96, 178
        <ol> (ordered list), 31, 178
        <ul> (unordered list), 31, 98
local servers, 349, 394
local sites, 390
    connecting to remote sites, 390
    publishing (putting) online, 402–404
    synchronizing with remote sites, 393, 404–405
local/network connections to remote sites, 390
lossy/lossless compression, 208–209

## M

margins
    CSS, 60–62
    HTML, 44
master/detail page sets, 372–374
    behaviors
        displaying multiple items, 376
        displaying record counts, 379–380
        go-to-detail-page, 383
        hiding paging controls, 378–379
        record paging, 377–378
    detail pages, 384–386
    displaying images, 374–376
    master pages, 372–374
    styling dynamic data, 380–382
Max Chars attribute, 308
McFarland, David Sawyer, 68
media/multimedia
    animation
        with Adobe Flash, 288
        basics, 288
        with HTML5, 288, 290–293
    tags
        <audio>, 34
        <figcaption>, 33
        <figure>, 33
        <img /> (image), 31
        <source>, 34
        <track>, 34
        <video>, 34
    video
        with Adobe Flash, 288–289, 294–297
        basics, 288
        with HTML5, 288, 293–294
menu bar, 4
menus/lists
    formatting, 175–178
    forms, 304, 306
        Spry widgets, 320–322
    interactive menus, 122–125
        visual effects, 127–128
    tags
        <li> (list), 31, 96, 178
        <ol> (ordered list), 31, 178
        <ul> (unordered list), 31, 98

## V

validation, forms, 307, 309–312

vector graphics, 204

vertical alignment, tables, 193

video

with Adobe Flash, 288–289, 294–297

basics, 288

with HTML5, 288, 293–294

`<video>` tags, 34, 294, 296

View menu, toolbar selection, 13

## W

W3Schools/other resources

browser statistics, 44, 73

Dreamweaver Marketplace & Exchange, behaviors, 270

HTML, 29

elements list, 35

local web server configuration, 349

operating systems, 73

screen resolutions and sizes, 73

SQL (Structured Query Language), 362

SVG graphics, 204

web form mail scripts, 328

WAMP/MAMP web servers, 349

web animation

with Adobe Flash, 288

basics, 288

with HTML5, 288, 290–293

Web Distributed Authoring and Versioning (WebDav), 390

Web Folders, 390

web servers

ASP (Active Server Pages)

Dreamweaver support, 4

.html extension, 357

web form mail scripts, 328

web server models, 348–349

ColdFusion

Dreamweaver support, 4

.html extension, 357

RDS (Remote Development Services), 390

web form mail scripts, 328

web server models, 348–349

local servers, 349

PHP (PHP Hypertext Processor), 349

data display, 367–368

database connections with MySQL, 354–358

Dreamweaver support, 4

.html extension, 357

recordsets, 362–367

testing servers, 350–352

web form actions, 324–325

web form mail scripts, 325–328

testing servers, 350–352, 369

web video

with Adobe Flash, 288–289, 294–297

basics, 288

with HTML5, 288, 293–294

WebDav (Web Distributed Authoring and Versioning), 390

WebM file format, 289, 294

webpages

behaviors

displaying multiple items, 376

displaying record counts, 379–380

go-to-detail-page, 383

hiding paging controls, 378–379

record paging, 377–378

repeat regions, 369–370

data display, 367–368, 371–372

testing servers, 369

design considerations, 75–76

detail pages, 384–386

layout sketches, 75–77

master/detail page sets

displaying images, 374–376

master pages, 372–374

styling dynamic data, 380–382

recordsets, 362–366

thumbnails, 75

wireframes, 77–78

web-safe colors, 207

websites

design concerns

Adobe Flash, lack of support for, 74

browsers commonly used, 73

customers' access methods and usage, 73–74

desktop, laptop, and mobile device challenges, 73–74

# AdobePress

# LEARN BY VIDEO

The **Learn by Video** series from video2brain and Adobe Press is the only Adobe-approved video courseware for the Adobe Certified Associate Level certification, and has quickly established itself as one of the most critically acclaimed training products available on the fundamentals of Adobe software.

**Learn by Video** offers up to 15 hours of high-quality HD video training presented by experienced trainers, as well as lesson files, assessment quizzes, and review materials. The DVD is bundled with a full-color printed booklet that provides supplemental information as well as a guide to the video topics.

For more information go to
www.adobepress.com/learnbyvideo

Table of Contents never more than a click away

Up to 15 hours of high-quality video training

Lesson files are included on the DVD

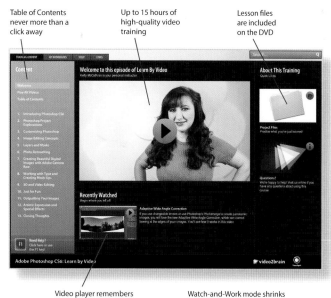

Video player remembers which movie you watched last

Watch-and-Work mode shrinks the video into a small window while you work in the software

## Titles

**Adobe Photoshop CS6: Learn by Video: Core Training in Visual Communication**
ISBN: 9780321840714

**Adobe Illustrator CS6: Learn by Video**
ISBN: 9780321840684

**Adobe InDesign CS6: Learn by Video**
ISBN: 9780321840691

**Adobe Flash Professional CS6: Learn by Video: Core Training in Rich Media Communication**
ISBN: 9780321840707

**Adobe Dreamweaver CS6: Learn by Video: Core Training in Web Communication**
ISBN: 9780321840370

**Adobe Premiere Pro CS6: Learn by Video: Core Training in Video Communication**
ISBN: 9780321840721

**Adobe After Effects CS6: Learn by Video**
ISBN: 9780321840387

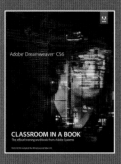

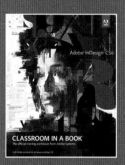

# The fastest, easiest, most comprehensive way to learn

**Classroom in a Book®**, the best-selling series of hands-on software training books, helps you learn the features of Adobe software quickly and easily.

The **Classroom in a Book** series offers what no other book or training program does—an official training series from Adobe Systems, developed with the support of Adobe product experts.

**To see a complete list of our Adobe® Creative Suite® 6 titles go to**
www.peachpit.com/adobecs6

**Adobe Photoshop CS6 Classroom in a Book**
ISBN: 9780321827333

**Adobe Illustrator CS6 Classroom in a Book**
ISBN: 9780321822482

**Adobe InDesign CS6 Classroom in a Book**
ISBN: 9780321822499

**Adobe Flash Professional CS6 Classroom in a Book**
ISBN: 9780321822512

**Adobe Dreamweaver CS6 Classroom in a Book**
ISBN: 9780321822451

**Adobe Muse Classroom in a Book**
ISBN: 9780321821362

**Adobe Fireworks CS6 Classroom in a Book**
ISBN: 9780321822444

**Adobe Premiere Pro CS6 Classroom in a Book**
ISBN: 9780321822475

**Adobe After Effects CS6 Classroom in a Book**
ISBN: 9780321822437

**Adobe Audition CS6 Classroom in a Book**
ISBN: 9780321832832

**Adobe Creative Suite 6 Design & Web Premium Classroom in a Book**
ISBN: 9780321822604

**Adobe Creative Suite 6 Production Premium Classroom in a Book**
ISBN: 9780321832689

**Adobe**Press